INVENTED LIVES

Also Edited by Mary Helen Washington

MIDNIGHT BIRDS:
Stories of Contemporary Black Women Writers (1980)

BLACK-EYED SUSANS:
Classic Stories By and About Black Women (1975)

Grateful acknowledgment is made for permission to reprint the following:

"Janie Crawford" by Alice Walker from *Good Night Willie Lee, I'll See You in the Morning,* Copyright © 1979 by Alice Walker. Reprinted by permission of Doubleday & Company, Inc.

Excerpts from *Jonah's Gourd Vine* by Zora Neale Hurston. Copyright © 1934 by Zora Neale Hurston. Copyright Renewed 1962 by John C. Hurston. Reprinted by permission of John C. Hurston.

Excerpts from *Their Eyes Were Watching God* by Zora Neale Hurston. Copyright © 1937 by J. B. Lippincott Company. Copyright Renewed 1965 by John C. Hurston and Joel Hurston. Reprinted by permission of John C. Hurston and Joel Hurston.

"I see the mask" by Sherley Anne Williams from *Some One Sweet Angel Chile,* Copyright © 1982 by Sherley Anne Williams. Reprinted by permission of William Morrow & Company.

Excerpts from *The Narrows* by Ann Petry. Copyright © 1953 by Ann Petry. Reprinted by permission of Ann Petry.

Excerpts from *The Living Is Easy* by Dorothy West. Copyright © 1948 by Dorothy West. Reprinted by permission of Dorothy West.

"Annie Allen" by Gwendolyn Brooks from *Annie Allen.* Copyright © 1949 by Gwendolyn Brooks. Reprinted by permission of Gwendolyn Brooks.

Excerpts from *Maud Martha* by Gwendolyn Brooks. Copyright © 1953 by Gwendolyn Brooks Blakely. Reprinted by permission of Gwendolyn Brooks.

Library of Congress Cataloging-in-Publication Data

Invented lives.

Includes bibliographies and index.
1. Short stories, American—Afro-American authors.
2. Short stories, American—Women authors.
3. American fiction—20th century.
4. Afro-American women—Fiction.
I. Washington, Mary Helen.
PS647.A35I58   1987   813'.008'09287   86-24143
ISBN: 0-385-18393-3

CONTENTS

ACKNOWLEDGMENTS

I have many people to thank for their assistance and encouragement in helping me to write and edit this book. The fellowship year at the Bunting Institute of Radcliffe College (1979–80) and the semester's fellowship at the Center for Research on Women at Wellesley College (1983) allowed me to continue my reading, thinking, and researching black women's literary history. During my semester as visiting professor at Mills College, I had the generous aid of Phyllis Bishof, librarian for the Afro-American and African Collections at the University of California at Berkeley.

I am grateful for the friends and colleagues who read and critiqued parts of this manuscript: Jean Fagan Yellin, Jean McMahon Humez, Linda Dittmar, Nellie McKay, Thad Davis, Fran Foster, and Richard Yarborough. Many thanks to colleagues who sent me their work in progress: Deborah McDowell, Hazel Carby, Valerie Smith, Jean Fagan Yellin, Carol McAlpine Watson. Thanks are certainly due my research assistants, Mia Carter and Lisa Schwartz, who did the leg work for the bibliographies (especially to Lisa who studied these writers carefully and made me realize the work that still needed to be done), and to my dedicated word processors Marilyn Cirafice and Roseanne Donahue, who are slowly bringing me into the age of technology.

More thanks: To Ponchita Argieard, Paulette Childress White, Sr. Barbara Johns, Sr. Maureen Aggeler, and Tommy Washington who believe in the value of my work. To Alice Walker who urges me to write with the passion she hears in my voice. To Genii Guinier who listened to parts of this manuscript as I was thinking it aloud and chose the title.

To Michelene Malson and Evelyn Moore who vacationed quietly around me as I worked at this on Martha's Vineyard and sometimes brought lunch to my desk. To my family who help me in ways they will never know: Myrna Mitchell, Bernadette Washington, Betty Ann Washington, David Washington, Byron Washington, and Mary Catherine Washington.

Finally, to my editors at Doubleday, Loretta Barrett and Gerald Gladney, whose wit, wisdom, and expertise navigated this project to a safe shore.

INTRODUCTION
"The Darkened Eye Restored:"
Notes Toward a Literary History
of Black Women

When Gwendolyn Brooks won the Pulitzer prize for her second book of poems, *Annie Allen*, in 1950, *Negro Digest* sent a male reporter who covered the story and wrote a brief "homey" article about the life of a Pulitzer-prize-winning poet. The article begins with a list of people who didn't believe Brooks had won the prize—her son, her mother, her husband, friends—even the poet herself. It then catalogs all the negative experiences Brooks had after winning the prize —phones ringing, people dropping in, work interrupted, the family overwhelmed. It mentions her husband, Henry Blakely, as a poet who devotes only occasional time to poetry because "he feels no one family can support two poets." We also learn that the poet was "shy and self conscious" (her terms) until she married Blakely who helped her to lose some of her "social backwardness" (the reporter's terms). The last paragraph of the article, devoted to the poet's nine-year-old son, includes one of the boy's poems (But not a line from the poet who has just won the Pulitzer!) and ends with the son's rejection of his mother's fame because it has upset his life: "All the attention is wearing off now and I sure am glad. I don't like to be so famous. You have too many people talking to you. You never have any peace."[1] The entire article was an act of sabotage, situating Brooks in a domestic milieu where her "proper" role as wife and mother could be asserted and her role as serious artist—a role this reporter obviously found too threatening to even consider—could be undercut.

Three years later when Brooks published her first—and

still her only novel—*Maud Martha* (1953), a novel about a woman's anger, repressions, and silences, the critical reviews were equally condescending and dismissive. Despite Brooks's stature as a Pulitzer-prize-winning poet, the reviews were short, ranging in length from one hundred and sixty to six hundred words, and many were unsigned. Here is a novel that deals with the most compelling themes in contemporary literature: the struggle to sustain one's identity against a racist and sexist society, the silences that result from repressed anger, the need to assert a creative life. Had *Maud Martha* been written by a man about a man's experience, it would have been considered a brilliant modernist text. But these reviewers, unable to place *Maud Martha* in any literary context, chose instead to concentrate on female cheerfulness, calling Maud Martha "a spunky and sophisticated Negro girl" who, they said, had a marvelous "ability to turn unhappiness and anger into a joke."[2]

Consider the way Ralph Ellison's first novel, *Invisible Man*, was received the year before *Maud Martha* when Ellison was still relatively unknown. *The New Republic, Crisis, The Nation, The New Yorker,* and *The Atlantic* published lengthy and signed reviews, ranging in length from six hundred to twenty-one hundred words. Wright Morris and Irving Howe were called in to write serious critical assessments for the *Times* and *The Nation.* Although Brooks's protagonist was never compared to any other literary character, Ellison's nameless hero was considered not only "the embodiment of the Negro race" but the "conscience of all races." The titles of Ellison's reviews—"Black & Blue," "Underground Notes," "Brother Betrayed," "Black Man's Burdens"—suggest the universality of the invisible man's struggle. The title of Brooks's reviews—"Young Girl Growing Up" and "Daydreams of Flight," beside being misleading, deny any relationship between the protagonist's personal experiences and the historical experiences of her people. Ellison himself was compared to Richard Wright, Dostoyevski, and Faulkner. Brooks, only to the unspecified "imagists." Most critically,

Ellison's work was placed in a tradition; it was described as an example of the "picaresque" tradition and the pilgrim/journey tradition by all reviews. (Later it would be considered a descendant of the slave narrative tradition.) *Maud Martha*, the reviewers said, "stood alone."[3]

Reading these reviews I was struck not only by their resistance to the deeper meaning in *Maud Martha* but by their absolute refusal to see Brooks's novel as part of any tradition in Afro-American or mainstream American literature. Is this because few critics could picture the questing figure, the powerful articulate voice in the tradition as a plain, dark-skinned housewife living in a kitchenette apartment on the south side of Chicago? As I have written earlier, I realize that the supreme confidence of the Ellison text—its epic sweep, its eloquent flow of words, its conscious manipulation of historical situations—invites its greater critical acceptance. By comparison, the *Maud Martha* test is hesitant, self-doubting, retentive, mute. Maud is restricted, for a good part of the novel, to a domestic life that seems narrow and limited—even to her. And, yet, if the terms *invisibility, double-consciousness, the black mask* have any meaning at all for the Afro-American literary tradition, then *Maud Martha*, whose protagonist is more intimately acquainted with the meanings of those words than any male character, belongs unquestionably to that tradition.

Tradition. Now there's a word that nags the feminist critic. A word that has so often been used to exclude or misrepresent women. It is always something of a shock to see black women, sharing equally (and sometimes more than equally) in the labor and strife of black people, expunged from the text when that history becomes shaped into what we call tradition. Why is the fugitive slave, the fiery orator, the political activist, the abolitionist always represented as a black *man?*[4] How does the heroic voice and heroic image of the black woman get suppressed in a culture that depended on her heroism for its survival? What we have to recognize is that the creation of the fiction of tradition is a matter of power, not justice, and that that power has always been in the hands of men—mostly white but some black. Women are the disinherited. Our "ritual journeys," our "articulate voices," our "symbolic spaces" are rarely the same as men's. Those differences and the assumption that those differences make women inherently inferior plus the appropriation by men of the power to define tradition account for women's absence from our written records.

In the early 1890s when a number of leading black intellectuals decided to form "an organization of Colored authors, scholars, and artists," with the expressed intent of raising "the standard of intellectual endeavor among American Negroes," one of the invited members wrote to declare himself "decidedly opposed to the admission of women to membership" because "literary matters and social matters do not mix." He need not have concerned himself since the distinguished luminaries, among them Alexander Crummell, Francis Grimké, and W. E. B. DuBois, proposed from the beginning that the American Negro Academy—a kind of think tank for that intellectual black elite called the Talented Tenth—be open only to "*men* of African descent."[5] Imagine, if you can, black women intellectuals and activists, who in the 1890s had taken on such issues as the moral integrity of black women, lynching, and the education of black youth, being considered social decorations. I mention this egregious example of sexism in the black intellectual community —which by and large was and still is far more egalitarian than their white counterparts—because it underscores an attitude toward black women that has helped to maintain and perpetuate a male-dominated literary and critical tradition. Women have worked assiduously in this tradition as writers, as editors, sometimes, though rarely, as critics, and yet every study of Afro-American narrative, every anthology of *the* Afro-American literary tradition has set forth a model of literary paternity in which each male author vies with his predecessor for greater authenticity, greater control over *his* voice, thus fulfilling the mission his *forefathers* left unfinished.

Women in this model are sometimes granted a place as a stepdaughter who prefigures and directs us to the real heirs (like Ellison and Wright) but they do not influence and determine the direction and shape of the literary canon.[6] Women's writing is considered singular and anomalous, not universal and representative, and for some mysterious reason, writing about black women is not considered as racially significant as writing about black men. Zora Neale Hurston was chastised by critic Benjamin Brawley because "Her interest . . . is not in solving problems, the chief concern being with individuals."[7] And, in his now-famous contemptuous review of Hurston's *Their Eyes Were Watching God*, Richard Wright objects to her novel because her characters (unlike his) live in a "safe and narrow orbit . . . between laughter and tears."[8] Male critics go to great lengths to explain the political naïveté or racial ambivalence of male writers while they harshly criticize women writers for the same kinds of shortcomings. In Wright's essay, "Literature of the Negro of the United States," he forgives George Moses Horton, an early black poet, for being "a split man," trapped in a culture of which he was not really a part; but Phillis Wheatley, he says, is fully culpable. She was, Wright claims, so fully at one with white colonial culture that she developed "innocently," free "to give utterance to what she felt without the humiliating pressure of the color line."[9]

Banished to the "nigger pews" in the Christian churches of Colonial Boston, deprived of the companionship of other blacks, totally under the control of whites, "torn by contrary instincts," Phillis Wheatley was never "at one with her culture." As a new generation of critics, led by William Robinson, Alice Walker, and Merle A. Richmond, has shown us, Phillis Wheatley was a young slave woman whose choice to be an artist in the repressive, racist era of Colonial America represents "the triumph of the artist amid catastrophe."[10]

With the exception of a handful of autobiographical narratives from the nineteenth century, the black woman's realities are virtually suppressed until the period of the Harlem Renaissance and later. Essentially the black woman as artist, as intellectual spokesperson for her own cultural apprenticeship, has not existed before, for anyone. At the source of her own symbol-making task, this community of writers confronts, therefore, a tradition of work that is quite recent, its continuities, broken and sporadic.[11]

The eight essays in this collection and the excerpts from the writings of these ten writers—Harriet Jacobs (Linda Brent), Frances Harper, Pauline Hopkins, Fannie Barrier Williams, Marita Bonner, Nella Larsen, Zora Neale Hurston, Ann Petry, Dorothy West, and Gwendolyn Brooks—represent an effort to piece together those "broken and sporadic" continuities that constitute black women's literary tradition. Without exception these writers have been dismissed by Afro-American literary critics until they were rediscovered and reevaluated by feminist critics. Examples: Linda Brent's slave narrative, *Incidents in the Life of a Slave Girl* (1860), was judged by male historians to be inauthentic because her story was "too melodramatic" and not "representative."[12] Contemporary feminist critics have documented Brent's life as not only entirely authentic but "representative" of the experience of many slave women. Except for Barbara Christian's *Black Women Novelists* and other texts that specifically deal with women writers, critical texts have never considered Frances Harper and Pauline Hopkins makers of early black literary traditions. Like many white women writers of the nineteenth century, they were dismissed as "sentimentalists," even though their male counterparts wrote similarly sentimental novels. Zora Hurston's *Their Eyes Were Watching God* was declared by Richard Wright to be a novel that carried "no theme, no message, no thought," and during the thirty years that Wright dominated the black literary scene, Hurston's novel was out of print.[13] Nella Larsen was also out of print for many years and was not until recently considered a major Harlem Renaissance writer. Ann Petry is usually analyzed as a disciple of Wright's school of social protest fiction, and Dorothy West has not been written about seriously since Robert Bone's *The Negro Novel in America* in 1965. Brooks's novel, *Maud Martha*, though it perfectly expresses the race alienation of the 1950s, was totally eclipsed by Ellison's *Invisible Man* and never considered a vital part of the Afro-American canon.

If there is a single distinguishing feature of the literature of black women—and this accounts for their lack of recognition—it is this: their literature is about black women; it takes the trouble to record the thoughts, words, feelings, and deeds of black women, experiences that make the realities of being black in America look very different from what men have written. There are no women in this tradition hibernating in dark holes contemplating their invisibility; there are no women dismembering the bodies or crushing the skulls of either women or men; and few, if any, women in the literature of black women succeed in heroic quests without the support of other women or men in their communities. Women talk to other women in this tradition, and their friendships with other women—mothers, sisters, grandmothers, friends, lovers—are vital to their growth and well-being. A common scene recurring in at least five of the eight fiction writers in this collection is one in which women (usually two) gather together in a small room to share intimacies that can be trusted only to a kindred female spirit. That intimacy is a tool, allowing women writers to represent women more fully. The friendship between Sappho and Dora in *Contending Forces*, Janie and Pheoby in *Their Eyes Were Watching God*, Linda and her grandmother in *Incidents in the Life of a Slave Girl*, Helga and Mrs. Hayes-Rore in *Quicksand*, Cleo and her sisters in *The Living Is Easy* emphasize this concern with female bonding and suggest that female relationships are an essential aspect of self-definition for women.

I do not want these writers to be misrepresented as apolitical because of their deep concern for the personal lives of

their characters. All of these texts are clearly involved with
issues of social justice: the rape of black women, the lynching of black men, slavery and Reconstruction, class distinctions among blacks, and all forms of discrimination against
black people. No romantic heroines, all of these women
work, and in nearly every one of these eight selections
women experience discrimination against them in the workplace, a subject that almost never surfaces in the writings of
men. At the beginning of *Contending Forces*, Sappho Clark
brings her stenography work home with her because blacks
are not allowed in the office. Iola Leroy is twice dismissed
from jobs when her co-workers discover her race. The educated Helga Crane seeks work as a domestic in Chicago
because black women are barred from the professions and
from clerical work. Maud Martha also finds work as a domestic where she encounters the brutal condescension of her
white employers. These examples have a special meaning
for me because in the 1920s my mother and my five aunts
migrated to Cleveland, Ohio, from Indianapolis and, in spite
of their many talents, they found every door except the
kitchen door closed to them. My youngest aunt was trained
as a bookkeeper and was so good at her work that her white
employer at Guardian Savings of Indianapolis allowed her to
work at the branch in a black area. The Cleveland Trust
Company was not so liberal, however, so in Cleveland (as
Toni Morrison asks, "What could go wrong in Ohio?") she
went to work in what is known in the black community as
"private family." Her thwarted career is not simply a narrow
personal tragedy. As these texts make clear to us—and they
are the only texts that tell this story—several generations of
competent and talented black women, all of whom *had* to
work, were denied access to the most ordinary kind of jobs
and therefore to any kind of economic freedom.

Women's sexuality is another subject treated very differ-
ently by women and men writers. In the male slave narrative
for example, sexuality is nearly always avoided, and when it
does surface it is to report the sexual abuse of female slaves

The male slave narrator was under no compulsion to discuss his own sexuality nor that of other men. As far as we know, the only slave narrator forced to admit a sexual life was Linda Brent who bore two children as a single woman rather than submit to forced concubinage. Her reluctance to publish *Incidents* because it was not the life of "a Heroine with no degradation associated with it" shows that sexuality literally made a woman an unfit subject for literature. In Harlem Renaissance literature, as Barbara Christian reminds us, only male writers felt free to celebrate exoticized sexuality: "The garb of uninhibited passion wears better on a male, who after all, does not have to carry the burden of the race's morality or lack of it."[14] In Renaissance literature, Nella Larsen does represent Helga as a sexual being but that treatment of sex is never celebratory. Helga's sexuality is constantly thwarted, ending as Hazel Carby notes, not in exotic passion but in biological entrapment. In *The Living Is Easy*, Cleo connects sexuality to women's repression and refuses any kind of sexual life, preferring instead emotional intimacy with her sisters and their children. The only woman in these excerpts who revels in her sexuality is Janie Crawford in *Their Eyes Were Watching God*, and, significantly, even in this seemingly idyllic treatment of erotic love, female sexuality is always associated with violence. Janie's mother and grandmother are sexually exploited and Janie is beaten by her glorious lover, Tea Cake, so that he can prove his superiority to other men. What do these stories say about female sexuality? It seems to me that all of them point to the fundamental issue of whether or not women can exert control over their sexuality. Helga Crane, for example, fights against the sexual attraction she feels for Dr. Anderson because that attraction makes her feel out of control. Cleo, who is controlled by her husband in all other aspects of her life, controls him by refusing sex. In *Contending Forces*, Sappho forces her lover to undergo a series of tests in order to determine the constancy of his love. And surely the clearest statement of women's anxiety about sexuality and the need for control over one's female body is made by Linda Brent when she tries to explain to her white female audience why she deliberately chose to bear two children outside of marriage to a white man who was not her owner: "It seems less degrading to give one's self, than to submit to compulsion. There is something akin to freedom in having a lover *who has no control over you*, [emphasis mine] except that which he gains by kindness and attachment."[15] Given this deep alienation from and anxiety about heterosexual relationships, we might wonder if any of these women considered taking women as lovers. If they did, they wrote about such affairs in private places—letters, journals, diaries, poetry—if they wrote about them at all. In a diary, which she kept in the 1920s and 1930s, Alice Dunbar-Nelson is more explicit about sexual intimacy among black women than any writer of that period that I know, but even her revelations are quite guarded: "And Fay, lovely little Fay. One day we saw each other, *one day*, and a year has passed. And still we cannot meet again . . ."[16]

The anxiety of black women writers over the representation of sexuality goes back to the nineteenth century and the prescription for womanly "virtues" which made slave women automatically immoral and less "feminine than white women," but that anxiety is evident even in contemporary texts many of which avoid any kind of sexual vulnerability or project the most extreme forms of sexual vulnerability onto children and poor women. Once again the issue is control, and control is bought by cordoning off those aspects of sexuality that threaten to make women feel powerless. If pleasure and danger are concomitant aspects of sexuality, it seems clear to me that black women writers have, out of historical necessity, registered far more of the latter than the former.

> For a woman to write, she must experiment with "altering and adapting the current shape of her thought without crushing or distorting it."[17]

Although each of the ten fiction writers in this collection in some way challenges conventional notions of what is possible for women characters, "dissenting" from traditions that demand female subordination, I want to single out Zora Neale Hurston and Gwendolyn Brooks for creating narrative strategies whose major concern is the empowerment of women. Both Hurston and Brooks enter fiction through a side door: Hurston was a folklorist and anthropologist; Brooks is primarily a poet. As outsiders both were freer to experiment with fictional forms, the result being that they were able to choose forms that resist female entrapment. Janie Crawford's quest in *Their Eyes Were Watching God* is to recover her own voice and her own sense of autonomy. By framing the story with Janie telling her tale to her friend Pheoby, Hurston makes Janie's self-conscious reflections on her life the central narrative concern. Though Hurston often denies this quest story in favor of the romantic plot, her interest in Janie's heroic potential is unmistakable. In *Maud Martha* Brooks also dislodges the romance plot, first by inventing a woman who does not fit the profile of a romantic heroine and then by making the death of romance essential to Maud's growth. Being a wife, "in every way considering and replenishing him," is in conflict with Maud's own desire for what she vaguely terms "more life." And finally the narrative form itself, as it enacts Maud's rage, her muteness, her indirection, places narrative emphasis on the unsparing, meticulous, courageous consciousness of Maud Martha, making that female consciousness the heroic center of the text. The text that was so arrogantly dismissed in 1953 returns, subversively, in the 1980s, with its rejection of male power, as a critique of the very patriarchal authority that sought its dismissal.

Obviously we will have to learn to read the Afro-American literary tradition in new ways, for continuing on in the old way is impossible. In the past ten or fifteen years the crucial task of reconstruction has been carried on by a number of scholars whose work has made it possible to document black women as artists, as intellectuals, as symbol makers. The continuities of this tradition, as Hortense Spillers tells us, are broken and sporadic, but the knitting together of these fragments has begun. As I look around at my own library shelves I see the texts that have helped to make *Invented Lives* possible. First those pioneering studies undertaken to pave the way for the rest of us: Barbara Christian's, *Black Women Novelists, The Development of a Tradition, 1892–1976;* the invaluable sourcebook, *All the Women Are White, All the Blacks Are Men, But Some of Us Are Brave,* edited by Gloria L. Hull, Patricia Bell Scott, and Barbara Smith; Marilyn Richardson's bibliography, *Black Women and Religion;* Ora Williams's bibliography, *American Black Women;* those early anthologies of black women's literature, *The Black Woman,* edited by Toni Cade Bambara; Pat Crutchfield Exum's *Keeping the Faith;* and *Sturdy Black Bridges: Visions of Black Women in Literature,* edited by Beverly Guy-Sheftall, Roseann P. Bell and Bettye J. Parker.

Robert Hemenway's biography, *Zora Neale Hurston: A Literary Biography,* and Alice Walker's *I Love Myself When I Am Laughing . . . And Then Again When I Am Looking Mean and Impressive: A Zora Neale Hurston Reader* are the major scholarly works that allowed us to reclaim Hurston. Two books on black women's spiritual autobiography, Jean McMahon Humez's *Gifts of Power,* an edition of the writings of Rebecca Jackson Cox, as well as William Andrews's *Sisters of the Spirit* have reclaimed a unique part of black women's early literary tradition. Gloria Hull's edition of Alice Dunbar-Nelson's diary, *Give Us Each Day,* and Dorothy Sterling's *We Are Your Sisters,* a documentary portrayal of nineteenth-century black women, provide evidence of the rich cultural history of black women that is to be found in nontraditional sources. Paula Giddings's history of black women, *When and Where I Enter: The Impact of Black Women on Race and Sex in America* documents the political, social, and literary work of black women.

Deborah E. McDowell's Beacon Press series on black women's fiction has already reissued a number of out-of-print novels, for example, *The Street, Like One of the Family,* and *Iola Leroy.* Rutgers University Press has reissued *Quicksand* and *Passing.* In 1987 a number of important works on black women will be published: Jean Fagan Yellin's definitive edition of Harriet Jacobs's *Incidents in the Life of a Slave Girl* and Hazel Carby's ground-breaking work on black women's narrative tradition: *Reconstructing Womanhood: The Emergence of the Afro-American Woman Novelist.*

As we continue the work of reconstructing a literary history that insists on black women as central to that history, as we reject the old male-dominated accounts of history, refusing to be cramped into the little spaces men have allotted women, we should be aware that this is an act of enlightenment, not simply repudiation. In her 1892 text on black women, *A Voice from the South,* Anna Julia Cooper says that a world in which the female is made subordinate is like a body with one eye bandaged. When the bandage is removed, the body is filled with light: "It sees a circle where before it saw a segment. The darkened eye restored, every member rejoices with it."[18] The making of a literary history in which black women are fully represented is a search for full vision, to create a circle where now we have but a segment.

NOTES

1. Frank Harriott, "The Life of a Pulitzer Poet," *Negro Digest* (August 1950): 14–16.

2. 1953 reviews of *Maud Martha: The New Yorker* (October 10, 1953), unsigned, 160 words; Hubert Creekmore, "Daydreams in Flight," New York *Times Book Review* (October 4, 1953), 400 words; Nicolas Monjo, "Young Girl Growing Up," *Saturday Review* (October 31, 1953), 140 words; and Coleman Rosenberger, New York *Herald Times,* (October 18, 1953), 600 words.

3. 1952 reviews of *Invisible Man:* George Mayberry, "Underground Notes," *The New Republic* (April 21, 1952), 600 words; Irving Howe, "A Negro in America," *The Nation* (May 10, 1952), 950 words; Anthony West, "Black Man's Burden," *The New Yorker* (May 31, 1952),

(unused)

2,100 words; C. J. Rolo, "Candide in Harlem," *The Atlantic* (July 1952), 450 words; Wright Morris, "The World Below," New York *Times Book Review* (April 13, 1952), 900 words; "Black & Blue," *Time* (April 14, 1952), 850 words; and J. E. Cassidy "A Brother Betrayed," *Commonweal* (May 2, 1952), 850 words.

1953 reviews of *Maud Martha*: *The New Yorker* (October 10, 1953), 160 words; Hubert Creekmore, "Daydreams in Flight," New York *Times Book Review* (October 4, 1953), 400 words; Nicolas Monjo "Young Girl Growing Up," *Saturday Review* (October 31, 1953); 140 words; and Coleman Rosenberger, New York *Herald Tribune* (October 18, 1953), 600 words.

The diction of the reviews, too, is revealing. The tone of *Invisible Man* was defined as "vigorous, imaginative, violently humorous and quietly tragic" *(New Republic)*, "searing and exalted" *(The Nation)*; while *Maud Martha* drew "freshness, warm cheerfulness . . . [and] vitality" (New York *Times*), "ingratiating" *(Saturday Review)*. Several reviews of Ellison used "gusto," for Brooks, "liveliness." Brooks's "Negro heroine" (New York *Times*), was characterized as a "young colored woman" *(Saturday Review)* and a "spunky and sophisticated Negro girl" (New York *Times)*; Ellison's character as a "hero" and "pilgrim" *(New Republic)*.

Matters of style received mixed response in both novels. *Maud Martha*'s "impressionistic style" was deemed "not quite sharp or firm enough" and her "remarkable gift" was seen (in the same review) as "mimicry" and an "ability to turn unhappiness and anger into a joke"—a gift that her style did not engender (New York *Times).* The *Saturday Review* said: "Its form is no more than a random narration of loosely assembled incidents" and called its "framework . . . somewhat ramshackle." Only the New York *Times* noticed a significance in her style, and likened the "flashes . . . of sensitive lightness" to Imagist poetics, as well as commenting on the "finer qualities of insight and rhythm."

Both authors are criticized along the same lines concerning form and style, but in the reviews of Brooks, her style is the topic that draws the most attention, and the review is favorable or unfavorable depending upon whether or not the reviewer is personally attracted to "impressionism." Ellison's novel is treated more seriously than Brooks's because his novel is seen as addressing a broader range of issues, despite his sometimes "hysterical" style.

This position is most apparent in Howe's review in *The Nation.* Howe asks serious questions about traditional literary devices, such as narrative stance and voice, and method of characterization, despite the book's lack of "finish." (Ellison's first-person narration is discussed by all reviewers, while Brooks's narrative style is hardly mentioned in any review.) Implicit in Howe's stance toward *Invisible*

Man is an assumption that this is a serious novel to be investigated rigorously in accordance with the (high) standards of the academy. Despite those qualities of tone and style that Howe criticizes it for, *Invisible Man* is important, finally, because it fits into the literary tradition of the epic journey of discovery. Howe calls it a "searing and exalted record of a Negro's journey toward contemporary America in search of success, companionship, and finally himself."

4. The extent to which black men are considered representative of the race was suggested to me most emphatically in *Black Women in Nineteenth-Century American Life: Their Words, Their Thoughts, Their Feelings,* ed. Bert James Loewenberg and Ruth Bogin (University Park: Pennsylvania State University Press, 1976). In their introduction, "Women, Blacks, History," the editors make this comment: "Not only do black women seldom appear in treatments of black history, but historians have been content to permit the male to represent the female in almost every significant category. Thus it is the male who is the representative abolitionist, fugitive slave, or political activist. The black male is the leader, the entrepreneur, the politician, the man of thought. When historians discuss black abolitionist writers and lecturers, they are men. David Walker, Charles Lenox Remond, and a procession of male stalwarts preempt the list in conventional accounts. Particularly later when black history was consciously written, it was the male, not the female, who recorded it. Women are conspicuous by their silence." (p. 4)

5. Alfred A. Moss, Jr., *The American Negro Academy: Voice of the Talented Tenth* (Baton Rouge: Louisiana State University Press, 1981). According to Moss, The American Negro Academy, the first major black American learned society was founded March 5, 1897 in Washington, D.C. The constitution of the ANA defined it as "an organization of authors, scholars, artists, and those distinguished in other walks of life, men of African descent, for the promotion of Letters, Science, and Art." While Dubois argued for a more democratic membership "because we find men who are not distinguished in science or literature or art are just the men we want," he did not, apparently argue for women. Theophilus G. Steward, one of the invited members, was the only one who specifically declared himself opposed to the admission of women. (pp. 38, 42)

6. Nearly every Afro-American literary history reads the tradition as primarily a male tradition, beginning with the male slave narrative as the source which generates the essential texts in the canon. With absolute predictability the Frederick Douglass 1845 *Narrative* is the text that issues the call, and the response comes back loud and clear from W. E. B. Du Bois, James Weldon Johnson, Richard Wright, James Baldwin, and Ralph Ellison. So firmly established is this male

hegemony that even men's arguments with one another (Wright, Baldwin, Ellison) get written into the tradition as a way of interpreting its development. As most feminist critics have noted, women writers cannot simply be inserted into the gaps, or be used to prefigure male writers, the tradition has to be conceptualized from a feminist viewpoint.

7. Benjamin Brawley, *The Negro Genius: A New Appraisal of the Achievement of the American Negro in Literature and the Fine Arts* (New York: Bibb and Tannen, 1969), p. 258. Of the thirteen portraits of writers and artists in this book, only two are of women.

8. Richard Wright, " 'Between Laughter and Tears,' " *New Masses* 5 (October 1937): 25–26.

9. Richard Wright, "The Literature of the Negro of the United States," in *White Man Listen!* (Garden City, N.Y.: Doubleday & Company, 1964), p. 76.

10. William Robinson, *Phillis Wheatley in the Black American Beginnings* (Detroit: Broadside Press, 1976); Alice Walker, "In Search of Our Mothers' Gardens," in *In Search of Our Mothers' Gardens: Womanist Prose* (New York: Harcourt Brace Jovanovich, 1983), pp. 231–43 and M. A. Richmond, *Bid the Vassal Soar: Interpretive Essays on the Life and Poetry of Phillis Wheatley and George Moses Horton* (Washington D.C.: Howard University Press, 1974).

11. Hortense J. Spillers, "A Hateful Passion, A Lost Love," *Feminist Studies* 9, no. 2 (Summer 1983): 297.

12. In *Reconstructing Womanhood: The Emergence of the Afro-American Woman Novelist* (New York: Oxford University Press, 1987), Hazel Carby discusses this dismissal of the Brent narrative by John Blassingame in *The Slave Community: Plantation Life in the Antebellum South* (New York: Oxford University Press, 1979).

13. Wright " 'Beyond Laughter and Tears.' "

14. Barbara Christian, *Black Women Novelists: The Development of a Tradition 1892–1976* (Westport, Conn.: Greenwood Press, 1980) p. 40.

15. Linda Brent, *Incidents in the Life of a Slave Girl*, ed. L. Maria Child (New York: Harcourt Brace Jovanovich, 1973), p. 55.

16. Gloria T. Hull, ed., *Give Us Each Day: The Diary of Alice Dunbar Nelson* (New York: W. W. Norton & Company, 1984), pp. 421–22

17. In *Writing Beyond the Ending: Narrative Strategies of Twentieth-Century Women Writers* (Bloomington: Indiana University Press, 1985) p. 32, Rachel Blau DuPlessis quotes Virginia Woolf's prescription

for women's writing, "Women and Fiction," in *Granite and Rainbow* (New York: Harcourt Brace and Company, 1958), p. 80.

18. Anna J. Cooper, *A Voice from the South by a Black Woman of the South* (Xenia, Oh.: Aldine Printing House, 1892), p. 123.

PART ONE

Oh slavery, slavery, my Daddy would say.
It ain't something in a book, Lue.
Even the good parts was awful.
                    —Lucille Clifton, *Generations*

INTRODUCTION

Meditations on History:
The Slave Woman's Voice

In 1861, with the help of two white abolitionists, Amy Post and Lydia Maria Child, Harriet Jacobs, abolitionist and ex-slave, published under the pseudonym, Linda Brent, an account of her life in slavery called *Incidents in the Life of a Slave Girl*, one of the few slave narratives written by a woman.[1] Working in New York as a nurse for the well-known magazinist, Nathaniel Parker Willis, Jacobs had to write her autobiography secretly at night when she could steal the time from her duties taking care of four small children in an eighteen-room house. The Willis' demanding social schedule exhausted everyone in the house. Jacobs wrote to Amy Post in 1853 that despite these continual interruptions, she was determined to get her story written: "Poor Hatty's name is so much in demand that I cannot accomplish much; if I could steal away and have two quiet months to myself, I would work night and day though it should all fall to the ground . . . As yet I have not written a single page by daylight."[2]

Twenty years after her escape from slavery, Harriet Jacobs published what may very well be the only slave narrative that deals primarily with the sexual exploitation of slave women. Linda Brent deliberately chooses to bear two children by a white man in order to escape the sexual harassment of her legal master, Dr. Flint, a choice that labels her a disgrace in the eyes of her family and her community and herself. Harriet Jacobs's narrative is unique in still other ways. Brent does not follow the usual pattern of the male fugitive slave who flees to freedom, leaving behind kith and kin. She is so reluctant to leave her children and grandmother that she hides out in a tiny garret at the top of her grandmother's house for several years. Nor is there any man-to-man physical confrontation between Brent and her owner; she exerts her power against Flint in more covert and clandestine ways.

And when she comes to write her story, she encounters a problem that no male slave autobiographer had to contend with. The male narrator was under no compulsion to discuss his sexuality or his sex life; he did not have to reveal the existence of children he may have fathered outside of marriage. However, neither Linda Brent's sexual exploitation nor her two half-white children could be ignored in the story of her bondage and her freedom. The male narrator could write his tale as a reclamation of his manhood, but under the terms of white society's ideals of chastity and sexual ignorance for women Brent certainly cannot claim "true" womanhood.[3] By the hypocritical standards of nineteenth-century Victorian morality, Brent was a scandalous woman with a disgraceful past. This question of a woman's shame over her sexuality is central to our understanding of Brent's narrative; for, unlike male slave narrators who wrote to show that they had the qualities valued and respected by other men—courage, mobility, rationality, and physical strength— Harriet Jacobs wrote to confess that she did not have the qualities valued in white women.[4] Writing again to her trusted friend, Amy Post, Jacobs struggled with her feelings of humiliation about her past life and anguished over whether she should expose herself by writing her life story:

> Your proposal to me has been thought over and over again, but not without some most painful remembrance. Dear Amy, if it was the life of a Heroine with no degradation associated with it! Far better to have been one of the starving poor of Ireland whose bones had to bleach on the highways than to have been a slave with the curse of slavery stamped upon yourself and Children. . . . I have tried for the last two years to conquer [my stubborn pride] and I feel that God has helped me on. I never would consent to give my past life to anyone without giving the whole truth. If it could help save another from my fate it would be selfish and unchristian in me to keep it back.[5]

Though she is unable to say so directly, Brent was a sexually experienced woman even at the age of fifteen. She tries to explain her sexual maturity discreetly: "The influences of slavery had had the same effect on me that they had on other young girls; they had made me prematurely knowing, concerning the ways of the world. I knew what I did, and I did it with deliberate calculation" (p. 56).

But Brent cannot savor the satisfaction of her actions because the very act of taking control of her life is also, for a woman, a fall from grace. Her grandmother nearly disowns her, Brent herself feels degraded, and, when she comes to write her story, she chooses to tell it in a form that made it impossible for her to discuss her sexual abuse openly.

Writing in the nineteenth century and in the form of the domestic sentimental novel, Brent had to observe conventions of decorum which demanded virginity, modesty, and delicacy of women.[6] Locked into these conventions, Brent presents Dr. Flint as a jealous lover and herself as a vulnerable, young woman undergoing a "perilous passage" rather than a slave whose sexual exploitation was legally sanctioned. Her use of romantic language seems more suited to a story of seduction than to the slave woman's life. As contemporary critics of the Brent narrative have demonstrated, Brent was obviously reaching for a form that would help her to establish rapport with her Northern white women readers, and they would most certainly have been familiar with the domestic novel. It was, in almost every way, a poor choice for her story, for a novel that described the perfect woman as the submissive, pious, and devoted wife of a white man "mocked the condition of the female slave."[7] If the domestic novel of sentiment and melodrama helped Brent to reach an audience of women who were familiar with this form, it also severely limited her ability to produce a written account of her life as profound as her own experiences.

But Harriet Jacobs did not allow the sentimental novel to reenslave her as some critics have said.[8] Her contemporary interpreters, Jean Fagan Yellin, Hazel Carby, Valerie Smith, and Joanne Braxton have demonstrated conclusively Brent's struggle to resist the ideological implications of the sentimental novel and the cult of true womanhood. It is an ideology, writes Carby, "that would deny her very existence as woman and as mother."[9] Yellin argues further that the Brent narrative actually defies the domestic novel's rules of sexual propriety:

> Despite her language (and what other one wonders was available to her?) this narrator does not characterize herself conventionally as a passive female victim. On the contrary, she asserts that she was—even when young and a slave—an effective moral agent, and she takes full responsibility for her actions.[10]

Brent's deliberate and knowing choice to take a white lover and to bear two children by him in order to foil Dr. Flint's plans to make her his mistress is, in some ways, an act of emancipation. That she sees it as a means to free herself is clear: "It seems less degrading to give one's self than to submit to compulsion. There is something akin to freedom in having a lover who has no control over you, except that which he gains by kindness and attachment" (p. 55).

Yellin also invites us to consider that "extraordinary sentence" in *Incidents* in which Brent, refusing to be bound by the standards and morality of white women, "proposes a new definition of female morality grounded in her own experience."[11] Having confessed her sexual experience and her willful use of it, Brent concludes, "Still, in looking back calmly, on the events of my life, I feel that the slave woman ought not to be judged by the same standard as others" (p. 56). These are neither the words nor the sentiment, nor the rhetoric, of the domestic novel or the novel of seduction.[12] The sentence is direct, powerful, unadorned; and it separates Linda Brent from the women of sentimental fiction. Brent makes that separation even more explicit when, at the end of her story, she eschews the sentimental novel's passive stance for one of power and autonomy: "Reader, my story ends with freedom; not in the usual way, with marriage. . and my children are now free."

In spite of Harriet Jacobs's twenty-year struggle to write her story; in spite of her status as social activist—she worked in the antislavery office and reading room in Rochester where she met Amy Post and other abolitionists—in spite of her work as a teacher and nurse with the newly freed people in Virginia, where she and her daughter Louisa organized sewing circles and schools; in spite of the book's enthusiastic reception at the time of its publication, Harriet Jacobs's narrative was considered by many twentieth-century scholars to be a fraud. In his 1972 edition of his landmark study of slave narratives, *Slave Testimony,* John Blassingame dismisses Jacobs's story as too melodramatic to be authentic. Using the male slave narrative as the standard, Blassingame cannot accept this "nonstandard" female slave narrative with its peculiar form, the many examples of "miscegenation and outraged virtue, unrequited love, and planter licentiousness [which] appear on practically every page." But, as Hazel Carby argues in her study of female slave narratives, this rejection of the female story is based on criteria that exclude the female experience:

> . . . issues of miscegenation, unrequited love, outraged virtue and planter licentiousness, are found foregrounded in diaries by southern white women while absent or in the background of the records of their planter husbands. Identifying such a difference should lead us to question and consider the significance of these issues in the lives of women as opposed to men not to the conclusion that the diaries are not credible because they deviate from the conventions of male authored texts.[13]

Black women wrote about 12 percent of the total number of extant slave narratives, but none of these is as well known as the narratives by men. The result has been that the life of the male slave has come to be representative, even though the female experience in slavery was sometimes radically different, as the Jacobs narrative documents.[14] What is also different—often radically—is the written form of their narratives. In male narratives, women play subordinate roles. Men leave them behind when they escape to the North, or they are pitiable subjects of brutal treatment, or benign nurturers who help the fugitive in his quest for freedom, or objects of sentimentality. Or, as in the case of the Frederick Douglass *Narrative*, they are simply rendered invisible. Douglass tells the story of his escape as though he were a solo artist—self-initiating, self-propelling, and self-sustaining—making the plunge into the dark night of freedom alone and unassisted. The testimony of his eldest daughter, Rosetta, tells quite a different story: that one Anna Murray, a free black woman of Baltimore, welcomed Frederick Bailey (as he was then known) into her circle of friends, that a romance developed between them, that not only did Anna make the sailor suit that Douglass wore in his daring escape disguised as a sailor, but that she used funds from her savings as a valued household worker to help him get safely to New York and, a week after his arrival, "she confidently joined in matrimony, this man, this escaped slave with a price on his head and then went on to face with him the double uncertainty of life in the North."[15] I have often wondered why none of this critical information about Anna Murray Douglass found its way into Douglass's poignant story. Like the Douglass *Narrative*, the plot of the standard male narrative, Valerie Smith points out, is not only "the journey from slavery to freedom, but also the journey from slavehood to manhood." She comments, "By mythologizing rugged individuality, physical strength, and geographical mobility, the narratives of men enshrine cultural definitions of masculinity."[16]

Narratives by women play an important part in allowing us to hear the voices of slave women; they show women as active agents rather than objects of pity, capable of interpreting their experiences and, like men, able to turn their victimization into triumph. Hazel Carby makes the point that women slave narrators describe their victimization in a context that also shows them fighting back:

> Narratives by black women foreground their active tales as historical agents as opposed to passive subjects, acting upon their own visions they make decisions over their own lives. They do also document their sufferings and brutal treatment *but in a context that is also the story of resistance* [emphasis mine].[17]

The Linda Brent narrative is such a story about a woman in the act of resistance. Her resistance took bizarre forms, but, however melodramatic her autobiography may seem by contemporary standards, we now know that the facts of her life presented in *Incidents* are irrefutable. According to Yellin, there is enough external evidence to establish beyond a doubt the truthfulness of Jacobs's account of her life.

In 1982 Yellin went to North Carolina, interviewed local historians, and worked in the state archives which enabled her to identify nearly all of the people and places in *Incidents*, including "Dr. Flint," who was a prominent North Carolina doctor, and, according to Yellin's findings, evidently capable of just the sort of tyranny presented in *Incidents*. Walking through Edenton, Yellin found the town exactly as Jacobs described it, the historic area where Jacobs lived so compact that it would be possible to look out of an attic window and observe many of the town's activities. Yellin says she has absolute faith in Jacobs's reconstruction of events in *Incidents*: "You can trust her. She's not ever wrong. She may be wrong on incidentals like the birth order of her mistress's children—after all she was a woman in her forties trying to remember what happened to her as a teenager—but she's never wrong in substance."[18]

Furthermore, the discovery of a cache of her letters showing her in the act of creating her narrative also proves that *Incidents* was indeed written by Harriet Jacobs. Through these letters we discover, for example, that, though she refused the aid of her proslavery employer, Nathaniel Willis,

Jacobs did ask Harriet Beecher Stowe to help her write her manuscript. Stowe, the prominent author of *Uncle Tom's Cabin*, suggested that she use Jacobs's story in *The Key to Uncle Tom's Cabin*, which Stowe was rushing to complete. Jacobs was firmly opposed to that idea and determined to be the author of her own life. She requested her employer, Mrs. Willis, to write to Stowe, saying "that I wished it to be a history of my life entirely by itself, which would do more good, and it needed no romance; but if she wanted some facts for her book, that I would be most happy to give her some."[19]

We know also from these letters and from her preface that Jacobs was embarrassed about the revelations of her sexual life. She expressed to Post her need for a woman to write an introduction to the book that would justify its sensational contents: "I have thought that I wanted some female friend to write a preface or some introductory remarks . . . yet believe me, dear friend, there are many painful things in . . . . . [my book] that make me shrink from asking this sacrifice from one so good and pure as yourself."[20] Jacobs was able to persuade Lydia Maria Child, another abolitionist, to write an introduction that was intended to influence white Northern women to accept her story in spite of its "indecorum." Child accepted the responsibility of presenting slavery "with the veil withdrawn" for the greater purpose of arousing Northern white women to exert their influence against slavery. And Jacobs finally agreed to publish her story that was "no fiction" in order to expose not just her own suffering, but "the condition of two millions of women at the South, still in bondage, suffering what I suffered, and most of them far worse" (p. xi).

While much of the current criticism and analysis of *Incidents* focuses on its relationship to the domestic novel and its subversion of that form, my own reading of *Incidents* would connect it to the tradition of the Afro-American slave narrative. For me, the pivotal moment in the Brent text, one consistently overlooked in feminist readings, is one that transcends the boundaries of gender and unites Brent with both male and female slave narrators determined to affirm a self in a world equally determined to annihilate that self. Near the end of her story, Brent becomes enraged when she learns that Mrs. Bruce has arranged to buy her from Dr. Flint. The buying and selling of Linda Brent—even if Mrs. Bruce's ultimate goal is to give her her freedom—is an act that demonstrates the white woman's power and the black woman's powerlessness; and Brent deeply resents being forced to acknowledge herself as chattel:

> The more my mind has become enlightened, the more difficult it was for me to consider myself an article of property; and to pay money to those who had so grievously oppressed me seemed like taking from my suffering the glory of triumph. I wrote to Mrs. Bruce, thanking her, but saying that being sold from one owner to another seemed too much like slavery; that such a great obligation could not be easily cancelled; and that I preferred to go to my brother in California. (p. 205)

This demonstration of anger, outrage, and obstinacy, as Brent calls it, is the moment of real triumph in the text. Brent refuses the role of pathetic victim as well as the role of grateful slave rescued by noble benefactor. Furthermore, her defiance links Brent to the tradition of narrators who finally throw off all the shackles of slavery and exert control over their own voice. As Marilyn Richardson says in her review of *Our Nig* (1859), the confrontation by which the black character claims a distinct sense of self "is one of the classic recurring scenes in all early black writing."[21] Brent's sense of herself as too enlightened to consider herself a piece of property reminds me of that turning point in Frederick Douglass's *Narrative* after which he tells us he could no longer consider himself a slave, even though legally he was still owned by a white man. Even when he is working for a "good" master, Douglass, like Brent, is beyond the point where he can consider anyone his "master": "I will give Mr.

Freeland the credit of being the best master I ever had, till I became my own *master* . . . . by this time I began to want to live *upon free land* as well as *with Freeland;* and I was no longer content, therefore, to live with him or any other slave-holder."[22]

The rhetoric in the Brent passage is also reminiscent of Douglass's *Narrative.* The balanced parallel phrases ("The more my mind had become enlightened, the more difficult it was for me to consider myself an article of property"); the powerful active voice ("I preferred to go to my brother in California"); the desire to claim her own moment of glory ("to pay money to those who had so grievously oppressed me seemed like taking from my suffering the glory of triumph")—these rhetorical patterns connect Brent to all those other figures in the slave narrative tradition who re-created a self and a voice in order to challenge a system that meant to destroy them.

Harriet Jacobs/Linda Brent was subjected to many kinds of imprisonment. She deliberately confined herself to a cramped attic space for many years in order to achieve freedom; she was confined by a slave narrative tradition that took the male's experiences as representative and marginalized the female's experiences; and she was rendered nearly invisible by a fictional tradition that made white skin a requirement for womanhood. She resisted all of these imprisonments to create a document that helps to answer the question, What was it like to be a *female* slave? In spite of the constraints against a black woman that made it nearly impossible for her to achieve authority in her own life as well as in the retelling of that life, Jacobs, nonetheless, succeeded in doing both.

NOTES

1. Harriet Jacobs, *Incidents in the Life of a Slave Girl* (New York: Harcourt Brace Jovanovich, 1973). Subsequent references will be to this edition.

2. Dorothy Sterling, ed., *We Are Your Sisters: Black Women in the Nineteenth Century* (New York: W. W. Norton Company, 1984), p. 80.

3. Barbara Welter describes the nineteenth-century notion of true womanhood in her essay, "The Cult of True Womanhood," *Dimity Convictions: The American Woman in the Nineteenth Century* (Athens: Ohio University Press, 1977), pp. 21–41.

4. As Jean Yellin points out in her reading of this essay, Jacobs's emphasis on herself as a devoted mother feeds into the Victorian idolatry of motherhood. While her sexual involvement precludes her from claiming true womanhood, her devotion to her children partly reclaims her. *Women and Sisters* (New Haven: Yale University Press, forthcoming).

5. Sterling, *We Are Your Sisters*, p. 75.

6. I do not wish to join the list of critics who have traditionally maligned the "domestic" or "sentimental" novel. The new scholarship on nineteenth-century American women's writing challenges the gender politics which has made terms like *sentimental* and *domestic* pejorative buzzwords used to ridicule and dismiss nineteenth-century women. Judith Fetterly's *Provisions: A Reader from 19th Century American Women* (Bloomington: Indiana University Press, 1985) and Lucy Freibert and Barbara A. White's *Hidden Hands; An Anthology of American Women Writers, 1790–1870* (New Brunswick, N.J.: Rutgers University Press, 1985) offer reassessments of the domestic novel which suggest that nineteenth-century women writers were no more sentimental or melodramatic than the men of their era, that, in fact, women were predominantly realistic writers, more overtly concerned with social and political issues than nineteenth-century American [white] men. (Qualification mine.)

7. Annette Niemtzow, "The Problematic of Self in Autobiography: The Example of the Slave Narrative," in *The Art of Slave Narrative: Original Essays in Criticism and Theory*, ed. John Sekora and Darwin T. Turner (Macomb, Ill.: Western Illinois University, 1982), p. 105.

8. In their essays in *The Art of Slave Narrative* both Niemtzow and Raymond Hedin conclude that Harriet Jacobs is unable to triumph over the conventions of the sentimental novel. In "Strategies of

Form in the American Slave Narrative," Hedin says women narrators had less reason than did men to undercut the genre of the sentimental novel because the vulnerable woman image could elicit the emotional responses they wanted from their largely female readers. Niemtzow says in "The Problematic of Self in Autobiography" that in her attempt to gain the virtues of true womanhood, Linda Brent allows the domestic novel to consume her authentic voice. I agree with Jean Fagan Yellin, Hazel Carby, and Valerie Smith who have conclusively proved that Brent does triumph over the limits of the form she has chosen.

9. Hazel Carby, *Reconstructing Womanhood: The Emergence of the Afro-American Woman Novelist* (New York: Oxford University Press, 1987).

10. Jean Yellin, "Text and Contexts of Harriet Jacobs's *Incidents in the Life of a Slave Girl: Written By Herself,"* in *The Slave's Narrative,* ed. Charles T. Davis and Henry Louis Gates, Jr., (New York: Oxford University Press, 1985), p. 273.

11. Ibid., p. 274.

12. Jean Yellin makes a distinction between the novel of seduction and what Nina Baym calls "women's fiction." Baym argues that "women's fiction," also called the domestic or sentimental novel, does show women as active. Women as passive victims are found more often in the novel of seduction.

13. In *Reconstructing Womanhood,* Hazel Carby rejects the notion of a representative narrative based on the male slave narrative. She argues that John Blassingame's *The Slave Community: Plantation Life in the Antebellum South* (New York: Oxford University Press, 1979), as well as other studies that exclude the female narrative are limited because they rely on a set of assumptions based on the experiences of men, pp. 74–75.

14. Sekora and Turner, *The Art of Slave Narrative,* a recent book of critical essays on the slave narrative, features a cover designed by Preston Jackson. Representing the slave is a large muscular man in a loincloth, his head bent from the weight of a heavy burden, his muscles straining to carry the load. Blassingame's *Slave Testimony* also features a picture of a man on the inside front page. As these images indicate, many interpretations and/or critical studies of the slave narrative imagined the representative slave as a man.

15. Sylvia Lyons Render, "Afro-American Women: The Outstanding and the Obscure," *The Quarterly Journal of the Library of Congress* (October 1975): 308.

16. Valerie Smith, "Narrative Authority in Twentieth-Century Afro-American Fiction" (Cambridge: Harvard University Press, 1987), forthcoming.

7. Carby, *Reconstructing Womanhood*, p. 22.

8. Telephone conversation with Jean Fagan Yellin, August 26, 985. Yellin's first documentation of the authenticity of *Incidents* was ne essay, "Written by Herself: Harriet Jacobs' Slave Narrative," *merican Literature* 53 (November 1981): 479–86. She has done an nnotated edition of *Incidents*, that establishes the real names of the eople in the narrative and further documents the authenticity of acobs's autobiography (Cambridge: Harvard University Press, 987).

9. Sterling, *We Are Your Sisters*, p. 77.

0. Yellin, "Written by Herself," pp. 485–86.

1. Marilyn Richardson, "The Shadow of Slavery," *The Women's eview of Books* 1, no. 1 (October 1983): 15.

2. Benjamin Quarles, ed., *Narrative of the Life of Frederick Douglass: n American Slave Written by Himself* (Cambridge: Harvard University ress, 1979), p. 116.

HARRIET JACOBS

The Perils of a
Slave Woman's Life

THE TRIALS OF GIRLHOOD

During the first years of my service in Dr. Flint's family, I was
accustomed to share some indulgences with the children of
my mistress. Though this seemed to me no more than right,
I was grateful for it, and tried to merit the kindness by the
faithful discharge of my duties. But I now entered on my
fifteenth year—a sad epoch in the life of a slave girl. My
master began to whisper foul words in my ear. Young as I
was, I could not remain ignorant of their import. I tried to
treat them with indifference or contempt. The master's age,
my extreme youth, and the fear that his conduct would be
reported to my grandmother, made him bear this treatment
for many months. He was a crafty man, and resorted to many
means to accomplish his purposes. Sometimes he had
stormy, terrific ways, that made his victims tremble; sometimes he assumed a gentleness that he thought must surely
subdue. Of the two, I preferred his stormy moods, although
they left me trembling. He tried his utmost to corrupt the
pure principles my grandmother had instilled. He peopled
my young mind with unclean images, such as only a vile
monster could think of. I turned from him with disgust and
hatred. But he was my master. I was compelled to live under
the same roof with him—where I saw a man forty years my
senior daily violating the most sacred commandments o

"The Perils of a Slave Woman's Life" from *Incidents in the Life of a
Slave Girl* (1860)

nature. He told me I was his property; that I must be subject to his will in all things. My soul revolted against the mean tyranny. But where could I turn for protection? No matter whether the slave girl be as black as ebony or as fair as her mistress. In either case, there is no shadow of law to protect her from insult, from violence, or even from death; all these are inflicted by fiends who bear the shape of men. The mistress, who ought to protect the helpless victim, has no other feelings towards her but those of jealousy and rage. The degradation, the wrongs, the vices, that grow out of slavery, are more than I can describe. They are greater than you would willingly believe. Surely, if you credited one half the truths that are told you concerning the helpless millions suffering in this cruel bondage, you at the north would not help to tighten the yoke. You surely would refuse to do for the master, on your own soil, the mean and cruel work which trained bloodhounds and the lowest class of whites do for him at the south.

Every where the years bring to all enough of sin and sorrow; but in slavery the very dawn of life is darkened by these shadows. Even the little child, who is accustomed to wait on her mistress and her children, will learn, before she is twelve years old, why it is that her mistress hates such and such a one among the slaves. Perhaps the child's own mother is among those hated ones. She listens to violent outbreaks of jealous passion, and cannot help understanding what is the cause. She will become prematurely knowing in evil things. Soon she will learn to tremble when she hears her master's footfall. She will be compelled to realize that she is no longer a child. If God has bestowed beauty upon her, it will prove her greatest curse. That which commands admiration in the white woman only hastens the degradation of the female slave. I know that some are too much brutalized by slavery to feel the humiliation of their position; but many slaves feel it most acutely, and shrink from the memory of it. I cannot tell how much I suffered in the presence of these wrongs, nor how I am still pained by the retrospect.

My master met me at every turn, reminding me that I belonged to him, and swearing by heaven and earth that he would compel me to submit to him. If I went out for a breath of fresh air, after a day of unwearied toil, his footsteps dogged me. If I knelt by my mother's grave, his dark shadow fell on me even there. The light heart which nature had given me became heavy with sad forebodings. The other slaves in my master's house noticed the change. Many of them pitied me; but none dared to ask the cause. They had no need to inquire. They knew too well the guilty practices under that roof; and they were aware that to speak of them was an offence that never went unpunished.

I longed for some one to confide in. I would have given the world to have laid my head on my grandmother's faithful bosom, and told her all my troubles. But Dr. Flint swore he would kill me, if I was not as silent as the grave. Then, although my grandmother was all in all to me, I feared her as well as loved her. I had been accustomed to look up to her with a respect bordering upon awe. I was very young, and felt shamefaced about telling her such impure things, especially as I knew her to be very strict on such subjects. Moreover, she was a woman of a high spirit. She was usually very quiet in her demeanor; but if her indignation was once roused, it was not very easily quelled. I had been told that she once chased a white gentleman with a loaded pistol, because he insulted one of her daughters. I dreaded the consequences of a violent outbreak; and both pride and fear kept me silent. But though I did not confide in my grandmother, and even evaded her vigilant watchfulness and inquiry, her presence in the neighborhood was some protection to me. Though she had been a slave, Dr. Flint was afraid of her. He dreaded her scorching rebukes. Moreover, she was known and patronized by many people; and he did not wish to have his villainy made public. It was lucky for me that I did not live on a distant plantation, but in a town not so large that the inhabitants were ignorant of each other's affairs. Bad as are the laws and customs in a slaveholding community, the doctor, as a professional man, deemed it prudent to keep up some outward show of decency.

O, what days and nights of fear and sorrow that man caused me! Reader, it is not to awaken sympathy for myself that I am telling you truthfully what I suffered in slavery. I do it to kindle a flame of compassion in your hearts for my sisters who are still in bondage, suffering as I once suffered.

I once saw two beautiful children playing together. One was a fair white child; the other was her slave, and also her sister. When I saw them embracing each other, and heard their joyous laughter, I turned sadly away from the lovely sight. I foresaw the inevitable blight that would fall on the little slave's heart. I knew how soon her laughter would be changed to sighs. The fair child grew up to be a still fairer woman. From childhood to womanhood her pathway was blooming with flowers, and overarched by a sunny sky. Scarcely one day of her life had been clouded when the sun rose on her happy bridal morning.

How had those years dealt with her slave sister, the little playmate of her childhood? She, also, was very beautiful; but the flowers and sunshine of love were not for her. She drank the cup of sin, and shame, and misery, whereof her persecuted race are compelled to drink.

In view of these things, why are ye silent, ye free men and women of the north? Why do your tongues falter in maintenance of the right? Would that I had more ability! But my heart is so full, and my pen is so weak! There are noble men and women who plead for us, striving to help those who cannot help themselves. God bless them! God give them strength and courage to go on! God bless those, every where, who are laboring to advance the cause of humanity!

THE JEALOUS MISTRESS

I would ten thousand times rather that my children should be the half-starved paupers of Ireland than to be the most pampered among the slaves of America. I would rather drudge out my life on a cotton plantation, till the grave opened to give me rest, than to live with an unprincipled master and a jealous mistress. The felon's home in a penitentiary is preferable. He may repent, and turn from the error of his ways, and so find peace; but it is not so with a favorite slave. She is not allowed to have any pride of character. It is deemed a crime in her to wish to be virtuous.

Mrs. Flint possessed the key to her husband's character before I was born. She might have used this knowledge to counsel and to screen the young and the innocent among her slaves; but for them she had no sympathy. They were the objects of her constant suspicion and malevolence. She watched her husband with unceasing vigilance; but he was well practised in means to evade it. What he could not find opportunity to say in words he manifested in signs. He invented more than were ever thought of in a deaf and dumb asylum. I let them pass, as if I did not understand what he meant; and many were the curses and threats bestowed on me for my stupidity. One day he caught me teaching myself to write. He frowned, as if he was not well pleased; but I suppose he came to the conclusion that such an accomplishment might help to advance his favorite scheme. Before long, notes were often slipped into my hand. I would return them, saying, "I can't read them, sir." "Can't you?" he replied; "then I must read them to you." He always finished the reading by asking, "Do you understand?" Sometimes he would complain of the heat of the tea room, and order his supper to be placed on a small table in the piazza. He would seat himself there with a well-satisfied smile, and tell me to stand by and brush away the flies. He would eat very slowly, pausing between the mouthfuls. These intervals were employed in describing the happiness I was so foolishly throwing away, and in threatening me with the penalty that finally awaited my stubborn disobedience. He boasted much of the forbearance he had exercised towards me, and reminded me that there was a limit to his patience. When I succeeded in avoiding opportunities for him to talk to me at home, I was ordered to come to his office, to do some errand. When there, I was obliged to stand and listen to such language as he saw fit to address to me. Sometimes I so openly expressed my contempt for him that he would become violently enraged, and I wondered why he did not strike me. Circumstanced as he was, he probably thought it was better policy to be forbearing. But the state of things grew worse and worse daily. In desperation I told him that I must and would apply to my grandmother for protection. He threatened me with death, and worse than death, if I made any complaint to her. Strange to say, I did not despair. I was naturally of a buoyant disposition, and always I had a hope of somehow getting out of his clutches. Like many a poor, simple slave before me, I trusted that some threads of joy would yet be woven into my dark destiny.

I had entered my sixteenth year, and every day it became more apparent that my presence was intolerable to Mrs. Flint. Angry words frequently passed between her and her husband. He had never punished me himself, and he would not allow any body else to punish me. In that respect, she was never satisfied; but, in her angry moods, no terms were too vile for her to bestow upon me. Yet I, whom she detested so bitterly, had far more pity for her than he had, whose duty it was to make her life happy. I never wronged her, or wished to wrong her; and one word of kindness from her would have brought me to her feet.

After repeated quarrels between the doctor and his wife, he announced his intention to take his youngest daughter, then four years old, to sleep in his apartment. It was necessary that a servant should sleep in the same room, to be on hand if the child stirred. I was selected for that office, and informed for what purpose that arrangement had been made. By managing to keep within sight of people, as much as possible, during the day time, I had hitherto succeeded in eluding my master, though a razor was often held to my throat to force me to change this line of policy. At night I slept by the side of my great aunt, where I felt safe. He was too prudent to come into her room. She was an old woman, and had been in the family many years. Moreover, as a married man, and a professional man, he deemed it necessary to save appearances in some degree. But he resolved to remove the obstacle in the way of his scheme; and he thought he had planned it so that he should evade suspicion. He was well aware how much I prized my refuge by the side of my old aunt, and he determined to dispossess me of it. The first night the dotor had the little child in his room alone. The next morning, I was ordered to take my station as nurse the following night. A kind Providence interposed in my favor. During the day Mrs. Flint heard of this new arrangement, and a storm followed. I rejoiced to hear it rage.

After a while my mistress sent for me to come to her room. Her first question was, "Did you know you were to sleep in the doctor's room?"

"Yes, ma'am."

"Who told you?"

"My master."

"Will you answer truly all the questions I ask?"

"Yes, ma'am."

"Tell me, then, as you hope to be forgiven, are you innocent of what I have accused you?"

"I am."

She handed me a Bible, and said, "Lay your hand on your heart, kiss this holy book, and swear before God that you tell me the truth."

I took the oath she required, and I did it with a clear conscience.

"You have taken God's holy word to testify your innocence," said she. "If you have deceived me, beware! Now take this stool, sit down, look me directly in the face, and tell me all that has passed between your master and you."

I did as she ordered. As I went on with my account her color changed frequently, she wept, and sometimes groaned. She spoke in tones so sad, that I was touched by her grief. The tears came to my eyes; but I was soon convinced that her emotions arose from anger and wounded pride. She felt that her marriage vows were desecrated, her dignity insulted; but she had no compassion for the poor victim of her husband's perfidy. She pitied herself as a martyr; but she was incapable of feeling for the condition of shame and misery in which her unfortunate, helpless slave was placed.

Yet perhaps she had some touch of feeling for me; for when the conference was ended, she spoke kindly, and promised to protect me. I should have been much comforted by this assurance if I could have had confidence in it; but my experiences in slavery had filled me with distrust. She was not a very refined woman, and had not much control over her passions. I was an object of her jealousy, and, consequently, of her hatred; and I knew I could not expect kindness or confidence from her under the circumstances in which I was placed. I could not blame her. Slaveholders' wives feel as other women would under similar circumstances. The fire of her temper kindled from small sparks, and now the flame became so intense that the doctor was obliged to give up his intended arrangement.

I knew I had ignited the torch, and I expected to suffer for it afterwards; but I felt too thankful to my mistress for the timely aid she rendered me to care much about that. She now took me to sleep in a room adjoining her own. There I was an object of her especial care, though not of her especial comfort, for she spent many a sleepless night to watch over me. Sometimes I woke up, and found her bending over me. At other times she whispered in my ear, as though it was her husband who was speaking to me, and listened to hear what I would answer. If she startled me, on such occasions, she would glide stealthily away; and the next morning she would tell me I had been talking in my sleep, and ask who I was talking to. At last, I began to be fearful for my life. It had been often threatened; and you can imagine, better than I can describe, what an unpleasant sensation it must produce to wake up in the dead of night and find a jealous woman bending over you. Terrible as this experience was, I had fears that it would give place to one more terrible.

My mistress grew weary of her vigils; they did not prove satisfactory. She changed her tactics. She now tried the trick of accusing my master of crime, in my presence, and gave my name as the author of the accusation. To my utter astonishment, he replied, "I don't believe it; but if she did acknowledge it, you tortured her into exposing me." Tortured into exposing him! Truly, Satan had no difficulty in distinguishing the color of his soul! I understood his object in making this false representation. It was to show me that I gained nothing by seeking the protection of my mistress; that the power was still all in his own hands. I pitied Mrs. Flint. She was a second wife, many years the junior of her husband; and the hoary-headed miscreant was enough to try the patience of a wiser and better woman. She was completely foiled, and knew not how to proceed. She would gladly have had me flogged for my supposed false oath; but, as I have already stated, the doctor never allowed any one to whip me. The old sinner was politic. The application of the lash might have led to remarks that would have exposed him in the eyes of his children and grandchildren. How often did I rejoice that I lived in a town where all the inhabitants knew each other! If I had been on a remote plantation, or lost among the multitude of a crowded city, I should not be a living woman at this day.

The secrets of slavery are concealed like those of the Inquisition. My master was, to my knowledge, the father of eleven slaves. But did the mothers dare to tell who was the father of their children? Did the other slaves dare to allude to it, except in whispers among themselves? No, indeed! They knew too well the terrible consequences.

My grandmother could not avoid seeing things which excited her suspicions. She was uneasy about me, and tried various ways to buy me; but the never-changing answer was always repeated: "Linda does not belong to *me*. She is my daughter's property, and I have no legal right to sell her." The conscientious man! He was too scrupulous to *sell* me; but he had no scruples whatever about committing a much greater wrong against the helpless young girl placed under his guardianship, as his daughter's property. Sometimes my persecutor would ask me whether I would like to be sold. I told him I would rather be sold to any body than to lead such a life as I did. On such occasions he would assume the air of a very injured individual, and reproach me for my ingratitude. "Did I not take you into the house, and make you the companion of my own children?" he would say. "Have I ever treated you like a negro? I have never allowed you to be punished, not even to please your mistress. And this is the recompense I get, you ungrateful girl!" I answered that he had reasons of his own for screening me from punishment, and that the course he pursued made my mistress hate me and persecute me. If I wept, he would say, "Poor child! Don't cry! don't cry! I will make peace for you with your mistress. Only let me arrange matters in my own way. Poor, foolish girl! you don't know what is for your own good. I would cherish you. I would make a lady of you. Now go, and think of all I have promised you."

I did think of it.

Reader, I draw no imaginary pictures of southern homes. I am telling you the plain truth. Yet when victims make their escape from this wild beast of Slavery, northerners consent to act the part of bloodhounds, and hunt the poor fugitive back into his den, "full of dead men's bones, and all uncleanness." Nay, more, they are not only willing, but proud, to give their daughters in marriage to slaveholders. The poor girls have romantic notions of a sunny clime, and of the flowering vines that all the year round shade a happy home. To what disappointments are they destined! The young wife soon learns that the husband in whose hands she has placed her happiness pays no regard to his marriage vows. Children of every shade of complexion play with her own fair babies, and too well she knows that they are born unto him of his own household. Jealousy and hatred enter the flowery home, and it is ravaged of its loveliness.

Southern women often marry a man knowing that he is the father of many little slaves. They do not trouble themselves about it. They regard such children as property, as marketable as the pigs on the plantation; and it is seldom that they do not make them aware of this by passing them into the slave-trader's hands as soon as possible, and thus getting them out of their sight. I am glad to say there are some honorable exceptions.

I have myself known two southern wives who exhorted their husbands to free those slaves towards whom they stood in a "parental relation;" and their request was granted. These husbands blushed before the superior nobleness of their wives' natures. Though they had only counselled them to do that which it was their duty to do, it commanded their respect, and rendered their conduct more exemplary. Concealment was at an end, and confidence took the place of distrust.

Though this bad institution deadens the moral sense, even in white women, to a fearful extent, it is not altogether extinct. I have heard southern ladies say of Mr. Such a one, "He not only thinks it no disgrace to be the father of those little niggers, but he is not ashamed to call himself their master. I declare, such things ought not to be tolerated in any decent society!"

THE LOVER

Why does the slave ever love? Why allow the tendrils of the heart to twine around objects which may at any moment be wrenched away by the hand of violence? When separations come by the hand of death, the pious soul can bow in resignation, and say, "Not my will, but thine be done, O Lord!" But when the ruthless hand of man strikes the blow, regardless of the misery he causes, it is hard to be submissive. I did not reason thus when I was a young girl. Youth will be youth. I loved, and I indulged the hope that the dark clouds around me would turn out a bright lining. I forgot that in the land of my birth the shadows are too dense for light to penetrate. A land

"Where laughter is not mirth; nor thought the mind;
  Nor words a language; nor e'en men mankind.
  Where cries reply to curses, shrieks to blows,
  And each is tortured in his separate hell."

There was in the neighborhood a young colored carpenter; a free-born man. We had been well acquainted in childhood, and frequently met together afterwards. We became mutually attached, and he proposed to marry me. I loved him with all the ardor of a young girl's first love. But when I reflected that I was a slave, and that the laws gave no sanction to the marriage of such, my heart sank within me. My lover wanted to buy me; but I knew that Dr. Flint was too wilful and arbitrary a man to consent to that arrangement. From him, I was sure of experiencing all sorts of opposition, and I had nothing to hope from my mistress. She would have been delighted to have got rid of me, but not in that way. It would have relieved her mind of a burden if she could have seen me sold to some distant state, but if I was married near home I should be just as much in her husband's power as I had previously been,—for the husband of a slave has no power to protect her. Moreover, my mistress, like many others, seemed to think that slaves had no right to any family ties of their own; that they were created merely to wait upon the family of the mistress. I once heard her abuse a young slave girl, who told her that a colored man wanted to make her his wife. "I will have you peeled and pickled, my lady," said she, "if I ever hear you mention that subject again. Do you suppose that I will have you tending *my* children with the children of that nigger?" The girl to whom she said this had a mulatto child, of course not acknowledged by its father. The poor black man who loved her would have been proud to acknowledge his helpless offspring.

Many and anxious were the thoughts I revolved in my mind. I was at a loss what to do. Above all things, I was desirous to spare my lover the insults that had cut so deeply into my own soul. I talked with my grandmother about it, and partly told her my fears. I did not dare to tell her the worst. She had long suspected all was not right, and if I confirmed her suspicions I knew a storm would rise that would prove the overthrow of all my hopes.

This love-dream had been my support through many trials; and I could not bear to run the risk of having it suddenly dissipated. There was a lady in the neighborhood, a particular friend of Dr. Flint's, who often visited the house. I had a great respect for her, and she had always manifested a friendly interest in me. Grandmother thought she would have great influence with the doctor. I went to this lady, and told her my story. I told her I was aware that my lover's being a free-born man would prove a great objection; but he wanted to buy me; and if Dr. Flint would consent to that arrangement, I felt sure he would be willing to pay any reasonable price. She knew that Mrs. Flint disliked me; therefore, I ventured to suggest that perhaps my mistress would approve of my being sold, as that would rid her of me. The lady listened with kindly sympathy, and promised to do her utmost to promote my wishes. She had an interview with he doctor, and I believe she pleaded my cause earnestly; but it was all to no purpose.

How I dreaded my master now! Every minute I expected to be summoned to his presence; but the day passed, and I heard nothing from him. The next morning, a message was brought to me: "Master wants you in his study." I found the door ajar, and I stood a moment gazing at the hateful man who claimed a right to rule me, body and soul. I entered, and tried to appear calm. I did not want him to know how my heart was bleeding. He looked fixedly at me, with an expression which seemed to say, "I have half a mind to kill you on the spot." At last he broke the silence, and that was a relief to both of us.

"So you want to be married, do you?" said he, "and to a free nigger."

"Yes, sir."

"Well, I'll soon convince you whether I am your master, or the nigger fellow you honor so highly. If you *must* have a husband, you may take up with one of my slaves."

What a situation I should be in, as the wife of one of *his* slaves, even if my heart had been interested!

I replied, "Don't you suppose, sir, that a slave can have some preference about marrying? Do you suppose that all men are alike to her?"

"Do you love this nigger?" said he, abruptly.

"Yes, sir."

"How dare you tell me so!" he exclaimed, in great wrath. After a slight pause, he added, "I supposed you thought more of yourself; that you felt above the insults of such puppies."

I replied, "If he is a puppy I am a puppy, for we are both of the negro race. It is right and honorable for us to love each other. The man you call a puppy never insulted me, sir; and he would not love me if he did not believe me to be a virtuous woman."

He sprang upon me like a tiger, and gave me a stunning blow. It was the first time he had ever struck me; and fear did

not enable me to control my anger. When I had recovered a
little from the effects, I exclaimed, "You have struck me for
answering you honestly. How I despise you!"

There was silence for some minutes. Perhaps he was de
ciding what should be my punishment; or, perhaps, he
wanted to give me time to reflect on what I had said, and to
whom I had said it. Finally, he asked, "Do you know what
you have said?"

"Yes, sir; but your treatment drove me to it."

"Do you know that I have a right to do as I like with you,—
that I can kill you, if I please?"

"You have tried to kill me, and I wish you had; but you
have no right to do as you like with me."

"Silence!" he exclaimed, in a thundering voice. "By heav
ens, girl, you forget yourself too far! Are you mad? If you
are, I will soon bring you to your senses. Do you think any
other master would bear what I have borne from you this
morning? Many masters would have killed you on the spot.
How would you like to be sent to jail for your insolence?"

"I know I have been disrespectful, sir," I replied; "but you
drove me to it; I couldn't help it. As for the jail, there would
be more peace for me there than there is here."

"You deserve to go there," said he, "and to be under such
treatment, that you would forget the meaning of the word
peace. It would do you good. It would take some of your high
notions out of you. But I am not ready to send you there yet,
notwithstanding your ingratitude for all my kindness and
forbearance. You have been the plague of my life. I have
wanted to make you happy, and I have been repaid with the
basest ingratitude; but though you have proved yourself
incapable of appreciating my kindness, I will be lenient to
wards you, Linda. I will give you one more chance to redeem
your character. If you behave yourself and do as I require, I
will forgive you and treat you as I always have done; but if
you disobey me, I will punish you as I would the meanest
slave on my plantation. Never let me hear that fellow's name
mentioned again. If I ever know of your speaking to him,

will cowhide you both; and if I catch him lurking about my premises, I will shoot him as soon as I would a dog. Do you hear what I say? I'll teach you a lesson about marriage and free niggers! Now go, and let this be the last time I have occasion to speak to you on this subject."

Reader, did you ever hate? I hope not. I never did but once; and I trust I never shall again. Somebody has called it "the atmosphere of hell;" and I believe it is so.

For a fortnight the doctor did not speak to me. He thought to mortify me; to make me feel that I had disgraced myself by receiving the honorable addresses of a respectable colored man, in preference to the base proposals of a white man. But though his lips disdained to address me, his eyes were very loquacious. No animal ever watched its prey more narrowly than he watched me. He knew that I could write, though he had failed to make me read his letters; and he was now troubled lest I should exchange letters with another man. After a while he became weary of silence; and I was sorry for it. One morning, as he passed through the hall, to leave the house, he contrived to thrust a note into my hand. I thought I had better read it, and spare myself the vexation of having him read it to me. It expressed regret for the blow he had given me, and reminded me that I myself was wholly to blame for it. He hoped I had become convinced of the injury I was doing myself by incurring his displeasure. He wrote that he had made up his mind to go to Louisiana; that he should take several slaves with him, and intended I should be one of the number. My mistress would remain where she was; therefore I should have nothing to fear from that quarter. If I merited kindness from him, he assured me that it would be lavishly bestowed. He begged me to think over the matter, and answer the following day.

The next morning I was called to carry a pair of scissors to his room. I laid them on the table, with the letter beside them. He thought it was my answer, and did not call me back. I went as usual to attend my young mistress to and from school. He met me in the street, and ordered me to stop at his office on my way back. When I entered, he showed me his letter, and asked me why I had not answered it. I replied, "I am your daughter's property, and it is in your power to send me, or take me, wherever you please." He said he was very glad to find me so willing to go, and that we should start early in the autumn. He had a large practice in the town, and I rather thought he had made up the story merely to frighten me. However that might be, I was determined that I would never go to Louisiana with him.

Summer passed away, and early in the autumn Dr. Flint's eldest son was sent to Louisiana to examine the country, with a view to emigrating. That news did not disturb me. I knew very well that I should not be sent with *him*. That I had not been taken to the plantation before this time, was owing to the fact that his son was there. He was jealous of his son; and jealousy of the overseer had kept him from punishing me by sending me into the fields to work. Is it strange that I was not proud of these protectors? As for the overseer, he was a man for whom I had less respect than I had for a bloodhound.

Young Mr. Flint did not bring back a favorable report of Louisiana, and I heard no more of that scheme. Soon after this, my lover met me at the corner of the street, and I stopped to speak to him. Looking up, I saw my master watching us from his window. I hurried home, trembling with fear. I was sent for, immediately, to go to his room. He met me with a blow. "When is mistress to be married?" said he, in a sneering tone. A shower of oaths and imprecations followed. How thankful I was that my lover was a free man! that my tyrant had no power to flog him for speaking to me in the street!

Again and again I revolved in my mind how all this would end. There was no hope that the doctor would consent to sell me on any terms. He had an iron will, and was determined to keep me, and to conquer me. My lover was an intelligent and religious man. Even if he could have obtained permission to marry me while I was a slave, the marriage would give him no power to protect me from my master. It would have made him miserable to witness the insults I should have been subjected to. And then, if we had children, I knew they must "follow the condition of the mother." What a terrible blight that would be on the heart of a free, intelligent father! For *his* sake, I felt that I ought not to link his fate with my own unhappy destiny. He was going to Savannah to see about a little property left him by an uncle; and hard as it was to bring my feelings to it, I earnestly entreated him not to come back. I advised him to go to the Free States, where his tongue would not be tied, and where his intelligence would be of more avail to him. He left me, still hoping the day would come when I could be bought. With me the lamp of hope had gone out. The dream of my girlhood was over. I felt lonely and desolate.

Still I was not stripped of all. I still had my good grandmother, and my affectionate brother. When he put his arms round my neck, and looked into my eyes, as if to read there the troubles I dared not tell, I felt that I still had something to love. But even that pleasant emotion was chilled by the reflection that he might be torn from me at any moment, by some sudden freak of my master. If he had known how we loved each other, I think he would have exulted in separating us. We often planned together how we could get to the north. But, as William remarked, such things are easier said than done. My movements were very closely watched, and we had no means of getting any money to defray our expenses. As for grandmother, she was strongly opposed to her children's undertaking any such project. She had not forgotten poor Benjamin's sufferings, and she was afraid that if another child tried to escape, he would have a similar or a worse fate. To me, nothing seemed more dreadful than my present life. I said to myself, "William *must* be free. He shall go to the north, and I will follow him." Many a slave sister has formed the same plans.

A PERILOUS PASSAGE IN
THE SLAVE GIRL'S LIFE

After my lover went away, Dr. Flint contrived a new plan. He seemed to have an idea that my fear of my mistress was his greatest obstacle. In the blandest tones, he told me that he was going to build a small house for me, in a secluded place four miles away from the town. I shuddered; but I was constrained to listen, while he talked of his intention to give me a home of my own, and to make a lady of me. Hitherto, I had escaped my dreaded fate, by being in the midst of people. My grandmother had already had high words with my master about me. She had told him pretty plainly what she thought of his character, and there was considerable gossip in the neighborhood about our affairs, to which the open-mouthed jealousy of Mrs. Flint contributed not a little. When my master said he was going to build a house for me, and that he could do it with little trouble and expense, I was in hopes something would happen to frustrate his scheme; but I soon heard that the house was actually begun. I vowed before my Maker that I would never enter it. I had rather toil on the planatation from dawn till dark; I had rather live and die in jail, than drag on, from day to day, through such a living death. I was determined that the master, whom I so hated and loathed, who had blighted the prospects of my youth, and made my life a desert, should not, after my long struggle with him, succeed at last in trampling his victim under his feet. I would do any thing, every thing, for the sake of defeating him. What *could* I do? I thought and thought, till I became desperate, and made a plunge into the abyss.

And now, reader, I come to a period in my unhappy life which I would gladly forget if I could. The remembrance fills me with sorrow and shame. It pains me to tell you of it; but I have promised to tell you the truth, and I will do it honestly let it cost me what it may. I will not try to screen myself behind the plea of compulsion from a master; for it was not so. Neither can I plead ignorance or thoughtlessness. For years, my master had done his utmost to pollute my mind with foul images, and to destroy the pure principles inculcated by my grandmother, and the good mistress of my childhood. The influences of slavery had had the same effect on me that they had on other young girls; they had made me prematurely knowing, concerning the evil ways of the world. I knew what I did, and I did it with deliberate calculation.

But, O, ye happy women, whose purity has been sheltered from childhood, who have been free to choose the objects of your affection, whose homes are protected by law, do not judge the poor desolate slave girl too severely! If slavery had been abolished, I, also, could have married the man of my choice; I could have had a home shielded by the laws; and I should have been spared the painful task of confessing what I am now about to relate; but all my prospects had been blighted by slavery. I wanted to keep myself pure; and, under the most adverse circumstances, I tried hard to preserve my self-respect; but I was struggling alone in the powerful grasp of the demon Slavery; and the monster proved too strong for me. I felt as if I was forsaken by God and man; as if all my efforts must be frustrated; and I became reckless in my despair.

I have told you that Dr. Flint's persecutions and his wife's jealousy had given rise to some gossip in the neighborhood. Among others, it chanced that a white unmarried gentleman had obtained some knowledge of the circumstances in which I was placed. He knew my grandmother, and often spoke to me in the street. He became interested for me, and asked questions about my master, which I answered in part. He expressed a great deal of sympathy, and a wish to aid me. He constantly sought opportunities to see me, and wrote to me frequently. I was a poor slave girl, only fifteen years old.

So much attention from a superior person was, of course, flattering; for human nature is the same in all. I also felt grateful for his sympathy, and encouraged by his kind words. It seemed to me a great thing to have such a friend. By degrees, a more tender feeling crept into my heart. He was an educated and eloquent gentleman; too eloquent, alas, for the poor slave girl who trusted in him. Of course I saw whither all this was tending. I knew the impassable gulf between us; but to be an object of interest to a man who is not married, and who is not her master, is agreeable to the pride and feelings of a slave, if her miserable situation has left her any pride or sentiment. It seems less degrading to give one's self, than to submit to compulsion. There is something akin to freedom in having a lover who has no control over you, except that which he gains by kindness and attachment. A master may treat you as rudely as he pleases, and you dare not speak; moreover, the wrong does not seem so great with an unmarried man, as with one who has a wife to be made unhappy. There may be sophistry in all this; but the condition of a slave confuses all principles of morality, and, in fact, renders the practice of them impossible.

When I found that my master had actually begun to build the lonely cottage, other feelings mixed with those I have described. Revenge, and calculations of interest, were added to flattered vanity and sincere gratitude for kindness. I knew nothing would enrage Dr. Flint so much as to know that I favored another; and it was something to triumph over my tyrant even in that small way. I thought he would revenge himself by selling me, and I was sure my friend, Mr. Sands, would buy me. He was a man of more generosity and feeling than my master, and I thought my freedom could be easily obtained from him. The crisis of my fate now came so near that I was desperate. I shuddered to think of being the mother of children that should be owned by my old tyrant. I knew that as soon as a new fancy took him, his victims were sold far off to get rid of them; especially if they had children. I had seen several women sold, with his babies at the breast. He never allowed his offspring by slaves to remain long in sight of himself and his wife. Of a man who was not my master I could ask to have my children well supported; and in this case, I felt confident I should obtain the boon. I also felt quite sure that they would be made free. With all these thoughts revolving in my mind, and seeing no other way of escaping the doom I so much dreaded, I made a headlong plunge. Pity me, and pardon me, O virtuous reader! You never knew what it is to be a slave; to be entirely unprotected by law or custom; to have the laws reduce you to the condition of a chattel, entirely subject to the will of another. You never exhausted your ingenuity in avoiding the snares, and eluding the power of a hated tyrant; you never shuddered at the sound of his footsteps, and trembled within hearing of his voice. I know I did wrong. No one can feel it more sensibly than I do. The painful and humiliating memory will haunt me to my dying day. Still, in looking back, calmly, on the events of my life, I feel that the slave woman ought not to be judged by the same standard as others.

The months passed on. I had many unhappy hours. I secretly mourned over the sorrow I was bringing on my grandmother, who had so tried to shield me from harm. I knew that I was the greatest comfort of her old age, and that it was a source of pride to her that I had not degraded myself, like most of the slaves. I wanted to confess to her that I was no longer worthy of her love; but could not utter the dreaded words.

As for Dr. Flint, I had a feeling of satisfaction and triumph in the thought of telling *him*. From time to time he told me of his intended arrangements, and I was silent. At last, he came and told me the cottage was completed, and ordered me to go to it. I told him I would never enter it. He said, "I have heard enough of such talk as that. You shall go, if you are carried by force; and you shall remain there."

I replied, "I will never go there. In a few months I shall be a mother."

He stood and looked at me in dumb amazement, and left the house without a word. I thought I should be happy in my triumph over him. But now that the truth was out, and my relatives would hear of it, I felt wretched. Humble as were their circumstances, they had pride in my good character. Now, how could I look them in the face? My self-respect was gone! I had resolved that I would be virtuous, though I was a slave. I had said, "Let the storm beat! I will brave it till I die." And now, how humiliated I felt!

I went to my grandmother. My lips moved to make confession, but the words stuck in my throat. I sat down in the shade of a tree at her door and began to sew. I think she saw something unusual was the matter with me. The mother of slaves is very watchful. She knows there is no security for her children. After they have entered their teens she lives in daily expectation of trouble. This leads to many questions. If the girl is of a sensitive nature, timidity keeps her from answering truthfully, and this well-meant course has a tendency to drive her from maternal counsels. Presently, in came my mistress, like a mad woman, and accused me concerning her husband. My grandmother, whose suspicions had been previously awakened, believed what she said. She exclaimed, "O Linda! has it come to this? I had rather see you dead than to see you as you now are. You are a disgrace to your dead mother." She tore from my fingers my mother's wedding ring and her silver thimble. "Go away!" she exclaimed, "and never come to my house, again." Her reproaches fell so hot and heavy, that they left me no chance to answer. Bitter tears, such as the eyes never shed but once, were my only answer. I rose from my seat, but fell back again, sobbing. She did not speak to me; but the tears were running down her furrowed cheeks, and they scorched me like fire. She had always been so kind to me! *So* kind! How I longed to throw myself at her feet, and tell her all the truth! But she had ordered me to go, and never to come there again. After a few minutes, I mustered strength, and started to obey her. With what feelings did I now close that little gate, which I used to open with such an eager hand in my childhood! It closed upon me with a sound I never heard before.

Where could I go? I was afraid to return to my master's. I walked on recklessly, not caring where I went, or what would become of me. When I had gone four or five miles, fatigue compelled me to stop. I sat down on the stump of an old tree. The stars were shining through the boughs above me. How they mocked me, with their bright, calm light! The hours passed by, and as I sat there alone a chilliness and deadly sickness came over me. I sank on the ground. My mind was full of horrid thoughts. I prayed to die; but the prayer was not answered. At last, with great effort I roused myself, and walked some distance further, to the house of a woman who had been a friend of my mother. When I told her why I was there, she spoke soothingly to me; but I could not be comforted. I thought I could bear my shame if I could only be reconciled to my grandmother. I longed to open my heart to her. I thought if she could know the real state of the case, and all I had been bearing for years, she would perhaps judge me less harshly. My friend advised me to send for her. I did so; but days of agonizing suspense passed before she came. Had she utterly forsaken me? No. She came at last. I knelt before her, and told her things that had poisoned my life; how long I had been persecuted; that I saw no way of escape; and in an hour of extremity I had become desperate. She listened in silence. I told her I would bear any thing and do any thing, if in time I had hopes of obtaining her forgiveness. I begged of her to pity me, for my dead mother's sake. And she did pity me. She did not say, "I forgive you;" but she looked at me lovingly, with her eyes full of tears. She laid her old hand gently on my head, and murmured, "Poor child! Poor child!"

THE NEW TIE TO LIFE

returned to my good grandmother's house. She had an interview with Mr. Sands. When she asked him why he could have have [sic] left her one ewe lamb,—whether there were not plenty of slaves who did not care about character,—he made no answer; but he spoke kind and encouraging words. He promised to care for my child, and to buy me, be the conditions what they might.

I had not seen Dr. Flint for five days. I had never seen him since I made the avowal to him. He talked of the disgrace I had brought on myself; how I had sinned against my master, and mortified my old grandmother. He intimated that if I had accepted his proposals, he, as a physician, could have saved me from exposure. He even condescended to pity me. Could he have offered wormwood more bitter? He, whose persecutions had been the cause of my sin!

"Linda," said he, "though you have been criminal towards me, I feel for you, and I can pardon you if you obey my wishes. Tell me whether the fellow you wanted to marry is the father of your child. If you deceive me, you shall feel the fires of hell."

I did not feel as proud as I had done. My strongest weapon with him was gone. I was lowered in my own estimation, and had resolved to bear his abuse in silence. But when he spoke contemptuously of the lover who had always treated me honorably; when I remembered that but for *him* I might have been a virtuous, free, and happy wife, I lost my patience. "I have sinned against God and myself," I replied; "but not against you."

He clinched his teeth, and muttered, "Curse you!" He came towards me, with ill-suppressed rage, and exclaimed, "You obstinate girl! I could grind your bones to powder! You have thrown yourself away on some worthless rascal. You are weak-minded, and have been easily persuaded by those who don't care a straw for you. The future will settle accounts between us. You are blinded now; but hereafter you will be convinced that your master was your best friend. My lenity towards you is a proof of it. I might have punished you in many ways. I might have had you whipped till you fell dead under the lash. But I wanted you to live; I would have bettered your condition. Others cannot do it. You are my slave. Your mistress, disgusted by your conduct, forbids you to return to the house; therefore I leave you here for the present; but I shall see you often. I will call tomorrow."

He came with frowning brows, that showed a dissatisfied state of mind. After asking about my health, he inquired whether my board was paid, and who visited me. He then went on to say that he had neglected his duty; that as a physician there were certain things that he ought to have explained to me. Then followed talk such as would have made the most shameless blush. He ordered me to stand up before him. I obeyed. "I command you," said he, "to tell me whether the father of your child is white or black." I hesitated. "Answer me this instant!" he exclaimed. I did answer. He sprang upon me like a wolf, and grabbed my arm as if he would have broken it. "Do you love him?" said he, in a hissing tone.

"I am thankful that I do not despise him," I replied.

He raised his hand to strike me; but it fell again. I don't know what arrested the blow. He sat down, with lips tightly compressed. At last he spoke. "I came here," said he, "to make you a friendly proposition; but your ingratitude chafes me beyond endurance. You turn aside all my good intentions towards you. I don't know what it is that keeps me from killing you." Again he rose, as if he had a mind to strike me.

But he resumed. "On one condition I will forgive your insolence and crime. You must henceforth have no communication of any kind with the father of your child. You must not ask any thing from him, or receive any thing from him. I will take care of you and your child. You had better promise this at once, and not wait till you are deserted by him. This is the last act of mercy I shall show towards you."

I said something about being unwilling to have my child supported by a man who had cursed it and me also. He rejoined, that a woman who had sunk to my level had no right to expect any thing else. He asked, for the last time, would I accept his kindness? I answered that I would not.

"Very well," said he; "then take the consequences of your wayward course. Never look to me for help. You are my slave, and shall always be my slave. I will never sell you, that you may depend upon."

Hope died away in my heart as he closed the door after him. I had calculated that in his rage he would sell me to a slave-trader; and I knew the father of my child was on the watch to buy me.

About this time my uncle Phillip was expected to return from a voyage. The day before his departure I had officiated as bridesmaid to a young friend. My heart was then ill at ease, but my smiling countenance did not betray it. Only a year had passed; but what fearful changes it had wrought! My heart had grown gray in misery. Lives that flash in sunshine, and lives that are born in tears, receive their hue from circumstances. None of us know what a year may bring forth.

I felt no joy when they told me my uncle had come. He wanted to see me, though he knew what had happened. I shrank from him at first; but at last consented that he should come to my room. He received me as he always had done. O, how my heart smote me when I felt his tears on my burning cheeks! The words of my grandmother came to my mind,— "Perhaps your mother and father are taken from the evil days to come." My disappointed heart could now praise God that it was so. But why, thought I, did my relatives ever cherish hopes for me? What was there to save me from the usual fate of slave girls? Many more beautiful and more intelligent than I had experienced a similar fate, or a far worse one. How could they hope that I should escape?

My uncle's stay was short, and I was not sorry for it. I was too ill in mind and body to enjoy my friends as I had done. For some weeks I was unable to leave my bed. I could not have any doctor but my master, and I would not have him sent for. At last, alarmed by my increasing illness, they sent for him. I was very weak and nervous; and as soon as he entered the room, I began to scream. They told him my state was very critical. He had no wish to hasten me out of the world, and he withdrew.

When my babe was born, they said it was premature. It weighed only four pounds; but God let it live. I heard the doctor say I could not survive till morning. I had often prayed for death; but now I did not want to die, unless my child could die too. Many weeks passed before I was able to leave my bed. I was a mere wreck of my former self. For a year there was scarcely a day when I was free from chills and fever. My babe also was sickly. His little limbs were often racked with pain. Dr. Flint continued his visits, to look after my health; and he did not fail to remind me that my child was an addition to his stock of slaves.

I felt too feeble to dispute with him, and listened to his remarks in silence. His visits were less frequent; but his busy spirit could not remain quiet. He employed my brother in his office, and he was made the medium of frequent notes and messages to me. William was a bright lad, and of much use to the doctor. He had learned to put up medicines, to leech, cup, and bleed. He had taught himself to read and spell. I was proud of my brother; and the old doctor suspected as much. One day, when I had not seen him for several weeks, I heard his steps approaching the door. I dreaded the encounter, and hid myself. He inquired for me, of course; but I was nowhere to be found. He went to his office, and despatched William with a note. The color mounted to my brother's face when he gave it to me; and he said, "Don't you hate me, Linda, for bringing you these things?" I told him I could not blame him; he was a slave, and obliged to obey his master's will. The note ordered me to come to his office. I went. He demanded to know where I was when he called. I told him I was at home. He flew into a passion, and said he knew better. Then he launched out upon his usual themes,—my crimes against him, and my ingratitude for his forbearance. The laws were laid down to me anew, and I was dismissed. I felt humiliated that my brother should stand by, and listen to such language as

would be addressed only to a slave. Poor boy! He was powerless to defend me; but I saw the tears, which he vainly
strove to keep back. This manifestation of feeling irritated
the doctor. William could do nothing to please him. One
morning he did not arrive at the office so early as usual; and
that circumstance afforded his master an opportunity to vent
his spleen. He was put in jail. The next day my brother sent a
trader to the doctor, with a request to be sold. His master
was greatly incensed at what he called his insolence. He said
he had put him there to reflect upon his bad conduct, and he
certainly was not giving any evidence of repentance. For two
days he harassed himself to find somebody to do his office
work; but every thing went wrong without William. He was
released, and ordered to take his old stand, with many
threats, if he was not careful about his future behavior.

As the months passed on, my boy improved in health.
When he was a year old, they called him beautiful. The little
vine was taking deep root in my existence, though its clinging fondness excited a mixture of love and pain. When I was
most sorely oppressed I found a solace in his smiles. I loved
to watch his infant slumbers; but always there was a dark
cloud over my enjoyment. I could never forget that he was a
slave. Sometimes I wished that he might die in infancy. God
tried me. My darling became very ill. The bright eyes grew
dull, and the little feet and hands were so icy cold that I
thought death had already touched them. I had prayed for
his death, but never so earnestly as I now prayed for his life;
and my prayer was heard. Alas, what mockery it is for a slave
mother to try to pray back her dying child to life! Death is
better than slavery. It was a sad thought that I had no name
to give my child. His father caressed him and treated him
kindly, whenever he had a chance to see him. He was not
unwilling that he should bear his name; but he had no legal
claim to it; and if I had bestowed it upon him, my master
would have regarded it as a new crime, a new piece of insolence, and would, perhaps, revenge it on the boy. O, the
serpent of Slavery has many and poisonous fangs!

ANOTHER LINK TO LIFE

I had not returned to my master's house since the birth of my child. The old man raved to have me thus removed from his immediate power; but his wife vowed, by all that was good and great, she would kill me if I came back; and he did not doubt her word. Sometimes he would stay away for a season. Then he would come and renew the old threadbare discourse about his forbearance and my ingratitude. He labored, most unnecessarily, to convince me that I had lowered myself. The venomous old reprobate had no need of descanting on that theme. I felt humiliated enough. My unconscious babe was the ever-present witness of my shame. I listened with silent contempt when he talked about my having forfeited *his* good opinion; but I shed bitter tears that I was no longer worthy of being respected by the good and pure. Alas! slavery still held me in its poisonous grasp. There was no chance for me to be respectable. There was no prospect of being able to lead a better life.

Sometimes, when my master found that I still refused to accept what he called his kind offers, he would threaten to sell my child. "Perhaps that will humble you," said he.

Humble *me!* Was I not already in the dust? But his threat lacerated my heart. I knew the law gave him power to fulfil it; for slaveholders have been cunning enough to enact that "the child shall follow the condition of the *mother*," not of the *father;* thus taking care that licentiousness shall not interfere with avarice. This reflection made me clasp my innocent babe all the more firmly to my heart. Horrid visions passed through my mind when I thought of his liability to fall into the slave-trader's hands. I wept over him, and said, "O my child! perhaps they will leave you in some cold cabin to die, and then throw you into a hole, as if you were a dog."

When Dr. Flint learned that I was again to be a mother, he

was exasperated beyond measure. He rushed from the house, and returned with a pair of shears. I had a fine head of hair; and he often railed about my pride of arranging it nicely. He cut every hair close to my head, storming and swearing all the time. I replied to some of his abuse, and he struck me. Some months before, he had pitched me down stairs in a fit of passion; and the injury I received was so serious that I was unable to turn myself in bed for many days. He then said, "Linda, I swear by God I will never raise my hand against you again;" but I knew that he would forget his promise.

After he discovered my situation, he was like a restless spirit from the pit. He came every day; and I was subjected to such insults as no pen can describe. I would not describe them if I could; they were too low, too revolting. I tried to keep them from my grandmother's knowledge as much as I could. I knew she had enough to sadden her life, without having my troubles to bear. When she saw the doctor treat me with violence, and heard him utter oaths terrible enough to palsy a man's tongue, she could not always hold her peace. It was natural and motherlike that she should try to defend me; but it only made matters worse.

When they told me my new-born babe was a girl, my heart was heavier than it had ever been before. Slavery is terrible for men; but it is far more terrible for women. Superadded to the burden common to all, *they* have wrongs, and sufferings, and mortifications peculiarly their own.

Dr. Flint had sworn that he would make me suffer, to my last day, for this new crime against *him,* as he called it; and as long as he had me in his power he kept his word. On the fourth day after the birth of my babe, he entered my room suddenly, and commanded me to rise and bring my baby to him. The nurse who took care of me had gone out of the room to prepare some nourishment, and I was alone. There was no alternative. I rose, took up my babe, and crossed the room to where he sat. "Now stand there," said he, "till I tell you to go back!" My child bore a strong resemblance to her father, and to the deceased Mrs. Sands, her grandmother. He noticed this; and while I stood before him, trembling with weakness, he heaped upon me and my little one every vile epithet he could think of. Even the grandmother in her grave did not escape his curses. In the midst of his vituperations I fainted at his feet. This recalled him to his senses. He took the baby from my arms, laid it on the bed, dashed cold water in my face, took me up, and shook me violently, to restore my consciousness before any one entered the room. Just then my grandmother came in, and he hurried out of the house. I suffered in consequence of this treatment; but I begged my friends to let me die, rather than send for the doctor. There was nothing I dreaded so much as his presence. My life was spared; and I was glad for the sake of my little ones. Had it not been for these ties to life, I should have been glad to be released by death, though I had lived only nineteen years.

Always it gave me a pang that my children had no lawful claim to a name. Their father offered his; but, if I had wished to accept the offer, I dared not while my master lived. Moreover, I knew it would not be accepted at their baptism. A Christian name they were at least entitled to; and we resolved to call my boy for our dear good Benjamin, who had gone far away from us.

My grandmother belonged to the church; and she was very desirous of having the children christened. I knew Dr. Flint would forbid it, and I did not venture to attempt it. But chance favored me. He was called to visit a patient out of town, and was obliged to be absent during Sunday. "Now is the time," said my grandmother; "we will take the children to church, and have them christened."

When I entered the church, recollections of my mother came over me, and I felt subdued in spirit. There she had presented me for baptism, without any reason to feel ashamed. She had been married, and had such legal rights as slavery allows to a slave. The vows had at least been sacred to *her*, and she had never violated them. I was glad she was not alive, to know under what different circumstances her grandchildren were presented for baptism. Why had my lot been so different from my mother's? *Her* master had died when she was a child; and she remained with her mistress till she married. She was never in the power of any master; and thus she escaped one class of the evils that generally fall upon slaves.

When my baby was about to be christened, the former mistress of my father stepped up to me, and proposed to give it her Christian name. To this I added the surname of my father, who had himself no legal right to it; for my grandfather on the paternal side was a white gentleman. What tangled skeins are the genealogies of slavery! I loved my father; but it mortified me to be obliged to bestow his name on my children.

When we left the church, my father's old mistress invited me to go home with her. She clasped a gold chain round my baby's neck. I thanked her for this kindness; but I did not like the emblem. I wanted no chain to be fastened on my daughter, not even if its links were of gold. How earnestly I prayed that she might never feel the weight of slavery's chain, whose iron entereth into the soul!

CONTINUED PERSECUTIONS

My children grew finely; and Dr. Flint would often say to me, with an exulting smile, "These brats will bring me a handsome sum of money one of these days."

I thought to myself that, God being my helper, they should never pass into his hands. It seemed to me I would rather see them killed than have them given up to his power. The money for the freedom of myself and my children could be obtained; but I derived no advantage from that circumstance. Dr. Flint loved money, but he loved power more. After much discussion, my friends resolved on making an other trial. There was a slaveholder about to leave for Texas, and he was commissioned to buy me. He was to begin with nine hundred dollars, and go up to twelve. My master refused his offers. "Sir," said he, "she don't belong to me. She is my daughter's property, and I have no right to sell her. I mistrust that you come from her paramour. If so, you may tell him that he cannot buy her for any money; neither can he buy her children."

The doctor came to see me the next day, and my heart beat quicker as he entered. I never had seen the old man tread with so majestic a step. He seated himself and looked at me with withering scorn. My children had learned to be afraid of him. The little one would shut her eyes and hide her face on my shoulder whenever she saw him; and Benny, who was now nearly five years old, often inquired, "What makes that bad man come here so many times? Does he want to hurt us?" I would clasp the dear boy in my arms, trusting that he would be free before he was old enough to solve the problem. And now, as the doctor sat there so grim and silent, the child left his play and came and nestled up by me. At last my tormentor spoke. "So you are left in disgust, are you?" said he. "It is no more than I expected. You remember I told you years ago that you would be treated so. So he is tired of you? Ha! ha! ha! The virtuous madam don't like to hear about it, does she? Ha! ha! ha!" There was a sting in his calling me virtuous madam. I no longer had the power of answering him as I had formerly done. He continued: "So it seems you are trying to get up another intrigue. Your new paramour came to me, and offered to buy you; but you may be assured you will not succeed. You are mine; and you shall be mine for life. There lives no human being that can take you out of slavery. I would have done it; but you rejected my kind offer."

I told him I did not wish to get up any intrigue; that I had never seen the man who offered to buy me.

"Do you tell me I lie?" exclaimed he, dragging me from my chair. "Will you say again that you never saw that man?"

I answered, "I do say so."

He clinched my arm with a volley of oaths. Ben began to scream, and I told him to go to his grandmother.

"Don't you stir a step, you little wretch!" said he. The child drew nearer to me, and put his arms round me, as if he wanted to protect me. This was too much for my enraged master. He caught him up and hurled him across the room. I thought he was dead, and rushed towards him to take him up.

"Not yet!" exclaimed the doctor. "Let him lie there till he comes to."

"Let me go! Let me go!" I screamed, "or I will raise the whole house." I struggled and got away; but he clinched me again. Somebody opened the door, and he released me. I picked up my insensible child, and when I turned my tormentor was gone. Anxiously I bent over the little form, so pale and still; and when the brown eyes at last opened, I don't know whether I was very happy.

All the doctor's former persecutions were renewed. He came morning, noon, and night. No jealous lover ever watched a rival more closely than he watched me and the unknown slaveholder, with whom he accused me of wishing to get up an intrigue. When my grandmother was out of the way he searched every room to find him.

In one of his visits, he happened to find a young girl, whom he had sold to a trader a few days previous. His statement was, that he sold her because she had been too familiar with the overseer. She had had a bitter life with him, and was glad to be sold. She had no mother, and no near ties. She had been torn from her family years before. A few friends had entered into bonds for her safety, if the trader would allow her to spend with them the time that intervened between her sale and the gathering up of his human stock. Such a favor was rarely granted. It saved the trader the expense of board and jail fees, and though the amount was small, it was a weighty consideration in a slave-trader's mind.

Dr. Flint always had an aversion to meeting slaves after he had sold them. He ordered Rose out of the house; but he was no longer her master, and she took no notice of him. For once the crushed Rose was the conqueror. His gray eyes flashed angrily upon her; but that was the extent of his power. "How came this girl here?" he exclaimed. "What right had you to allow it, when you knew I had sold her?"

I answered "This is my grandmother's house, and Rose came to see her. I have no right to turn any body out of doors, that comes here for honest purposes."

He gave me the blow that would have fallen upon Rose if she had still been his slave. My grandmother's attention had been attracted by loud voices, and she entered in time to see a second blow dealt. She was not a woman to let such an outrage, in her own house, go unrebuked. The doctor undertook to explain that I had been insolent. Her indignant feelings rose higher and higher, and finally boiled over in words. "Get out of my house!" she exclaimed. "Go home, and take care of your wife and children, and you will have enough to do, without watching my family."

He threw the birth of my children in her face, and accused her of sanctioning the life I was leading. She told him I was living with her by compulsion of his wife; that he needn't accuse her, for he was the one to blame; he was the one who had caused all the trouble. She grew more and more excited as she went on. "I tell you what, Dr. Flint," said she, "you ain't got many more years to live, and you'd better be saying your prayers. It will take 'em all, and more too, to wash the dirt off your soul."

"Do you know whom you are talking to?" he exclaimed.

She replied, "Yes, I know very well who I am talking to."

He left the house in a great rage. I looked at my grandmother. Our eyes met. Their angry expression had passed away, but she looked sorrowful and weary—weary of incessant strife. I wondered that it did not lessen her love for me; but if it did she never showed it. She was always kind, always ready to sympathize with my troubles. There might have been peace and contentment in that humble home if it had not been for the demon Slavery.

The winter passed undisturbed by the doctor. The beautiful spring came; and when Nature resumes her loveliness, the human soul is apt to revive also. My drooping hopes came to life again with the flowers. I was dreaming of freedom again; more for my children's sake than my own. I planned and I planned. Obstacles hit against plans. There seemed no way of overcoming them; and yet I hoped.

Back came the wily doctor. I was not at home when he called. A friend had invited me to a small party, and to gratify her I went. To my great consternation, a messenger came in haste to say that Dr. Flint was at my grandmother's, and insisted on seeing me. They did not tell him where I was, or he would have come and raised a disturbance in my friend's house. They sent me a dark wrapper; I threw it on and hurried home. My speed did not save me; the doctor had gone away in anger. I dreaded the morning, but I could not delay it; it came, warm and bright. At an early hour the doctor came and asked me where I had been last night. I told him. He did not believe me, and sent to my friend's house to ascertain the facts. He came in the afternoon to assure me he was satisfied that I had spoken the truth. He seemed to be in a facetious mood, and I expected some jeers were coming. "I suppose you need some recreation," said he, "but I am surprised at your being there, among those negroes. It was not the place for *you*. Are you *allowed* to visit such people?"

I understood this covert fling at the white gentleman who was my friend; but I merely replied, "I went to visit my friends, and any company they keep is good enough for me."

He went on to say, "I have seen very little of you of late, but my interest in you in [sic] unchanged. When I said I would have no more mercy on you I was rash. I recall my words. Linda, you desire freedom for yourself and your children, and you can obtain it only through me. If you agree to what I am about to propose, you and they shall be free. There must be no communication of any kind between you and their father. I will procure a cottage, where you and the children can live together. Your labor shall be light, such as sewing for my family. Think what is offered you, Linda—a home and freedom! Let the past be forgotten. If I have been harsh with you at times, your wilfulness drove me to it. You know I exact obedience from my own children, and I consider you as yet a child."

He paused for an answer, but I remained silent.

"Why don't you speak?" said he. "What more do you wait for?"

"Nothing, sir."

"Then you accept my offer?"

"No, sir."

His anger was ready to break loose; but he succeeded in curbing it, and replied, "You have answered without thought. But I must let you know there are two sides to my proposition; if you reject the bright side, you will be obliged to take the dark one. You must either accept my offer, or you and your children shall be sent to your young master's plantation, there to remain till your young mistress is married; and your children shall fare like the rest of the negro children. I give you a week to consider of it."

He was shrewd; but I knew he was not to be trusted. I told him I was ready to give my answer now.

"I will not receive it now," he replied. "You act too much from impulse. Remember that you and your children can be free a week from to-day if you choose."

On what a monstrous chance hung the destiny of my children! I knew that my master's offer was a snare, and that if I entered it escape would be impossible. As for his promise, I knew him so well that I was sure if he gave me free papers, they would be so managed as to have no legal value. The alternative was inevitable. I resolved to go to the plantation. But then I thought how completely I should be in in [sic] his power, and the prospect was apalling. Even if I should kneel before him, and implore him to spare me, for the sake of my

children, I knew he would spurn me with his foot, and m
weakness would be his triumph.

Before the week expired, I heard that young Mr. Flint wa
about to be married to a lady of his own stamp. I foresaw th
position I should occupy in his establishment. I had onc
been sent to the plantation for punishment, and fear of th
son had induced the father to recall me very soon. My min
was made up; I was resolved that I would foil my master an
save my children, or I would perish in the attempt. I kept m
plans to myself; I knew that friends would try to dissuade m
from them, and I would not wound their feelings by re
jecting their advice.

On the decisive day the doctor came, and said he hoped
had made a wise choice.

"I am ready to go to the plantation, sir," I replied.

"Have you thought how important your decision is (
your children?" said he.

I told him I had.

"Very well. Go to the plantation, and my curse go wi
you," he replied. "Your boy shall be put to work, and he sha
soon be sold; and your girl shall be raised for the purpose (
selling well. Go your own ways!" He left the room wi
curses, not to be repeated.

As I stood rooted to the spot, my grandmother came an
said, "Linda, child, what did you tell him?"

I answered that I was going to the plantation.

"*Must* you go?" said she. "Can't something be done (
stop it?"

I told her it was useless to try; but she begged me not (
give up. She said she would go to the doctor, and remin
him how long and how faithfully she had served in the fan
ily, and how she had taken her own baby from her breast (
nourish his wife. She would tell him I had been out of th
family so long they would not miss me; that she would pa
them for my time, and the money would procure a woma
who had more strength for the situation than I had. I begge
her not to go; but she persisted in saying, "He will listen (

me, Linda." She went, and was treated as I expected. He coolly listened to what she said, but denied her request. He told her that what he did was for my good, that my feelings were entirely above my situation, and that on the plantation I would receive treatment that was suitable to my behavior.

My grandmother was much cast down. I had my secret hopes; but I must fight my battle alone. I had a woman's pride, and a mother's love for my children; and I resolved that out of the darkness of this hour a brighter dawn should rise for them. My master had power and law on his side; I had a determined will. There is might in each.

SCENES AT THE PLANTATION

Early the next morning I left my grandmother's with my youngest child. My boy was ill, and I left him behind. I had many sad thoughts as the old wagon jolted on. Hitherto, I had suffered alone; now, my little one was to be treated as a slave. As we drew near the great house, I thought of the time when I was formerly sent there out of revenge. I wondered for what purpose I was now sent. I could not tell. I resolved to obey orders so far as duty required; but within myself, I determined to make my stay as short as possible. Mr. Flint was waiting to receive us, and told me to follow him up stairs to receive orders for the day. My little Ellen was left below in the kitchen. It was a change for her, who had always been so carefully tended. My young master said she might amuse herself in the yard. This was kind of him, since the child was hateful to his sight. My task was to fit up the house for the reception of the bride. In the midst of sheets, tablecloths, towels, drapery, and carpeting, my head was as busy planning, as were my fingers with the needle. At noon I was allowed to go to Ellen. She had sobbed herself to sleep. I heard Mr. Flint say to a neighbor, "I've got her down here, and I'll soon take the town notions out of her head. My father is partly to blame for her nonsense. He ought to have broken her in long ago." The remark was made within my hearing, and it would have been quite as manly to have made it to my face. He *had* said things to my face which might, or might not, have surprised his neighbor if he had known of them. He was "a chip of [*sic*] the old block."

I resolved to give him no cause to accuse me of being too much of a lady, so far as work was concerned. I worked day and night, with wretchedness before me. When I say down beside my child, I felt how much easier it would be to see her die than to see her master beat her about, as I daily saw him beat other little ones. The spirit of the mothers was so crushed by the lash, that they stood by, without courage to remonstrate. How much more must I suffer, before I should be "broke in" to that degree?

I wished to appear as contented as possible. Sometimes I had an opportunity to send a few lines home; and this brought up recollections that made it difficult, for a time, to seem calm and indifferent to my lot. Notwithstanding my efforts, I saw that Mr. Flint regarded me with a suspicious eye. Ellen broke down under the trials of her new life. Separated from me, with no one to look after her, she wandered about, and in a few days cried herself sick. One day, she sat under the window where I was at work, crying that weary cry which makes a mother's heart bleed. I was obliged to steel myself to bear it. After a while it ceased. I looked out, and she was gone. As it was near noon, I ventured to go down in search of her. The great house was raised two feet above the ground. I looked under it, and saw her about midway, fast asleep. I crept under and drew her out. As I held her in my arms, I thought how well it would be for her if she never waked up; and I uttered my thought aloud. I was startled to hear someone say, "Did you speak to me?" I looked up, and saw Mr. Flint standing beside me. He said nothing further, but turned, frowning, away. That night he sent Ellen a biscuit and a cup of sweetened milk. This generosity surprised me. I learned afterwards, that in the afternoon he had killed a large snake, which crept from under the house; and I supposed that incident had prompted his unusual kindness.

The next morning the old cart was loaded with shingles for town. I put Ellen into it, and sent her to her grandmother. Mr. Flint said I ought to have asked his permission. I told him the child was sick, and required attention which I had no time to give. He let it pass; for he was aware that I had accomplished much work in a little time.

I had been three weeks on the plantation, when I planned a visit home. It must be at night, after every body was in bed. I was six miles from town, and the road was very dreary. I was to go with a young man, who, I knew, often stole to town to see his mother. One night, when all was quiet, we started. Fear gave speed to our steps, and we were not long in performing the journey. I arrived at my grandmother's. Her bed room was on the first floor, and the window was open, the weather being warm. I spoke to her and she awoke. She let me in and closed the window, lest some late passer-by should see me. A light was brought, and the whole household gathered round me, some smiling and some crying. I went to look at my children, and thanked God for their happy sleep. The tears fell as I leaned over them. As I moved to leave, Benny stirred. I turned back, and whispered, "Mother is here." After digging at his eyes with his little fist, they opened, and he sat up in bed, looking at me curiously. Having satisfied himself that it was I, he exclaimed, "O mother! you ain't dead, are you? They didn't cut off your head at the plantation, did they?"

My time was up too soon, and my guide was waiting for me. I laid Benny back in his bed, and dried his tears by a promise to come again soon. Rapidly we retraced our steps back to the plantation. About half way we were met by a company of four patrols. Luckily we heard their horses' hoofs before they came in sight, and we had time to hide behind a large tree. They passed, hallooing and shouting in a manner that indicated a recent carousal. How thankful we were that they had not their dogs with them! We hastened our footsteps, and when we arrived on the plantation we heard the sound of the hand-mill. The slaves were grinding their corn. We were safely in the house before the horn summoned them to their labor. I divided my little parcel of food with my guide, knowing that he had lost the chance of grinding his corn, and must toil all day in the field.

Mr. Flint often took an inspection of the house, to see that no one was idle. The entire management of the work was trusted to me, because he knew nothing about it; and rather than hire a superintendent he contented himself with my arrangements. He had often urged upon his father the necessity of having me at the plantation to take charge of his affairs, and make clothes for the slaves; but the old man knew him too well to consent to that arrangement.

When I had been working a month at the plantation, the great aunt of Mr. Flint came to make him a visit. This was the good old lady who paid fifty dollars for my grandmother, for the purpose of making her free, when she stood on the auction block. My grandmother loved this old lady, whom we all called Miss Fanny. She often came to take tea with us. On such occasions the table was spread with a snow-white cloth, and the china cups and silver spoons were taken from the old-fashioned buffet. There were hot muffins, tea rusks, and delicious sweetmeats. My grandmother kept two cows, and the fresh cream was Miss Fanny's delight. She invariably declared that it was the best in town. The old ladies had cosey times together. They would work and chat, and sometimes, while talking over old times, their spectacles would get dim with tears, and would have to be taken off and wiped. When Miss Fanny bade me good by, her bag was filled with grandmother's best cakes, and she was urged to come again soon.

There had been a time when Dr. Flint's wife came to take tea with us, and when her children were also sent to have a feast of "Aunt Marthy's" nice cooking. But after I became an object of her jealousy and spite, she was angry with grandmother for giving a shelter to me and my children. She would not even speak to her in the street. This wounded my grandmother's feelings, for she could not retain ill will against the woman whom she had nourished with her milk when a babe. The doctor's wife would gladly have prevented our intercourse with Miss Fanny if she could have done it, but fortunately she was not dependent on the bounty of the Flints. She had enough to be independent; and that is more than can ever be gained from charity, however lavish it may be.

Miss Fanny was endeared to me by many recollections, and I was rejoiced to see her at the plantation. The warmth of her large, loyal heart made the house seem pleasanter while she was in it. She staid a week, and I had many talks with her. She said her principal object in coming was to see how I was treated, and whether any thing could be done for me. She inquired whether she could help me in any way. I told her I believed not. She condoled with me in her own peculiar way; saying she wished that I and all my grandmother's family were at rest in our graves, for not until then should she feel any peace about us. The good old soul did not dream that I was planning to bestow peace upon her, with regard to myself and my children; not by death, but by securing our freedom.

Again and again I had traversed those dreary twelve miles, to and from the town; and all the way, I was meditating upon some means of escape for myself and my children. My friends had made every effort that ingenuity could devise to effect our purchase, but all their plans had proved abortive. Dr. Flint was suspicious, and determined not to loosen his grasp upon us. I could have made my escape alone; but it was more for my helpless children than for myself that I longed for freedom. Though the boon would have been precious to me, above all price, I would not have taken it at the expense of leaving them in slavery. Every trial I endured, every sacrifice I made for their sakes, drew them closer to my heart, and gave me fresh courage to beat back the dark waves that rolled and rolled over me in a seemingly endless night of storms.

[Editor's note] Realizing that she can never free her children while she is in Dr. Flint's power, Linda plans to escape. With the help of neighbors, friends, and family, she hides out in an attic shed above her grandmother's house, where she remains for several years: "I hardly expect that the reader will credit me, when I affirm that I lived in that little dismal hole, almost deprived of light and air, and with no space to move my limbs, for nearly seven years. But in fact; and to me a sad one, even now; for my body still suffers from the effects of that long imprisonment, to say nothing of my soul." Finally friends and family arrange her escape to the North, where she is reunited with her children who were purchased from Flint by their white father. In New York, Brent becomes a children's nurse in the Bruce household (Mr. Bruce is magazinist Nathaniel Parker Willis), and, when the Flints begin to pursue her, Mrs. Bruce purchases Brent's freedom.

FREE AT LAST

Mrs. Bruce, and every member of her family, were exceedingly kind to me. I was thankful for the blessings of my lot, yet I could not always wear a cheerful countenance. I was doing harm to no one; on the contrary, I was doing all the good I could in my small way; yet I could never go out to breathe God's free air without trepidation at my heart. This seemed hard; and I could not think it was a right state of things in any civilized country.

From time to time I received news from my good old grandmother. She could not write; but she employed others to write for her. The following is an extract from one of her last letters:—

"Dear Daughter: I cannot hope to see you again on earth; but I pray to God to unite us above, where pain will no more rack this feeble body of mine; where sorrow and parting from my children will be no more. God has promised these things if we are faithful unto the end. My age and feeble health deprive me of going to church now; but God is with me here at home. Thank your brother for his kindness. Give much love to him, and tell him to remember the Creator in the days of his youth, and strive to meet me in the Father's kingdom. Love to Ellen and Benjamin. Don't neglect him. Tell him for me, to be a good boy. Strive, my child, to train them for God's children. May he protect and provide for you, is the prayer of your loving old mother."

These letters both cheered and saddened me. I was always glad to have tidings from the kind, faithful old friend of my unhappy youth; but her messages of love made my heart yearn to see her before she died, and I mourned over the fact that it was impossible. Some months after I returned from my flight to New England, I received a letter from her, in which she wrote, "Dr. Flint is dead. He has left a distressed family. Poor old man! I hope he made his peace with God."

I remembered how he had defrauded my grandmother of the hard earnings she had loaned; how he had tried to cheat her out of the freedom her mistress had promised her, and how he had persecuted her children; and I thought to myself that she was a better Christian than I was, if she could entirely forgive him. I cannot say, with truth, that the news of my old master's death softened my feelings towards him. There are wrongs which even the grave does not bury. The man was odious to me while he lived, and his memory is odious now.

His departure from this world did not diminish my danger. He had threatened my grandmother that his heirs should hold me in slavery after he was gone; that I never should be free so long as a child of his survived. As for Mrs. Flint, I had seen her in deeper afflictions than I supposed the loss of her husband would be, for she had buried several children; yet I never saw any signs of softening in her heart. The doctor had died in embarrassed circumstances, and had little to will to his heirs, except such property as he was unable to grasp. I was well aware what I had to expect from the family of Flints; and my fears were confirmed by a letter from the south, warning me to be on my guard, because Mrs Flint openly declared that her daughter could not afford to lose so valuable a slave as I was.

I kept close watch of the newspapers for arrivals; but one Saturday night, being much occupied, I forgot to examine the Evening Express as usual. I went down into the parlor for it, early in the morning, and found the boy about to kindle a fire with it. I took it from him and examined the list of arrivals. Reader, if you have never been a slave, you can not imagine the acute sensation of suffering at my heart when I read the names of Mr. and Mrs. Dodge, at a hotel in Courtland Street. It was a third-rate hotel, and that circumstance convinced me of the truth of what I had heard, that they were short of funds and had need of my value, as *they* valued me; and that was by dollars and cents. I hastened with the paper to Mrs. Bruce. Her heart and hand were always open to every one in distress, and she always warmly sympathized with mine. It was impossible to tell how near the enemy was. He might have passed and repassed the house while we were sleeping. He might at that moment be waiting to pounce upon me if I ventured out of doors. I had never seen the husband of my young mistress, and therefore could not distinguish him from any other stranger. A carriage was hastily ordered; and, closely veiled, I followed Mrs Bruce, taking the baby again with me into exile. After various turnings and crossings, and returnings, the carriage stopped at the house of one of Mrs. Bruce's friends, where I was kindly received. Mrs. Bruce returned immediately, to instruct the domestics what to say if any one came to inquire for me.

It was lucky for me that the evening paper was not burned

up before I had a chance to examine the list of arrivals. It was not long after Mrs. Bruce's return to her house, before several people came to inquire for me. One inquired for me, another asked for my daughter Ellen, and another said he had a letter from my grandmother, which he was requested to deliver in person.

They were told, "She *has* lived here, but she has left."

"How long ago?"

"I don't know, sir."

"Do you know where she went?"

"I do not, sir." And the door was closed.

This Mr. Dodge, who claimed me as his property, was originally a Yankee pedler in the south; then he became a merchant, and finally a slaveholder. He managed to get introduced into what was called the first society, and married Miss Emily Flint. A quarrel arose between him and her brother, and the brother cowhided him. This led to a family feud, and he proposed to remove to Virginia. Dr. Flint left him no property, and his own means had become circumscribed, while a wife and children depended upon him for support. Under these circumstances, it was very natural that he should make an effort to put me into his pocket.

I had a colored friend, a man from my native place, in whom I had the most implicit confidence. I sent for him, and told him that Mr. and Mrs. Dodge had arrived in New York. I proposed that he should call upon them to make inquiries about his friends at the south, with whom Dr. Flint's family were well acquainted. He thought there was no impropriety in his doing so, and he consented. He went to the hotel, and knocked at the door of Mr. Dodge's room, which was opened by the gentleman himself, who gruffly inquired, "What brought you here? How came you to know I was in the city?"

"Your arrival was published in the evening papers, sir; and I called to ask Mrs. Dodge about my friends at home. I didn't suppose it would give any offence."

"Where's that negro girl, that belongs to my wife?"

"What girl, sir?"

"You know well enough. I mean Linda, that ran away from Dr. Flint's plantation, some years ago. I dare say you've seen her, and know where she is."

"Yes, sir, I've seen her, and know where she is. She is out of your reach, sir."

"Tell me where she is, or bring her to me, and I will give her a chance to buy her freedom."

"I don't think it would be of any use, sir. I have heard her say she would go to the ends of the earth, rather than pay any man or woman for her freedom, because she thinks she has a right to it. Besides, she couldn't do it, if she would, for she has spent her earnings to educate her children."

This made Mr. Dodge very angry, and some high words passed between them. My friend was afraid to come where I was; but in the course of the day I received a note from him. I supposed they had not come from the south, in the winter, for a pleasure excursion; and now the nature of their business was very plain.

Mrs. Bruce came to me and entreated me to leave the city the next morning. She said her house was watched, and it was possible that some clew to me might be obtained. I refused to take her advice. She pleaded with an earnest tenderness, that ought to have moved me; but I was in a bitter, disheartened mood. I was weary of flying from pillar to post. I had been chased during half my life, and it seemed as if the chase was never to end. There I sat, in that great city, guiltless of crime, yet not daring to worship God in any of the churches. I heard the bells ringing for afternoon service, and, with contemptuous sarcasm, I said, "Will the preachers take for their text, 'Proclaim liberty to the captive, and the opening of prison doors to them that are bound'? or will they preach from the text, 'Do unto others as ye would they should do unto you'?" Oppressed Poles and Hungarians could find a safe refuge in that city; John Mitchell* was free

* John Mitchel (1815–1875)—the name is spelled with a single *l*— Irish nationalist and advocate of armed resistance to England, was transported from Ireland to Van Dieman's Land (Tasmania) but

to proclaim in the City Hall his desire for "a plantation well stocked with slaves;" but there I sat, an oppressed American, not daring to show my face. God forgive the black and bitter thoughts I indulged on that Sabbath day! The Scripture says, "Oppression makes even a wise man mad;" and I was not wise.

I had been told that Mr. Dodge said his wife had never signed away her right to my children, and if he could not get me, he would take them. This it was, more than any thing else, that roused such a tempest in my soul. Benjamin was with his uncle William in California, but my innocent young daughter had come to spend a vacation with me. I thought of what I had suffered in slavery at her age, and my heart was like a tiger's when a hunter tries to seize her young.

Dear Mrs. Bruce! I seem to see the expression of her face, as she turned away discouraged by my obstinate mood. Finding her expostulations unavailing, she sent Ellen to entreat me. When ten o'clock in the evening arrived and Ellen had not returned, this watchful and unwearied friend became anxious. She came to us in a carriage, bringing a well-filled trunk for my journey—trusting that by this time I would listen to reason. I yielded to her, as I ought to have done before.

The next day, baby and I set out in a heavy snow storm, bound for New England again. I received letters from the City of Iniquity, addressed to me under an assumed name. In a few days one came from Mrs. Bruce, informing me that my new master was still searching for me, and that she intended to put an end to this persecution by buying my free-

---

escaped. In New York in 1853 he established a paper dedicated to the cause of Irish freedom, yet he opposed the abolitionists and came out in favor of slavery. He then moved to Knoxville, where he published a paper serving slavery interests. His sons fought in the Confederate army. "His intense nationalism," wrote a biographer in *Dictionary of American Biography*, "prevented his feeling any spirit of kinship with other men working in similar causes; for liberty in the abstract and humanity at large he cared nothing. . . ." W. T.

dom. I felt grateful for the kindness that prompted this offer, but the idea was not so pleasant to me as might have been expected. The more my mind had become enlightened, the more difficult it was for me to consider myself an article of property; and to pay money to those who had so grievously oppressed me seemed like taking from my sufferings the glory of triumph. I wrote to Mrs. Bruce, thanking her, but saying that being sold from one owner to another seemed too much like slavery; that such a great obligation could not be easily cancelled; and that I preferred to go to my brother in California.

Without my knowledge, Mrs. Bruce employed a gentleman in New York to enter into negotiations with Mr. Dodge. He proposed to pay three hundred dollars down, if Mr. Dodge would sell me, and enter into obligations to relinquish all claim to me or my children forever after. He who called himself my master said he scorned so small an offer for such a valuable servant. The gentleman replied, "You can do as you choose, sir. If you reject this offer you will never get any thing; for the woman has friends who will convey her and her children out of the country."

Mr. Dodge concluded that "half a loaf was better than no bread," and he agreed to the proffered terms. By the next mail I received this brief letter from Mrs. Bruce: "I am rejoiced to tell you that the money for your freedom has been paid to Mr. Dodge. Come home to-morrow. I long to see you and my sweet babe."

My brain reeled as I read these lines. A gentleman near me said, "It's true; I have seen the bill of sale." "The bill of sale!" Those words struck me like a blow. So I was *sold* at last! A human being *sold* in the free city of New York! The bill of sale is on record, and future generations will learn from it that women were articles of traffic in New York, late in the nineteenth century of the Christian religion. It may hereafter prove a useful document to antiquaries, who are seeking to measure the progress of civilization in the United States. well know the value of that bit of paper; but much as I love freedom, I do not like to look upon it. I am deeply grateful to the generous friend who procured it, but I despise the miscreant who demanded payment for what never rightfully belonged to him or his.

I had objected to having my freedom bought, yet I must confess that when it was done I felt as if a heavy load had been lifted from my weary shoulders. When I rode home in the cars I was no longer afraid to unveil my face and look at people as they passed. I should have been glad to have met Daniel Dodge himself; to have had him seen me and known me, that he might have mourned over the untoward circumstances which compelled him to sell me for three hundred dollars.

When I reached home, the arms of my benefactress were thrown round me, and our tears mingled. As soon as she could speak, she said, "O Linda, I'm *so* glad it's all over! You wrote to me as if you thought you were going to be transferred from one owner to another. But I did not buy you for your services. I should have done just the same, if you had been going to sail for California to-morrow. I should, at least, have the satisfaction of knowing that you left me a free woman."

My heart was exceedingly full. I remembered how my poor father had tried to buy me, when I was a small child, and how he had been disappointed. I hoped his spirit was rejoicing over me now. I remembered how my good old grandmother had laid up her earnings to purchase me in later years, and how often her plans had been frustrated. How that faithful, loving old heart would leap for joy, if she could look on me and my children now that we were free! My relatives had been foiled in all their efforts, but God had raised me up a friend among strangers, who had bestowed on me the precious, long-desired boon. Friend! It is a common word, often lightly used. Like other good and beautiful things, it may be tarnished by careless handling; but when I speak of Mrs. Bruce as my friend, the word is sacred.

My grandmother lived to rejoice in my freedom; but not

long after, a letter came with a black seal. She had gone "where the wicked cease from troubling, and the weary are at rest."

Time passed on, and a paper came to me from the south, containing an obituary notice of my uncle Phillip. It was the only case I ever knew of such an honor conferred upon a colored person. It was written by one of his friends, and contained these words: "Now that death has laid him low, they call him a good man and a useful citizen; but what are eulogies to the black man, when the world has faded from his vision? It does not require man's praise to obtain rest in God's kingdom." So they called a colored man a *citizen!* Strange words to be uttered in that region!

Reader, my story ends with freedom; not in the usual way, with marriage. I and my children are now free! We are as free from the power of slaveholders as are the white people of the north; and though that, according to my ideas, is not saying a great deal, it is a vast improvement in *my* condition. The dream of my life is not yet realized. I do not sit with my children in a home of my own. I still long for a hearthstone of my own, however humble. I wish it for my children's sake far more than for my own. But God so orders circumstances as to keep me with my friend Mrs. Bruce. Love, duty, gratitude, also bind me to her side. It is a privilege to serve her who pities my oppressed people, and who has bestowed the inestimable boon of freedom on me and my children.

BIBLIOGRAPHIC NOTES

Until the 1980s most critical commentary focuses on the debate over the authenticity of Jacobs's narrative. *The Negro Caravan,* eds. Sterling Brown, Ulysses Lee and Arthur P Davis (New York: The Citadel Press, 1941) and Arna Bontemps, "The Slave Narrative: An American Genre" in

Great Slave Narratives ed. Arna Bontemps (Boston: Beacon Press, 1969) strongly question its validity; Vernon Loggins's The Negro Author: His Development in America (NY: Columbia, 1931) accepts Jacobs as the author as does Marion W. Starling, "The Slave Narrative: Its Place in American Literary History." (Ph.D. diss. New York University, 1946). In "Critical Essay on Sources" in The Slave Community: Plantation Life in the Antebellum South (New York: Oxford University Press, 1979) John Blassingame presents an argument against the authenticity of Incidents, a position he later backs away from.

Contemporary criticism, benefiting from Jean Fagan Yellin's discovery of correspondence between Jacobs and the narrative's editor, Lydia Maria Child, takes the validity of Incidents for granted and the focus of the criticism has now shifted. Yellin's essay, "Text and Contexts of Harriet Jacobs' Incidents in the Life of a Slave Girl: Written by Herself" in The Slave's Narrative, Ed. Charles T. Davis and Henry Louis Gates, Jr., (New York: Oxford University Press, 1985) recounts Jacobs's efforts to write and publish the book and stresses the limits of Child's editorial role. Yellin views Jacobs's main subject as the "sexual oppression of slavery" and demonstrates the need for a "multiple context" analysis using black women's and American history and letters. Frances Smith Foster's Witnessing Slavery (Westport, Conn.: Greenwood Press, 1979) uses Incidents to exemplify the use of sentimental conventions common to many slave narratives. She also mentions several themes that place Jacobs firmly in the tradition of the slave narrative. Hazel Carby, in her comprehensive book on women slave narratives, Reconstructing Womanhood: The Emergence of the Afro-American Woman Novelist (New York: Oxford University Press, 1987), argues that Jacobs's use of the convention of eighteenth-century polite English letters actually served to question this literary form, thus subverting both the form and content of the era's dominant sexual ideology. The "gap" between the Richardsonian form—the "public plot of (female) weakness"—and Jacobs's themes of struggle, strength, and an alternative

PART TWO

But yet, as meanly as she is thought of;
hindered as she is in all directions, she is
always doing some thing of merit and
credit that is not expected of her.
She is irrepressible. She is insulted,
but she holds up her head; she is
scorned, but she proudly demands
respect. Thus it has come to pass
that the most interesting girl of
this country is the colored girl.

—Fannie Barrier Williams,
The Colored Girl

INTRODUCTION

Uplifting the Women and the Race: The Forerunners—Harper and Hopkins

The literature of black women at the turn of the century is a literature frozen into self-consciousness by the need to defend black women and men against the vicious and prevailing stereotypes that mark nineteenth-century American cultural thought.[1] Nearly a century later, it is difficult to imagine the universal acceptance of black inferiority in American life at the turn of the century. Minstrel shows caricatured blacks as ignorant, lazy, childlike, and cowardly. Plantation literature, written by proslavery diehards, created the stereotypes of the contented slave, the tragic mulatto, the noble savage, and the submissive Christian. Reconstruction writers produced more vicious stereotypes—the brutal rapist, the treacherous mulatto, the corrupt politician.[2] While most of these stereotypes were aimed at black men, the most common attack on the image of black women was to portray them as immoral women, licentious and oversexed, whose insatiable appetites were responsible for the bestial nature of the black man. At a time when the popular literature of the day attempted to create for white women an idealized "true woman," chaste and loving, in the center of the sacred trinity of marriage, home, and family, black women were exploited as sexually promiscuous, so base as to be disinclined toward the virtues of true womanhood. Only thirty-five years out of an enslavement that made legal marriage or protection against rape impossible, the black woman, declared Fannie Barrier Williams, is the only woman in America for whom virtue was not an ornament and a necessity.[3] So widespread was the image of black women as sexually immoral that virtually every black woman who took up a pen felt obligated to defend black women against these charges. In her 1897 speech to the Society of Christian Endeavor entitled "The Awakening of the Afro-American Woman," Victoria Earle Matthews was incensed at these renewed efforts by the same white patriarchal structure that had instituted slavery to demoralize "this woman who had stood upon the auction block possessed of no rights that a white man was bound to respect, and none which he did respect."[4] But, while women race leaders like Williams and Matthews expressed righteous indignation at a patriarchy that first enslaved black women and then crucified them for the effects of slavery, their arguments implied that, having been degraded by slavery, black women could not be expected to exhibit the qualities of virtuousness expected of white women. Speaking before a largely white Christian society, Matthews expressed this sense of past disgrace: "What a past was ours! There was no attribute of womanhood which had not been sullied—aye, which had not been despoiled in the crucible of slavery . . . It had destroyed, more than in men, all that a woman holds sacred, all that ennobles womanhood."[5] With a race to uplift and every poisonous slander against its women and men used to justify continued oppression, black women race leaders could hardly be expected to reject the ideals set up for "true women" for what they were: a fanatical method of sexual repression prescribed by white men to oppress and control women.

Considering the powerful text of race hatred that preached black inferiority and black immorality, it is no wonder that every black writer was condemned to write against that text. This motivation is at the heart of the problem of black fiction of that time. How can one imagine oneself in a period of such total debasement of the race? As Raymond Hedin puts it, "The notion of black inferiority has become the 'countertext' of black writing."[6] Black women writers, however, shouldered an additional burden. As profoundly disturbed as black men of 1900 were about their own oppression, they were not always willing to accept black women as equals. When leading black intellectuals, including Francis Grimké, W. E. B. Du Bois and Alexander Crummell, formed the prestigious American Negro Academy in 1897 "for the promotion of Literature, Science, and Art," they decided that black women were not competent for such an intellectual atmosphere and limited their membership to "men of African descent." There were other examples of such sexism. George Henry Murray stated categorically in a 1905 article written for *Colored American Magazine* that women were by nature "inferior in intellectual capacity to men" and declared that with their limited intellectual abilities, women should not be expected to produce any real scholarship.[7]

Black women writers at the turn of the century wrote under great pressures: to a white audience whose tastes were honed by the sentimental novel and whose conceptions of blacks were shaped by *Uncle Tom's Cabin;* to a limited black audience who desperately needed positive black role models; and to an audience whose notions of female propriety and female inferiority made it nearly impossible to imagine a complex woman character. Two of the best-known women writers of this period—Frances Harper and Pauline Hopkins—enlisted their fiction in the battle to counter the negative images of blacks and women. Hopkins, who was editor of the *Colored American Magazine,* published in Boston from 1902 to 1904, was explicit about the purposes of fiction. She writes in her preface to her first novel, *Contending Forces* (1900), that blacks must use fiction to preserve race memories: "It is a record of growth and development from generation to generation. *No one will do this for us: we must ourselves develop the men and women who will faithfully portray the inmost thoughts and feelings of the Negro with all the fire and romance which lie dormant in our history.*"[8] Frances Harper, who was most famous as an eloquent lecturer, first on behalf of the slave, then for the freedpeople, was equally intent on the uplift of women and the race. Typical of black fiction of that period, Harper's novel *Iola Leroy* (1892) features elevated superheroes, both male and female. Trying to imitate the popular form of the sentimental novel while also struggling to represent black

life and preserve its humanity, Harper and Hopkins exem
plify the artistic dilemmas of the black writer of that time, ;
dilemma that Arlene Elder says is unique in American fic
tion:

> Their author's acceptance of prevailing, popular literar
> forms pulls them toward the empty flights of romanti
> fiction, while their urgency to continue the antebellum
> Black tradition of speaking the stark truth insistently tug
> them back to their roots. In no other body of American
> writing are form and content so fiercely at war.[9]

Because women characters play a central role in thei
fiction, Harper and Hopkins share a certain uniqueness
among nineteenth-century black novelists. In contrast t
their famous male contemporaries—Charles Chesnutt, Pau
Laurence Dunbar, and William Wells Brown—Harper an
Hopkins put women's lives, women's activities, women'
feelings into the foreground of their fiction. They revers
the image of the tragic mulatto heroine, devising ways fo
their heroines to become political and social activists. The
reject the sentimental novel's ideal of marriage as an emo
tional and economic refuge for the helpless female; thei
women heroes marry men for support in their work of racia
uplift or they choose race uplift over marriage. Relation
ships between women are also foregrounded. We see a de
veloping friendship between Sappho and Dora in Hopkins
Contending Forces and between Iola and Aunt Linda in Har
per's *Iola Leroy.* Although neither of these novels meet
today's requirements for feminist fiction, at least there i
some focus on women's interaction with other women, som
interest in women's political views, and an insistence o
women's independence.

In spite of their attempts to give their women autonom
and power, both Harper and Hopkins were influenced b
the "Cult of True Womanhood," which demanded tha
women satisfy the obligations of affectional and domesti
life. In Harper's most well-known short story, "The Tw

Offers" (1859), her sympathies are clearly with Janette, the intellectual and artist who gains personal as well as economic independence as a successful, though unmarried, career woman.[10] But Harper still feels it necessary to justify Janette's life as a single woman by showing that Janette's true fulfillment is not in her career as a writer but in the higher mission as an advocate of the "downtrodden slave." While Janette will not belong to one man—this seems too chancy a proposition—she will be loved in a broader way by a world "full of warm, loving hearts" and her own will "beat in unison with them." As Barbara Welter points out in her study of the true womanhood cult, unmarried women could become "true women" through lives of unselfish service.[11] Thus, Harper's liberated career woman turns out to be a true woman in disguise, "the fires of her genius" contained and domesticated by love, duty, and religious principles.

Iola Leroy, Harper's first novel, published in 1892, more than thirty years after "The Two Offers," though it has a highly melodramatic plot, complete with idealized mulatto heroes, sudden reversals of fortune, the bad punished and the good rewarded, gives its main character a more powerful and unambiguously heroic role than Harper gives Janette. Perhaps because Iola is black and also a race leader Harper felt greater urgency to allow Iola freedom from the restrictions placed on women in fiction.

Iola first appears in the novel as a beautiful mulatto slave who is rescued from her cruel master by the Union Army and sent to work as a nurse in a Union camp. There she meets Dr. Gresham, the hospital physician and a wealthy white man, who falls in love with this beautiful, dedicated woman; but Iola refuses to marry Gresham because he is white. After the war, through a series of coincidences, fortuitous and unexplained, Iola is reunited with her entire family. She goes North with her uncle Robert where she continues to look for work despite the racial discrimination she encounters. In the North she meets another handsome physician, Dr. Frank Latimer, a black man who is light enough to pass for white. Having found a doctor with the right color and character, Iola marries him. By insisting that Iola choose between Dr. Gresham and Dr. Latimer (Iola's brother makes a similar choice between entering the Army as a white man or a black man), Harper politicizes marriage, making the love between Iola and Latimer not just a romantic attraction but a bond that allows them to support each other in working for the race:

> Kindred hopes and tastes had knit their hearts; grand and noble purposes were lighting up their lives; and they esteemed it a blessed privilege to stand on the threshold of a new era and labor for those who had passed from the old oligarchy of slavery into the new commonwealth of freedom.[12]

As a black woman directed by race loyalty, Iola is given a political role that Janette does not have. Iola speaks out against slavery; she refuses to marry a white man and abandon her commitment to the race; she acknowledges voluntarily her kinship to black people; she insists that to struggle for the race is a greater privilege than being white. As a political spokesperson, she criticizes the hypocritical Christian churches which refuse to minister to blacks. In succeeding generations of black writers, mulatto characters, like the ex-colored man in James Weldon Johnson's *Autobiography of an Ex-Coloured Man* (1912) and Helga Crane in Nella Larsen's *Quicksand* (1928), will be much more vulnerable in their marginality and far less able to articulate a political position that allows them Iola's power and triumph. Harper herself expressed the same clarity and conviction about her racial role: "After all, whether they encourage or discourage me, I belong to this race, and when it is down I belong to a down race; when it is up I belong to a risen race."[13]

In some ways Pauline Hopkins's novel *Contending Forces* published eight years later and by a black publisher, The Colored Co-operative Publishing Company, is not as pro gressive as *Iola Leroy*. Hopkins is less militant than Harper, less able to express her anger toward whites, and much more ambivalent toward her women characters. In his study of nineteenth-century Afro-American fiction, Richard Yarborough says that her association with a black publisher should have freed Hopkins from the influence that white editors exerted on other black writers: "Hopkins did not have to shape her fiction to meet unsympathetic or hostile readers. Knowing that her publisher was committed to reaching a black audience must have given her even more confidence to write what and how she saw fit."[14]

With such freedom to speak directly to a sympathetic black audience, why is Hopkins still a prisoner to an ideology that ultimately supports white superiority? She wants the race judged by its "little circles of educated men and women," black families like the Smiths in *Contending Forces*, whose thrift, industry, and hygienic cleanliness, along with a generous "infusion of white blood," account for their prosperity. In their autonomous black world they encounter little direct racism. Will Smith, a philosophy major at Harvard College, apparently does not experience any discrimination there. There is a strong sense of social hierarchy in Hopkins, with light-skinned blacks at the top and dialect-speaking dark-skinned blacks at the bottom. Her women characters also suffer from her hierarchical values, becoming less politically active and less central to the story as men take over the political affairs of the community.

In a sense, Hopkins could not depend on the easier solutions that were available to Harper, who was a member of an older generation and whose philosophy of life was formed during the Abolitionist struggle. In her absolute sense of the righteousness of her cause, Harper simply calls down divine retribution on evil whites. In her fiction the old masters and mistresses find the tables turned after the war, they lose their property, and/or drink themselves to death, while their former slaves live long and healthy lives. Hopkins did not find a way to express her anger directly so she contained it, usually confining her characters to a safe, all-black world where whites cannot affect them. Hopkins's response to the subject of lynching is to assign her character long, rational, controlled arguments that conclude that the solution to lynching is not to use "brute force" but to appeal for justice and try to influence public opinion.[15] In her Afterword to a reprint edition of *Contending Forces*, Gwendolyn Brooks correctly identifies the problem of submerged anger in Hopkins's work: "It is true that Pauline Hopkins can and does involve herself with black anger, but the texture, range, scope, the slashing red and scream and curse and *out-there* hurt that overwhelm us as Wright, Ellison and Haley deal with us, are not to be found in *Contending Forces*."[16] Brooks might have added her own name to the list of modern black writers whose anger overwhelms; her novel *Maud Martha*, is a countertext to *Contending Forces*. Brooks confronts what Hopkins must avoid at all costs: the fear of one's own inferiority in the face of a powerful racist white world, the inability to summon rage, the need to find a voice to maintain one's sanity and one's identity.

Avoidance and ambivalence also characterize Hopkins's treatment of women, and yet she quite consciously selects strategies to give her women freedom. In *Contending Forces* women develop friendships, they live in a little community in Ma Smith's house, they are intelligent, and they have work. Dora and her mother run a boardinghouse, and Sappho, whom we hear clicking away on her typewriter before she actually appears in the story, is a stenographer, an important choice because it is one of the first nonnurturing professions black women have in fiction. In one of the early scenes showing the beginning of their new friendship, Sappho and Dora are enclosed in a warm room during a winter storm, discussing everything from men to politics. Hopkins clearly intends for Sappho to represent the militant politics of Du Bois which are in opposition to the ideas of Arthur Lewis, who is modeled after Booker T. Washington. Taking Du Bois's position, Sappho argues for the franchise, for respect and equality without which "we become aliens in the very land of our birth." She rejects the Washingtonian program of "industrial education and the exclusion of politics," calling Lewis (and, presumably, Washington), an "insufferable prig."[17]

If Hopkins liberates her women in some ways, she also manages to undermine them in others. Sappho and Dora have their discussion within the confines of Sappho's bedroom, but when the public debates take place in *Contending Forces*, there are no women present. Hopkins also diminishes the stature of the women's friendship by describing it as "playing company like children." In fact, everything in the room is diminutive: their *small* feet, the *little* tea kettle, the *small* table, the *little* stove, the *thin* pieces of bread, and even Dora and Sappho, who are afraid to eat for fear they will gain weight. Hopkins's fear of women getting bigger and taking on roles of authority and prominence is quite obvious in her description of Mrs. Willis, an intellectual, feminist, and race leader, and, potentially, one of the most powerful women in this text. At the end of Willis's thoughtful and sensitive lecture on the advancement of colored women, Sappho is moved to confide in the older women; but just as she is about to do so, Hopkins reverses gears, charges Mrs. Willis with being "forced and insincere," and replaces Sappho's attraction with "a wave of repulsion toward this woman." Richard Yarborough also notes that Hopkins's discomfort with Mrs. Willis suggests some real threat that Willis poses:

> Hopkins is obviously attracted to the woman's strength of mind and forthright feminist political views. However, the extent of her ambitious drives seems somehow unsettling to the author . . . It is evident, however, that this powerful figure fascinates Hopkins far more than her small role in the novel might indicate.[18]

The short story, "Bro'r Abr'm Jimson's Wedding," published in *Colored American Magazine* in 1901, which features dialect-speaking, "folk" characters, represents a less re-

pressed Pauline Hopkins, less inhibited by white models and
less inclined to drain her characters, particularly her women,
of all real emotion. Perhaps because she does not take her
folk characters as seriously as she does her middle-class
blacks, or perhaps because the magazine was aimed at a
black audience, Hopkins allows these characters to behave
much more realistically than the nearly white superheroes of
her novel. Andy Nash pushing the Irish woman into a bowl
of lobster because she calls him a "nigger," the widow Nash
scheming for revenge on the man who dumped her for a
younger woman, and Brother Jimson's hypocritical piety are
far more believable than the noble, straight-laced, white-
approved characters in *Contending Forces*. There are other
ruptures in this short story that Hopkins does not allow in
her novel. When the racial antagonism between blacks and
the Irish explodes into violence and only the blacks are
punished, the widow Nash expresses anger over this injustice in language that Hopkins carefully excludes from the
novel: "White folks can run agin the law all the time an' they
never gits caught, but a nigger!" Hopkins is also less influenced in this story by sentimental conventions and the cult
of true womanhood which makes for some important
changes in her women characters. Women have a powerful
presence in this story. They control the plot and determine
its direction in ways that the more passive women in *Contending Forces* are never allowed. The widow Nash, Caramel Johnson, and Jane Jimson are not restricted by any notion of a
woman's place or female decorum: "I'm jes' coaxin' the
Lord to keep me sweet," Sister Nash says to Jimson immediately before she confronts him with his treachery. Even
though Caramel is a ploy to activate the rivalry between two
men—Brother Jimson and Andy Nash—her presence domi-
nates the story and her determination to snare a wealthy
husband sets up the chain of narrative events. This story also
makes us aware of the economic disparity between men and
women; for even in this prospering little community, women
do the low-paid, backbreaking work and are dependent on

the "leading men with money" who do not always live up to their ideals or the community's expectations.

In her book on Afro-American fiction of the nineteenth century, *The Hindered Hand*, Arlene Elder makes it very clear that the artistic choices of these writers were very limited. The need to use their writing as a vehicle to uplift the race, as a weapon against oppression, the lack of support for them as professional writers, a white audience whose attitudes about blacks were shaped by minstrel shows and plantation literature made it nearly impossible for most turn-of-the-century black writers to create freely. There was one way, however, Elder says these writers were able to find artistic freedom: "through their occasional acceptance of the liberating, subversive weapon of African-American folklore."[19]

In small ways both Harper and Hopkins did manage to subvert the literary conventions that stifled black writers. Frances Harper's experience as an antislavery orator influenced the voice of *Iola Leroy* as much as the sentimental novel did. Pauline Hopkins's rare excursion into the world of unassimilated blacks provides a humor, realism, and racial awareness not available in her genteel fiction. And in creating women who are intelligent and powerful, and making them central to their narratives, both Hopkins and Harper consciously resisted one of the most pervasive myths in patriarchal culture.

NOTES

1. Hazel Carby's introduction to a new edition of *Iola Leroy* (Boston: Beacon Press, 1987) establishes a new critical direction for scholarship on Frances Harper and, indeed, for all nineteenth-century black women writers. What Carby makes indisputably clear is that misinterpretations of Harper stem from a particular ideological position in Afro-American literary criticism, one that maintains that art and ideology must remain separate, that either condemns, ignores, ridicules, or misreads—whether knowingly or unknowingly—writers who use the novel as social protest. Carby's brilliant reinterpre-

tation of Harper casts great doubt on all previous scholarship on
Harper. She reminds us that the 1890s was a period of intense
intellectual and political activity for black women and that as one of
these extraordinary intellectuals Harper crafted *Iola Leroy* "with the
same political intensity that she gave to her lectures, speeches, and
articles." Thus Harper's narrative strategy is not so much to defend
the race against stereotypical portrayals as to represent a world in
which a new social order, displacing a racist white patriarchal order,
prevails. Carby maintains that Iola finds her rightful place, not by
finding a husband, but by searchng for and finding her maternal
family; characters who can pass for white choose to take their place
in the black race; black intellectuals debate the political issues that
were of consequence for the race during that time. Carby also offers
a political explanation for the mulatto figure which occurs so frequently in nineteenth-century black fiction. She sees this figure
functioning to displace the rigidity of Jim Crow in the South, en-
abling "an exploration of the social relations between the races."
While she is critical of the limitations of the novel, Carby finally
assesses *Iola Leroy* as "an integral part of Frances Harper's vision of a
'woman's era': an 'uprising' of women to establish an alternative
moral and social order." (pp. ix–xxvi.)

2. Sterling A. Brown, "A Century of Negro Portraiture in American
Literature," in *Black Voices: An Anthology of Afro-American Literature*, ed.
Abraham Chapman (New York: New American Library, 1968), p.
567.

3. Fannie Barrier Williams, "The Intellectual Progress of the
Colored Women of the United States Since the Emancipation Proc-
lamation," *World's Congress of Representative Women*, ed. May Wright
Sewall (Chicago, 1893), pp 696–711, in *Black Women in Nineteenth-
Century American Life: Their Words, Their Thoughts, Their Feelings*, ed.
Bert James Loewenberg and Ruth Bogin (University Park: Pennsyl-
vania State University Press, 1975), p. 272.

4. Victoria Earle Matthews, "The Awakening of the Afro-American
Woman" (Address delivered to the Annual Convention of the Society of Christian Endeavor, San Francisco, 11 July 1897).

5. Ibid., p.6.

6. Raymond Hedin, "The Structuring of Emotion in Black American Fiction," *Novel* 16 (Fall 1982):36.

7. George Henry Murray, "Educated Colored Men and White
Women," *Colored American Magazine* 8, no. 2 (February 1905):94.

8. Pauline Hopkins, *Contending Forces: A Romance Illustrative of Negro
Life North and South* (Boston: The Colored Co-operative Publishing
Co., 1900), pp. 13–14.

8. Arlene Elder, *The "Hindred Hand": Cultural Implications of Early Afro-American Fiction* (Westport, Conn.: Greenwood Press, 1978), pp. 36–37.

10. Harper imbues Janette with qualities she certainly must have possessed herself, and, in some respects, Janette's life is very much like Harper's: "Her path for a while ws marked with struggle and trial, but instead of uselessly repining she met them bravely and her life became not a thing of ease and indulgence, but of conquest, victory and accomplishments." Orphaned in 1828 at age three, Harper began to earn her own living as a domestic by the time she was fourteen. She was raised by an aunt and uncle in Baltimore, where she attended her uncle's school for free blacks. She worked for a few years as a teacher, but in 1853, shortly after Maryland passed a law allowing free blacks entering that state to be sold as slaves, she began work as an antislavery lecturer. She married in 1864, but, after her husband's death four years later, she resumed her career lecturing to the newly freed people, particularly to black women whom she never charged a fee. The most popular black poet of her day, Harper was well known for her poetry dealing with the grief and tragedy of slavery and for her novel *Iola Leroy* which went into three editions.

11. Barbara Welter points out in her study of the "cult of true womanhood" that the virtues of true womanhood could be achieved in any state of life, not just in marriage:

> But although marriage was best, it was not absolutely necessary. The women's magazines tried to remove the stigma from being an "Old Maid." They advised no marriage at all rather than an unhappy one contracted out of selfish motives. Their stories showed maiden ladies as unselfish ministers to the sick, teachers of the young, or moral preceptors with their pens, beloved of the entire village. Usually the life of single blessedness resulted from the premature death of a fiancé, or was chosen through fidelity to some high mission. ("The Cult of True Womanhood, 1820–1860," in *Dimity Convictions: The American Woman in the Nineteenth Century* [Athens: Ohio University Press, 1976], p. 37)

12. Frances Harper, *Iola Leroy, or Shadows Uplifted* (New York: AMS Press, 1971), p. 271.

13. Gerda Lerner, ed., *Black Women in White America: A Documentary History* (New York: Pantheon Books, 1972), pp. 535–36.

14. Richard A. Yarborough, "The Depiction of Blacks in the Early Afro-American Novel" (Ph.D. diss., Stanford University, 1980), p. 477.

15. Hedin, "Structuring of Emotion," p. 37. Hedin's essay catalogues the strategies black fiction writers since the slave narratives

FRANCES ELLEN WATKINS HARPER

Iola

DIVERGING PATHS

On the eve of his departure from the city of P——, Dr. Gresham called on Iola, and found her alone. They talked awhile of reminiscences of the war and hospital life, when Dr. Gresham, approaching Iola, said:—

"Miss Leroy, I am glad the great object of your life is accomplished, and that you have found all your relatives. Years have passed since we parted, years in which I have vainly tried to get a trace of you and have been baffled, but I have found you at last!" Clasping her hand in his, he continued, "I would it were so that I should never lose you again! Iola, will you not grant me the privilege of holding this hand as mine all through the future of our lives? Your search for your mother is ended. She is well cared for. Are you not free at last to share with me my Northern home, free to be mine as nothing else on earth is mine." Dr. Gresham looked eagerly on Iola's face, and tried to read its varying expression. "Iola, I learned to love you in the hospital. I have tried to forget you, but it has been all in vain. Your image is just as deeply engraven on my heart as it was the day we parted."

"Doctor," she replied, sadly, but firmly, as she withdrew her hand from his, "I feel now as I felt then, that there is an insurmountable barrier between us."

"What is it, Iola?" asked Dr. Gresham, anxiously.

"It is the public opinion which assigns me a place with the colored people."

"Iola" from *Iola Leroy* (1892)

"But what right has public opinion to interfere with our marriage relations? Why should we yield to its behests?"

"Because it is stronger than we are, and we cannot run counter to it without suffering its penalties."

"And what are they, Iola? Shadows that you merely dread?"

"No! no! the penalties of social ostracism North and South, except here and there some grand and noble exceptions. I do not think that you fully realize how much prejudice against colored people permeates society, lowers the tone of our religion, and reacts upon the life of the nation. After freedom came, mamma was living in the city of A——, and wanted to unite with a Christian church there. She made application for membership. She passed her examination as a candidate, and was received as a church member. When she was about to make her first communion, she unintentionally took her seat at the head of the column. The elder who was administering the communion gave her the bread in the order in which she sat, but before he gave her the wine some one touched him on the shoulder and whispered a word in his ear. He then passed mamma by, gave the cup to others, and then returned to her. From that rite connected with the holiest memories of earth, my poor mother returned humiliated and depressed."

"What a shame!" exclaimed Dr. Gresham, indignantly.

"I have seen," continued Iola, "the same spirit manifested in the North. Mamma once attempted to do missionary work in this city. One day she found an outcast colored girl, whom she wished to rescue. She took her to an asylum for fallen women and made an application for her, but was refused. Colored girls were not received there. Soon after mamma found among the colored people an outcast white girl. Mamma's sympathies, unfettered by class distinction, were aroused in her behalf, and, in company with two white ladies, she went with the girl to that same refuge. For her the door was freely opened and admittance readily granted. It was as if two women were sinking in the quicksands, and on the solid land stood other women with life-lines in their hands, seeing the deadly sands slowly creeping up around the hapless victims. To one they readily threw the lines of deliverance, but for the other there was not one strand of salvation. Sometime since, to the same asylum, came a poor fallen girl who had escaped from the clutches of a wicked woman. For her the door would have been opened, had not the vile woman from whom she was escaping followed her to that place of refuge and revealed the fact that she belonged to the colored race. That fact was enough to close the door upon her, and to send her back to sin and to suffer, and perhaps to die as a wretched outcast. And yet in this city where a number of charities are advertised, I do not think there is one of them which, in appealing to the public, talks more religion than the managers of this asylum. This prejudice against the colored race environs our lives and mocks our aspirations."

"Iola, I see no use in your persisting that you are colored when your eyes are as blue and complexion as white as mine."

"Doctor, were I your wife, are there not people who would caress me as a white woman who would shrink from me in scorn if they knew I had one drop of negro blood in my veins? When mistaken for a white woman, I should hear things alleged against the race at which my blood would boil. No, Doctor, I am not willing to live under a shadow of concealment which I thoroughly hate as if the blood in my veins were an undetected crime of my soul."

"Iola, dear, surely you paint the picture too darkly."

"Doctor, I have painted it with my heart's blood. It is easier to outgrow the dishonor of crime than the disabilities of color. You have created in this country an aristocracy of color wide enough to include the South with its treason and Utah with its abominations, but too narrow to include the best and bravest colored man who bared his breast to the bullets of the enemy during your fratricidal strife. Is not the most arrant Rebel to-day more acceptable to you than the most faithful colored man?"

"No! no!" exclaimed Dr. Gresham, vehemently. "You are wrong. I belong to the Grand Army of the Republic. We have no separate State Posts for the colored people, and, were such a thing proposed, the majority of our members, I believe, would be against it. In Congress colored men have the same seats as white men, and the color line is slowly fading out in our public institutions."

"But how is it in the Church?" asked Iola.

"The Church is naturally conservative. It preserves old truths, even if it is somewhat slow in embracing new ideas. It has its social as well as its spiritual side. Society is woman's realm. The majority of church members are women, who are said to be the aristocratic element of our country. I fear that one of the last strongholds of this racial prejudice will be found beneath the shadow of some of our churches. I think, on account of this social question, that large bodies of Christian temperance women and other reformers, in trying to reach the colored people even for their own good, will be quicker to form separate associations than our National Grand Army, whose ranks are open to black and white, liberals and conservatives, saints and agnostics. But, Iola, we have drifted far away from the question. No one has a right to interfere with our marriage if we do not infringe on the rights of others."

"Doctor," she replied, gently, "I feel that our paths must diverge. My life-work is planned. I intend spending my future among the colored people of the South."

"My dear friend," he replied, anxiously, "I am afraid that you are destined to sad disappointment. When the novelty wears off you will be disillusioned, and, I fear, when the time comes that you can no longer serve them they will forget your services and remember only your failings."

"But, Doctor, they need me; and I am sure when I taught among them they were very grateful for my services."

"I think," he replied, "these people are more thankful than grateful."

"I do not think so; and if I did it would not hinder me from doing all in my power to help them. I do not expect all the finest traits of character to spring from the hot-beds of slavery and caste. What matters it if they do forget the singer, so they don't forget the song? No, Doctor, I don't think that I could best serve my race by forsaking them and marrying you."

"Iola," he exclaimed, passionately, "if you love your race, as you call it, work for it, live for it, suffer for it, and, if need be, die for it; but don't marry for it. Your education has unfitted you for social life among them."

"It was," replied Iola, "through their unrequited toil that I was educated, while they were compelled to live in ignorance. I am indebted to them for the power I have to serve them. I wish other Southern women felt as I do. I think they could do so much to help the colored people at their doors if they would look at their opportunities in the light of the face of Jesus Christ. Nor am I wholly unselfish in allying myself with the colored people. All the rest of my family have done so. My dear grandmother is one of the excellent of the earth, and we all love her too much to ignore our relationship with her. I did not choose my lot in life, and the simplest thing I can do is to accept the situation and do the best I can."

"And is this your settled purpose?" he asked, sadly.

"It is, Doctor," she replied, tenderly but firmly. "I see no other. I must serve the race which needs me most."

"Perhaps you are right," he replied; "but I cannot help feeling sad that our paths, which met so pleasantly, should diverge so painfully. And yet, not only the freedmen, but the whole country, need such helpful, self-sacrificing teachers as you will prove; and if earnest prayers and holy wishes can brighten your path, your lines will fall in the pleasantest places."

As he rose to go, sympathy, love, and admiration were blended in the parting look he gave her; but he felt it was useless to attempt to divert her from her purpose. He knew that for the true reconstruction of the country something more was needed than bayonets and bullets, or the schemes of selfish politicians or plotting demagogues. He knew that the South needed the surrender of the best brain and heart of the country to build, above the wastes of war, more stately temples of thought and action.

DR. LATROBE'S MISTAKE

On the morning previous to their departure for their respective homes, Dr. Gresham met Dr. Latrobe in the parlor of the Concordia.

"How," asked Dr. Gresham, "did you like Dr. Latimer's paper?"

"Very much, indeed. It was excellent. He is a very talented young man. He sits next to me at lunch and I have conversed with him several times. He is very genial and attractive, only he seems to be rather cranky on the negro question. I hope if he comes South that he will not make the mistake of mixing up with the negroes. It would be throwing away his influence and ruining his prospects. He seems to be well versed in science and literature and would make a very delightful accession to our social life."

"I think," replied Dr. Gresham, "that he is an honor to our profession. He is one of the finest specimens of our young manhood."

Just then Dr. Latimer entered the room. Dr. Latrobe arose and, greeting him cordially, said: "I was delighted with your paper; it was full of thought and suggestion."

"Thank you," answered Dr. Latimer, "it was my aim to make it so."

"And you succeeded admirably," replied Dr. Latrobe. "I could not help thinking how much we owe to heredity and environment."

"Yes," said Dr. Gresham. "Continental Europe yearly sends to our shores subjects to be developed into citizens. Emancipation has given us millions of new citizens, and to them our influence and example should be a blessing and not a curse."

"Well," said Dr. Latimer, "I intend to go South, and help those who so much need helpers from their own ranks."

"I hope," answered Dr. Latrobe, "that if you go South you will only sustain business relations with the negroes, and not commit the folly of equalizing yourself with them."

"Why not?" asked Dr. Latimer, steadily looking him in the eye.

"Because in equalizing yourself with them you drag us down; and our social customs must be kept intact."

"You have been associating with me at the convention for several days; I do not see that the contact has dragged you down, has it?"

"You! What has that got to do with associating with niggers?" asked Dr. Latrobe, curtly.

"The blood of that race is coursing through my veins. I am one of them," replied Dr. Latimer, proudly raising his head.

"You!" exclaimed Dr. Latrobe, with an air of profound astonishment and crimsoning face.

"Yes;" interposed Dr. Gresham, laughing heartily at Dr. Latrobe's discomfiture. "He belongs to that negro race both by blood and choice. His father's mother made overtures to receive him as her grandson and heir, but he has nobly refused to forsake his mother's people and has cast his lot with them."

"And I," said Dr. Latimer, "would have despised myself if I had done otherwise."

"Well, well," said Dr. Latrobe, rising, "I was never so deceived before. Good morning!"

Dr. Latrobe had thought he was clear-sighted enough to detect the presence of negro blood when all physical traces had disappeared. But he had associated with Dr. Latimer for several days, and admired his talent, without suspecting for one moment his racial connection. He could not help feeling a sense of vexation at the signal mistake he had made.

Dr. Frank Latimer was the natural grandson of a Southern lady, in whose family his mother had been a slave. The blood of a proud aristocratic ancestry was flowing through his veins, and generations of blood admixture had effaced all trace of his negro lineage. His complexion was blonde, his eye bright and piercing, his lips firm and well moulded; his manner very affable; his intellect active and well stored with information. He was a man capable of winning in life through his rich gifts of inheritance and acquirements. When freedom came, his mother, like Hagar of old, went out into the wide world to seek a living for herself and child. Through years of poverty she labored to educate her child, and saw the glad fruition of her hopes when her son graduated as an M. D. from the University of P——.

After his graduation he met his father's mother, who recognized him by his resemblance to her dear, departed son. All the mother love in her lonely heart awoke, and she was willing to overlook "the missing link of matrimony," and adopt him as her heir, if he would ignore his identity with the colored race.

Before him loomed all the possibilities which only birth and blood can give a white man in our Democratic country. But he was a man of too much sterling worth of character to be willing to forsake his mother's race for the richest advantages his grandmother could bestow.

Dr. Gresham had met Dr. Latimer at the beginning of the convention, and had been attracted to him by his frank and genial manner. One morning, when conversing with him, Dr. Gresham had learned some of the salient points of his history, which, instead of repelling him, had only deepened his admiration for the young doctor. He was much amused when he saw the pleasant acquaintanceship between him and Dr. Latrobe, but they agreed to be silent about his racial connection until the time came when they were ready to divulge it; and they were hugely delighted at his signal blunder.

VISITORS FROM THE SOUTH

"Mamma is not well," said Iola to Robert. "I spoke to her about sending for a doctor, but she objected and I did not insist."

"I will ask Dr. Latimer, whom I met at the Concordia, to step in. He is a splendid young fellow. I wish we had thousands like him."

In the evening the doctor called. Without appearing to make a professional visit he engaged Marie in conversation, watched her carefully, and came to the conclusion that her failing health proceeded more from mental than physical causes.

"I am so uneasy about Harry," said Mrs. Leroy. "He is so fearless and outspoken. I do wish the attention of the whole nation could be turned to the curel barbarisms which are a national disgrace. I think the term 'bloody shirt' is one of the most heartless phrases ever invented to divert attention from cruel wrongs and dreadful outrages."

Just then Iola came in and was introduced by her uncle to Dr. Latimer, to whom the introduction was a sudden and unexpected pleasure.

After an interchange of courtesies, Marie resumed the conversation, saying: "Harry wrote me only last week that a young friend of his had lost his situation because he refused to have his pupils strew flowers on the streets through which Jefferson Davis was to pass."

"I think," said Dr. Latimer, indignantly, "that the Israelites had just as much right to scatter flowers over the bodies of the Egyptians, when the waves threw back their corpses on the shores of the Red Sea, as these children had to strew the path of Jefferson Davis with flowers. We want our boys to grow up manly citizens, and not cringing sycophants. When do you expect your son, Mrs. Leroy?"

"Some time next week," answered Marie.

"And his presence will do you more good than all the medicine in my chest."

"I hope, Doctor," said Mrs. Leroy, "that we will not lose sight of you, now that your professional visit is ended; for I believe your visit was the result of a conspiracy between Iola and her uncle."

Dr. Latimer laughed, as he answered, "Ah, Mrs. Leroy, I see you have found us all out."

"Oh, Doctor," exclaimed Iola, with pleasing excitement, "there is a young lady coming here to visit me next week. Her name is Miss Lucille Delany, and she is my ideal woman. She is grand, brave, intellectual, and religious."

"Is that so? She would make some man an excellent wife," replied Dr. Latimer.

"Now isn't that perfectly manlike," answered Iola, smiling. "Mamma, what do you think of that? Did any of you gentlemen ever see a young woman of much ability that you did not look upon as a flotsam all adrift until some man had appropriated her?"

"I think, Miss Leroy, that the world's work, if shared, is better done than when it is performed alone. Don't you think your life-work will be better done if some one shares it with you?" asked Dr. Latimer, slowly, and with a smile in his eyes.

"That would depend on the person who shared it," said Iola, faintly blushing.

"Here," said Robert, a few evenings after this conversation, as he handed Iola a couple of letters, "is something which will please you."

Iola took the letters, and, after reading one of them, said: "Miss Delany and Harry will be here on Wednesday; and this one is an invitation which also adds to my enjoyment."

"What is it?" asked Marie; "an invitation to a hop or a german?"

"No; but something which I value far more. We are all invited to Mr. Stillman's to a *conversazione.*"

"What is the object?"

"His object is to gather some of the thinkers and leaders of the race to consult on subjects of vital interest to our welfare. He has invited Dr. Latimer, Professor Gradnor, of North Carolina, Mr. Forest, of New York, Hon. Dugdale, Revs. Carmicle, Cantnor, Tunster, Professor Langhorne, of Georgia, and a few ladies, Mrs. Watson, Miss Brown, and others."

"I am glad that it is neither a hop nor a german," said Iola, "but something for which I have been longing."

"Why, Iola," asked Robert, "don't you believe in young people having a good time?"

"Oh, yes," answered Iola, seriously, "I believe in young people having amusements and recreations; but the times are too serious for us to attempt to make our lives a long holiday."

"Well, Iola," answered Robert, "this is the first holiday we have had in two hundred and fifty years, and you shouldn't be too exacting."

"Yes," replied Marie, "human beings naturally crave enjoyment, and if not furnished with good amusements they are apt to gravitate to low pleasures."

"Some one," said Robert, "has said that the Indian belongs to an old race and looks gloomily back to the past, and that the negro belongs to a young race and looks hopefully towards the future."

"If that be so," replied Marie, "our race-life corresponds more to the follies of youth than the faults of maturer years."

On Dr. Latimer's next visit he was much pleased to see a great change in Marie's appearance. Her eye had grown brighter, her step more elastic, and the anxiety had faded from her face. Harry had arrived, and with him came Miss Delany.

"Good evening, Dr. Latimer," said Iola, cheerily, as she entered the room with Miss Lucille Delany. "This is my

friend, Miss Delany, from Georgia. Were she not present
would say she is one of the grandest women in America.

"I am very much pleased to meet you," said Dr. Latimer
cordially; "I have heard Miss Leroy speak of you. We wer
expecting you," he added, with a smile.

Just then Harry entered the room, and Iola presented hir
to Dr. Latimer, saying, "This is my brother, about whor
mamma was so anxious."

"Had you a pleasant journey?" asked Dr. Latimer, afte
the first greetings were over.

"Not especially," answered Miss Delany. "Southern road
are not always very pleasant to travel. When Mr. Leroy en
tered the cars at A——, where he was known, had he take
his seat among the white people he would have been re
manded to the colored car."

"But after awhile," said Harry, "as Miss Delany and mysel
were sitting together, laughing and chatting, a colored ma
entered the car, and, mistaking me for a white man, aske
the conductor to have me removed, and I had to insist that
was colored in order to be permitted to remain. It would b
ludicrous, if it were not vexatious, to be too white to b
black, and too black to be white."

"Caste plays such fantastic tricks in this country," said D
Latimer.

"I tell Mr. Leroy," said Miss Delany, "that when he re
turns he must put a label on himself, saying, 'I am a colore
man,' to prevent annoyance."

DAWNING AFFECTIONS

"Doctor," said Iola, as they walked home from the *conversaz
one*, "I wish I could do something more for our people than
am doing. I taught in the South till failing health compelle
me to change my employment. But, now that I am well an

strong, I would like to do something of lasting service for the race."

"Why not," asked Dr. Latimer, "write a good, strong book which would be helpful to them? I think there is an amount of dormant talent among us, and a large field from which to gather materials for such a book."

"I would do it, willingly, if I could; but one needs both leisure and money to make a successful book. There is material among us for the broadest comedies and the deepest tragedies, but, besides money and leisure, it needs patience, perseverance, courage, and the hand of an artist to weave it into the literature of the country."

"Miss Leroy, you have a large and rich experience; you possess a vivid imagination and glowing fancy. Write, out of the fullness of your heart, a book to inspire men and women with a deeper sense of justice and humanity."

"Doctor," replied Iola, "I would do it if I could, not for the money it might bring, but for the good it might do. But who believes any good can come out of the black Nazareth?"

"Miss Leroy, out of the race must come its own thinkers and writers. Authors belonging to the white race have written good racial books, for which I am deeply grateful, but it seems to be almost impossible for a white man to put himself completely in our place. No man can feel the iron which enters another man's soul."

"Well, Doctor, when I write a book I shall take you for the hero of my story."

"Why, what have I done," asked Dr. Latimer, in a surprised tone, "that you should impale me on your pen?"

"You have done nobly," answered Iola, "in refusing your grandmother's offer."

"I only did my duty," he modestly replied.

"But," said Iola, "when others are trying to slip out from the race and pass into the white basis, I cannot help admiring one who acts as if he felt that the weaker the race is the closer he would cling to it."

"My mother," replied Dr. Latimer, "faithful and true, belongs to that race. Where else should I be? But I know a young lady who could have cast her lot with the favored race, yet chose to take her place with the freed people, as their teacher, friend, and adviser. This young lady was alone in the world. She had been fearfully wronged, and to her stricken heart came a brilliant offer of love, home, and social position. But she bound her heart to the mast of duty, closed her ears to the syren song, and could not be lured from her purpose."

A startled look stole over Iola's face, and, lifting her eyes to his, she faltered:—

"Do you know her?"

"Yes, I know her and admire her; and she ought to be made the subject of a soul-inspiring story. Do you know of whom I speak?"

"How should I, Doctor? I am sure you have not made me your confidante," she responded, demurely; then she quickly turned and tripped up the steps of her home, which she had just reached.

After this conversation Dr. Latimer became a frequent visitor at Iola's home, and a firm friend of her brother. Harry was at that age when, for the young and inexperienced, vice puts on her fairest guise and most seductive smiles. Dr. Latimer's wider knowledge and larger experience made his friendship for Harry very valuable, and the service he rendered him made him a favorite and ever-welcome guest in the family.

"Are you all alone," asked Robert, one night, as he entered the cosy little parlor where Iola sat reading. "Where are the rest of the folks?"

"Mamma and grandma have gone to bed," answered Iola. "Harry and Lucille are at the concert. They are passionately fond of music, and find facilities here that they do not have in the South. They wouldn't go to hear a seraph where they must take a negro seat. I was too tired to go. Besides, 'two company and three's a crowd,'" she added, significantly.

"I reckon you struck the nail on the head that time," said

obert, laughing. "But you have not been alone all the time. ust as I reached the corner I saw Dr. Latimer leaving the oor. I see he still continues his visits. Who is his patient ow?"

"Oh, Uncle Robert," said Iola, smiling and flushing, "he is ut with Harry and Lucille part of the time, and drops in now nd then to see us all."

"Well," said Robert, "I suppose the case is now an affair of ae heart. But I cannot blame him for it," he added, looking ndly on the beautiful face of his niece, which sorrow had ouched only to chisel into more loveliness. "How do you ke him?"

"I must have within me," answered Iola, with unaffected uthfulness, "a large amount of hero worship. The charac- rs of the Old Testament I most admire are Moses and ehemiah. They were willing to put aside their own advan- ges for their race and country. Dr. Latimer comes up to my leal of a high, heroic manhood."

"I think," answered Robert, smiling archly, "he would be elighted to hear your opinion of him."

"I tell him," continued Iola, "that he belongs to the days f chivalry. But he smiles and says, 'he only belongs to the ays of hard-pan service.' "

"Some one," said Robert, "was saying to-day that he ood in his own light when he refused his grandmother's ffer to receive him as her son."

"I think," said Iola, "it was the grandest hour of his life hen he made that decision. I have admired him ever since I eard his story."

"But, Iola, think of the advantages he set aside. It was no acrifice for me to remain colored, with my lack of education nd race sympathies, but Dr. Latimer had doors open to him s a white man which are forever closed to a colored man. To e born white in this country is to be born to an inheritance f privileges, to hold in your hands the keys that open before ou the doors of every occupation, advantage, opportunity, nd achievement."

"I know that, uncle," answered Iola; "but even these a
vantages are too dearly bought if they mean loss of hono
true manliness, and self respect. He could not have retaine
these had he ignored his mother and lived under a veil
concealment, constantly haunted by a dread of detectio
The gain would not have been worth the cost. It were bett
that he should walk the ruggedest paths of life a true m
than tread the softest carpets a moral cripple."

"I am afraid," said Robert, laying his hand caressing
upon her head, "that we are destined to lose the light of o
home."

"Oh, uncle, how you talk! I never dreamed of what you a
thinking," answered Iola, half reproachfully.

"And how," asked Robert, "do you know what I am thir
ing about?"

"My dear uncle, I'm not blind."

"Neither am I," replied Robert, significantly, as he left t
room.

Iola's admiration for Dr. Latimer was not a one-sid
affair. Day after day she was filling a larger place in his hea
The touch of her hand thrilled him with emotion. Her ligl
est words were an entrancing melody to his ear. Her nobl
sentiments found a response in his heart. In their desire
help the race their hearts beat in loving unison. One gra
and noble purpose was giving tone and color to their liv
and strengthening the bonds of affection between them.

WOOING AND WEDDING

Harry's vacation had been very pleasant. Miss Delany, wi
her fine conversational powers and ready wit, had add
much to his enjoyment. Robert had given his mother t
pleasantest room in the house, and in the evening the fam
would gather around her, tell her the news of the day, re
to her from the Bible, join with her in thanksgiving

mercies received and in prayer for protection through the night. Harry was very grateful to Dr. Latimer for the kindly interest he had shown in accompanying Miss Delany and himself to places of interest and amusement. He was grateful, too, that in the city of P—— doors were open to them which were barred against them in the South.

The bright, beautiful days of summer were gliding into autumn, with its glorious wealth of foliage, and the time was approaching for the departure of Harry and Miss Delany to their respective schools, when Dr. Latimer received several letters from North Carolina, urging him to come South, as physicians were greatly needed there. Although his practice was lucrative in the city of P——, he resolved he would go where his services were most needed.

A few evenings before he started he called at the house, and made an engagement to drive Iola to the park.

At the time appointed he drove up to the door in his fine equipage. Iola stepped gracefully in and sat quietly by his side to enjoy the loveliness of the scenery and the gorgeous grandeur of the setting sun.

"I expect to go South," said Dr. Latimer, as he drove slowly along.

"Ah, indeed," said Iola, assuming an air of interest, while a shadow flitted over her face. "Where do you expect to pitch your tent?"

"In the city of C——, North Carolina," he answered.

"Oh, I wish," she exclaimed, "that you were going to Georgia, where you could take care of that high-spirited brother of mine."

"I suppose if he were to hear you he would laugh, and say that he could take care of himself. But I know a better plan than that."

"What is it?" asked Iola, innocently.

"That you will commit yourself, instead of your brother, to my care."

"Oh, dear," replied Iola, drawing a long breath. "What would mamma say?"

"That she would willingly resign you, I hope."

"And what would grandma and Uncle Robert say?" again asked Iola.

"That they would cheerfully acquiesce. Now, what would I say if they all consent?"

"I don't know," modestly responded Iola.

"Well," replied Dr. Latimer, "I would say:—

> "Could deeds my love discover,
> Could valor gain thy charms,
> To prove myself thy lover
> I'd face a world in arms."

"And prove a good soldier," added Iola, smiling, "when there is no battle to fight."

"Iola, I am in earnest," said Dr. Latimer, passionately. "In the work to which I am devoted every burden will be lighter, every path smoother, if brightened and blessed with your companionship."

A sober expression swept over Iola's face, and, dropping her eyes, she said: "I must have time to think."

Quietly they rode along the river bank until Dr. Latimer broke the silence by saying:—

"Miss Iola, I think that you brood too much over the condition of our people."

"Perhaps I do," she replied, "but they never burn a man in the South that they do not kindle a fire around my soul."

"I am afraid," replied Dr. Latimer, "that you will grow morbid and nervous. Most of our people take life easily—why shouldn't you?"

"Because," she answered, "I can see breakers ahead which they do not."

"Oh, give yourself no uneasiness. They will catch the fire and fever of the nineteenth century soon enough. I have heard several of our ministers say that it is chiefly men of disreputable characters who are made the subjects of violence and lynch-law."

"Suppose it is so," responded Iola, feelingly. "If these

men believe in eternal punishment they ought to feel a greater concern for the wretched sinner who is hurried out of time with all his sins upon his head, than for the godly man who passes through violence to endless rest."

"That is true; and I am not counseling you to be selfish; but, Miss Iola, had you not better look out for yourself?"

"Thank you, Doctor, I am feeling quite well."

"I know it, but your devotion to study and work is too intense," he replied.

"I am preparing to teach, and must spend my leisure time in study. Mr. Cloten is an excellent employer, and treats his employes as if they had hearts as well as hands. But to be an expert accountant is not the best use to which I can put my life."

"As a teacher you will need strong health and calm nerves. You had better let me prescribe for you. You need," he added, with a merry twinkle in his eyes, "change of air, change of scene, and change of name."

"Well, Doctor," said Iola, laughing, "that is the newest nostrum out. Had you not better apply for a patent?"

"Oh," replied Dr. Latimer, with affected gravity, "you know you must have unlimited faith in your physician."

"So you wish me to try the faith cure?" asked Iola, laughing.

"Yes, faith in me," responded Dr. Latimer, seriously.

"Oh, here we are at home!" exclaimed Iola. "This has been a glorious evening, Doctor. I am indebted to you for a great pleasure. I am extremely grateful."

"You are perfectly welcome," replied Dr. Latimer. "The pleasure has been mutual, I assure you."

"Will you not come in?" asked Iola.

Tying his horse, he accompanied Iola into the parlor. Seating himself near her, he poured into her ears words eloquent with love and tenderness.

"Iola," he said, "I am not an adept in courtly phrases. I am a plain man, who believes in love and truth. In asking you to share my lot, I am not inviting you to a life of ease and luxury, for year after year I may have to struggle to keep the wolf from the door, but your presence would make my home one of the brightest spots on earth, and one of the fairest types of heaven. Am I presumptuous in hoping that your love will become the crowning joy of my life?"

His words were more than a tender strain wooing her to love and happiness, they were a clarion call to a life of high and holy worth, a call which found a response in her heart. Her hand lay limp in his. She did not withdraw it, but, raising her lustrous eyes to his, she softly answered: "Frank, I love you."

After he had gone, Iola sat by the window, gazing at the splendid stars, her heart quietly throbbing with a delicious sense of joy and love. She had admired Dr. Gresham and, had there been no barrier in her way, she might have learned to love him; but Dr. Latimer had grown irresistibly upon her heart. There were depths in her nature that Dr. Gresham had never fathomed; aspirations in her soul with which he had never mingled. But as the waves leap up to the strand, so her soul went out to Dr. Latimer. Between their lives were no impeding barriers, no inclination impelling one way and duty compelling another. Kindred hopes and tastes had knit their hearts; grand and noble purposes were lighting up their lives; and they esteemed it a blessed privilege to stand on the threshold of a new era and labor for those who had passed from the old oligarchy of slavery into the new commonwealth of freedom.

BIBLIOGRAPHIC NOTES

Criticism of Frances Harper is mostly concerned with her poetry. Discussions of *Iola Leroy*, when they appear, are very brief and resemble apologies more than analyses. Typical of this treatment are Robert Bone's two paragraphs on Harper in *The Negro Novel in America* (New Haven: Yale University Press, 1965), in which the novel's lack of urgency of protest is excused because of Harper's advanced age. At age sixty-seven, Harper, says Bone, did not have the social consciousness of her contemporaries. (p. 32)

Serious consideration of *Iola Leroy* has only recently appeared. Barbara Christian, *Black Women Novelists: The Making of a Tradition, 1892–1976* (Westport, Conn.: Greenwood Press, 1980), discusses the stereotypes that Harper attempted to refute and demonstrates Harper's contention that black women must be involved in race uplift work. She also points out that Iola is not a tragic heroine and discusses the importance of Harper's subversion of that tradition that emphasizes weakness of women and their inability to succeed in either a white or black world. Richard Yarborough, "The Depiction of Blacks in the Early Afro-American Novel" (Ph.D. diss., Stanford University, 1980), also discusses Harper's attempts to counteract revisionist histories of the Civil War and myths of happy plantation life.

Carol McAlpine Watson's new book *Prologue: The Novels of Black American Women 1891–1965* (Westport, Conn.: Greenwood Press, 1985) contains a lengthy study of Harper, concentrating on Harper's appeal to a democratic Christian vision of racial equality. Elizabeth Ammons has done considerable research on Harper and has published several articles, one of which, "Stowe's Dream of the Mother-Savior: *Uncle Tom's Cabin* and American Women Writers Before the 1920's," is in Eric Sundquist, ed., *Five New Essays on Uncle Tom's Cabin* (Cambridge: Cambridge University Press, 1985). Here, she places *Iola Leroy* in the canon of important works by women writers and compares elements of plot and theme with *Uncle Tom's Cabin.* Ammons's analysis focuses on Harper's redefinition of motherhood as politically as well as morally aware, and she discusses the implications of this redefinition of motherhood for black female heroes.

Frances Smith Foster is preparing a critical edition of Harper's work for the Feminist Press. There is a new edition of

Frances Harper's novel *Iola Leroy*, with an introduction by Hazel Carby (Boston: Beacon Press, 1987). Barbara Christian's "The Use of History: Frances Harper's *Iola Leroy, Shadows Uplifted*" in *Black Feminist Criticism: Perspectives on Black Women Writers* (New York: Pergamon Press, 1985, pp. 165-70), examines the dilemmas of a political writer like Harper who was forced to conform to the tenets of the romance novel.

dom. It was a new view of the possibilities and probabiliti
which the future might open to her people. Long she stru
gled with thoughts which represented to her but vaguely
life beyond anything of which she had ever dreamed.

Sappho generally carried her work home in the mornin
but ten o'clock would find her seated at her desk and reac
to begin her task anew. Some days she was unoccupied; b
this did not happen very frequently. These free days wer
the gala days of her existence, when under Dora's guidanc
she explored various points of interest, and learned fro
observation the great plan of life as practiced in an intell
gent, liberty-loving community. Here in the free air of Ne
England's freest city, Sappho drank great draughts of free
dom's subtle elixir. Dora was interested and amused i
watching the changes on the mirror-like face of her frien
whenever her attention was arrested by a new phenomeno
It was strange to see this girl, resembling nothing so much a
a lily in its beautiful purity, shrink from entering a place o
public resort for fear of insult. It was difficult to convince he
that she might enter a restaurant frequented by educate
whites and meet with nothing but the greatest courtesy; th
she might take part in the glorious service at fashionab
Trinity and be received with punctilious politeness. To th
woman, denied association with the vast sources of inform
tion, which are heirlooms to the lowliest inhabitant of Bo
ton, the noble piles, which represented the halls of learnin
and the massive grandeur of the library, free to all, seeme
to invite her to a full participation in their intellectual joy
She had seen nothing like them. Statuary, paintings, scul
tures,—all appealed to her beauty-loving nature. The hi
den springs of spirituality were satisfied and at rest, claimi
kinship with the great minds of the past, whose never-dyi
works breathed perennial life in the atmosphere of the qui
halls.

Now was the beginning of the storm season in New E
gland, and on stormy days the two girls would sit before t
fire in Sappho's room and talk of the many things dear

women, while they embroidered or stitched. So they sat one cold, snowy day. The storm had started the afternoon before and had raged with unceasing fury all night,—snow and rain which the increasing cold quickly turned into cutting sleet. Morning had brought relief from the high winds, and the temperature had moderated somewhat; but the snow still fell steadily, drifting into huge piles, which made the streets impassable. It was the first great storm Sappho had seen. It was impossible for her to leave home, so she begged Dora to pass the day with her and play "company," like the children. Dora was nothing loathe; and as soon as her morning duties were finished, she told her mother that she was going visiting and would not be at home until tea time. By eleven o'clock they had locked the door of Sappho's room to keep out all intruders, had mended the fire until the little stove gave out a delicious warmth, and had drawn the window curtains close to keep out stray currents of air. Sappho's couch was drawn close beside the stove, while Dora's small person was most cosily bestowed in her favorite rocking-chair.

It was a very convenient stove that Sappho had in her room. The ornamental top could be turned back on its movable hinge, and there was a flat stove cover ready to hold any vessel and heat its contents to just the right temperature. Sappho was prouder of that stove than a daughter of Fortune would have been of the most expensive silver chafing-dish. It was very near lunch time, so the top was turned back, and the little copper teakettle was beginning to sing its welcome song. Dora had placed a small, round table between the couch and the rocker. A service for two was set out in dainty china dishes, cream and sugar looking doubly tempting as it gleamed and glistened in the delicate ware. One plate was piled with thinly cut slices of bread and butter, another held slices of pink ham.

Sappho lay back among her cushions, lazily stretching her little slippered feet toward the warm stove, where the fire burned so cheerily and glowed so invitingly as it shone through the isinglass door. She folded her arms above her head and turned an admiring gaze on the brown face of her friend, who swayed gently back and forth in her rocking-chair, her feet on a hassock, and a scarlet afghan wrapped about her knees. Dora was telling Sappho all about her engagement to John Langley and their plans for the future.

"I think you will be happy, Dora, if you love him. All things are possible if love is the foundation stone," said Sappho, after a slight pause, as she nestled among her pillows. Dora was sitting bolt upright with the usual business-like look upon her face.

"I like him well enough to marry him, but I don't believe there's enough sentiment in me to make love a great passion, such as we read of in books. Do you believe marriage is the beautiful state it is painted by writers?"

"Why, yes," laughed Sappho; "I wouldn't believe anything else for your sake, my little brownie."

"No joking, Sappho; this is dead earnest. Don't you ever expect to marry, and don't you speculate about the pros and cons and the maybes and perhapses of the situation?" asked Dora, as she filled the cups with steaming cocoa and passed one to her friend.

"Dora, you little gourmand, what have you got in the refrigerator?" A box ingeniously nailed to the window seat outside, and filled with shelves, and having a substantial door, was the ice-box, or refrigerator, where Sappho kept materials handy for a quick lunch. Dora closed the window and returned quickly to her seat, placing a glass dish on the table as she did so.

"It's only part of a cream pie that ma had left last night. I thought it would help out nicely with our lunch."

"What, again!" said Sappho significantly. "That's the fourth time this week, and here it is but Friday. You'll be as fat as a seal, and then John P. won't want you at any price. Take warning, and depart from the error of your ways before it is too late."

Dora laughed guiltily and said, as she drew a box from her

apron pocket: "Well, here are John's chocolate bonbons that he brought last night. I suppose you won't want me to touch *them*, for fear of getting fat."

Sappho shook her head in mock despair. "And your teeth, your beautiful white teeth, where will they be shortly if you persist in eating a pound of bonbons every day? Think of your fate, Dora, and pause in your reckless career—forty inches about the waist and only scraggy snags to show me when you grin!"

"Thank heaven I'll never come to that while there's a dentist in the city of Boston! I'll eat all the bonbons I want in spite of you, Sappho, and if you don't hurry I'll eat your slice of cream pie, too." At this dire threat there ensued a scramble for the pie, mingled with peals of merry laughter, until all rosy and sparkling, Sappho emerged from the fray with the dish containing her share of the dainty held high in the air.

Presently lunch was over, and they resumed their old positions, prepared to "take comfort."

"You haven't answered my question yet, Sappho."

"To tell you the truth, I had forgotten your remark, Dora; what was it?"

"I suspect that is a bit of a fib to keep me from teasing you about getting married. What I want to know is: Do you ever mean to marry, or are you going to pine in single blessedness on my hands and be a bachelor-maid to the end?"

"Well," replied Sappho, with a comical twist to her face, "in the words of Unc' Gulliver, 'I mote, an' then agin I moten't.' "

"What troubles me is having a man bothering around. Now I tell John P. that I'm busy, or something like that, and I'm rid of him; but after you marry a man, he's on your hands for good and all. I'm wondering if my love could stand the test."

"That's queer talk for an engaged girl, with a fine, handsome fellow to court her. Why, Dora, 'I'm s'prised at yer!' " laughed Sappho gaily.

"I'm not ashamed of John P.'s appearance in company; he

looks all right; but when one is terribly in love one is supposed to want the dear object always near; but matches,—
love matches,—my child, turn out so badly that a girl hesi-
tates to 'git jined to eny man fer betterer or worserer,' as Dr.
Peters says. Then I get tired of a man so soon! (This with a
doleful sigh.) I dread to think of being tied to John for good
and all; I know I'll be sick of him inside of a week. I do
despair of ever being like other girls."

Sappho laughed outright at the woe-begone countenance
before her.

"It is generally the other way: the men get tired of us first.
A woman loves one man, and is true to him through all
eternity."

"That's just what makes me feel so *unsexed,* so to speak; I
like John's looks. He's the style among all the girls in our set.
I like to know that I can claim him before them all. It's fun to
see 'em fluttering around him, kindly trying to put my nose
out of joint. I must say that I feel real *comfortable* to spoil
sport by walking off with him just when they think they've
got things running as they wish. Yes, it's real *comfortable* to
know that they're all as jealous as can be. But for all that, I
know I'll get tired of him."

"Let us hope not, if you have really made up your mind to
marry him. Dora, sometimes I am afraid that you mean what
you say. I notice that you call him 'John P.' What's the P
for?"

"Pollock—John Pollock Langley. His grandfather was his
father's master, and Pollock was his name," sang Dora, as
she rocked gently to and fro. "Now, there's Arthur Lewis,"
she continued; "he's jolly fun. He isn't a fascinator, or anything of that sort; he's just good."

"Who is he?" asked Sappho, with languid interest.

"Properly speaking, he's Dr. Arthur Lewis. We were children together, although he is five years older than I. He's a
fine scholar and a great business man. He has a large industrial school in Louisiana. He's gone up in the world, I tell
you, since we made mud pies on the back doorsteps; but I

never think of him except as old Arthur, who used to drag me to school on his sled."

There was a gleam of fun in Sappho's eyes, as she said demurely: "You seem to know all about him. Was he ever a lover of yours?"

"Lover! no, indeed!" Dora flushed vividly under her brown skin. "The idea of Arthur as my lover is too absurd."

"Excuse me, dear, for my mistake," said Sappho mischievously. "I didn't know but that he might be the mysterious link which would join love, marriage and the necessary man in a harmonious whole."

"Well," said Dora, after a slight pause, blushing furiously, "I don't say he wouldn't like the rôle. You'll see him soon; he's coming to Boston on business in a few weeks. Oh, we've had rare times together." She sighed and smiled, lost for the moment in pleasant memories. Sappho smiled, too, in sympathy with her mood.

"Ah, yes; I think I understand. Poor John!"

"John's all right. Don't shed any tears over him," said Dora testily. They sat awhile in silence, listening to the sound of the whirling frozen flakes wind-driven against the window panes. It was scarce three o'clock, but darkness was beginning to envelop the city, and it was already a pleasant twilight in the room.

"Tell me about Dr. Lewis and his work, Dora," said Sappho presently. "Do you know, he interests me exceedingly."

"I don't really understand Arthur's hobbies, but I believe that he is supposed to be doing a great work in the Black Belt. His argument is, as I understand it, that industrial education and the exclusion of politics will cure all our race troubles."

"I doubt it," returned Sappho quickly, with an impatient toss of the head. "That reasoning might be practically illustrated with benefit to us for a few years in the South, but to my mind would not effect a permanent cure for race troubles if we are willing to admit that human nature is the same in us as in others. The time will come when our men will grow away from the trammels of narrow prejudice, and desire the same treatment that is accorded to other men. Why, one can but see that any degree of education and development will not fail of such a result."

"I am willing to confess that the subject is a little deep for me," replied Dora. "I'm not the least bit of a politician, and I generally accept whatever the men tell me as right; but I know that there is something very wrong in our lives, and nothing seems to remedy the evils under which the colored man labors."

"But you can see, can't you, that if our men are deprived of the franchise, we become aliens in the very land of our birth?"

"Arthur says that would be better for us; the great loss of life would cease, and we should be at peace with the whites."

"Ah, how can he argue so falsely! I have lived beneath the system of oppression in the South. If we lose the franchise, at the same time we shall lose the respect of all other citizens. Temporizing will not benefit us; rather, it will leave us branded as cowards, not worthy a freeman's respect—an alien people, without a country and without a home."

Dora gazed at her friend with admiration, and wished that she had a kodak, so that she might catch just the expression that lighted her eyes and glowed in a bright color upon her cheeks.

"I predict some fun when you and Arthur meet. I'll just start you both out some night, and you'll be spitting at each other like two cats inside of five minutes. Arthur thinks that women should be seen and not heard, where politics is under discussion."

"Insufferable prig!" exclaimed Sappho, with snapping eyes.

"Oh, no, he isn't; Arthur's all right. But you see he is living South; his work is there, and he must keep in with the whites of the section where his work lies, or all he has accomplished will go for naught, and perhaps his life might be forfeited, too."

"I see. The mess of pottage and the birthright."

"Bless you! not so bad as that; but money makes the mare go," returned Dora, with a wink at her friend, and a shrewd business look on her bright little Yankee face. "I say to you, as Arthur says to me when I tell him what I think of his system: 'If you want honey, you must have money.' I don't know anything about politics, as I said before, but my opinion won't cost you anything: when we can say that lots of our men are as rich as Jews, there'll be no question about the franchise, and my idea is that Arthur'll be one of the Jews."

"Oh!" exclaimed Sappho disgustedly, as she resumed her lounging position.

"Sappho, how did you come to take up stenography? I should have thought you would have preferred teaching."

"I had to live, my dear; I could not teach school, because my education does not include a college course. I could not do housework, because my constitution is naturally weak."

It was noticeable in these confidential chats that Sappho never spoke of her early life. Dora had confided to her friend every event of importance that had occurred in her young life; and, in harmless gossip, had related the history of all the friends who visited the house intimately; but all this had begot no like unburdening to eager ears of the early history of her friend. Wonderful to relate, however, Dora did not resent this reserve, which she could see was studied. It spoke well for the sincerity of the love that had taken root in her heart for Sappho, that it subdued her inquisitiveness, and she gladly accepted her friendship without asking troublesome questions.

"How did you finally succeed in getting work? I have always heard that it was very difficult for colored girls to find employment in offices where your class of work is required."

"And so it is, my dear. I sometimes think that if I lose the work I am on, I shall not try for another position. I shall never forget the day I started out to find work: the first place that I visited was all right until the man found I was colored; then he said that his wife wanted a nurse girl, and he had no doubt she would be glad to hire me, for I looked good-tempered. At the second place where I ventured to intrude the proprietor said: 'Yes; we want a stenographer, but we've no work for your kind.' However, that was preferable to the insulting familiarity which some men assumed. It was dreadful! I don't like to think about it. Father Andrew induced the man for whom I am working to employ me. I do not interfere with the other help, because I take my work home; many of the other clerks have never seen me, and so the proprietor runs no risk of being bothered with complaints from them. He treats me very well, too."

"I have heard many girls tell much the same tale about other lines of business," said Dora. "It makes me content to do the work of this house, and not complain."

"You ought to thank God every day for such a refuge as you have in your home."

"I cannot understand people. Here in the North we are allowed every privilege. There seems to be no prejudice until we seek employment; then every door is closed against us. Can you explain this?"

"No, I cannot; to my way of thinking the whole thing is a Chinese puzzle."

"Bless my soul! Just look at that clock!" exclaimed Dora, as she scrambled to her feet and began gathering up her scattered property. "Five o'clock, and tea to get. Sappho, you've been lazy enough for one day. Come downstairs and help me get tea. The boys will be here in no time, as hungry as bears."

Piloted by Dora, Sappho became well acquainted with ancient landmarks of peculiar interest to the colored people. They visited the home for aged women on M—— Street, and read and sang to the occupants. They visited St. Monica's Hospital, and carried clothes, flowers, and a little money saved from the cost of contemplated Easter finery. They scattered brightness along with charitable acts wherever a case of want was brought to their attention.

THE SEWING-CIRCLE

Where village statesmen talked with looks profound,
Imagination fondly stoops to trace
The parlor splendors of that festive place.

Yes! let the rich deride, the proud disdain,
These simple blessings of the lowly train;
To me more dear,
One native charm than all the gloss of art.

—GOLDSMITH

Ma Smith was a member of the church referred to in the last
chapter, the most prominent one of color in New England. It
was situated in the heart of the West End, and was a very
valuable piece of property. Every winter this church gave
many entertainments to aid in paying off the mortgage,
which at this time amounted to about eight thousand dollars. Mrs. Smith, as the chairman of the board of steward-
esses, was inaugurating a fair—one that should eclipse anything of a similar nature ever attempted by the colored
people, and numerous sewing-circles were being held
among the members all over the city. Parlor entertainments
where an admission fee of ten cents was collected from every
patron, were also greatly in vogue, and the money thus
obtained was put into a fund to defray the expense of pur-
chasing eatables and decorations, and paying for the printing of tickets, circulars, etc., for the fair. The strongest forces
of the colored people in the vicinity were to combine and
lend their aid in making a supreme effort to clear this magnificent property.

Boston contains a number of well-to-do families of color
whose tax-bills show a most comfortable return each year to
the city treasury. Strange as it may seem, these well-to-do
people, in goodly numbers, distribute themselves and their
children among the various Episcopal churches with which
the city abounds, the government of which holds out the

welcome hand to the brother in black, who is drawn to unite his fortunes with the members of this particular denomination. It may be true that the beautiful ritual of the church is responsible in some measure for this. Colored people are nothing if not beauty-lovers, and for such a people the grandeur of the service has great attractions. But in justice to this church one must acknowledge that it has been instrumental in doing much toward helping this race to help itself, along the lines of brotherly interest.

These people were well represented within the precincts of Mrs. Smith's pretty parlor one afternoon, all desirous of lending their aid to help along the great project.

As we have said, Mrs. Smith occupied the back parlor of the house as her chamber, and within this room the matrons had assembled to take charge of the cutting out of different garments; and here, too, the sewing machine was placed ready for use. In the parlor proper all the young ladies were seated ready to perform any service which might be required of them in the way of putting garments together.

By two o'clock all the members of the sewing-circle were in their places. The parlor was crowded. Mrs. Willis, the brilliant widow of a bright Negro politician, had charge of the girls, and after the sewing had been given out the first business of the meeting was to go over events of interest to the Negro race which had transpired during the week throughout the country. These facts had been previously tabulated upon a blackboard which was placed upon an easel, and occupied a conspicuous position in the room. Each one was supposed to contribute anything of interest that she had read or heard in that time for the benefit of all. After these points had been gone over, Mrs. Willis gave a talk upon some topic of interest. At six o'clock tea was to be served in the kitchen, the company taking refreshment in squads of five. At eight o'clock all unfinished work would be folded and packed away in the convenient little Boston bag to be finished at home, and the male friends of the various ladies were expected to put in an appearance. Music and recitations were to be enjoyed for two hours, ice cream and cake being sold for the benefit of the cause.

Mrs. Willis was a good example of a class of women of color that came into existence at the close of the Civil War. She was not a *rara avis,* but one of many possibilities which the future will develop from among the colored women of New England. Every city or town from Maine to New York has its Mrs. Willis. Keen in her analysis of human nature, most people realized, after a short acquaintance, in which they ran the gamut of emotions from strong attraction to repulsion, that she had sifted them thoroughly, while they had gained nothing in return. Shrewd in business matters, many a subtle business man had been worsted by her apparent womanly weakness and charming simplicity. With little money, she yet contrived to live in quiet elegance, even including the little journeys from place to place, so adroitly managed as to increase her influence at home and her fame abroad. Well-read and thoroughly conversant with all current topics, she impressed one as having been liberally educated and polished by travel, whereas a high-school course more than covered all her opportunities.

Even today it is erroneously believed that all racial development among colored people has taken place since emancipation. It is impossible of belief for some, that little circles of educated men and women of color have existed since the Revolutionary War. Some of these people were born free, some have lost the memory of servitude in the dim past; a greater number by far were recruited from the energetic slaves of the South, who toiled when they should have slept, for the money that purchased their freedom, or else they boldly took the rights which man denied. Mrs. Willis was one from among these classes. The history of her descent could not be traced, but somewhere, somehow, a strain of white blood had filtered through the African stream. At sixty odd she was vigorous, well-preserved, broad and comfortable in appearance, with an aureole of white hair crowning a pleasant face.

She had loved her husband with a love ambitious for his advancement. His foot on the stairs mounting to the two-room tenement which constituted their home in the early years of married life, had sent a thrill to her very heart as she sat sewing baby clothes for the always expected addition to the family. But twenty years make a difference in all our lives. It brought many changes to the colored people of New England—social and business changes. Politics had become the open sesame for the ambitious Negro. A seat in the Legislature then was not a dream to this man, urged by the loving woman behind him. Other offices of trust were quickly offered him when his worth became known. He grasped his opportunity; grew richer, more polished, less social, and the family broadened out and overflowed from old familiar "West End" environments across the River Charles into the aristocratic suburbs of Cambridge. Death comes to us all.

Money, the sinews of living and social standing, she did not possess upon her husband's death. Therefore she was forced to begin a weary pilgrimage—a hunt for the means to help her breast the social tide. The best opening, she decided after looking carefully about her, was in the great cause of the evolution of true womanhood in the work of the "Woman Question" as embodied in marriage and suffrage. She could talk dashingly on many themes, for which she had received much applause in by-gone days, when in private life she had held forth in the drawing-room of some Back Bay philanthropist who sought to use her talents as an attraction for a worthy charitable object, the discovery of a rare species of versatility in the Negro character being a sure drawing-card. It was her boast that she had made the fortunes of her family and settled her children well in life. The advancement of the colored woman should be the new problem in the woman question that should float her upon its tide into the prosperity she desired. And she succeeded well in her plans: conceived in selfishness, they yet bore glorious fruit in the formation of clubs of colored women banded together for

charity, for study, for every reason under God's glorious
heavens that can better the condition of mankind.

Trivialities are not to be despised. Inborn love implanted
in a woman's heart for a luxurious, esthetic home life, running on well-oiled wheels amid flowers, sunshine, books and
priceless pamphlets, easy chairs and French gowns, may be
the means of developing a Paderewski or freeing a race from
servitude. It was amusing to watch the way in which she
governed societies and held her position. In her hands com-
mittees were as wax, and loud murmurings against the tyranny of her rule died down to judicious whispers. If a vote
went contrary to her desires, it was in her absence. Thus she
became the pivot about which all the social and intellectual
life of the colored people of her section revolved. No one
had yet been found with the temerity to contest her position,
which, like a title of nobility, bade fair to descend to her
children. It was thought that she might be eclipsed by the
younger and more brilliant women students on the strength
of their alma mater, but she still held her own by sheer force
of will-power and indomitable pluck.

The subject of the talk at this meeting was: "The place
which the virtuous woman occupies in upbuilding a race."
After a few explanatory remarks, Mrs. Willis said:

"I am particularly anxious that you should think upon this
matter seriously, because of its intrinsic value to all of us as
race women. I am not less anxious because you represent
the coming factors of our race. Shortly, you must fill the
positions now occupied by your mothers, and it will rest with
you and your children to refute the charges brought against
us as to our moral irresponsibility, and the low moral standard maintained by us in comparison with other races."

"Did I understand you to say that the Negro woman in her
native state is truly a virtuous woman?" asked Sappho, who
had been very silent during the bustle attending the opening
of the meeting.

"Travelers tell us that the native African woman is impreg-
nable in her virtue," replied Mrs. Willis.

"So we have sacrificed that attribute in order to acquire civilization," chimed in Dora.

"No, not 'sacrificed,' but pushed one side by the force of circumstances. Let us thank God that it *is* an essential attribute peculiar to us—a racial characteristic which is slumbering but not lost," replied Mrs. Willis. "But let us not forget the definition of virtue—'Strength to do the right thing under all temptations.' Our ideas of virtue are too narrow. We confine them to that conduct which is ruled by our animal passions alone. It goes deeper than that—general excellence in every duty of life is what we may call virtue."

"Do you think, then, that Negro women will be held responsible for all the lack of virtue that is being laid to their charge today? I mean, do you think that God will hold us responsible for the *illegitimacy* with which our race has been obliged, as it were, to flood the world?" asked Sappho.

"I believe that we shall not be held responsible for wrongs which we have *unconsciously* committed, or which we have committed under *compulsion.* We are virtuous or non-virtuous only when we have a *choice* under temptation. We cannot by any means apply the word to a little child who has never been exposed to temptation, nor to the Supreme Being 'who cannot be tempted with evil.' So with the African brought to these shores against his will—the state of morality which implies willpower on his part does not exist, therefore he is not a responsible being. The sin and its punishment lies with the person *consciously* false to his *knowledge* of right. From this we deduce the truism that 'the civility of no race is perfect whilst another race is degraded.' "

"I shall never forget my feelings," chimed in Anna Stevens, a school teacher of a very studious temperament, "at certain remarks made by the Rev. John Thomas at one of his noonday lectures in the Temple. He was speaking on 'Different Races,' and had in his vigorous style been sweeping his audience with him at a high elevation of thought which was dazzling to the faculties, and almost impossible to follow in some points. Suddenly he touched upon the Negro, and with impressive gesture and lowered voice thanked God that the mulatto race was dying out, because it was a mongrel mixture which combined the worst elements of two races. Lo, the poor mulatto! despised by the blacks of his own race, scorned by the whites! Let him go out and hang himself!" In her indignation Anna forgot the scissors, and bit her thread off viciously with her little white teeth.

Mrs. Willis smiled as she said calmly: "My dear Anna, I would not worry about the fate of the mulatto, for the fate of the mulatto will be the fate of the entire race. Did you never think that today the black race on this continent has developed into a race of mulattoes?"

"Why, Mrs. Willis!" came in a chorus of voices.

"Yes," continued Mrs. Willis, still smiling. "It is an incontrovertible truth that there is no such thing as an unmixed black on the American continent. Just bear in mind that we cannot tell by a person's complexion whether he be dark or light in blood, for by the working of the natural laws the white father and black mother produce the mulatto offspring; the black father and white mother the mulatto offspring also, while the *black father* and *quadroon* mother produce the black child, which to the eye alone is a child of unmixed black blood. I will venture to say that out of a hundred apparently pure black men not one will be able to trace an unmixed flow of African blood since landing upon these shores! What an unhappy example of the frailty of all human intellects, when such a man and scholar as Doctor Thomas could so far allow his prejudices to dominate his better judgment as to add one straw to the burden which is popularly supposed to rest upon the unhappy mulattoes of a despised race," finished the lady, with a dangerous flash of her large dark eyes.

"Mrs. Willis," said Dora, with a scornful little laugh, "I am not unhappy, and I am a mulatto. I just enjoy my life, and I don't want to die before my time comes, either. There are lots of good things left on earth to be enjoyed even by mulattoes, and I want my share."

"Yes, my dear; and I hope you may all live and take comfort in the proper joys of your lives. While we are all content to accept life, and enjoy it along the lines which God has laid down for us as individuals as well as a race, we shall be happy and get the best out of life. Now, let me close this talk by asking you to remember one maxim written of your race by a good man: 'Happiness and social position are not to be gained by pushing.' Let the world, by its need of us along certain lines, and our intrinsic fitness for these lines, push us into the niche which God has prepared for us. So shall our lives be beautified and our race raised in the civilization of the future as we grow away from all these prejudices which have been the instruments of our advancement according to the intention of an All-seeing Omnipotence, from the beginning. Never mind our poverty, ignorance, and the slights and injuries which we bear at the hands of a higher race. With the thought ever before us of what the Master suffered to raise all humanity to its present degree of prosperity and intelligence, let us cultivate, while we go about our daily tasks, no matter how inferior they may seem to us, beauty of the soul and mind, which being transmitted to our children by the law of heredity, shall improve the race by eliminating *immorality* from our midst and raising *morality* and virtue to their true place. Thirty-five years of liberty have made us a new people. The marks of servitude and oppression are dropping slowly from us; let us hasten the transformation of the body by the nobility of the soul."

> For of the soul the body form doth take,
> For soul is form and doth the body make,

quoted Dora.

"Yes," said Mrs. Willis with a smile, "that is the idea exactly, and well expressed. Now I hope that through the coming week you will think of what we have talked about this afternoon, for it is of the very first importance to all people, but particularly so to young folks."

Sappho, who had been thoughtfully embroidering pansies

on white linen, now leaned back in her chair for a moment and said: "Mrs. Willis, here *[sic]* is one thing which puzzles me—how are we to overcome the nature which is given us? I mean how can we eliminate passion from our lives, and emerge into the purity which marked the life of Christ? So many of us desire purity and think to have found it, but in a moment of passion, or under the pressure of circumstances which we cannot control, we commit some horrid sin, and the taint of it sticks and will not leave us, and we grow to loathe ourselves."

"Passion, my dear Miss Clark, is a state in which the will lies dormant, and all other desires become subservient to one. Enthusiasm for any one object or duty may become a passion. I believe that in some degree passion may be beneficial, but we must guard ourselves against a sinful growth of any appetite. All work of whatever character, as I look at it, needs a certain amount of absorbing interest to become successful, and it is here that the Christian life gains its greatest glory in teaching us how to keep ourselves from abusing any of our human attributes. We are not held responsible for compulsory sin, only for the sin that is pleasant to our thoughts and palatable to our appetites. All desires and hopes with which we are endowed are good in the sight of God, only it is left for us to discover their right uses. Do I cover your ground?"

"Yes and no," replied Sappho; "but perhaps at some future time you will be good enough to talk with me personally upon this subject."

"Dear child, sit here by me. It is a blessing to look at you. Beauty like yours is inspiring. You seem to be troubled; what is it? If I can comfort or strengthen, it is all I ask." She pressed the girl's hand in hers and drew her into a secluded corner. For a moment the flood-gates of suppressed feeling flew open in the girl's heart, and she longed to lean her head on that motherly breast and unburden her sorrows there.

"Mrs. Willis, I am troubled greatly," she said at length.

"I am *so* sorry; tell me, my love, what it is all about."

Just as the barriers of Sappho's reserve seemed about to be swept away, there followed, almost instantly, a wave of repulsion toward this woman and her effusiveness, so forced and insincere. Sappho was very impressionable, and yielded readily to the influence which fell like a cold shadow between them. She drew back as from an abyss suddenly beheld stretching before her.

"On second thoughts, I think I ought to correct my remarks. It is not really *trouble*, but more a desire to confirm me in my own ideas."

"Well, if you feel you are right, dear girl, stand for the uplifting of the race and womanhood. Do not shrink from duty."

"It was simply a thought raised by your remarks on morality. I once knew a woman who had sinned. No one in the community in which she lived knew it but herself. She married a man who would have despised her had he known her story; but as it is, she is looked upon as a pattern of virtue for all women."

"And then what?" asked Mrs. Willis, with a searching glance at the fair face beside her.

"Ought she not to have told her husband before marriage? Was it not her duty to have thrown herself upon his clemency?"

"I think not," replied Mrs. Willis dryly. "See here, my dear, I am a practical woman of the world, and I think your young woman builded wiser than she knew. I am of the opinion that most men are like the lower animals in many things—they don't always know what is for their best good. If the husband had been left to himself, he probably would not have married the one woman in the world best fitted to be his wife. I think in her case she did her duty."

"Ah, that word 'duty.' What is our duty?" queried the girl, with a sad droop to the sensitive mouth. "It is so hard to know our duty. We are told that all hidden things shall be revealed. Must repented and atoned-for sin rise at last to be our curse?"

"Here is a point, dear girl. God does not look upon the constitution of sin as we do. His judgment is not ours; ours is finite, his infinite. *Your* duty is not to be morbid, thinking these thoughts that have puzzled older heads than yours. *Your* duty is, also, to be happy and bright for the good of those about you. Just blossom like the flowers, have faith and *trust.*" At this point the entrance of the men made an interruption, and Mrs. Willis disappeared in a crowd of other matrons. Sappho was impressed in spite of herself, by the woman's words. She sat buried in deep thought.

There was evidently more in this woman than appeared upon the surface. With all the centuries of civilization and culture that have come to this grand old world, no man has yet been found able to trace the windings of God's inscrutable ways. There are men and women whose seeming uselessness fit perfectly into the warp and woof of Destiny's web. All things work together for good.

PAULINE E. HOPKINS

Bro'r Abr'm Jimson's Wedding
A Christmas Story

It was a Sunday in early spring the first time that Caramel Johnson dawned on the congregation of ——— Church in a populous New England City.

The Afro-Americans of that city are well-to-do, being of a frugal nature, and considering it a lasting disgrace for any man among them, desirous of social standing in the community, not to make himself comfortable in this world's goods against the coming time, when old age creeps on apace and renders him unfit for active business.

Therefore the members of the said church had not waited to be exhorted by reformers to own their unpretentious homes and small farms outside the city limits, but they vied with each other in efforts to accumulate a small competency urged thereto by a realization of what pressing needs the future might bring, or that might have been because of the constant example of white neighbors, and a due respect for the dignity which *their* foresight had brought to the superior race.

Of course, these small Vanderbilts and Astors of a darker hue must have a place of worship in accord with their worldly prosperity, and so it fell out that ——— church was the richest plum in the ecclesiastical pudding, and greatly sought by scholarly divines as a resting place for four years, —the extent of the time-limit allowed by conference to the men who must be provided with suitable charges according to the demands of their energy and scholarship.

"Bro'r Abr'm Jimson's Wedding: A Christmas Story" (1901)

The attendance was unusually large for morning service, and a restless movement was noticeable all through the sermon. How strange a thing is nature; the change of the seasons announces itself in all humanity as well as in the trees and flowers, the grass, and in the atmosphere. Something within us responds instantly to the touch of kinship that dwells in all life.

The air, soft and balmy, laden with rich promise for the future, came through the massive, half-open windows, stealing in refreshing waves upon the congregation. The sunlight fell through the colored glass of the windows in prismatic hues, and dancing all over the lofty star-gemmed ceiling, painted the hue of the broad vault of heaven, creeping down in crinkling shadows to touch the deep garnet cushions of the sacred desk, and the rich wood of the altar with a hint of gold.

The offertory was ended. The silvery cadences of a rich soprano voice still lingered on the air, "O, Worship the Lord in the beauty of holiness." There was a suppressed feeling of expectation, but not the faintest rustle as the minister rose in the pulpit, and after a solemn pause, gave the usual invitation:

"If there is anyone in this congregation desiring to unite with this church, either by letter or on probation, please come forward to the altar."

The words had not died upon his lips when a woman started from her seat near the door and passed up the main aisle. There was a sudden commotion on all sides. Many heads were turned—it takes so little to interest a church audience. The girls in the choir-box leaned over the rail, nudged each other and giggled, while the men said to one another, "She's a stunner, and no mistake."

The candidate for membership, meanwhile, had reached the altar railing and stood before the man of God, to whom she had handed her letter from a former Sabbath home, with head decorously bowed as became the time and the holy place. There was no denying the fact that she was a pretty girl; brown of skin, small of feature, with an ever-lurking gleam of laughter in eyes coal black. Her figure was slender and beautifully moulded, with a seductive grace in the undulating walk and erect carriage. But the chief charm of the sparkling dark face lay in its intelligence, and the responsive play of facial expression which was enhanced by two mischievous dimples pressed into the rounded cheeks by the caressing fingers of the god of Love.

The minister whispered to the candidate, coughed, blew his nose on his snowy clerical handkerchief, and, finally turned to the expectant congregation:

"Sister Chocolate Caramel Johnson—"

He was interrupted by a snicker and a suppressed laugh again from the choir-box, and an audible whisper which sounded distinctly throughout the quiet church,—

"I'd get the Legislature to change that if it was mine, 'deed I would!" then silence profound caused by the reverend's stern glance of reproval bent on the offenders in the choir box.

"Such levity will not be allowed among the members of the choir. If it occurs again, I shall ask the choir master for the names of the offenders and have their places taken by those more worthy to be gospel singers."

Thereupon Mrs. Tilly Anderson whispered to Mrs. Nancy Tobias that, "them choir gals is the mos' deceivines' hussies in the church, an' for my part, I'm glad the pastor called 'em down. That sister's too good lookin' for 'em, an' they'll be after her like er pack o' houn's, min' me, Sis' Tobias."

Sister Tobias ducked her head in her lap and shook her fat sides in laughing appreciation of the sister's foresight.

Order being restored the minister proceeded:

"Sister Chocolate Caramel Johnson brings a letter to us from our sister church in Nashville, Tennessee. She has been a member in good standing for ten years, having been received into fellowship at ten years of age. She leaves them now, much to her regret, to pursue the study of music at one of the large conservatories in this city, and they recommend

er to our love and care. You know the contents of the letter.
.ll in favor of giving Sister Johnson the right hand of fellow-
hip, please manifest the same by a rising vote." The whole
ongregation rose.

"Contrary minded? None. The ayes have it. Be seated,
riends. Sister Johnson, it gives me great pleasure to receive
ou into this church. I welcome you to its joys and sorrows.
May God bless you, Brother Jimson?" (Brother Jimson
tepped from his seat to the pastor's side.) "I assign this
ister to your class. Sister Johnson, this is Brother Jimson,
our future spiritual teacher."

Brother Jimson shook the hand of his new member,
armly, and she returned to her seat. The minister pro-
ounced the benediction over the waiting congregation; the
rgan burst into richest melody. Slowly the crowd of wor-
hippers dispersed.

Abraham Jimson had made his money as a janitor for the
vealthy people of the city. He was a bachelor, and when
eproved by some good Christian brother for still dwelling
n single blessedness always offered as an excuse that he had
een too busy to think of a wife, but that now he was "well
xed," pecuniarily, he would begin to "look over" his lady
riends for a suitable companion.

He owned a house in the suburbs and a fine brick dwell-
ng-house in the city proper. He was a trustee of prominence
n the church, in fact, its "solid man," and his opinion was
ought and his advice acted upon by his associates on the
Board. It was felt that any lady in the congregation would be
roud to know herself his choice.

When Caramel Johnson received the right hand of fellow-
hip, her aunt, the widow Maria Nash, was ahead in the race
or the wealthy class-leader. It had been neck-and-neck for a
vhile between her and Sister Viney Peters, but, finally it had
ettled down to Sister Maria with a hundred to one, among
he sporting members of the Board, that she carried off the
rize, for Sister Maria owned a house adjoining Brother
imson's in the suburbs, and property counts these days.

Sister Nash had "no idea" when she sent for her niece to come to B. that the latter would prove a rival; her son Andy was as good as engaged to Caramel. But it is always the unexpected that happens. Caramel came, and Brother Jimson had no eyes for the charms of other women after he had gazed into her coal black orbs, and watched her dimples come and go.

Caramel decided to accept a position as housemaid in order to help defray the expenses of her tuition at the conservatory, and Brother Jimson interested himself so warmly in her behalf that she soon had a situation in the home of his richest patron where it was handy for him to chat with her about the business of the church, and the welfare of her soul in general. Things progressed very smoothly until the fall when one day Sister Maria had occasion to call, unexpectedly, on her niece and found Brother Jimson basking in her smiles while he enjoyed a sumptuous dinner of roast chicken and fixings.

To say that Sister Maria was "set way back" would not accurately describe her feelings; but from that time Abraham Jimson knew that he had a secret foe in the Widow Nash.

Before many weeks had passed it was publicly known that Brother Jimson would lead Caramel Johnson to the altar "come Christmas." There was much sly speculation as to the "widder's gittin' left," and how she took it from those who had cast hopeless glances toward the chief man of the church. Great preparations were set on foot for the wedding festivities. The bride's trousseau was a present from the groom and included a white satin wedding gown and a costly gold watch. The town house was refurnished and a trip to New York was in contemplation.

"Hump!" grunted Sister Nash when told the rumors, "there's no fool like an ol' fool. Car'mel's a han'ful he'll fin' ef he gits her."

"I reckon he'll git her all right, Sis' Nash," laughed the neighbor, who had run in to talk over the news.

"I've said my word an' I ain't goin' change it, Sis'r. Min' me, I says, *ef he gits her*, an, I mean it."

Andy Nash was also a member of Brother Jimson's class; he possessed, too, a strong sweet baritone voice which made him a great value to the choir. He was an immense success in the social life of the city, and had created sad havoc with the hearts of the colored girls; he could have his pick of the best of them because of his graceful figure and fine easy manners. Until Caramel had been dazzled by the wealth of her elderly lover, she had considered herself fortunate as the lady of his choice.

It was Sunday, three weeks before the wedding that Andy resolved to have it out with Caramel.

"She's been hot an' she's been col', an' now she's luke warm, an' today ends it before this gent-man sleeps," he told himself as he stood before the glass and tied his pale blue silk tie in a stunning knot, and settled his glossy tile at a becoming angle.

Brother Jimson's class was a popular one and had a large membership; the hour spent there was much enjoyed, even by visitors. Andy went into the vestry early resolved to meet Caramel if possible. She was there, at the back of the room sitting alone on a settee. Andy immediately seated himself in the vacant place by her side. There were whispers and much head-shaking among the few early worshippers, all of whom knew the story of the young fellow's romance and his disappointment.

As he dropped into the seat beside her, Caramel turned her large eyes on him intently, speculatively, with a doubtful sort of curiosity suggested in her expression, as to how he took her flagrant desertion.

"Howdy, Car'mel?" was his greeting without a shade of resentment.

"I'm well; no need to ask how you are," was the quick response. There was a mixture of cordiality and coquetry in her manner. Her eyes narrowed and glittered under lowered lids, as she gave him a long side-glance. How could she help showing her admiration for the supple young giant beside her? "Surely," she told herself, "I'll have long time enough to git sick of old rheumatics," her pet name for her elderly lover.

"I ain't sick much," was Andy surly reply.

He leaned his elbow on the back of the settee and gave his recreant sweetheart a flaming glance of mingled love and hate, oblivious to the presence of the assembled class-members.

"You ain't over friendly these days, Car'mel, but I gits news of your capers 'roun' 'bout some of the members."

"My—Yes?" she answered as she flashed her great eyes at him in pretended surprise. He laughed a laugh not good to hear.

"Yes," he drawled. Then he added with sudden energy, "Are you goin' to tie up to old Rheumatism sure 'nuff, come Chris'mas?"

"Come Chris'mas, Andy, I be. I hate to tell you but I have to do it."

He recoiled as from a blow. As for the girl, she found a keen relish in the situation: it flattered her vanity.

"How comes it you've changed your mind, Car'mel, 'bout you an' me? You've tol' me often that I was your first choice."

"We—ll," she drawled, glancing uneasily about her and avoiding her aunt's gaze, which she knew was bent upon her every movement, "I did reckon once I would. But a man with money suits me best, an' you ain't got a cent."

"No more have you. You ain't no better than other women to work an' help a man along, is you?"

The color flamed an instant in her face turning the dusky skin to a deep, dull red.

"Andy Nash, you always was a fool, an' as ignerunt as a wil' Injun. I mean to have a sure nuff brick house an' plenty of money. That makes people respec' you. Why don' you quit bein' so shifless and save your money. You ain't worth your salt."

"Your head's turned with pianorer-playin' an' livin' up North. Ef you'll turn *him* off an' come back home, I'll turn over a new leaf. Car'mel," his voice was soft and persuasive enough now.

She had risen to her feet; her eyes flashed, her face was full of pride.

"I won't. I've quit likin' you, Andy Nash."

"Are you in earnest?" he asked, also rising from his seat.

"Dead earnes'."

"Then there's no more to be said."

He spoke calmly, not raising his voice above a whisper. She stared at him in surprise. Then he added as he swung on his heel preparatory to leaving her:

"You ain't got him yet, my gal. But remember, I'm waitin' for you when you need me."

While this whispered conference was taking place in the back of the vestry, Brother Jimson had entered, and many an anxious glance he cast in the direction of the couple. Andy made his way slowly to his mother's side as Brother Jimson rose in his place to open the meeting. There was a commotion on all sides as the members rustled down on their knees for prayer. Widow Nash whispered to her son as they knelt side by side:

"How did you make out, Andy?"

"Didn't make out at all, mammy; she's as obstinate as a mule."

"Well, then, there's only one thing mo' to do."

Andy was unpleasant company for the remainder of the day. He sought, but found nothing to palliate Caramel's treachery. He had only surly, bitter words for his companions who ventured to address him, as the outward expression of inward tumult. The more he brooded over his wrongs the worse he felt. When he went to work on Monday morning he was feeling vicious. He had made up his mind to do something desperate. The wedding should not come off. He would be avenged.

Andy went about his work at the hotel in gloomy silence

unlike his usual gay hilarity. It happened that all the femal
help at the great hostelry was white, and on that particula
Monday morning was the duty of Bridget McCarthy's watc
to clean the floors. Bridget was also not in the best c
humors, for Pat McClosky, her special company, had gone t
the priest's with her rival, Kate Connerton, on Sunday afte
noon, and Bridget had not yet got over the effects of a stron
rum punch taken to quiet her nerves after hearing the new

Bridget had scrubbed a wide swath of the marble floc
when Andy came through with a rush order carried in scier
tific style high above his head, balanced on one hand. Inter
upon satisfying the guest who was princely in his "tips,
Andy's unwary feet became entangled in the maelstrom c
brooms, scrubbing-brushes and pails. In an instant the "or
der" was sliding over the floor in a general mix-up.

To say Bridget was mad wouldn't do her state justice. Sh
forgot herself and her surroundings and relieved her fee
ings in elegant Irish, ending a tirade of abuse by callin
Andy a "wall-eyed, bandy-legged nagur."

Andy couldn't stand that from "common, po' whit
trash," so calling all his science into play he struck ou
straight from the shoulder with his right, and brought her
swinging blow on the mouth, which seated her neatly in th
five-gallon bowl of freshly made lobster salad which har
pened to be standing on the floor behind her.

There was a wail from the kitchen force that reached t
every department. It being the busiest hour of the day whe
they served dinner, the dish-washers and scrubbers went o
a strike against the "nagur who struck Bridget McCarthy, th
baste," mingled with cries of "lynch him!" Instantly th
great basement floor was a battle ground. Every colore
man seized whatever was handiest and ranged himself b
Andy's side, and stood ready to receive the onslaught of th
Irish brigade. For the sake of peace, and sorely against h

"Baste" is "beast" as Hopkins tries to imitate an Irish brogue.

inclinations, the proprietor surrendered Andy to the police on a charge of assault and battery.

On Wednesday morning of that eventful week, Brother Jimson wended his way to his house in the suburbs to collect the rent. Unseen by the eye of man, he was wrestling with a problem that had shadowed his life for many years. No one on earth suspected him unless it might be the widow. Brother Jimson boasted of his consistent Christian life— rolled his piety like a sweet morsel beneath his tongue, and had deluded himself into thinking that *he* could do no sin. There were scoffers in the church who doubted the genuineness of his pretentions, and he believed that there was a movement on foot against his power led by Widow Nash.

Brother Jimson groaned in bitterness of spirit. His only fear was that he might be parted from Caramel. If he lost her he felt that all happiness in life was over for him, anxiety gave him a sickening feeling of unrest. He was tormented, too, by jealousy; and when he was called upon by Andy's anxious mother to rescue her son from the clutches of the law, he had promised her fair enough, but in reality resolved to do nothing but—tell the judge that Andy was a dangerous character whom it was best to quell by severity. The pastor and all the other influential members of the church were at court on Tuesday, but Brother Jimson was conspicuous by his absence.

Today Brother Jimson resolved to call on Sister Nash, and as he had heard nothing of the outcome of the trial, make cautious inquiries concerning that, and also sound her on the subject nearest his heart.

He opened the gate and walked down the side path to the back door. From within came the rhythmic sound of a rubbing board. The brother knocked, and then cleared his throat with a preliminary cough.

"Come," called a voice within. As the door swung open it revealed the spare form of the widow, who with sleeves rolled above her elbows stood at the tub cutting her way through piles of foaming suds.

"Mornin', Sis' Nash! How's all?"

"That you, Bro'r Jimson? How's yourself? Take a cheer an' make yourself to home."

"Cert'nly, Sis' Nash, don' care ef I do," and the good brother scanned the sister with an eagle eye. "Yas'm I'm purty tol'rable these days, thank God. Bleeg'd to you, Sister, I jes' will stop an' res' myself befo' I repair myself back to the city." He seated himself in the most comfortable chair in the room, tilted it on the two back legs against the wall, lit his pipe and with a grunt of satisfaction settled back to watch the white rings of smoke curl about his head.

"These are mighty ticklish times, Sister. How's you continue on the journey? Is you strong in the faith?"

"I've got the faith, my brother, but I ain't on on mountain top this week. I'm way down in the valley; I'm jes' coaxin' the Lord to keep me sweet," and Sister Nash wiped the ends from her hands and prodded the clothes in the boiler with the clothes-stick, added fresh pieces and went on with her work.

"This is a worl' strewed with wrecks an' floatin' with tears. It's the valley of tribulation. May your faith continue. I hear Jim Jinkins has bought a farm up Taunton way."

"Wan'ter know!"

"Doctor tells me Bro'r Waters is comin' after Chris-mus. They do say as how he's stirrin' up things turrible; he's easin' his min' on this lynchin' business, an' it's high time—high time."

"Sho! Don' say so! What you reck'n he's goin tell us now, Brother Jimson?"

"Suthin' 'stonishin', Sister; it'll stir the country from end to end. Yes'm the Council is powerful strong as an organization."

"Sho! sho!" and the "thrub, thrub" of the board could be heard a mile away.

The conversation flagged. Evidently Widow Nash was not in a talkative mood that morning. The brother was disappointed.

"Well, it's mighty comfort'ble here, but I mus' be goin'."

"What's your hurry, Brother Jimson?"

"Business, Sister, business," and the brother brought his chair forward preparatory to rising. "Where's Andy? How'd he come out of that little difficulty?"

"Locked up."

"You don' mean to say he's in jail?"

"Yes, he's in jail 'tell I git's his bail."

"What might the sentence be, Sister?"

"Twenty dollars fine or six months at the Islan'." There was silence for a moment, broken only by the "thrub, thrub" of the washboard, while the smoke curled upward from Brother Jimson's pipe as he enjoyed a few last puffs.

"These are mighty ticklish times, Sister. Po' Andy, the way of the transgressor is hard."

Sister Nash took her hands out of the tub and stood with arms akimbo, a statue of Justice carved in ebony. Her voice was like the trump of doom.

"Yes; an' men like you is the cause of it. You leadin' men with money an' chances don' do your duty. I arst you, I arst you fair, to go down to the jedge an' bail that po' chile out. Did you go? No; you hard-faced old devil, you lef him be there, an' I had to git the money from my white folks. Yes, an' I'm breakin' my back now, over that pile of clo's to pay that twenty dollars. Um! all the trouble comes to us women."

"That's so, Sister; that's the livin' truth," murmured Brother Jimson furtively watching the rising storm and wondering where the lightning of her speech would strike next.

"I tell you that it is our receiptfulness to each other is the reason we don' prosper an' God's a-punishin' us with fire an' with sward 'cause we's so jealous an' snaky to each other."

"That's so, Sister; that's the livin' truth."

"Yes, sir; a nigger's boun' to be a nigger 'tell the trump of doom. You kin skin him, but he's a nigger still. Broad-cloth, iled shirts an' money won' make him more or less, no, sir."

"That's so, Sister; that's jes' so."

"A nigger can't help himself. White folks can run agin the law all the time an' they never gits caught, but a nigger! Every time he opens his mouth he puts his foot in it—got to hit that po' white trash gal in the mouth an' git jailed an' leave his po'r ol' mother to work her fingers to the secon' jint to get him out. Um!"

"These are mighty ticklish times, Sister. Man's boun' to sin; it's his nat'ral state. I hope this will teach Andy humility of the sperit."

"A little humility'd be good for yourself, Abra'm Jimson." Sister Nash ceased her sobs and set her teeth hard.

"Lord, Sister Nash, what compar'son is there 'twixt me an' a worthless nigger like Andy? My business is with the salt of the earth, an' so I have dwelt ever since I was consecrated."

"Salt of the earth! But ef the salt have los' its saver how you goin' salt it ergin? No, sir, you cain't do it; it mus' be cas' out an' trodded under foot of men. That's who's goin' happen you Abe Jimson, hyar me? An' I'd like to trod on you with my foot, an' every ol' good fer nuthin' bag o' salt like you," shouted Sister Nash. "You're a snake in the grass; you done stole the boy's gal an' then try to git him sent to the Islan'. You cain't deny it, fer the jedge done tol' me all you said, you ol' rhinoceros-hided hypercrite. Salt of the earth! You!"

Brother Jimson regretted that Widow Nash had found him out. Slowly he turned, settling his hat on the back of his head.

"Good mornin', Sister Nash. I ain't no hard feelin's agains' you. I too near to the kingdom to let trifles jar me. My bowels of compassion yearns over you, Sister, a pilgrim an' a stranger in this unfriendly worl'."

No answer from Sister Nash. Brother Jimson lingered.

"Good mornin', Sister." Still no answer.

"I hope to see you at the weddin', Sister."

"Keep on hopin', I'll be there. That gal's my own sister' chile. What in time she wants of a rheumatic ol' sap-head lik you for, beats me. I wouldn't marry you for no money, myself; no, sir; it's my belief that you've done goophered her."

"Yes, Sister; I've hearn tell of people refusin' befo' they was ask'd," he retorted, giving her a sly look.

For answer the widow grabbed the clothes-stick and flung it at him in speechless rage.

"My, what a temper it's got," remarked Brother Jimson soothingly as he dodged the shovel, the broom, the coal-hod and the stove-covers. But he sighed with relief as he turned into the street and caught the faint sound of the washboard now resumed.

To a New Englander the season of snow and ice with its clear biting atmosphere, is the ideal time for the great festival. Christmas morning dawned in royal splendor; the sun kissed the snowy streets and turned the icicles into brilliant stalactites. The bells rang a joyous call from every steeple, and soon the churches were crowded with eager worshippers—eager to hear again the oft-repeated, the wonderful story on which the heart of the whole Christian world feeds its faith and hope. Words of tender faith, marvellous in their simplicity fell from the lips of a world-renowned preacher, and touched the hearts of the listening multitude:

"The winter sunshine is not more bright and clear than the atmosphere of living joy, which stretching back between our eyes and that picture of Bethlehem, shows us its beauty in unstained freshness. And as we open once again those chapters of the gospel in which the ever fresh and living picture stands, there seems from year to year always to come some newer, brighter meaning into the words that tell the tale.

"St. Matthew says that when Jesus was born in Bethlehem the wise men came from the East to Jerusalem. The East means man's search after God; Jerusalem means God's search after man. The East means the religion of the devout soul; Jerusalem means the religion of the merciful God. The

East means Job's cry, 'Oh, that I knew where I might find him!' Jerusalem means 'Immanuel—God with us.' "

Then the deep-toned organ joined the grand chorus of human voices in a fervent hymn of praise and thanksgiving:

> Lo! the Morning Star appeareth,
>   O'er the world His beams are cast;
> He the Alpha and Omega,
>   He, the Great, the First the Last!
> Hallelujah! hallelujah!
>   Let the heavenly portal ring!
> Christ is born, the Prince of glory!
> Christ the Lord, Messiah, King!

Everyone of the prominence in church circles had been bidden to the Jimson wedding. The presents were many and costly. Early after service on Christmas morning the vestry room was taken in hand by leading sisters to prepare the tables for the supper, for on account of the host of friends bidden to the feast, the reception was to be held in the vestry.

The tables groaned beneath their loads of turkey, salads, pies, puddings, cakes and fancy ices.

Yards and yards of evergreen wreaths encircled the granite pillars; the altar was banked with potted plants and cut flowers. It was a beautiful sight. The main aisle was roped off for the invited guests with white satin ribbons.

Brother Jimson's patrons were to be present in a body, and they had sent the bride a solid silver service, so magnificent that the sisters could only sigh with envy.

The ceremony was to take place at seven sharp. Long before that hour the ushers in full evening dress were ready to receive the guests. Sister Maria Nash was among the first to arrive, and even the Queen of Sheba was not arrayed like unto her. At fifteen minutes before the hour, the organist began an elaborate instrumental performance. There was an expectant hush and much head-turning when the music changed to the familiar strains of the "Wedding March."

The minister took his place inside the railing ready to receive the party. The groom waited at the altar.

First came the ushers, then the maids of honor, then the flower girl—daughter of a prominent member—carrying a basket of flowers which she scattered before the bride, who was on the arm of the best man. In the bustle and confusion incident to the entrance of the wedding party no one noticed a group of strangers accompanied by Andy Nash enter and occupy seats near the door.

The service began. All was quiet. The pastor's words fell clearly upon the listening ears. He had reached the words: "If any man can show just cause, etc.," when like a thunder-clap came a voice from the back part of the house—an angry excited voice, and a woman of ponderous avoirdupois advanced up the aisle.

"Hol' on that, pastor, hol' on! A man cain't have but one wife 'cause it's agin' the law. I'm Abe Jimson's lawful wife, an' hyars his six children—all boys—to pint out their daddy." In an instant the assembly was in confusion.

"My soul," exclaimed Viney Peters, "the ol' serpent! An' to think how near I come to takin' up with him. I'm glad I ain't Car'mel."

Sis'r Maria said nothing, but a smile of triumph lit up her countenance.

"Brother Jimson, is this true?" demanded the minister, sternly. But Abraham Jimson was past answering. His face was ashen, his teeth chattering, his hair standing on end. His shaking limbs refused to uphold his weight; he sank upon his knees on the steps of the altar.

But now a hand was laid upon his shoulder and Mrs. Jimson hauled him upon his feet with a jerk.

"Abe Jimson, you know me. You run'd 'way from me up North fifteen year ago, an' you hid yourself like a groun' hog in a hole, but I've got you. There'll be no new wife in the Jimson family this week. I'm yer fus' wife and I'll be yer las' one. Git up hyar now, you mis'able sinner an' tell the pastor who I be." Brother Jimson meekly obeyed the clarion voice.

His sanctified air had vanished; his pride humbled into the dust.

"Pastor," came in trembling tones from his quivering lips. "These are mighty ticklish times." He paused. A deep silence followed his words. "I'm a weak-kneed, mis'able sinner. I have fallen under temptation. This is Ma' Jane, my wife, an' these hyar boys is my sons, God forgive me."

The bride, who had been forgotten now, broke in:

"Abraham Jimson, you ought to be hung. I'm going to sue you for breach of promise." It was a fatal remark. Mrs. Jimson turned upon her.

"You will, will you? Sue him, will you? I'll make a choc'late Car'mel of you befo' I'm done with you, you 'ceitful hussy, hoodooin' hones' men from thar wives."

She sprang upon the girl, tearing, biting, rendering. The satin gown and gossamer veil were reduced to rags. Caramel emitted a series of ear-splitting shrieks, but the biting and tearing went on. How it might have ended no one can tell if Andy had not sprang over the backs of the pews and grappled with the infuriated woman.

The excitement was intense. Men and women struggled to get out of the church. Some jumped from the windows and others crawled under the pews, where they were secure from violence. In the midst of the melee, Brother Jimson disappeared and was never seen again, and Mrs. Jimson came into possession of his property by due process of law.

In the church Abraham Jimson's wedding and his fall from grace is still spoken of in eloquent whispers.

In the home of Mrs. Andy Nash a motto adorns the parlor walls worked in scarlet wool and handsomely framed in gilt. The text reads: "Ye are the salt of the earth; there is nothing hidden that shall not be revealed."

BIBLIOGRAPHIC NOTES

Despite her singular position as writer, editor, publisher, and activist in turn-of-the-century Boston, few sources of information about Pauline Hopkins's life exist. The *Dictionary of American Negro Biography*, ed. Rayford W. Logan and Michael R. Winston (New York: Norton, 1982), carries a well-informed encyclopedia entry listing most of her publications and touching on reactions to her work and ideas by her contemporaries and more recent critics. This piece also correctly identifies the reason behind her resignation from *Colored American Magazine* as part of the struggle between W. E. B. Du Bois and Booker T. Washington for control of the Negro press. This ouster by forces associated with Washington is thoroughly and insightfully discussed in Abby Arthur Johnson and Ronald Maberry Johnson, "Away from Accommodation: Radical Editors and Protest Journalism, 1900–1910," *Journal of Negro History* 62 (October 1977): 325–29. Here, Hopkins comes alive, shaping *Colored American Magazine* according to her Du Boisean predilections in the face of powerful accommodationist forces and indignant white readers. More insight is shown here into Hopkins's activist role and literary concerns than in most other evaluations, but because of the larger scope of the article, no mention is made of Hopkins after 1905, twenty-five years before her death in 1930. Two briefer accounts also exist but their authors seem unaware of her role in the Du Bois-Washington controversy, reporting that Hopkins left the magazine because of poor health. One of them, Ann Allen Shockley's character sketch, "Pauline Elizabeth Hopkins: A Biographical Excursion into Obscurity," *Phylon* 33 (1972): 22–26, is helpful because it is the only source to mention the titles of her short stories. The other entry, Lina Mainiero, ed., *American Women Writers: A Critical Reference Guide from Colonial Times to the Present*, vol. 2 (New York: Ungar, 1980), pp. 325–327, is the sole entry to mention her support for limited suffrage but fails to note Hopkins's stated reticence to enter into political alliance with white women as the reason behind her qualification.

The exclusion of Hopkins from the critical canon of black women writers is most evident. If she is mentioned at all—and many more omit than include her—discussion is limited to the novel *Contending Forces*. More attention is paid to the preface (in which Hopkins asserts the need for black literary independence) than to the text itself. Vernon Loggins, *The Negro Author, His Development in America to 1900* (Port Washington, N.Y.: Kennikat Press, 1964), compares the novel to Harper's *Iola Leroy*, citing both for exaggeration, overcomplicated plots, and sentimentality.

Robert A. Bone, *The Negro Novel in America* (New Haven: Yale University Press, 1965) includes Hopkins in his analysis of early Negro novelists, devoting a few paragraphs to her middle-class standards, minor comic characters, and her underlying belief in white superiority. In this whipping-girl role he devised for Hopkins, Bone criticizes her for many traits also found in male novelists to whom he gives more time and more serious analysis. Also brief, but more insightful, is Judith Berzon's *Neither White nor Black* (New York: New York University Press, 1978), which comments on the influence of Du Bois on Hopkins.

Claudia Tate's essay, "Pauline Hopkins: Our Literary Foremother," in *Conjuring Black Women, Fiction, and Literary Tradition*, ed. Marjorie Pryse and Hortense Spillers (Bloomington: Indiana University Press, 1985), gives comprehensive summaries of Hopkins's fiction, including her serialized novels, and notes the change from the serious racial theme of *Contending Forces* to the escapist fiction of Hopkins's later novels.

The fullest and most helpful analysis of Hopkins is in Richard Yarborough's "The Depiction of Blacks in the Early

Afro-American Novel" (Ph.D. diss., Stanford University, 1980). It is an excellent summary of critics' response to Hopkins, and an analysis of *Contending Forces* and two of the serialized short novels.

FANNIE BARRIER WILLIAMS

The Colored Girl

What becomes of the colored girl? This is a question that cannot fail to be of interest to men and women everywhere, who have at heart the well-being of all the people.

That the term "colored girl" is almost a term of reproach in the social life of America is all too true; she is not known and hence not believed in; she belongs to a race that is best designated by the term "problem," and she lives beneath the shadow of that problem which envelopes and obscures her.

The colored girl may have character, beauty and charms ineffable, but she is not in vogue. The muses of song, poetry and art do not woo and exalt her. She is not permitted or supposed to typify the higher ideals that make life something higher, sweeter and more spiritual than a mere existence. Man's instinctive homage at the shrine of womankind draws a line of color, which places her forever outside its mystic circle.

The white manhood of America sustains no kindly or respectful feeling for the colored girl; great nature has made her what she is, and the laws of men have made for her a class below the level of other women. The women of other races bask in the clear sunlight of man's chivalry, admiration, and even worship, while the colored woman abides in the shadow of his contempt, mistrust or indifference.

How much easier it would be to be a good christian and to be loyal to the better instincts of manhood, if these girls of color were not like other girls in heart, brain and soul. Yet her presence is inevitable. The character of American womanhood is, in spite of itself, affected by the presence of the colored girl. The current of her aspirations finds a subtle connection with the aspirations of the thousands who socially feel themselves to be beyond and above her. Nay, more; those who meanly malign and humiliate her are unconsciously sapping the sweetness and light out of their own lives. The colored girl is a cause as well as an effect. We cannot comprehend the term American womanhood without including the colored girl. Thanks to the All wise Creator of men and things, the law of life is infinitely deeper than the law of society. The ties of kinship and love continually cross and recross the color line of man-made prejudices. The woman beautiful, the woman courageous, the woman capable is neither white nor colored; she is bound to be loved and admired in spite of all the meannesses that are of human origin. For, after all, "color is only sink deep." Has the colored girl the heart, spirit and subtle tenderness of womanhood? Such a question would be impertinent in an age where human life meant something too sacred to be loved or scorned, according to color.

It is because of this tyranny of race prejudice that the colored girl is called upon to endure and overcome more difficulties than confront any other women in our country. In law, religion and ethics, she is entitled to everything, but in practice there are always forces at work that would deny her anything. But yet, as meanly as she is thought of; hindered as she is in all directions, she is always doing something of merit and credit that is not expected of her. She is irrepressible. She is insulted, but she holds up her head; she is scorned, but she proudly demands respect. Thus has it come to pass that the most interesting girl of this country is the colored girl. Upon her devolves the marvelous task of establishing the social status of the race. Black men may work and save and build, but all their labor and all their savings and creations will not make a strong foundation for the social life of the race without the pure heart, cultivated mind and home-making spirit of the colored woman. It is a heart aching task, but the colored girl must and will accomplish it.

At this hour when a thousand social ills beset her, she is taking hold of life in a serious and helpful spirit. It is becoming more and more evident that she is not afraid of the age in which she lives nor its problems. She is a daughter of misfortune but she contributes her full share to the joys of the life about her. She is the very heart of the race problem. She is beginning to realize that the very character of our social fabric depends upon the quality of her womanliness.

It would seem trite to recount her services to the cause of education. Take the colored girl out of our schools and all progress would cease. As an educator she does more work with less compensation than any other teacher in the country. Follow her, if you will, into the remote corners of the schoolless South, and you will find material for such a story of gentle martyrdom as would forever put to shame those who hold our girls in light esteem. As a teacher and guide to thousands who have had no moral training in home and school, she has fully earned the right to be, at least, respected. No class of our people have so quickly caught and appropriated the self-sacrificing devotion of the pioneer New England teacher, as the colored girl. She has shown in cases innumerable that she can abandon social pleasures, good salaries, ordinary comforts and the flattery of men for the sacred cause of bringing light out of darkness to the masses. Would you know the real heroines of the colored race, do not look for them among the well dressed throngs that parade our streets and fill our churches, but look in obscure places like Mt. Meigs in Alabama, the settlement in Georgia under the benign direction of Miss Julia Jackson, or in the alleys of South Washington, where Mrs. Fernandez works, prays and waits. Here you will find women of real consecration and the spirit of Jane Addams, working with as well as for the unfortunate all around them. This type of colored girl is increasing every day in numbers and influence. She will some day become the heart and the very life of everything that is best amongst us. This is a work that calls for courage, patience, love, and the best qualities of the human heart, because it must be wrought out in the midst of the very worst conditions and emphasized by example, as well as by teaching and precept.

Yet there are men and women who profess to be fair and just who still insist that the colored girl is without character. It is true that we have our trifling girls, and in this respect we are thoroughly human.

While we believe that the colored girl of character amongst us is a constantly increasing factor in our progress, she has but few ways of making herself known beyond her immediate environment. She has inspired no novels. Those who write for the press and magazines seldom think of this dark-skinned girl who is persistently breaking through the petty tyrannies of cast into the light of recognition. She has enterprise and ambition that are always in advance of her opportunities. At this very moment she is knocking at every door through which other women, less equipped than she, have passed on from one achievement to another.

In Chicago, for example, where the color line is quite rigidly drawn against the colored girl in almost every direction, still it is possible to find her pluckily challenging this humiliating color line, and in many surprising instances with success. I know of more than a score of girls who are holding positions of high responsibility, which were at first denied to them as beyond their reach. These positions so won and held were never intended for them; to seek them was considered an impertinence, and to hope for them was an absurdity. Nothing daunted, these young women, conscious of their own deserving, would not admit or act upon the presumption that they were not as good and capable as other girls who were not really superior to them. It is certainly not too much to say that the colored girl is fast developing character and spirit sufficient to make her own way and win the respect and confidence of those who once refused even to consider her claims of character and fitness.

What the colored girl craves, above all things, is to be respected and believed in. This is more important than position and opportunities. In fact there can be for her no such thing as opportunity, unless she can win the respect of those who have it in their power to humiliate her. How can she win this respect? This question is addressed to colored men quite as much as to white men. I believe that as a general thing we hold our girls too cheaply. Too many colored men entertain very careless, if not contemptible, opinions of the colored girl. They are apt to look to other races for their types of beauty and character. For the most part the chivalry of colored men for colored women has in it but little heart and no strength of protection. They ought to appreciate that a colored girl of character and intelligence is a very precious asset in our social life, and they should act accordingly.

Among the Jewish people, for example, their women are safe-guarded and exalted in ways that make their character and womanhood sacred. The colored girl has already done enough for herself and her race to deserve at least the colored man's respect. We have all too many colored men who hold the degrading opinions of ignorant white men, that all colored girls are alike. They lose sight of the fact that colored girls like other girls are apt to be just as pure, noble and sweet as the best of our men shall insist upon their being. How rare are the reported instances of colored men resenting any slur or insult upon their own women. Colored women can never be all that they would be until colored men shall begin to exalt their character and beauty and to throw about them the chivalry of love and protection which shall command the recognition and respect of all the world. There is something fundamentally wrong in our social instincts and sentiments, if we fail to recognize the ever enlarging difference between the pure and impure, the upright and degraded of colored women.

The colored girl of character and accomplishments is

abroad in the land. She wants and deserves many things, but the greatest of her needs is the respect and confidence of those who should exalt and respect her. Is the colored man brave enough to stand out and say to all the world, "Thus far and no farther in your attempt to insult and degrade our women"?

It is not in any mere sentimental sense that this plea is made for a more generous respect for colored women by colored men. Our women have comparatively none of the social pharaphernalia and settings that command general admiration. If they are to be respected and admired to their full deserving, it must be for what they are and not for what they have. In this respect they are unlike the women of other races. The very unpopularity of their complexion obscures their merits.

The colored man, as well as the white man, is more apt to be attracted by womanly appearance than by womanly merit. For example, there are at this hour thousands of superior young colored women in this country who are compelled to fill occupations far below their accomplishments and deservings. Are they respected and admired because of the courage of their determination not to be idle? Scarcely. Those who make up and are responsible for what is called the higher life amongst us are apt to scorn the colored girl who works with her hands. Only the parlor girl finds social favor. This sort of borrowed snobbishness is responsible for the going wrong of many of our girls.

What our girls and women have a right to demand from our best men is that they cease to imitate the artificial standards of other people and create a race standard of their own. In no other way can we make prominent and important the colored girl of character and intelligence. What the colored girl needs today is encouragement to do whatever her hands find to do, and be protected and honored for it. If the colored girl of character and intelligence must cook, who shall say that she is not as deserving of the honors of the best

PART THREE

Every Black woman in America lives
her life somewhere along a wide curve
of ancient and unexpressed angers.

—Audre Lorde, *Sister Outsider*

feeling uncomfortable among black people and unable to sort out their racial identity. We might justifiably wonder, is there anything relevant, in the lives of women who arrogantly expected to live in Harlem, in the middle-class enclave of Sugar Hill, to summer at resorts like Idlewild in Michigan, to join exclusive black clubs and sororities? Weren't the interests that preoccupied Larsen in her work just the spoiled tantrums of "little yellow dream children" grown up?

But during the 1920s, Larsen's novels were perceived as "uplift novels," novels that proved that blacks were intelligent, refined, morally upright—and therefore equal to whites. The novel about the fair-skinned woman who challenged color lines to improve her social situation was viewed as a kind of protest against a rigid caste system which denied blacks social mobility. Even militant activists like W. E. B. Du Bois approved of fiction that represented the struggles of the black elite; Du Bois in fact thought the black bourgeoisie —the "Talented Tenth," as he referred to them—would lead the race into the American mainstream. Novelist Jessie Fauset, another of Larsen's contemporaries, also wrote novels of social uplift which present educated and aspiring blacks desperately intent on upward mobility. But Fauset's novels never shatter the illusions and pretenses of middle-class respectability; they essentially confirm the necessity for black people to struggle harder to attain it. Larsen's novels go far beyond the elitism of other novels of the "Talented Tenth." They are not about the barriers to black social mobility and class privilege; they are about the chaos in the world of the black elite, the emptiness in the climb to bourgeois respectability. They are about the women in that world who are inhibited and stunted by cultural scripts that deny them any "awakenings" and punish them for their defiance.

While Larsen's fiction reflects the spiritual vacuity of the black bourgeoisie, her sense of marginality must certainly have been drawn from her own life. Larsen's mother was a white woman from Denmark; her father, a black West Indian.

Widowed when Larsen was a young girl, her mother remarried, this time to "one of her own kind." In the new all-white family—father, mother, and second daughter—Larsen's blackness was an embarrassment. In a 1929 newspaper interview Larsen confirms a painful isolation from them: "I don't see my family much now. It might make it awkward for them, particularly my half-sister." Larsen was constantly trying to negotiate two very separate worlds. She studied at Fisk, the black college in Nashville where she was in the high school. For several years she audited courses at the University of Copenhagen, where her white relatives lived. Little is known about her three-year sojourn in Europe, though the autobiographical character, Helga Crane, the mulatto outcast in *Quicksand,* suggests some possible scenarios. Perhaps, like Helga, she was received warmly by her Danish relatives and treated as something of a curiosity, her dark skin standing out in vivid relief against so many pale blonds. Helga grows discontent playing the role of exotic freak and finds herself longing desperately to be surrounded by brown laughing faces and to be immersed in the warm spontaneity of black Harlem life. A similar experience probably accounts for Larsen's abrupt departure from Tuskegee for New York. There she worked as a librarian from 1921 to 1926, during which time she wrote the only two books she would ever publish.

Nella Larsen won a Guggenheim in 1930, the first black woman to win a creative writing award from that foundation, and she traveled to Spain to work on a third novel. It was never published. Instead Nella Larsen entered into a thirty-year silence. She worked as a supervising nurse at Beth Israel Hospital in Manhattan, neither passing for white nor identifying with blacks. She died in obscurity in Manhattan in 1964.[2]

There are a few clues as to why Nella Larsen fell silent as a literary voice. In 1930 she was accused of plagiarizing a story that was published in *Forum* magazine. Though she was supported by her editor, who had seen several drafts of the story, she was nonetheless devastated by the criticism. Then she was divorced from her husband, Dr. Elmer Imes, a physicist at Fisk University. The divorce was crudely sensationalized by one widely read black newspaper. The Baltimore *Afro-American* reported "rumors" that Professor Imes was involved with a white woman and that Larsen's frequent trips to Europe had helped to cause the breakup and added that the speculation at Fisk was that Larsen had tried to kill herself by jumping out of a window.

These two events of public shame, plus a fragile and vulnerable personality, a sense of oddness that made her seem strange to her friends, and a deep-seated ambivalence about her racial status combined to reinforce her sense of herself as the outsider and may finally have pushed her into a life of obscurity.

Always there is the ambivalence about her racial identity. In her personal correspondence Larsen is detached and aloof speaking about "the Negroes" as though she were observing a comic opera, and yet there is the unmistakable race pride as she observes the style and coping power of poor blacks in the South. She once wrote in a letter to Carl Van Vechten, a white novelist and critic of the Harlem Renaissance period, that she found poor Southern blacks quaint and amusing: "I've never seen anything quite so true to what's expected. Mostly black and good-natured and apparently quite shiftless, frightfully clean and decked out in the most appalling colors, but somehow just right. Terribly poor." Then she hastens to add that the poor whites by comparison are tragic and depressing.

What happens to a writer who is legally black but internally identifies with both blacks and whites, who is supposed to be content as a member of the black elite but feels suffocated by its narrowness, who is emotionally rooted in the black experience and yet wants to live in the whole world not confined to a few square blocks and the mentality that make up Sugar Hill?

Her two novels give no indication that Nella Larsen ever

solved the problem of duality. The lives of all Larsen's major women characters—Helga Crane, Clare Kendry, and Irene Redfield—end in self-destruction. As middle-class black women of the 1920s, they are marginal to both black and white worlds. Like strange plants trying to sustain themselves without roots or nourishment, they are detached and isolated from the black community. Helga Crane feels claustrophobic in the black Southern college and in black Harlem where she is forced to observe taboos and conventions that constrict her spirit. She says that the proscription against wearing bright colors (because bright colors supposedly emphasize a dark-skinned woman's blackness) amuses her, but she also sees it as one of the innumerable internal controls people already under severe restraints must submit to. Even more intolerable for Helga is the absolute law against any kind of interracial mixing, which Helga's Harlem friends consider an act of disloyalty to the race. One woman in *Quicksand* is ostracized because she is seen dancing publicly with white men. Helga is never able to completely deny her blackness, so she lives with resentment and rancor at having to "ghettoize" her own life.

In Larsen's second novel, *Passing*, one can see most clearly how she failed to resolve the dilemma of the marginal woman. The central character, Clare Kendry, is married to a white man and has been passing for white all of her married life. Passionate and daring, the mysterious Clare lives in both the black and white worlds, but on the fringes, feeling no permanent allegiance to either. Why does Clare pass? Because it enables her to marry a man of means. Because she, like most other black women of the 1920s if they achieved middle-class status, did so by virtue of a man's presence in her life, by virtue of his status—a grandfather who owned an undertaking business, a father who became a doctor, a husband elected to public office. "Passing" becomes, in Larsen's terms, a metaphor for the risk-taking experience, the life lived without the support other black women cling to in order to survive in a white and male-dominated society. But *passing,* as a word that can also connote death—in the black community dying is often referred to as "passing"—it also expresses Larsen's ambivalence about Clare's choice. She does in fact die as a result of passing for white.

The very choice of "passing" as a symbol or metaphor or deliverance for women reflects Larsen's failure to deal with the problem of marginality. "Passing" is an obscene form of salvation. The woman who passes is required to deny everything about her past: her girlhood, her family, places with memories, folk customs, folk rhymes, her language, the entire long line of people who have gone before her. She lives in terror of discovery—what if she has a child with a dark complexion, what if she runs into an old school friend, how does she listen placidly to racial slurs? And more, where does the woman who passes find the equanimity to live by the privileged status that is based on the oppression of her own people?

Larsen's heroines are all finally destroyed somewhere down the paths they choose. Helga Crane loses herself in a loveless marriage to an old black preacher by whom she has five children in as many years. She finally retreats into illness and silence, eventually admitting to herself a suppressed hatred for her husband. Irene Redfield suspects an affair between her friend Clare (recently surfaced from the white world) and her black physician husband. In the novel's melodramatic ending, she pushes Clare off the balcony of a high-rise apartment and then sinks into unconsciousness when she is questioned about Clare's death.

And Nella Larsen, who created Helga and Irene, chose oblivion for herself. From the little we know of the last thirty years of her life, she handled the problem of marginality by default, living entirely without any racial or cultural identity. Her exile was so complete that one of her biographers,

Thadious Davis, couldn't find an obituary for her: "I couldn't even bury Nella Larsen," she said.

But unlike the women in her novels, Larsen did not die from her marginality. She lived for seventy years, was an active part of the high-stepping Harlem Renaissance, traveled abroad, and worked as a nurse for forty years. She was an "unconventional" woman in the 1920s: she wore her dresses short, smoked cigarettes, rejected religion, and lived in defiance of the rules that most black women of her education and means were bound by. She lived the conflicts of the marginal woman and felt them passionately. Why didn't she leave us the greater legacy of the mature model, the perceptions of a woman who confronts pain, alienation, and isolation, and grapples with these conundrums until new insight has been forged from the struggle? Why didn't she continue to write after 1929?

If there are any answers to these questions, we have to look to Larsen's fiction to find them. Both her novels end with images of numbness, suffocation, and invisibility. Certainly these images reflect the constrictions and limitations of the world a middle-class black woman inhabited in the 1920s, a world even more restricted than that in Ralph Ellison's *Invisible Man*, another novel about marginality and the Afro-American experience.

The "Invisible Man" at least has the choice of a range of work options, mobility, and political activism. Who can imagine a black woman character replicating the intense activities of a black man, who—in literature and life—is at least sometimes physically free to hop a freight North or to highball it down the track from coast to coast as a Pullman porter, to organize and lead political movements without apology, to wield the tools of an occupation other than personal service and earn a living by sheer physical skill? And the characters in the literature of white women move through a variety of places and experiences with relative ease when compared to black women. They can be artists in

Europe, or illustrators in New York, or farmers in Iowa without suffering the permanent loss of community. At the heart of *Quicksand* and the Bonner essay is a quality of passivity, of resignation, of suppressed anger that results from the stifling of desire and energy. Bonner is more explicit than Larsen in articulating this repression:

> For you know that—being a woman—you cannot twice a month or twice a year, for that matter, break away to see or hear anything in a city that is supposed to see and hear too much.
> That's being a woman. A woman of any color . . . .
> And, you know, being a woman, you have to go about it gently and quietly, to find out and to discover just what is wrong. Just what can be done.

In their insistence that black women are estranged from the right to aspire and achieve in the wide world of thought and action, *Quicksand* and *Passing* (as well as the Bonner essay) are brilliant witnesses to the position of a colored woman in a white, male world.

She did not solve her own problems, but Larsen made us understand as no one did before her that the image of the middle-class black woman as a coldly self-centered snob, chattering irrelevantly at bridge club and sorority meetings, was as much a mask as the grin on the face of Stepin Fetchit. The women in her novels, like Larsen, are driven to emotional and psychological extremes in their attempts to handle ambivalence, marginality, racism, and sexism. She has shown us that behind the carefully manicured exterior, behind the appearance of security is a woman who hears the beating of her wings against a walled prison.

NOTES

1. Marita O. Bonner, "On Being Young—a Woman—and Colored," *Crisis* 31 (December 1925): 63–65.
2. According to Larsen's biographer, Thadious Davis, even the dat

of Larsen's birth is a mystery. It appears to be 1891 rather than 1893, as is generally given, but no birth certificate has been found. Davis, a professor of English at the University of North Carolina in Chapel Hill, is working on the biography of Larsen, which will bring to light much of what is now unknown about Larsen.

MARITA O. BONNER

On Being Young—
a Woman—and Colored

You start out after you have gone from kindergarten to sheepskin covered with sundry Latin phrases.

At least you know what you want life to give you. A career as fixed and as calmly brilliant as the North Star. The one real thing that money buys. Time. Time to do things. A house that can be as delectably out of order and as easily put in order as the doll-house of "playing-house" days. And of course, a husband you can look up to without looking down on yourself.

Somehow you feel like a kitten in a sunny catnip field that sees sleek, plump brown field mice and yellow baby chicks sitting coyly, side by side, under each leaf. A desire to dash three or four ways seizes you.

That's Youth.

But you know that things learned need testing—acid testing—to see if they are really after all, an interwoven part of you. All your life you have heard of the debt you owe "Your People" because you have managed to have the things they have not largely had.

So you find a spot where there are hordes of them—of course below the Line—to be your catnip field while you close your eyes to mice and chickens alike.

If you have never lived among your own, you feel prodigal. Some warm untouched current flows through them—through you—and drags you out into the deep waters of a new sea of human foibles and mannerisms; of a peculiar

"On Being Young—a Woman—and Colored" (1925)

psychology and prejudices. And one day you find yourself entangled—enmeshed—pinioned in the seaweed of a Black Ghetto.

Not a Ghetto, placid like the Strasse that flows, outwardly unperturbed and calm in a stream of religious belief, but a peculiar group. Cut off, flung together, shoved aside in a bundle because of color and with no more in common.

Unless color is, after all, the real bond.

Milling around like live fish in a basket. Those at the bottom crushed into a sort of stupid apathy by the weight of those on top. Those on top leaping, leaping; leaping to scale the sides; to get out.

There are two "colored" movies, innumerable parties—and cards. Cards played so intensely that it fascinates and repulses at once.

Movies.

Movies worthy and worthless—but not even a low-caste spoken stage.

Parties, plentiful. Music and dancing and much that is wit and color and gaiety. But they are like the richest chocolate; stuffed costly chocolates that make the taste go stale if you have too many of them. That make plain whole bread taste like ashes.

There are all the earmarks of a group within a group. Cut off all around from ingress from or egress to other groups. A sameness of type. The smug self-satisfaction of an inner measurement; a measurement by standards known within a limited group and not those of an unlimited, seeing, world. . . . Like the blind, blind mice. Mice whose eyes have been blinded.

Strange longing seizes hold of you. You wish yourself back where you can lay your dollar down and sit in a dollar seat to hear voices, strings, reeds that have lifted the World out, up, beyond things that have bodies and walls. Where you can marvel at new marbles and bronzes and flat colors that will make men forget that things exist in a flesh more often than in spirit. Where you can sink your body in a cushioned seat and sink your soul at the same time into a section of life set before you on the boards for a few hours.

You hear that up at New York this is to be seen; that, to be heard.

You decide the next train will take you there.

You decide the next second that that train will not take you, nor the next—nor the next for some time to come.

For you know that—being a woman—you cannot twice a month or twice a year, for that matter, break away to see or hear anything in a city that is supposed to see and hear too much.

That's being a woman. A woman of any color.

You decide that something is wrong with a world that stifles and chokes; that cuts off and stunts; hedging in, pressing down on eyes, ears and throat. Somehow all wrong.

You wonder how it happens there that—say five hundred miles from the Bay State—Anglo Saxon intelligence is so warped and stunted.

How judgment and discernment are bred out of the race. And what has become of discrimination? Discrimination of the right sort. Discrimination that the best minds have told you weighs shadows and nuances and spiritual differences before it catalogues. The kind they have taught you all of your life was best: that looks clearly past generalization and past appearance to dissect, to dig down to the real heart of matters. That casts aside rapid summary conclusions, drawn from primary inference, as Daniel did the spiced meats.

Why can't they then perceive that there is a difference in the glance from a pair of eyes that look, mildly docile, at "white ladies" and those that, impersonally and perceptively —aware of distinctions—see only women who happen to be white?

Why do they see a colored woman only as a gross collection of desires, all uncontrolled, reaching out for their Apollos and the Quasimodos with avid indiscrimination?

Why unless you talk in staccato squawks—brittle as sea-shells—unless you "champ" gum—unless you cover two yards square when you laugh—unless your taste runs to violent colors—impossible perfumes and more impossible clothes—are you a feminine Caliban craving to pass for Ariel?

An empty imitation of an empty invitation. A mime; a sham; a copy-cat. A hollow re-echo. A froth, a foam. A fleck of the ashes of superficiality?

Everything you touch or taste now is like the flesh of an unripe persimmon.

. . . Do you need to be told what that is being. . . ?

Old ideas, old fundamentals seem worm-eaten, out-grown, worthless, bitter; fit for the scrap-heap of Wisdom.

What you had thought tangible and practical has turned out to be a collection of "blue-flower" theories.

If they have not discovered how to use their accumulation of facts, they are useless to you in Their world.

Every part of you becomes bitter.

But—"In Heaven's name, do not grow bitter. Be bigger than they are",—exhort white friends who have never had to draw breath in a Jim-Crow train. Who have never had petty putrid insult dragged over them—drawing blood—like pebbled sand on your body where the skin is tenderest. On your body where the skin is thinnest and tenderest.

You long to explode and hurt everything white; friendly; unfriendly. But you know that you cannot live with a chip on your shoulder even if you can manage a smile around your eyes—without getting steely and brittle and losing the soft-ness that makes you a woman.

For chips make you bend your body to balance them. And once you bend, you lose your poise, your balance, and the chip gets into you. The real you. You get hard.

. . . And many things in you can ossify. . . .

And you know, being a woman, you have to go about it gently and quietly, to find out and to discover just what is wrong. Just what can be done.

You see clearly that they have acquired things.

Money; money. Money to build with, money to destroy. Money to swim in. Money to drown in. Money.

An ascendancy of wisdom. An incalculable hoard of wisdom in all fields, in all things collected from all quarters of humanity.

A stupendous mass of things.

Things.

So, too, the Greeks. . . . Things.

And the Romans. . . .

And you wonder and wonder why they have not discovered how to handle deftly and skillfully, Wisdom, stored up for them—like the honey for the Gods on Olympus—since time unknown.

You wonder and you wonder until you wander out into Infinity, where—if it is to be found anywhere—Truth really exists.

The Greeks had possessions, culture. They were lost because they did not understand.

The Romans owned more than anyone else. Trampled under the heel of Vandals and Civilization, because they would not understand.

Greeks. Would not understand.

Romans. Would not understand.

"They." Will not understand.

So you find, they have shut Wisdom up and have forgotten to find the key that will let her out. They have trapped, trammeled, lashed her to sea and earth and air to bring every treasure to her. But she sulks themselves with thews and thongs and theories. They have ransacked and will not work for a world with a whitish hue because it has snubbed her twin sister, Understanding.

You see clearly—off there is Infinity—Understanding. Standing alone, waiting for someone to really want her.

But she is so far out there is no way to snatch at her and drag her in.

So—being a woman—you can wait.

You must sit quietly without a chip. Not sodden—and

eighted as if your feet were cast in the iron of your soul.
Iot wasting strength in enervating gestures as if two hun-
red years of bonds and whips had really tricked you into
ervous uncertainty.

But quiet; quiet. Like Buddha—who brown like I am—sat
ntirely at ease, entirely sure of himself; motionless and
nowing, a thousand years before the white man knew there
as so very much difference between feet and hands.

Motionless on the outside. But inside?

Silent.

Still . . . "Perhaps Buddha is a woman."

So you too. Still; quiet; with a smile, ever so slight, at the
yes so that Life will flow into and not by you. And you can
ather, as it passes, the essences, the overtones, the tints, the
hadows; draw understanding to your self.

And then you can, when Time is ripe, swoop to your feet—
t your full height—at a single gesture.

Ready to go where?

Why . . . Wherever God motions.

NELLA LARSEN

Helga Crane

I

Helga Crane sat alone in her room, which at that hour, eigh
in the evening, was in soft gloom. Only a single readin
lamp, dimmed by a great black and red shade, made a poo
of light on the blue Chinese carpet, on the bright covers o
the books which she had taken down from their long shelves
on the white pages of the opened one selected, on the shin
ing brass bowl crowded with many-colored nasturtiums be
side her on the low table, and on the oriental silk whic
covered the stool at her slim feet. It was a comfortable room
furnished with rare and intensely personal taste, floode
with Southern sun in the day, but shadowy just then with th
drawn curtains and single shaded light. Large, too. So larg
that the spot where Helga sat was a small oasis in a desert o
darkness. And eerily quiet. But that was what she liked afte
her taxing day's work, after the hard classes, in which sh
gave willingly and unsparingly of herself with no apparen
return. She loved this tranquillity, this quiet, following th
fret and strain of the long hours spent among fellow mem
bers of a carelessly unkind and gossiping faculty, followin
the strenuous rigidity of conduct required in this huge edu
cational community of which she was an insignificant par
This was her rest, this intentional isolation for a short whil
in the evening, this little time in her own attractive roor
with her own books. To the rapping of other teachers, bear
ing fresh scandals, or seeking information, or other mor

"Helga Crane" from *Quicksand* (1928)

oncrete favors, or merely talk, at that hour Helga Crane
never opened her door.

An observer would have thought her well fitted to that
raming of light and shade. A slight girl of twenty-two years,
with narrow, sloping shoulders and delicate, but well-
turned, arms and legs, she had, none the less, an air of
radiant, careless health. In vivid green and gold negligee
and glistening brocaded mules, deep sunk in the big high-
backed chair, against whose dark tapestry her sharply cut
face, with skin like yellow satin, was distinctly outlined, she
was—to use a hackneyed word—attractive. Black, very broad
brows over soft, yet penetrating, dark eyes, and a pretty
mouth, whose sensitive and sensuous lips had a slight questioning petulance and a tiny dissatisfied droop, were the
features on which the observer's attention would fasten;
though her nose was good, her ears delicately chiseled, and
her curly blue-black hair plentiful and always straying in a
little wayward, delightful way. Just then it was tumbled, falling unrestrained about her face and on to her shoulders.

Helga Crane tried not to think of her work and the school
as she sat there. Ever since her arrival in Naxos she had
striven to keep these ends of the days from the intrusion of
irritating thoughts and worries. Usually she was successful.
But not this evening. Of the books which she had taken from
their places she had decided on Marmaduke Pickthall's *Saïd
the Fisherman*. She wanted forgetfulness, complete mental
relaxation, rest from thought of any kind. For the day had
been more than usually crowded with distasteful encounters
and stupid perversities. The sultry hot Southern spring had
left her strangely tired, and a little unnerved. And annoying
beyond all other happenings had been that affair of the noon
period, now again thrusting itself on her already irritated
mind.

She had counted on a few spare minutes in which to in-
dulge in the sweet pleasure of a bath and a fresh, cool
change of clothing. And instead her luncheon time had been
shortened, as had that of everyone else, and immediately

after the hurried gulping down of a heavy hot meal th
hundreds of students and teachers had been herded into th
sun-baked chapel to listen to the banal, the patronizing, an
even the insulting remarks of one of the renowned whit
preachers of the state.

Helga shuddered a little as she recalled some of the state
ments made by that holy white man of God to the black fol
sitting so respectfully before him.

This was, he had told them with obvious sectional pride
the finest school for Negroes anywhere in the country, nort
or south; in fact, it was better even than a great many school
for white children. And he had dared any Northerner t
come south and after looking upon this great institution t
say that the Southerner mistreated the Negro. And he ha
said that if all Negroes would only take a leaf out of the boo
of Naxos and conduct themselves in the manner of th
Naxos products, there would be no race problem, becaus
Naxos Negroes knew what was expected of them. They ha
good sense and they had good taste. They knew enough t
stay in their places and that, said the preacher, showed goo
taste. He spoke of his great admiration for the Negro race
no other race in so short a time had made so much progres:
but he had urgently besought them to know when and wher
to stop. He hoped, he sincerely hoped, that they wouldn
become avaricious and grasping, thinking only of adding t
their earthly goods, for that would be a sin in the sight
Almighty God. And then he had spoken of contentmen
embellishing his words with scriptural quotations and poin
ing out to them that it was their duty to be satisfied in th
estate to which they had been called, hewers of wood an
drawers of water. And then he had prayed.

Sitting there in her room, long hours after, Helga agai
felt a surge of hot anger and seething resentment. And agai
it subsided in amazement at the memory of the considerabl
applause which had greeted the speaker just before he ha
asked his God's blessing upon them.

The South. Naxos. Negro education. Suddenly she hate

them all. Strange, too, for this was the thing which she had
ardently desired to share in, to be a part of this monument to
one man's genius and vision. She pinned a scrap of paper
about the bulb under the lamp's shade, for, having dis-
carded her book, in the certainty that in such a mood even
Saïd and his audacious villainy could not charm her, she
wanted an even more soothing darkness. She wished it were
vacation, so that she might get away for a time.

"No, forever!" she said aloud.

The minutes gathered into hours, but still she sat motionless, a disdainful smile or an angry frown passing now and
then across her face. Somewhere in the room a little clock
ticked time away. Somewhere outside, a whippoorwill
wailed. Evening died. A sweet smell of early Southern flowers rushed in on a newly-risen breeze which suddenly parted
the thin silk curtains at the opened windows. A slender, frail
glass vase fell from the sill with a tingling crash, but Helga
Crane did not shift her position. And the night grew cooler,
and older.

At last she stirred, uncertainly, but with an overpowering
desire for action of some sort. A second she hesitated, then
rose abruptly and pressed the electric switch with determined firmness, flooding suddenly the shadowy room with a
white glare of light. Next she made a quick nervous tour to
the end of the long room, paused a moment before the old
bow-legged secretary that held with almost articulate protest
her school-teacher paraphernalia of drab books and papers.
Frantically Helga Crane clutched at the lot and then flung
them violently, scornfully toward the wastebasket. It received a part, allowing the rest to spill untidily over the floor.
The girl smiled ironically, seeing in the mess a simile of her
own earnest endeavor to inculcate knowledge into her indifferent classes.

Yes, it was like that; a few of the ideas which she tried to
put into the minds behind those baffling ebony, bronze, and
gold faces reached their destination. The others were left
scattered about. And, like the gay, indifferent wastebasket, it

wasn't their fault. No, it wasn't the fault of those minds back of the diverse colored faces. It was, rather, the fault of the method, the general idea behind the system. Like her own hurried shot at the basket, the aim was bad, the material drab and badly prepared for its purpose.

This great community, she thought, was no longer a school. It had grown into a machine. It was now a show place in the black belt, exemplification of the white man's magnanimity, refutation of the black man's inefficiency. Life had died out of it. It was, Helga decided, now only a big knife with cruelly sharp edges ruthlessly cutting all to a pattern, the white man's pattern. Teachers as well as students were subjected to the paring process, for it tolerated no innovations, no individualisms. Ideas it rejected, and looked with open hostility on one and all who had the temerity to offer a suggestion or ever so mildly express a disapproval. Enthusiasm, spontaneity, if not actually suppressed, were at least openly regretted as unladylike or ungentlemanly qualities. The place was smug and fat with self-satisfaction.

A peculiar characteristic trait, cold, slowly accumulated unreason in which all values were distorted or else ceased to exist, had with surprising ferociousness shaken the bulwarks of that self-restraint which was also, curiously, a part of her nature. And now that it had waned as quickly as it had risen, she smiled again, and this time the smile held a faint amusement, which wiped away the little hardness which had congealed her lovely face. Nevertheless she was soothed by the impetuous discharge of violence, and a sigh of relief came from her.

She said aloud, quietly, dispassionately: "Well, I'm through with that," and, shutting off the hard, bright blaze of the overhead lights, went back to her chair and settled down with an odd gesture of sudden soft collapse, like a person who had been for months fighting the devil and then unexpectedly had turned round and agreed to do his bidding.

Helga Crane had taught in Naxos for almost two years, at

first with the keen joy and zest of those immature people who have dreamed dreams of doing good to their fellow men. But gradually this zest was blotted out, giving place to a deep hatred for the trivial hypocrisies and careless cruelties which were, unintentionally perhaps, a part of the Naxos policy of uplift. Yet she had continued to try not only to teach, but to befriend those happy singing children, whose charm and distinctiveness the school was so surely ready to destroy. Instinctively Helga was aware that their smiling submissiveness covered many poignant heartaches and perhaps much secret contempt for their instructors. But she was powerless. In Naxos between teacher and student, between condescending authority and smoldering resentment, the gulf was too great, and too few had tried to cross it. It couldn't be spanned by one sympathetic teacher. It was useless to offer her atom of friendship, which under the existing conditions was neither wanted nor understood.

Nor was the general atmosphere of Naxos, its air of self-righteousness and intolerant dislike of difference, the best of mediums for a pretty, solitary girl with no family connections. Helga's essentially likable and charming personality was smudged out. She had felt this for a long time. Now she faced with determination that other truth which she had refused to formulate in her thoughts, the fact that she was utterly unfitted for teaching, even for mere existence, in Naxos. She was a failure here. She had, she conceded now, been silly, obstinate, to persist for so long. A failure. Therefore, no need, no use, to say longer. Suddenly she longed for immediate departure. How good, she thought, to go now, tonight!—and frowned to remember how impossible that would be. "The dignitaries," she said, "are not in their offices, and there will be yards and yards of red tape to unwind, gigantic, impressive spools of it."

And there was James Vayle to be told, and much-needed money to be got. James, she decided, had better be told at once. She looked at the clock racing indifferently on. No, too late. It would have to be tomorrow.

She hated to admit that money was the most serious difficulty. Knowing full well that it was important, she nevertheless rebelled at the unalterable truth that it could influence her actions, block her desires. A sordid necessity to be grappled with. With Helga it was almost a superstition that to concede to money its importance magnified its power. Still, in spite of her reluctance and distaste, her financial situation would have to be faced, and plans made, if she were to get away from Naxos with anything like the haste she now so ardently desired.

Most of her earnings had gone into clothes, into books, into the furnishings of the room which held her. All her life Helga Crane had loved and longed for nice things. Indeed, it was this craving, this urge for beauty which had helped to bring her into disfavor in Naxos—"pride" and "vanity" her detractors called it.

The sum owing to her by the school would just a little more than buy her ticket back to Chicago. It was too near the end of the school term to hope to get teaching-work anywhere. If she couldn't find something else, she would have to ask Uncle Peter for a loan. Uncle Peter was, she knew, the one relative who thought kindly, or even calmly, of her. Her step-father, her step-brothers and sisters, and the numerous cousins, aunts, and other uncles could not be even remotely considered. She laughed a little, scornfully, reflecting that the antagonism was mutual, or, perhaps, just a trifle keener on her side than on theirs. They feared and hated her. She pitied and despised them. Uncle Peter was different. In his contemptuous way he was fond of her. Her beautiful, unhappy mother had been his favorite sister. Even so, Helga Crane knew that he would be more likely to help her because her need would strengthen his oft-repeated conviction that because of her Negro blood she would never amount to anything, than from motives of affection or loving memory. This knowledge, in its present aspect of truth, irritated her to an astonishing degree. She regarded Uncle Peter almost vindictively, although always he had been extraordinarily generous with her and she fully intended to ask his assistance. "A beggar," she thought ruefully, "cannot expect to choose."

Returning to James Vayle, her thoughts took on the frigidity of complete determination. Her resolution to end her stay in Naxos would of course inevitably end her engagement to James. She had been engaged to him since her first semester there, when both had been new workers, and both were lonely. Together they had discussed their work and problems in adjustment, and had drifted into a closer relationship. Bitterly she reflected that James had speedily and with entire ease fitted into his niche. He was now completely "naturalized," as they used laughingly to call it. Helga, on the other hand, had never quite achieved the unmistakable Naxos mold, would never achieve it, in spite of much trying. She could neither conform, nor be happy in her unconformity. This she saw clearly now, and with cold anger at all the past futile effort. What a waste! How pathetically she had struggled in those first months and with what small success. A lack somewhere. Always she had considered it a lack of understanding on the part of the community, but in her present new revolt she realized that the fault had been partly hers. A lack of acquiescence. She hadn't really wanted to be made over. This thought bred a sense of shame, a feeling of ironical disillusion. Evidently there were parts of her she couldn't be proud of. The revealing picture of her past striving was too humiliating. It was as if she had deliberately planned to steal an ugly thing, for which she had no desire, and had been found out.

Ironically she visualized the discomfort of James Vayle. How her maladjustment had bothered him! She had a faint notion that it was behind his ready assent to her suggestion anent a longer engagement than, originally, they had planned. He was liked and approved of in Naxos and loathed the idea that the girl he was to marry couldn't manage to win liking and approval also. Instinctively Helga had known that secretly he had placed the blame upon her. How right he had been! Certainly his attitude had gradually changed, though he still gave her his attentions. Naxos pleased him and he had become content with life as it was lived there. No longer lonely, he was now one of the community and so beyond the need or the desire to discuss its affairs and its failings with an outsider. She was, she knew, in a queer indefinite way, a disturbing factor. She knew too that a something held him, a something against which he was powerless. The idea that she was in but one nameless way necessary to him filled her with a sensation amounting almost to shame. And yet his mute helplessness against that ancient appeal by which she held him pleased her and fed her vanity—gave her a feeling of power. At the same time she shrank away from it, subtly aware of possibilities she herself couldn't predict.

Helga's own feelings defeated inquiry, but honestly confronted, all pretense brushed aside, the dominant one, she suspected, was relief. At least, she felt no regret that tomorrow would mark the end of any claim she had upon him. The surety that the meeting would be a clash annoyed her, for she had no talent for quarreling—when possible she preferred to flee. That was all.

The family of James Vayle, in near-by Atlanta, would be glad. They had never liked the engagement, had never liked Helga Crane. Her own lack of family disconcerted them. No family. That was the crux of the whole matter. For Helga, it accounted for everything, her failure here in Naxos, her former loneliness in Nashville. It even accounted for her engagement to James. Negro society, she had learned, was as complicated and as rigid in its ramifications as the highest strata of white society. If you couldn't prove your ancestry and connections, you were tolerated, but you didn't "belong." You could be queer, or even attractive, or bad, or brilliant, or even love beauty and such nonsense if you were a Rankin, or a Leslie, or a Scoville; in other words, if you had a family. But if you were just plain Helga Crane, of whom nobody had ever heard, it was presumptuous of you to be anything but inconspicuous and conformable.

To relinquish James Vayle would most certainly be social suicide, for the Vayles were people of consequence. The fact that they were a "first family" had been one of James's attractions for the obscure Helga. She had wanted social background, but—she had not imagined that it could be so stuffy.

She made a quick movement of impatience and stood up. As she did so, the room whirled about her in an impish, hateful way. Familiar objects seemed suddenly unhappily distant. Faintness closed about her like a vise. She swayed, her small, slender hands gripping the chair arms for support. In a moment the faintness receded, leaving in its wake a sharp resentment at the trick which her strained nerves had played upon her. And after a moment's rest she got hurriedly into bed, leaving her room disorderly for the first time.

Books and papers scattered about the floor, fragile stockings and underthings and the startling green and gold negligee dripping about on chairs and stool, met the encounter of the amazed eyes of the girl who came in the morning to awaken Helga Crane.

II

She woke in the morning unrefreshed and with that feeling of half-terrified apprehension peculiar to Christmas and birthday mornings. A long moment she lay puzzling under the sun streaming in a golden flow through the yellow curtains. Then her mind returned to the night before. She had decided to leave Naxos. That was it.

Sharply she began to probe her decision. Reviewing the situation carefully, frankly, she felt no wish to change her resolution. Except—that it would be inconvenient. Much as she wanted to shake the dust of the place from her feet forever, she realized that there would be difficulties. Red tape. James Vayle. Money. Other work. Regretfully she was forced to acknowledge that it would be vastly better to wait until June, the close of the school year. Not so long, really. Half of March, April, May, some of June. Surely she could endure for that much longer conditions which she had borne for nearly two years. By an effort of will, her will, it could be done.

But this reflection, sensible, expedient, though it was, did not reconcile her. To remain seemed too hard. Could she do it? Was it possible in the present rebellious state of her feelings? The uneasy sense of being engaged with some formidable antagonist, nameless and ununderstood, startled her. It wasn't, she was suddenly aware, merely the school and its ways and its decorous stupid people that oppressed her. There was something else, some other more ruthless force, a quality within herself, which was frustrating her, had always frustrated her, kept her from getting the things she had wanted. Still wanted.

But just what did she want? Barring a desire for material security, gracious ways of living, a profusion of lovely clothes, and a goodly share of envious admiration, Helga Crane didn't know, couldn't tell. But there was, she knew, something else. Happiness, she supposed. Whatever that might be. What, exactly, she wondered, was happiness. Very positively she wanted it. Yet her conception of it had no tangibility. She couldn't define it, isolate it, and contemplate it as she could some other abstract things. Hatred, for instance. Or kindness.

The strident ringing of a bell somewhere in the building brought back the fierce resentment of the night. It crystallized her wavering determination.

From long habit her biscuit-coloured feet had slipped mechanically out from under the covers at the bell's first unkind jangle. Leisurely she drew them back and her cold anger vanished as she decided that, now, it didn't at all matter if she failed to appear at the monotonous distasteful breakfast which was provided for her by the school as part of her wages.

In the corridor beyond her door was a medley of noises incident to the rising and preparing for the day at the same hour of many schoolgirls—foolish giggling, indistinguishable snatches of merry conversation, distant gurgle of running water, patter of slippered feet, low-pitched singing, good-natured admonitions to hurry, slamming of doors, clatter of various unnamable articles, and—suddenly—calamitous silence.

Helga ducked her head under the covers in the vain attempt to shut out what she knew would fill the pregnant silence—the sharp sarcastic voice of the dormitory matron. It came.

"Well! Even if every last one of you did come from homes where you weren't taught any manners, you might at least try to pretend that you're capable of learning some here, now that you have the opportunity. Who slammed the shower-baths door?"

Silence.

"Well, you needn't trouble to answer. It's rude, as all of you know. But it's just as well, because none of you can tell the truth. Now hurry up. Don't let me hear of a single one of you being late for breakfast. If I do there'll be extra work for everybody on Saturday. And *please* at least try to act like ladies and not like savages from the backwoods."

On her side of the door, Helga was wondering if it had ever occurred to the lean and desiccated Miss MacGooden that most of her charges had actually come from the backwoods. Quite recently too. Miss MacGooden, humorless, prim, ugly, with a face like dried leather, prided herself on being a "lady" from one of the best families—an uncle had been a congressman in the period of the Reconstruction. She was therefore, Helga Crane reflected, perhaps unable to perceive that the inducement to act like a lady, her own acrimonious example, was slight, if not altogether negative. And thinking on Miss MacGooden's "ladyness," Helga grinned a little as she remembered that one's expressed reason for never having married, or intending to marry. There were, so she had been given to understand, things in the matrimonial state that were of necessity entirely too repulsive for a lady of delicate and sensitive nature to submit to.

Soon the forcibly shut-off noises began to be heard again, as the evidently vanishing image of Miss MacGooden evaporated from the short memories of the ladies-in-making. Preparations for the intake of the day's quota of learning went on again. Almost naturally.

"So much for that!" said Helga, getting herself out of bed.

She walked to the window and stood looking down into the great quadrangle below, at the multitude of students streaming from the six big dormitories which, two each, flanked three of its sides, and assembling into neat phalanxes preparatory to marching in military order to the sorry breakfast in Jones Hall on the fourth side. Here and there a male member of the faculty, important and resplendent in the regalia of an army officer, would pause in his prancing or strutting, to jerk a negligent or offending student into the proper attitude or place. The massed phalanxes increased in size and number, blotting out pavements, bare earth, and grass. And about it all was a depressing silence, a sullenness almost, until with a horrible abruptness the waiting band blared into "The Star Spangled Banner." The goosestep began. Left, right. Left, right. Forward! March! The automatons moved. The squares disintegrated into fours. Into twos. Disappeared into the gaping doors of Jones Hall. After the last pair of marchers had entered, the huge doors were closed. A few unlucky latecomers, apparently already discouraged, tugged half-heartedly at the knobs, and finding, as they had evidently expected, that they were indeed barred out, turned resignedly away.

Helga Crane turned away from the window, a shadow dimming the pale amber loveliness of her face. Seven o'clock it was now. At twelve those children who by some accident had been a little minute or two late would have their first meal after five hours of work and so-called education. Discipline, it was called.

There came a light knocking on her door.

"Come in," invited Helga unenthusiastically. The door opened to admit Margaret Creighton, another teacher in the English department and to Helga the most congenial member of the whole Naxos faculty. Margaret, she felt, appreciated her.

Seeing Helga still in night robe seated on the bedside in a mass of cushions, idly dangling a mule across bare toes like one with all the time in the world before her, she exclaimed in dismay: "Helga Crane, do you know what time it is? Why, it's long after half past seven. The students—"

"Yes, I know," said Helga defiantly, "the students are coming out from breakfast. Well, let them. I, for one, wish that there was some way that they could forever stay out from the poisonous stuff thrown at them, literally thrown at them, Margaret Creighton, for food. Poor things."

Margaret laughed. "That's just ridiculous sentiment, Helga, and you know it. But you haven't had any breakfast, yourself. Jim Vayle asked if you were sick. Of course nobody knew. You never tell anybody anything about yourself. I said I'd look in on you."

"Thanks awfully," Helga responded, indifferently. She was watching the sunlight dissolve from thick orange into pale yellow. Slowly it crept across the room, wiping out in its path the morning shadows. She wasn't interested in what the other was saying.

"If you don't hurry, you'll be late to your first class. Can I help you?" Margaret offered uncertainly. She was a little afraid of Helga. Nearly everyone was.

"No. Thanks all the same." Then quickly in another, warmer tone: "I do mean it. Thanks, a thousand times, Margaret. I'm really awfully grateful, but—you see, it's like this, I'm not going to be late to my class. I'm not going to be there at all."

The visiting girl, standing in relief, like old walnut against the buff-colored wall, darted a quick glance at Helga. Plainly she was curious. But she only said formally: "Oh, then you *are* sick." For something there was about Helga which discouraged questionings.

No, Helga wasn't sick. Not physically. She was merely disgusted. Fed up with Naxos. If that could be called sickness. The truth was that she had made up her mind to leave. That very day. She could no longer abide being connected with a place of shame, lies, hypocrisy, cruelty, servility, and snobbishness. "It ought," she concluded, "to be shut down by law."

"But, Helga, you can't go now. Not in the middle of the term." The kindly Margaret was distressed.

"But I can. And I am. Today."

"They'll never let you," prophesied Margaret.

"*They* can't stop me. Trains leave here for civilization every day. All that's needed is money," Helga pointed out.

"Yes, of course. Everybody knows that. What I mean is that you'll only hurt yourself in your profession. They won't give you a reference if you jump up and leave like this now. At this time of the year. You'll be put on the black list. And you'll find it hard to get another teaching-job. Naxos has enormous influence in the South. Better wait till school closes."

"Heaven forbid," answered Helga fervently, "that I should ever again want work anywhere in the South! I hate it." And fell silent, wondering for the hundredth time just what form of vanity it was that had induced an intelligent girl like Margaret Creighton to turn what was probably nice live crinkly hair, perfectly suited to her smooth dark skin and agreeable round features, into a dead straight, greasy, ugly mass.

Looking up from her watch, Margaret said: "Well, I've really got to run, or I'll be late myself. And since I'm staying— Better think it over, Helga. There's no place like

Naxos, you know. Pretty good salaries, decent rooms, plenty of men, and all that. Ta-ta." The door slid to behind her.

But in another moment it opened. She was back. "I do wish you'd stay. It's nice having you here, Helga. We all think so. Even the dead ones. We need a few decorations to brighten our sad lives." And again she was gone.

Helga was unmoved. She was no longer concerned with what anyone in Naxos might think of her, for she was now in love with the piquancy of leaving. Automatically her fingers adjusted the Chinese-looking pillows on the low couch that served for her bed. Her mind was busy with plans for departure. Packing, money, trains, and—could she get a berth?

III

On one side of the long, white, hot sand road that split the flat green, there was a little shade, for it was bordered with trees. Helga Crane walked there so that the sun could not so easily get at her. As she went slowly across the empty campus she was conscious of a vague tenderness for the scene spread out before her. It was so incredibly lovely, so appealing, and so facile. The trees in their spring beauty sent through her restive mind a sharp thrill of pleasure. Seductive, charming, and beckoning as cities were, they had not this easy unhuman loveliness. The trees, she thought, on city avenues and boulevards, in city parks and gardens, were tamed, held prisoners in a surrounding maze of human beings. Here they were free. It was human beings who were prisoners. It was too bad. In the midst of all this radiant life. They weren't, she knew, even conscious of its presence. Perhaps there was too much of it, and therefore it was less than nothing.

In response to her insistent demand she had been told that Dr. Anderson could give her twenty minutes at eleven o'clock. Well, she supposed that she could say all that she had to say in twenty minutes, though she resented being limited. Twenty minutes. In Naxos, she was as unimportant as that.

He was a new man, this principal, for whom Helga remembered feeling unaccountably sorry, when last September he had first been appointed to Naxos as its head. For some reason she had liked him, although she had seen little of him; he was so frequently away on publicity and money-raising tours. And as yet he had made but few and slight changes in the running of the school. Now she was a little irritated at finding herself wondering just how she was going to tell him of her decision. What did it matter to him? Why should she mind if it did? But there returned to her that indistinct sense of sympathy for the remote silent man with the tired gray eyes, and she wondered again by what fluke of fate such a man, apparently a humane and understanding person, had chanced into the command of this cruel educational machine. Suddenly, her own resolve loomed as an almost direct unkindness. This increased her annoyance and discomfort. A sense of defeat, of being cheated of justification, closed down on her. Absurd!

She arrived at the administration building in a mild rage, as unreasonable as it was futile, but once inside she had a sudden attack of nerves at the prospect of traversing that great outer room which was the workplace of some twenty odd people. This was a disease from which Helga had suffered at intervals all her life, and it was a point of honor, almost, with her never to give way to it. So, instead of turning away, as she felt inclined, she walked on, outwardly indifferent. Half-way down the long aisle which divided the room, the principal's secretary, a huge black man, surged toward her.

"Good-morning, Miss Crane, Dr. Anderson will see you in a few moments. Sit down right here."

She felt the inquiry in the shuttered eyes. For some reason this dissipated her self-consciousness and restored her poise. Thanking him, she seated herself, really careless now of the glances of the stenographers, book-keepers, clerks. Their curiosity and slightly veiled hostility no longer touched her. Her coming departure had released her from the need for conciliation which had irked her for so long. It was pleasant to Helga Crane to be able to sit calmly looking out of the window on to the smooth lawn, where a few leaves quite prematurely fallen dotted the grass, for once uncaring whether the frock which she wore roused disapproval or envy.

Turning from the window, her gaze wandered contemptuously over the dull attire of the women workers. Drab colors, mostly navy blue, black, brown, unrelieved, save for a scrap of white or tan about the hands and necks. Fragments of a speech made by the dean of women floated through her thoughts—"Bright colors are vulgar"—"Black, gray, brown, and navy blue are the most becoming colors for colored people"—"Dark-complected people shouldn't wear yellow, or green or red."—The dean was a woman from one of the "first families"—a great "race" woman; she, Helga Crane, a despised mulatto, but something intuitive, some unanalyzed driving spirit of loyalty to the inherent racial need for gorgeousness told her that bright colours *were* fitting and that dark-complexioned people *should* wear yellow, green, and red. Black, brown, and gray were ruinous to them, actually destroyed the luminous tones lurking in their dusky skins. One of the loveliest sights Helga had ever seen had been a sooty black girl decked out in a flaming orange dress, which a horrified matron had next day consigned to the dyer. Why, she wondered, didn't someone write *A Plea for Color?*

These people yapped loudly of race, of race consciousness, of race pride, and yet suppressed its most delightful manifestations, love of color, joy of rhythmic motion, naïve, spontaneous laughter. Harmony, radiance, and simplicity, all the essentials of spiritual beauty in the race they had marked for destruction.

She came back to her own problems. Clothes had been one of her difficulties in Naxos. Helga Crane loved clothes, elaborate ones. Nevertheless, she had tried not to offend. But with small success, for, although she had affected the deceptively simple variety, the hawk eyes of dean and matrons had detected the subtle difference from their own irreproachably conventional garments. Too, they felt that the colors were queer; dark purples, royal blues, rich greens, deep reds, in soft, luxurious woolens, or heavy, clinging silks. And the trimmings—when Helga used them at all—seemed to them odd. Old laces, strange embroideries, dim brocades. Her faultless, slim shoes made them uncomfortable and her small plain hats seemed to them positively indecent. Helga smiled inwardly at the thought that whenever there was an evening affair for the faculty, the dear ladies probably held their breaths until she made her appearance. They existed in constant fear that she might turn out in an evening dress. The proper evening wear in Naxos was afternoon attire. And one could, if one wished, garnish the hair with flowers.

Quick, muted footfalls sounded. The secretary had returned.

"Dr. Anderson will see you now, Miss Crane."

She rose, followed, and was ushered into the guarded sanctum, without having decided just what she was to say. For a moment she felt behind her the open doorway and then the gentle impact of its closing. Before her at a great desk her eyes picked out the figure of a man, at first blurred slightly in outline in that dimmer light. At his "Miss Crane?" her lips formed for speech, but no sound came. She was aware of inward confusion. For her the situation seemed charged, unaccountably, with strangeness and something very like hysteria. An almost overpowering desire to laugh seized her. Then, miraculously, a complete ease, such as she had never known in Naxos, possessed her. She smiled, nodded in answer to his questioning salutation, and with a gracious "Thank you" dropped into the chair which he indicated. She looked at him frankly now, this man still young, thirty-five perhaps, and found it easy to go on in the vein of a simple statement.

"Dr. Anderson, I'm sorry to have to confess that I've failed in my job here. I've made up my mind to leave. Today."

A short, almost imperceptible silence, then a deep voice of peculiarly pleasing resonance, asking gently: "You don't like Naxos, Miss Crane?"

She evaded. "Naxos, the place? Yes, I like it. Who wouldn't like it? It's so beautiful. But I—well—I don't seem to fit here."

The man smiled, just a little. "The school? You don't like the school?"

The words burst from her. "No, I don't like it. I hate it!"

"Why?" The question was detached, too detached.

In the girl blazed a desire to wound. There he sat, staring dreamily out of the window, blatantly unconcerned with her or her answer. Well, she'd tell him. She pronounced each word with deliberate slowness.

"Well, for one thing, I hate hypocrisy. I hate cruelty to students, and to teachers who can't fight back. I hate back-biting, and sneaking, and petty jealousy. Naxos? It's hardly a place at all. It's more like some loathsome, venomous disease. Ugh! Everybody spending his time in a malicious hunting for the weaknesses of others, spying, grudging, scratching."

"I see. And you don't think it might help to cure us, to have someone who doesn't approve of these things stay with us? Even just one person, Miss Crane?"

She wondered if this last was irony. She suspected it was humor and so ignored the half-pleading note in his voice.

"No, I don't! It doesn't do the disease any good. Only irritates it. And it makes me unhappy, dissatisfied. It isn't pleasant to be always made to appear in the wrong, even when I know I'm right."

His gaze was on her now, searching. "Queer," she thought, "how some brown people have gray eyes. Gives them a strange, unexpected appearance. A little frightening."

The man said, kindly: "Ah, you're unhappy. And for reasons you've stated?"

"Yes, partly. Then, too, the people here don't like me. They don't think I'm in the spirit of the work. And I'm not, not if it means suppression of individuality and beauty."

"And does it?"

"Well, it seems to work out that way."

"How old are you, Miss Crane?"

She resented this, but she told him, speaking with what curtness she could command only the bare figure: "Twenty-three."

"Twenty-three. I see. Some day you'll learn that lies, injustice, and hypocrisy are a part of every ordinary community. Most people achieve a sort of protective immunity, a kind of callousness, toward them. If they didn't, they couldn't endure. I think there's less of these evils here than in most places, but because we're trying to do such a big thing, to aim so high, the ugly things show more, they irk some of us more. Service is like clean white linen, even the tiniest speck shows." He went on, explaining, amplifying, pleading.

Helga Crane was silent, feeling a mystifying yearning which sang and throbbed in her. She felt again that urge for service, not now for her people, but for this man who was talking so earnestly of his work, his plans, his hopes. An insistent need to be a part of them sprang in her. With compunction tweaking at her heart for even having entertained the notion of deserting him, she resolved not only to remain until June, but to return next year. She was shamed, yet stirred. It was not sacrifice she felt now, but actual desire to stay, and to come back next year.

He came, at last, to the end of the long speech, only part of which she heard. "You see, you understand?" he urged.

"Yes, oh yes, I do."

"What we need is more people like you, people with a

sense of values, and proportion, an appreciation of the rarer things of life. You have something to give which we badly need here in Naxos. You mustn't desert us, Miss Crane."

She nodded, silent. He had won her. She knew that she would stay. "It's an elusive something," he went on. "Perhaps I can best explain it by the use of that trite phrase, 'You're a lady.' You have dignity and breeding."

At these words turmoil rose again in Helga Crane. The intricate pattern of the rug which she had been studying escaped her. The shamed feeling which had been her penance evaporated. Only a lacerated pride remained. She took firm hold of the chair arms to still the trembling of her fingers.

"If you're speaking of family, Dr. Anderson, why, I haven't any. I was born in a Chicago slum."

The man chose his words, carefully he thought. "That doesn't at all matter, Miss Crane. Financial, economic circumstances can't destroy tendencies inherited from good stock. You yourself prove that!"

Concerned with her own angry thoughts, which scurried here and there like trapped rats, Helga missed the import of his words. Her own words, her answer, fell like drops of hail.

"The joke is on you, Dr. Anderson. My father was a gambler who deserted my mother, a white immigrant. It is even uncertain that they were married. As I said at first, I don't belong here. I shall be leaving at once. This afternoon. Good-morning."

IV

Long, soft white clouds, clouds like shreds of incredibly fine cotton, streaked the blue of the early evening sky. Over the flying landscape hung a very faint mist, disturbed now and then by a languid breeze. But no coolness invaded the heat of the train rushing north. The open windows of the stuffy day coach, where Helga Crane sat with others of her race, seemed only to intensify her discomfort. Her head ached with a steady pounding pain. This, added to her wounds of the spirit, made traveling something little short of a medieval torture. Desperately she was trying to right the confusion in her mind. The temper of the morning's interview rose before her like an ugly mutilated creature crawling horribly over the flying landscape of her thoughts. It was no use. The ugly thing pressed down on her, held her. Leaning back, she tried to doze as others were doing. The futility of her effort exasperated her.

Just what had happened to her there in that cool dim room under the quizzical gaze of those piercing gray eyes? Whatever it was had been so powerful, so compelling, that but for a few chance words she would still be in Naxos. And why had she permitted herself to be jolted into a rage so fierce, so illogical, so disastrous, that now after it was spent she sat despondent, sunk in shameful contrition? As she reviewed the manner of her departure from his presence, it seemed increasingly rude.

She didn't, she told herself, after all, like this Dr. Anderson. He was too controlled, too sure of himself and others. She detested cool, perfectly controlled people. Well, it didn't matter. He didn't matter. But she could not put him from her mind. She set it down to annoyance because of the cold discourtesy of her abrupt action. She disliked rudeness in anyone.

She had outraged her own pride, and she had terribly wronged her mother by her insidious implication. Why? Her thoughts lingered with her mother, long dead. A fair Scandinavian girl in love with life, with love, with passion, dreaming, and risking all in one blind surrender. A cruel sacrifice. In forgetting all but love she had forgotten, or perhaps never known, that some things the world never forgives. But as Helga knew, she had remembered, or had learned in suffering and longing all the rest of her life. Her daughter hoped she had been happy, happy beyond most human creatures, in the little time it had lasted, the little time before that gay suave scoundrel, Helga's father, had left her. But Helga Crane doubted it. How could she have been? A girl gently bred, fresh from an older, more polished civilization, flung into poverty, sordidness, and dissipation. She visualized her now, sad, cold, and—yes, remote. The tragic cruelties of the years had left her a little pathetic, a little hard, and a little unapproachable.

That second marriage, to a man of her own race, but not of her own kind—so passionately, so instinctively resented by Helga even at the trivial age of six—she now understood as a grievous necessity. Even foolish, despised women must have food and clothing; even unloved little Negro girls must be somehow provided for. Memory, flown back to those years following the marriage, dealt her torturing stabs. Before her rose the pictures of her mother's careful management to avoid those ugly scarifying quarrels which even at this far-off time caused an uncontrollable shudder, her own childish self-effacement, the savage unkindness of her step-brothers and sisters, and the jealous, malicious hatred of her mother's husband. Summers, winters, years, passing in one long, changeless stretch of aching misery of soul. Her mother's death, when Helga was fifteen. Her rescue by Uncle Peter, who had sent her to school, a school for Negroes, where for the first time she could breathe freely, where she discovered that because one was dark, one was not necessarily loathsome, and could, therefore, consider oneself without repulsion.

Six years. She had been happy there, as happy as a child unused to happiness dared be. There had been always a feeling of strangeness, of outsideness, and one of holding her breath for fear that it wouldn't last. It hadn't. It had dwindled gradually into eclipse of painful isolation. As she grew older, she became gradually aware of a difference between herself and the girls about her. They had mothers, fathers, brothers, and sisters of whom they spoke frequently, and who sometimes visited them. They went home for the vacations which Helga spent in the city where the school was located. They visited each other and knew many of the same people. Discontent for which there was no remedy crept upon her, and she was glad almost when these most peaceful years which she had yet known came to their end. She had been happier, but still horribly lonely.

She had looked forward with pleasant expectancy to working in Naxos when the chance came. And now this! What was it that stood in her way? Helga Crane couldn't explain it, put a name to it. She had tried in the early afternoon in her gentle but staccato talk with James Vayle. Even to herself her explanation had sounded inane and insufficient; no wonder James had been impatient and unbelieving. During their brief and unsatisfactory conversation she had had an odd feeling that he felt somehow cheated. And more than once she had been aware of a suggestion of suspicion in his attitude, a feeling that he was being duped, that he suspected her of some hidden purpose which he was attempting to discover.

Well, that was over. She would never be married to James Vayle now. It flashed upon her that, even had she remained in Naxos, she would never have been married to him. She couldn't have married him. Gradually, too, there stole into her thoughts of him a curious sensation of repugnance, for which she was at a loss to account. It was new, something unfelt before. Certainly she had never loved him overwhelmingly, not, for example, as her mother must have loved her father, but she *had* liked him, and she had expected to love him, after their marriage. People generally did love then, she imagined. No, she had not loved James, but she had wanted to. Acute nausea rose in her as she recalled the slight quivering of his lips sometimes when her hands had unexpectedly touched his; the throbbing vein in his forehead on a gay day when they had wandered off alone across the low hills and she had allowed him frequent kisses under the shelter of some low-hanging willows. Now she shivered a little, even in the hot train, as if she had suddenly come out from a warm scented place into cool, clear air. She must have been mad, she thought; but she couldn't tell why she thought so. This, too, bothered her.

Laughing conversation buzzed about her. Across the aisle a bronze baby, with bright staring eyes, began a fretful whining, which its young mother essayed to silence by a low droning croon. In the seat just beyond, a black and tan young pair were absorbed in the eating of a cold fried chicken, audibly crunching the ends of the crisp, browned bones. A little distance away a tired laborer slept noisily. Near him two children dropped the peelings of oranges and bananas on the already soiled floor. The smell of stale food and ancient tobacco irritated Helga like a physical pain. A man, a white man, strode through the packed car and spat twice, once in the exact centre of the dingy door panel, and once into the receptacle which held the drinking-water. Instantly Helga became aware of stinging thirst. Her eyes sought the small watch at her wrist. Ten hours to Chicago. Would she be lucky enough to prevail upon the conductor to let her occupy a berth, or would she have to remain here all night, without sleep, without food, without drink, and with that disgusting door panel to which her purposely averted eyes were constantly, involuntarily straying?

Her first effort was unsuccessful. An ill-natured "No, you know you can't," was the answer to her inquiry. But farther on along the road, there was a change of men. Her rebuff had made her reluctant to try again, but the entry of a farmer carrying a basket containing live chickens, which he deposited on the seat (the only vacant one) beside her, strengthened her weakened courage. Timidly, she approached the new conductor, an elderly gray-mustached man of pleasant appearance, who subjected her to a keen, appraising look, and then promised to see what could be done. She thanked him, gratefully, and went back to her shared seat, to wait anxiously. After half an hour he returned, saying he could "fix her up," there was a section she could have, adding: "It'll cost you ten dollars." She murmured: "All right.

Thank you." It was twice the price, and she needed every penny, but she knew she was fortunate to get it even at that, and so was very thankful, as she followed his tall, loping figure out of that car and through seemingly endless others, and at last into one where she could rest a little.

She undressed and lay down, her thoughts still busy with the morning's encounter. Why hadn't she grasped his meaning? Why, if she said so much, hadn't she said more about herself and her mother? He would, she was sure, have understood, even sympathized. Why had she lost her temper and given way to angry half-truths?—Angry half-truths—Angry half—

V

Gray Chicago seethed, surged, and scurried about her. Helga shivered a little, drawing her light coat closer. She had forgotten how cold March could be under the pale skies of the North. But she liked it, this blustering wind. She would even have welcomed snow, for it would more clearly have marked the contrast between this freedom and the cage which Naxos had been to her. Not but what it was marked plainly enough by the noise, the dash, the crowds.

Helga Crane, who had been born in this dirty, mad, hurrying city had no home here. She had not even any friends here. It would have to be, she decided, the Young Women's Christian Association. "Oh dear! The uplift. Poor, poor colored people. Well, no use stewing about it. I'll get a taxi to take me out, bag and baggage, then I'll have a hot bath and a really good meal, peep into the shops—mustn't buy anything—and then for Uncle Peter. Guess I won't phone. More effective if I surprise him."

It was late, very late, almost evening, when finally Helga turned her steps northward, in the direction of Uncle Peter's home. She had put it off as long as she could, for she detested her errand. The fact that one day had shown her its acute necessity did not decrease her distaste. As she approached the North Side, the distaste grew. Arrived at last at the familiar door of the old stone house, her confidence in Uncle Peter's welcome deserted her. She gave the bell a timid push and then decided to turn away, to go back to her room and phone, or, better yet, to write. But before she could retreat, the door was opened by a strange red-faced maid, dressed primly in black and white. This increased Helga's mistrust. Where, she wondered, was the ancient Rose, who had, ever since she could remember, served her uncle.

The hostile "Well?" of this new servant forcibly recalled the reason for her presence there. She said firmly: "Mr. Nilssen, please."

"Mr. Nilssen's not in," was the pert retort. "Will you see Mrs. Nilssen?"

Helga was startled. "Mrs. Nilssen! I beg your pardon, did you say Mrs. Nilssen?"

"I did," answered the maid shortly, beginning to close the door.

"What is it, Ida?" A woman's soft voice sounded from within.

"Someone for Mr. Nilssen, m'am." The girl looked embarrassed.

In Helga's face the blood rose in a deep-red stain. She explained: "Helga Crane, his niece."

"She says she's his niece, m'am."

"Well, have her come in."

There was no escape. She stood in the large reception hall, and was annoyed to find herself actually trembling. A woman, tall, exquisitely gowned, with shining gray hair piled high, came forward murmuring in a puzzled voice: "His niece, did you say?"

"Yes, Helga Crane. My mother was his sister, Karen Nilssen. I've been away. I didn't know Uncle Peter had mar-

ried." Sensitive to atmosphere, Helga had felt at once the
latent antagonism in the woman's manner.

"Oh, yes! I remember about you now. I'd forgotten for a
moment. *Well*, he isn't exactly your uncle, is he? Your mother
wasn't married, was she? I mean, to your father?"

"I—I don't know," stammered the girl, feeling pushed
down to the uttermost depths of ignominy.

"Of course she wasn't." The clear, low voice held a positive note. "Mr. Nilssen has been very kind to you, supported
you, sent you to school. But you mustn't expect anything
else. And you mustn't come here any more. It—well, frankly,
it isn't convenient. I'm sure an intelligent girl like yourself
can understand that."

"Of course," Helga agreed, coldly, freezingly, but her lips
quivered. She wanted to get away as quickly as possible. She
reached the door. There was a second of complete silence,
then Mrs. Nilssen's voice, a little agitated: "And please remember that my husband is not your uncle. No indeed!
Why, that, that would make me your aunt! He's not—"

But at last the knob had turned in Helga's fumbling hand.
She gave a little unpremeditated laugh and slipped out.
When she was in the street, she ran. Her only impulse was to
get as far away from her uncle's house, and this woman, his
wife, who so plainly wished to dissociate herself from the
outrage of her very existence. She was torn with mad fright,
an emotion against which she knew but two weapons: to kick
and scream, or to flee.

The day had lengthened. It was evening and much colder,
but Helga Crane was unconscious of any change, so shaken
she was and burning. The wind cut her like a knife, but she
did not feel it. She ceased her frantic running, aware at last
of the curious glances of passersby. At one spot, for a moment less frequented than others, she stopped to give heed
to her disordered appearance. Here a man, well groomed
and pleasant-spoken, accosted her. On such occasions she
was wont to reply scathingly, but, tonight, his pale Caucasian

face struck her breaking faculties as too droll. Laughing harshly, she threw at him the words: "You're not my uncle."

He retired in haste, probably thinking her drunk, or possibly a little mad.

Night fell, while Helga Crane in the rushing swiftness of a roaring elevated train sat numb. It was as if all the bogies and goblins that had beset her unloved, unloving, and unhappy childhood had come to life with tenfold power to hurt and frighten. For the wound was deeper in that her long freedom from their presence had rendered her the more vulnerable. Worst of all was the fact that under the stinging hurt she understood and sympathized with Mrs. Nilssen's point of view, as always she had been able to understand her mother's, her stepfather's, and his children's points of view. She saw herself for an obscene sore in all their lives, at all costs to be hidden. She understood, even while she resented. It would have been easier if she had not.

Later in the bare silence of her tiny room she remembered the unaccomplished object of her visit. Money. Characteristically, while admitting its necessity, and even its undeniable desirability, she dismissed its importance. Its elusive quality she had as yet never known. She would find work of some kind. Perhaps the library. The idea clung. Yes, certainly the library. She knew books and loved them.

She stood intently looking down into the glimmering street, far below, swarming with people, merging into little eddies and disengaging themselves to pursue their own individual ways. A few minutes later she stood in the doorway, drawn by an uncontrollable desire to mingle with the crowd. The purple sky showed tremulous clouds piled up, drifting here and there with a sort of endless lack of purpose. Very like the myriad human beings pressing hurriedly on. Looking at these, Helga caught herself wondering who they were, what they did, and of what they thought. What was passing behind those dark molds of flesh. Did they really think at all? Yet, as she stepped out into the moving multi-colored crowd, there came to her a queer feeling of enthusiasm, as if she were tasting some agreeable, exotic food—sweetbreads, smothered with truffles and mushrooms—perhaps. And, oddly enough, she felt, too, that she had come home. She, Helga Crane, who had no home.

VI

Helga woke to the sound of rain. The day was leaden gray, and misty black, and dullish white. She was not surprised, the night had promised it. She made a little frown, remembering that it was today that she was to search for work.

She dressed herself carefully, in the plainest garments she possessed, a suit of fine blue twill faultlessly tailored, from whose left pocket peeped a gay kerchief, an unadorned, heavy silk blouse, a small, smart, fawn-colored hat, and slim, brown oxfords, and chose a brown umbrella. In a nearby street she sought out an appealing little restaurant, which she had noted in her last night's ramble through the neighborhood, for the thick cups and the queer dark silver of the Young Women's Christian Association distressed her.

After a slight breakfast she made her way to the library, that ugly, gray building, where was housed much knowledge and a little wisdom, on interminable shelves. The friendly person at the desk in the hall bestowed on her a kindly smile when Helga stated her business and asked for directions.

"The corridor to your left, then the second door to your right," she was told.

Outside the indicated door, for half a second she hesitated, then braced herself and went in. In less than a quarter of an hour she came out, in surprised disappointment. "Library training"—"civil service"—"library school"—"classification" — "cataloguing" — "probation period" —flitted through her mind.

"How erudite they must be!" she remarked sarcastically to herself, and ignored the smiling curiosity of the desk person as she went through the hall to the street. For a long moment she stood on the high stone steps above the avenue, then shrugged her shoulders and stepped down. It *was* a disappointment, but of course there were other things. She would find something else. But what? Teaching, even substitute teaching, was hopeless now, in March. She had no business training, and the shops didn't employ colored clerks or sales-people, not even the smaller ones. She couldn't sew, she couldn't cook. Well, she *could* do housework, or wait on tables, for a short time at least. Until she got a little money together. With this thought she remembered that the Young Women's Christian Association maintained an employment agency.

"Of course, the very thing!" She exclaimed, aloud. "I'll go straight back."

But, though the day was still dreary, rain had ceased to fall, and Helga, instead of returning, spent hours in aimless strolling about the hustling streets of the Loop district. When at last she did retrace her steps, the business day had ended, and the employment office was closed. This frightened her a little, this and the fact that she had spent money, too much money, for a book and a tapestry purse, things which she wanted, but did not need and certainly could not afford. Regretful and dismayed, she resolved to go without her dinner, as a self-inflicted penance, as well as an economy —and she would be at the employment office the first thing tomorrow morning.

But it was not until three days more had passed that Helga Crane sought the Association, or any other employment office. And then it was sheer necessity that drove her there, for her money had dwindled to a ridiculous sum. She had put off the hated moment, had assured herself that she was tired, needed a bit of vacation, was due one. It had been pleasant, the leisure, the walks, the lake, the shops and streets with their gay colors, their movement, after the great quiet of Naxos. Now she was panicky.

In the office a few nondescript women sat scattered about

on the long rows of chairs. Some were plainly uninterested, others wore an air of acute expectancy, which disturbed Helga. Behind a desk two alert young women, both wearing a superior air, were busy writing upon and filing countless white cards. Now and then one stopped to answer the telephone.

"Y.W.C.A. employment. . . . Yes. . . . Spell it, please. . . . Sleep in or out? Thirty dollars? . . . Thank you, I'll send one right over."

Or, "I'm awfully sorry, we haven't anybody right now, but I'll send you the first one that comes in."

Their manners were obtrusively business-like, but they ignored the already embarrassed Helga. Diffidently she approached the desk. The darker of the two looked up and turned on a little smile.

"Yes?" she inquired.

"I wonder if you can help me? I want work," Helga stated simply.

"Maybe. What kind? Have you references?"

Helga explained. She was a teacher. A graduate of Devon. Had been teaching in Naxos.

The girl was not interested. "Our kind of work wouldn't do for you," she kept repeating at the end of each of Helga's statements. "Domestic mostly."

When Helga said that she was willing to accept work of any kind, a slight, almost imperceptible change crept into her manner and her perfunctory smile disappeared. She repeated her question about the reference. On learning that Helga had none, she said sharply, finally: "I'm sorry, but we never send out help without references."

With a feeling that she had been slapped, Helga Crane hurried out. After some lunch she sought out an employment agency on State Street. An hour passed in patient sitting. Then came her turn to be interviewed. She said, simply, that she wanted work, work of any kind. A competent young woman, whose eyes stared frog-like from great tortoise-shell-rimmed glasses, regarded her with an appraising look and asked for her history, past and present, not forgetting the "references." Helga told her that she was a graduate of Devon, had taught in Naxos. But even before she arrived at the explanation of the lack of references, the other's interest in her had faded.

"I'm sorry, but we have nothing that you would be interested in," she said and motioned to the next seeker, who immediately came forward, proffering several much worn papers.

"References," thought Helga, resentfully, bitterly, as she went out the door into the crowded garish street in search of another agency, where her visit was equally vain.

Days of this sort of thing. Weeks of it. And of the futile scanning and answering of newspaper advertisements. She traversed acres of streets, but it seemed that in that whole energetic place nobody wanted her services. At least not the kind that she offered. A few men, both white and black, offered her money, but the price of the money was too dear. Helga Crane did not feel inclined to pay it.

She began to feel terrified and lost. And she was a little hungry too, for her small money was dwindling and she felt the need to economize somehow. Food was the easiest.

In the midst of her search for work she felt horribly lonely too. This sense of loneliness increased, it grew to appalling proportions, encompassing her, shutting her off from all of life around her. Devastated she was, and always on the verge of weeping. It made her feel small and insignificant that in all the climbing massed city no one cared one whit about her.

Helga Crane was not religious. She took nothing on trust. Nevertheless on Sundays she attended the very fashionable, very high services in the Negro Episcopal church on Michigan Avenue. She hoped that some good Christian would speak to her, invite her to return, or inquire kindly if she was a stranger in the city. None did, and she became bitter, distrusting religion more than ever. She was herself unconscious of that faint hint of offishness which hung about her and repelled advances, an arrogance that stirred in people a peculiar irritation. They noticed her, admired her clothes, but that was all, for the self-sufficient uninterested manner adopted instinctively as a protective measure for her acute sensitiveness, in her child days, still clung to her.

An agitated feeling of disaster closed in on her, tightened. Then, one afternoon, coming in from the discouraging round of agencies and the vain answering of newspaper wants to the stark neatness of her room, she found between door and sill a small folded note. Spreading it open, she read:

MISS CRANE:

Please come into the employment office as soon as you return.

IDA ROSS

Helga spent some time in the contemplation of this note. She was afraid to hope. Its possibilities made her feel a little hysterical. Finally, after removing the dirt of the dusty streets, she went down, down to that room where she had first felt the smallness of her commercial value. Subsequent failures had augmented her feeling of incompetence, but she resented the fact that these clerks were evidently aware of her unsuccess. It required all the pride and indifferent hauteur she could summon to support her in their presence. Her additional arrogance passed unnoticed by those for whom it was assumed. They were interested only in the business for which they had summoned her, that of procuring a traveling-companion for a lecturing female on her way to a convention.

"She wants," Miss Ross told Helga, "someone intelligent, someone who can help her get her speeches in order on the train. We thought of you right away. Of course, it isn't permanent. She'll pay your expenses and there'll be twenty-five dollars besides. She leaves tomorrow. Here's her address.

You're to go to see her at five o'clock. It's after four now. I'll phone that you're on your way."

The presumptuousness of their certainty that she would snatch at the opportunity galled Helga. She became aware of a desire to be disagreeable. The inclination to fling the address of the lecturing female in their face stirred in her, but she remembered the lone five-dollar bill in the rare old tapestry purse swinging from her arm. She couldn't afford anger. So she thanked them very politely and set out for the home of Mrs. Hayes-Rore on Grand Boulevard, knowing full well that she intended to take the job, if the lecturing one would take her. Twenty-five dollars was not to be looked at with nose in air when one was the owner of but five. And meals—meals for four days at least.

Mrs. Hayes-Rore proved to be a plump lemon-colored woman with badly straightened hair and dirty finger-nails. Her direct, penetrating gaze was somewhat formidable. Notebook in hand, she gave Helga the impression of having risen early for consultation with other harassed authorities on the race problem, and having been in conference on the subject all day. Evidently, she had had little time or thought for the careful donning of the five-years-behind-the-mode garments which covered her, and which even in their youth could hardly have fitted or suited her. She had a tart personality, and prying. She approved of Helga, after asking her endless questions about her education and her opinions on the race problem, none of which she was permitted to answer for Mrs. Hayes-Rore either went on to the next or answered the question herself by remarking: "Not that it matters, if you can only do what I want done, and the girls at the 'Y' said that you could. I'm on the Board of Managers, and I know they wouldn't send me anybody who wasn't all right." After this had been repeated twice in a booming, oratorical voice, Helga felt that the Association secretaries had taken an awful chance in sending a person about whom they knew as little as they did about her.

"Yes, I'm sure you'll do. I don't really need ideas, I've

plenty of my own. It's just a matter of getting someone to
help me get my speeches in order, correct and condense
them, you know. I leave at eleven in the morning. Can you
be ready by then? . . . That's good. Better be here at nine.
Now, don't disappoint me. I'm depending on you."

As she stepped into the street and made her way skillfully
through the impassioned human traffic, Helga reviewed the
plan which she had formed, while in the lecturing one's
presence, to remain in New York. There would be twenty-
five dollars, and perhaps the amount of her return ticket.
Enough for a start. Surely she could get work there. Everybody did. Anyway, she would have a reference.

With her decision she felt reborn. She began happily to
paint the future in vivid colors. The world had changed to
silver, and life ceased to be a struggle and became a gay
adventure. Even the advertisements in the shop windows
seemed to shine with radiance.

Curious about Mrs. Hayes-Rore, on her return to the "Y"
she went into the employment office, ostensibly to thank the
girls and to report that that important woman would take
her. Was there, she inquired, anything that she needed to
know? Mrs. Hayes-Rore had appeared to put such faith in
their recommendation of her that she felt almost obliged to
give satisfaction. And she added: "I didn't get much chance
to ask questions. She seemed so—er—busy."

Both the girls laughed. Helga laughed with them, surprised that she hadn't perceived before how really likable
they were.

"We'll be through here in ten minutes. If you're not busy,
come in and have your supper with us and we'll tell you
about her," promised Miss Ross.

VII

Having finally turned her attention to Helga Crane, Fortune now seemed determined to smile, to make amends for her shameful neglect. One had, Helga decided, only to touch the right button, to press the right spring, in order to attract the jade's notice.

For Helga that spring had been Mrs. Hayes-Rore. Ever afterwards on recalling that day on which with wellnigh empty purse and apprehensive heart she had made her way from the Young Women's Christian Association to the Grand Boulevard home of Mrs. Hayes-Rore, always she wondered at her own lack of astuteness in not seeing in the woman someone who by a few words was to have a part in the shaping of her life.

The husband of Mrs. Hayes-Rore had at one time been a dark thread in the soiled fabric of Chicago's South Side politics, who, departing this life hurriedly and unexpectedly and a little mysteriously, and somewhat before the whole of his suddenly acquired wealth had had time to vanish, had left his widow comfortably established with money and some of that prestige which in Negro circles had been his. All this Helga had learned from the secretaries at the "Y." And from numerous remarks dropped by Mrs. Hayes-Rore herself she was able to fill in the details more or less adequately.

On the train that carried them to New York, Helga had made short work of correcting and condensing the speeches, which Mrs. Hayes-Rore as a prominent "race" woman and an authority on the problem was to deliver before several meetings of the annual convention of the Negro Women's League of Clubs, convening the next week in New York. These speeches proved to be merely patchworks of others' speeches and opinions. Helga had heard other lecturers say the same things in Devon and again in Naxos. Ideas, phrases, and even whole sentences and paragraphs were lifted bodily from previous orations and published works of Wendell Phillips, Frederick Douglass, Booker T. Washington, and other doctors of the race's ills. For variety Mrs. Hayes-Rore had seasoned hers with a peppery dash of Du Bois and a few vinegary statements of her own. Aside from these it was, Helga reflected, the same old thing.

But Mrs. Hayes-Rore was to her, after the first short, awkward period, interesting. Her dark eyes, bright and investigating, had, Helga noted, a humorous gleam, and something in the way she held her untidy head gave the impression of a cat watching its prey so that when she struck, if she so decided, the blow would be unerringly effective. Helga, looking up from a last reading of the speeches, was aware that she was being studied. Her employer sat leaning back, the tips of her fingers pressed together, her head a bit on one side, her small inquisitive eyes boring into the girl before her. And as the train hurled itself frantically toward smoke-infested Newark, she decided to strike.

"Now tell me," she commanded, "how is it that a nice girl like you can rush off on a wildgoose chase like this at a moment's notice. I should think your people'd object, or'd make inquiries, or something."

At that command Helga Crane could not help sliding down her eyes to hide the anger that had risen in them. Was she to be forever explaining her people—or lack of them. But she said courteously enough, even managing a hard little smile: "Well you see, Mrs. Hayes-Rore, I haven't any people. There's only me, so I can do as I please."

"Ha!" said Mrs. Hayes-Rore.

Terrific, thought Helga Crane, the power of that sound from the lips of this woman. How, she wondered, had she succeeded in investing it with so much incredulity.

"If you didn't have people, you wouldn't be living. Everybody has people, Miss Crane. Everybody."

"I haven't, Mrs. Hayes-Rore."

Mrs. Hayes-Rore screwed up her eyes. "Well, that

mighty mysterious, and I detest mysteries." She shrugged, and into those eyes there now came with alarming quickness an accusing criticism.

"It isn't," Helga said defensively, "a mystery. It's a fact and a mighty unpleasant one. Inconvenient too," and she laughed a little, not wishing to cry.

Her tormentor, in sudden embarrassment, turned her sharp eyes to the window. She seemed intent on the miles of red clay sliding past. After a moment, however, she asked gently: "You wouldn't like to tell me about it, would you? It seems to bother you. And I'm interested in girls."

Annoyed, but still hanging, for the sake of the twenty-five dollars, to her self-control, Helga gave her head a little toss and flung out her hands in a helpless, beaten way. Then she shrugged. What did it matter? "Oh, well, if you really want to know. I assure you, it's nothing interesting. Or nasty," she added maliciously. "It's just plain horrid. For me." And she began mockingly to relate her story.

But as she went on, again she had that sore sensation of revolt, and again the torment which she had gone through loomed before her as something brutal and undeserved. Passionately, tearfully, incoherently, the final words tumbled from her quivering petulant lips.

The other woman still looked out of the window, apparently so interested in the outer aspect of the drab sections of the Jersey manufacturing city through which they were passing that, the better to see, she had now so turned her head that only an ear and a small portion of cheek were visible.

During the little pause that followed Helga's recital, the faces of the two women, which had been bare, seemed to harden. It was almost as if they had slipped on masks. The girl wished to hide her turbulent feeling and to appear indifferent to Mrs. Hayes-Rore's opinion of her story. The woman felt that the story, dealing as it did with race intermingling and possibly adultery, was beyond definite discussion. For among black people, as among white people, it is tacitly understood that these things are not mentioned—and therefore they do not exist.

Sliding adroitly out from under the precarious subject to a safer, more decent one, Mrs. Hayes-Rore asked Helga what she was thinking of doing when she got back to Chicago. Had she anything in mind?

Helga, it appeared, hadn't. The truth was she had been thinking of staying in New York. Maybe she could find something there. Everybody seemed to. At least she could make the attempt.

Mrs. Hayes-Rore sighed, for no obvious reason. "Um, maybe I can help you. I know people in New York. Do you?"

"No."

"New York's the lonesomest place in the world if you don't know anybody."

"It couldn't possibly be worse than Chicago," said Helga savagely, giving the table support a violent kick.

They were running into the shadow of the tunnel. Mrs. Hayes-Rore murmured thoughtfully: "You'd better come uptown and stay with me a few days. I may need you. Something may turn up."

It was one of those vicious mornings, windy and bright. There seemed to Helga, as they emerged from the depths of the vast station, to be a whirling malice in the sharp air of this shining city. Mrs. Hayes-Rore's words about its terrible loneliness shot through her mind. She felt its aggressive unfriendliness. Even the great buildings, the flying cabs, and the swirling crowds seemed manifestations of purposed malevolence. And for that first short minute she was awed and frightened and inclined to turn back to that other city, which, though not kind, was yet not strange. This New York seemed somehow more appalling, more scornful, in some inexplicable way even more terrible and uncaring than Chicago. Threatening almost. Ugly. Yes, perhaps she'd better turn back.

The feeling passed, escaped in the surprise of what Mrs. Hayes-Rore was saying. Her oratorical voice boomed above the city's roar. "I suppose I ought really to have phoned Anne from the station. About you, I mean. Well, it doesn't matter. She's got plenty of room. Lives alone in a big house, which is something Negroes in New York don't do. They fill 'em up with lodgers usually. But Anne's funny. Nice, though. You'll like her, and it will be good for you to know her if you're going to stay in New York. She's a widow, my husband's sister's son's wife. The war, you know."

"Oh," protested Helga Crane, with a feeling of acute misgiving, "but won't she be annoyed and inconvenienced by having me brought in on her like this? I supposed we were going to the 'Y' or a hotel or something like that. Oughtn't we really to stop and phone?"

The woman at her side in the swaying cab smiled, a peculiar invincible, self-reliant smile, but gave Helga Crane's suggestion no other attention. Plainly she was a person accustomed to having things her way. She merely went on talking of other plans. "I think maybe I can get you some work. With a new Negro insurance company. They're after me to put quite a tidy sum into it. Well, I'll just tell them that they may as well take you with the money," and she laughed.

"Thanks awfully," Helga said, "but will they like it? I mean being made to take me because of the money."

"They're not being made," contradicted Mrs. Hayes-Rore. "I intended to let them have the money anyway, and I'll tell Mr. Darling so—after he takes you. They ought to be glad to get you. Colored organizations always need more brains as well as more money. Don't worry. And don't thank me again. You haven't got the job yet, you know."

There was a little silence, during which Helga gave herself up to the distraction of watching the strange city and the strange crowds, trying hard to put out of her mind the vision of an easier future which her companion's words had conjured up; for, as had been pointed out, it was, as yet, only a possibility.

Turning out of the park into the broad thoroughfare of Lenox Avenue, Mrs. Hayes-Rore said in a too carefully ca-

sual manner: "And, by the way, I wouldn't mention that my
people are white, if I were you. Colored people won't understand it, and after all it's your own business. When you've
lived as long as I have, you'll know that what others don't
know can't hurt you. I'll just tell Anne that you're a friend of
mine whose mother's dead. That'll place you well enough
and it's all true. I never tell lies. She can fill in the gaps to suit
herself and anyone curious enough to ask."

"Thanks," Helga said again. And so great was her gratitude that she reached out and took her new friend's slightly
soiled hand in one of her own fastidious ones, and retained it
until their cab turned into a pleasant tree-lined street and
came to a halt before one of the dignified houses in the
center of the block. Here they got out.

In after years Helga Crane had only to close her eyes to
see herself standing apprehensively in the small cream-
colored hall, the floor of which was covered with deep silver-
hued carpet; to see Mrs. Hayes-Rore pecking the cheek of
the tall slim creature beautifully dressed in a cool green
tailored frock; to hear herself being introduced to "my
niece, Mrs. Grey" and "Miss Crane, a little friend of mine
whose mother's died, and I think perhaps a while in New
York will be good for her"; to feel her hand grasped in quick
sympathy, and to hear Anne Grey's pleasant voice, with its
faint note of wistfulness, saying: "I'm so sorry, and I'm glad
Aunt Jeanette brought you here. Did you have a good trip?
I'm sure you must be worn out. I'll have Lillie take you right
up." And to feel like a criminal.

VIII

A year thick with various adventures had sped by since that
spring day on which Helga Crane had set out away from
Chicago's indifferent unkindness for New York in the company of Mrs. Hayes-Rore. New York she had found not so

unkind, not so unfriendly, not so indifferent. There she had been happy, and secured work, had made acquaintances and another friend. Again she had had that strange transforming experience, this time not so fleetingly, that magic sense of having come home. Harlem, teeming black Harlem, had welcomed her and lulled her into something that was, she was certain, peace and contentment.

The request and recommendation of Mrs. Hayes-Rore had been sufficient for her to obtain work with the insurance company in which that energetic woman was interested. And through Anne it had been possible for her to meet and to know people with tastes and ideas similar to her own. Their sophisticated cynical talk, their elaborate parties, the unobrusive correctness of their clothes and homes, all appealed to her craving for smartness, for enjoyment. Soon she was able to reflect with a flicker of amusement on that constant feeling of humiliation and inferiority which had encompassed her in Naxos. Her New York friends looked with contempt and scorn on Naxos and all its works. This gave Helga a pleasant sense of avengement. Any shreds of self-consciousness or apprehension which at first she may have felt vanished quickly, escaped in the keenness of her joy at seeming at last to belong somewhere. For she considered that she had, as she put it, "found herself."

Between Anne Grey and Helga Crane there had sprung one of those immediate and peculiarly sympathetic friendships. Uneasy at first, Helga had been relieved that Anne had never returned to the uncomfortable subject of her mother's death so intentionally mentioned on their first meeting by Mrs. Hayes-Rore, beyond a tremulous brief: "You won't talk to me about it, will you? I can't bear the thought of death. Nobody ever talks to me about it. My husband, you know." This Helga discovered to be true. Later, when she knew Anne better, she suspected that it was a bit of a pose assumed for the purpose of doing away with the necessity of speaking regretfully of a husband who had been perhaps not too greatly loved.

After the first pleasant weeks, feeling that her obligation
to Anne was already too great, Helga began to look about
for a permanent place to live. It was, she found, difficult. She
eschewed the "Y" as too bare, impersonal, and restrictive.
Nor did furnished rooms or the idea of a solitary or a shared
apartment appeal to her. So she rejoiced when one day
Anne, looking up from her book, said lightly: "Helga, since
you're going to be in New York, why don't you stay here with
me? I don't usually take people. It's too disrupting. Still, it *is*
sort of pleasant having somebody in the house and I don't
seem to mind you. You don't bore me, or bother me. If you'd
like to stay—Think it over."

Helga didn't, of course, require to think it over, because
lodgment in Anne's home was in complete accord with what
she designated as her "aesthetic sense." Even Helga Crane
approved of Anne's house and the furnishings which so
admirably graced the big cream-colored rooms. Beds with
long, tapering posts to which tremendous age lent dignity
and interest, bonneted old highboys, tables that might be by
Duncan Phyfe, rare spindle-legged chairs, and others whose
ladder backs gracefully climbed the delicate wall panels.
These historic things mingled harmoniously and comfortably with brass-bound Chinese tea-chests, luxurious deep
chairs and davenports, tiny tables of gay color, a lacquered
jade-green settee with gleaming black satin cushions, lustrous Eastern rugs, ancient copper, Japanese prints, some
fine etchings, a profusion of precious bric-a-brac, and endless shelves filled with books.

Anne Grey herself was, as Helga expressed it, "almost too
good to be true." Thirty, maybe, brownly beautiful, she had
the face of a golden Madonna, grave and calm and sweet
with shining black hair and eyes. She carried herself as
queens are reputed to bear themselves, and probably do
not. Her manners were as agreeably gentle as her own soft
name. She possessed an impeccably fastidious taste in
clothes, knowing what suited her and wearing it with an air
of unconscious assurance. The unusual thing, a native New

Yorker, she was also a person of distinction, financially independent, well connected and much sought after. And she
was interesting, an odd confusion of wit and intense earnest-
ness; a vivid and remarkable person. Yes, undoubtedly,
Anne was almost too good to be true. She was almost perfect.

Thus established, secure, comfortable, Helga soon became thoroughly absorbed in the distracting interests of life
in New York. Her secretarial work with the Negro insurance
company filled her day. Books, the theater, parties, used up
the nights. Gradually in the charm of this new and delightful
pattern of her life she lost that tantalizing oppression of
loneliness and isolation which always, it seemed, had been a
part of her existence.

But, while the continuously gorgeous panorama of Harlem fascinated her, thrilled her, the sober mad rush of white
New York failed entirely to stir her. Like thousands of other
Harlem dwellers, she patronized its shops, its theaters, its art
galleries, and its restaurants, and read its papers, without
considering herself a part of the monster. And she was satisfied, unenvious. For her this Harlem was enough. Of that
white world, so distant, so near, she asked only indifference.
No, not at all did she crave, from those pale and powerful
people, awareness. Sinister folk, she considered them, who
had stolen her birthright. Their past contribution to her life,
which had been but shame and grief, she had hidden away
from brown folk in a locked closet, "never," she told herself,
"to be reopened."

Some day she intended to marry one of those alluring
brown or yellow men who danced attendance on her. Already financially successful, any one of them could give to
her the things which she had now come to desire, a home
like Anne's, cars of expensive makes such as lined the avenue, clothes and furs from Bendel's and Revillon Frères',
servants, and leisure.

Always her forehead wrinkled in distaste whenever, involuntarily, which was somehow frequently, her mind turned

on the speculative gray eyes and visionary uplifting plans of
Dr. Anderson. That other, James Vayle, had slipped absolutely from her consciousness. Of him she never thought.
Helga Crane meant, now, to have a home and perhaps
laughing, appealing dark-eyed children in Harlem. Her existence was bounded by Central Park, Fifth Avenue, St. Nicho-
las Park, and One Hundred and Forty-fifth Street. Not at all
narrow life, as Negroes live it, as Helga Crane knew it. Everything was there, vice and goodness, sadness and gayety,
ignorance and wisdom, ugliness and beauty, poverty and
richness. And it seemed to her that somehow of goodness,
gayety, wisdom, and beauty always there was a little more
than of vice, sadness, ignorance, and ugliness. It was only
riches that did not quite transcend poverty.

"But," said Helga Crane, "what of that? Money isn't everything. It isn't even the half of everything. And here we
have so much else—and by ourselves. It's only outside of
Harlem among those others that money really counts for
everything."

In the actuality of the pleasant present and the delightful
vision of an agreeable future she was contented, and happy.
She did not analyze this contentment, this happiness, but
vaguely, without putting it into words or even so tangible a
thing as a thought, she knew it sprang from a sense of freedom, a release from the feeling of smallness which had
hedged her in, first during her sorry, unchildlike childhood
among hostile white folk in Chicago, and later during her
uncomfortable sojourn among snobbish black folk in Naxos.

IX

But it didn't last, this happiness of Helga Crane's.

Little by little the signs of spring appeared, but strangely
the enchantment of the season, so enthusiastically, so lavishly greeted by the gay dwellers of Harlem, filled her only

with restlessness. Somewhere, within her, in a deep recess, crouched discontent. She began to lose confidence in the fullness of her life, the glow began to fade from her conception of it. As the days multiplied, her need of something, something vaguely familiar, but which she could not put a name to and hold for definite examination, became almost intolerable. She went through moments of overwhelming anguish. She felt shut in, trapped. "Perhaps I'm tired, need a tonic, or something," she reflected. So she consulted a physician, who, after a long, solemn examination, said that there was nothing wrong, nothing at all. "A change of scene, perhaps for a week or so, or a few days away from work," would put her straight most likely. Helga tried this, tried them both, but it was no good. All interest had gone out of living. Nothing seemed any good. She became a little frightened, and then shocked to discover that, for some unknown reason, it was of herself she was afraid.

Spring grew into summer, languidly at first, then flauntingly. Without awareness on her part, Helga Crane began to draw away from those contacts which had so delighted her. More and more she made lonely excursions to places outside of Harlem. A sensation of estrangement and isolation encompassed her. As the days became hotter and the streets more swarming, a kind of repulsion came upon her. She recoiled in aversion from the sight of the grinning faces and from the sound of the easy laughter of all these people who strolled, aimlessly now, it seemed, up and down the avenues. Not only did the crowds of nameless folk on the street annoy her, she began also actually to dislike her friends.

Even the gentle Anne distressed her. Perhaps because Anne was obsessed by the race problem and fed her obsession. She frequented all the meetings of protest, subscribed to all the complaining magazines, and read all the lurid newspapers spewed out by the Negro yellow press. She talked, wept, and ground her teeth dramatically about the wrongs and shames of her race. At times she lashed her fury to surprising heights for one by nature so placid and gentle.

And, though she would not, even to herself, have admitted it, she reveled in this orgy of protest.

"Social inequality," "Equal opportunity for all," were her slogans, often and emphatically repeated. Anne preached these things and honestly thought that she believed them, but she considered it an affront to the race, and to all the vari-colored peoples that made Lenox and Seventh Avenues the rich spectacles which they were, for any Negro to receive on terms of equality any white person.

"To me," asserted Anne Grey, "the most wretched Negro prostitute that walks One Hundred and Thirty-fifth Street is more than any president of these United States, not excepting Abraham Lincoln." But she turned up her finely carved nose at their lusty churches, their picturesque parades, their naïve clowning on the streets. She would not have desired or even have been willing to live in any section outside the black belt, and she would have refused scornfully, had they been tendered, any invitation from white folk. She hated white people with a deep and burning hatred, with the kind of hatred which, finding itself held in sufficiently numerous groups, was capable some day, on some great provocation, of bursting into dangerously malignant flames.

But she aped their clothes, their manners, and their gracious ways of living. While proclaiming loudly the undiluted good of all things Negro, she yet disliked the songs, the dances, and the softly blurred speech of the race. Toward these things she showed only a disdainful contempt, tinged sometimes with a faint amusement. Like the despised people of the white race, she preferred Pavlova to Florence Mills, John McCormack to Taylor Gordon, Walter Hampden to Paul Robeson. Theoretically, however, she stood for the immediate advancement of all things Negroid, and was in revolt against social inequality.

Helga had been entertained by this racial ardor in one so little affected by racial prejudice as Anne, and by her inconsistencies. But suddenly these things irked her with a great irksomeness and she wanted to be free of this constant prattling of the incongruities, the injustices, the stupidities, the viciousness of white people. It stirred memories, probed hidden wounds, whose poignant ache bred in her surprising oppression and corroded the fabric of her quietism. Sometimes it took all her self-control to keep from tossing sarcastically at Anne Ibsen's remark about there being assuredly something very wrong with the drains, but after all there were other parts of the edifice.

It was at this period of restiveness that Helga met again Dr. Anderson. She was gone, unwillingly, to a meeting, a health meeting, held in a large church—as were most of Harlem's uplift activities—as a substitute for her employer, Mr. Darling. Making her tardy arrival during a tedious discourse by a pompous saffron-hued physician, she was led by the irritated usher, whom she had roused from a nap in which he had been pleasantly freed from the intricacies of Negro health statistics, to a very front seat. Complete silence ensued while she subsided into her chair. The offended doctor looked at the ceiling, at the floor, and accusingly at Helga, and finally continued his lengthy discourse. When at last he had ended and Helga had dared to remove her eyes from his sweating face and look about, she saw with a sudden thrill that Robert Anderson was among her nearest neighbors. A peculiar, not wholly disagreeable, quiver ran down her spine. She felt an odd little faintness. The blood rushed to her face. She tried to jeer at herself for being so moved by the encounter.

He, meanwhile, she observed, watched her gravely. And having caught her attention, he smiled a little and nodded.

When all who so desired had spouted to their heart's content—if to little purpose—and the meeting was finally over, Anderson detached himself from the circle of admiring friends and acquaintances that had gathered around him and caught up with Helga half-way down the long aisle leading out to fresher air.

"I wondered if you were really going to cut me. I see you

were," he began, with that half-quizzical smile which she remembered so well.

She laughed. "Oh, I didn't think you'd remember me." Then she added: "Pleasantly, I mean."

The man laughed too. But they couldn't talk yet. People kept breaking in on them. At last, however, they were at the door, and then he suggested that they share a taxi "for the sake of a little breeze." Helga assented.

Constraint fell upon them when they emerged into the hot street, made seemingly hotter by a low-hanging golden moon and the hundreds of blazing electric lights. For a moment, before hailing a taxi, they stood together looking at the slow moving mass of perspiring human beings. Neither spoke, but Helga was conscious of the man's steady gaze. The prominent gray eyes were fixed upon her, studying her, appraising her. Many times since turning her back on Naxos she had in fancy rehearsed this scene, this re-encounter. Now she found that rehearsal helped not at all. It was so absolutely different from anything that she had imagined.

In the open taxi they talked of impersonal things, books, places, the fascination of New York, of Harlem. But underneath the exchange of small talk lay another conversation of which Helga Crane was sharply aware. She was aware, too, of a strange ill-defined emotion, a vague yearning rising within her. And she experienced a sensation of consternation and keen regret when with a lurching jerk the cab pulled up before the house in One Hundred and Thirty-ninth Street. So soon, she thought.

But she held out her hand calmly, coolly. Cordially she asked him to call some time. "It is," she said, "a pleasure to renew our acquaintance." Was it, she was wondering, merely an acquaintance?

He responded seriously that he too thought it a pleasure, and added: "You haven't changed. You're still seeking for something, I think."

At his speech there dropped from her that vague feeling of yearning, that longing for sympathy and understanding which his presence evoked. She felt a sharp stinging sensation and a recurrence of that anger and defiant desire to hurt which had so seared her on that past morning in Naxos. She searched for a biting remark, but, finding none venomous enough, she merely laughed a little rude and scornful laugh and, throwing up her small head, bade him an impatient good-night and ran quickly up the steps.

Afterwards she lay for long hours without undressing, thinking angry self-accusing thoughts, recalling and reconstructing that other explosive contact. That memory filled her with a sort of aching delirium. A thousand indefinite longings beset her. Eagerly she desired to see him again to right herself in his thoughts. Far into the night she lay planning speeches for their next meeting, so that it was long before drowsiness advanced upon her.

When he did call, Sunday, three days later, she put him off on Anne and went out, pleading an engagement, which until then she had not meant to keep. Until the very moment of his entrance she had had no intention of running away, but something, some imp of contumacy, drove her from his presence, though she longed to stay. Again abruptly had come the uncontrollable wish to wound. Later, with a sense of helplessness and inevitability, she realized that the weapon which she had chosen had been a boomerang, for she herself had felt the keen disappointment of the denial. Better to have stayed and hurled polite sarcasms at him. She might then at least have had the joy of seeing him wince.

In this spirit she made her way to the corner and turned into Seventh Avenue. The warmth of the sun, though gentle on that afternoon, had nevertheless kissed the street into marvelous light and color. Now and then, greeting an acquaintance, or stopping to chat with a friend, Helga was all the time seeing its soft shining brightness on the buildings along its sides or on the gleaming bronze, gold, and copper faces of its promenaders. And another vision, too, came haunting Helga Crane; level gray eyes set down in a brown face which stared out at her, coolly, quizzically, disturbingly. And she was not happy.

The tea to which she had so suddenly made up her mind to go she found boring beyond endurance, insipid drinks, dull conversation, stupid men. The aimless talk glanced from John Wellinger's lawsuit for discrimination because of race against a downtown restaurant and the advantages of living in Europe, especially France, to the significance, if any, of the Garvey movement. Then it sped to a favorite Negro dancer who had just then secured a foothold on the stage of a current white musical comedy, to other shows, to a new book touching on Negroes. Thence to costumes for a coming masquerade dance, to a new jazz song, to Yvette Dawson's engagement to a Boston lawyer who had seen her one night at a party and proposed to her the next day at noon. Then back again to racial discrimination.

Why, Helga wondered, with unreasoning exasperation, didn't they find something else to talk of? Why must the race problem always creep in? She refused to go on to another gathering. It would, she thought, be simply the same old thing.

On her arrival home she was more disappointed than she cared to admit to find the house in darkness and even Anne gone off somewhere. She would have liked that night to have talked with Anne. Get her opinion of Dr. Anderson.

Anne it was who the next day told her that he had given up his work in Naxos; or rather that Naxos had given him up. He had been too liberal, too lenient, for education as it was inflicted in Naxos. Now he was permanently in New York, employed as welfare worker by some big manufacturing concern, which gave employment to hundreds of Negro men.

"Uplift," sniffed Helga contemptuously, and fled before the onslaught of Anne's harangue on the needs and ills of the race.

X

With the waning summer the acute sensitiveness of Helga Crane's frayed nerves grew keener. There were days when the mere sight of the serene tan and brown faces about her stung her like a personal insult. The care-free quality of their laughter roused in her the desire to scream at them: "Fools, fools! Stupid fools!" This passionate and unreasoning protest gained in intensity, swallowing up all else like some dense fog. Life became for her only a hateful place where one lived in intimacy with people one would not have chosen had one been given choice. It was, too, an excruciating agony. She was continually out of temper. Anne, thank the gods! was away, but her nearing return filled Helga with dismay.

Arriving at work one sultry day, hot and dispirited, she found waiting a letter, a letter from Uncle Peter. It had originally been sent to Naxos, and from there it had made the journey back to Chicago to the Young Women's Christian Association, and then to Mrs. Hayes-Rore. That busy woman had at last found time between conventions and lectures to readdress it and had sent it on to New York. Four months, at last it had been on its travels. Helga felt no curiosity as to its contents, only annoyance at the long delay, as she ripped open the thin edge of the envelope, and for a space sat staring at the peculiar foreign script of her uncle.

715 Sheridan Road
Chicago, Ill.

DEAR HELGA:

It is now over a year since you made your unfortunate call here. It was unfortunate for us all, you, Mrs. Nilssen, and myself. But of course you couldn't know. I blame myself. I should have written you of my marriage.

I have looked for a letter, or some word from you; evidently, with your usual penetration, you understood thoroughly that I must terminate my outward relation with you. You were always a keen one.

Of course I am sorry, but it can't be helped. My wife must be considered, and she feels very strongly about this.

You know, of course, that I wish you the best of luck. But take an old man's advice and don't do as your mother did. Why don't you run over and visit your Aunt Katrina? She always wanted you. Maria Kirkeplads, No. 2, will find her.

I enclose what I intended to leave you at my death. It is better and more convenient that you get it now. I wish it were more, but even this little may come in handy for a rainy day.

Best wishes for your luck.

PETER NILSSEN

Beside the brief, friendly, but none the less final, letter there was a check for five thousand dollars. Helga Crane's first feeling was one of unreality. This changed almost immediately into one of relief, of liberation. It was stronger than the mere security from present financial worry which the check promised. Money as money was still not very important to Helga. But later, while on an errand in the big general office of the society, her puzzled bewilderment fled. Here the inscrutability of the dozen or more brown faces, all cast from the same indefinite mold, and so like her own, seemed pressing forward against her. Abruptly it flashed upon her that the harrowing irritation of the past weeks was a smoldering hatred. Then, she was overcome by another, so actual, so sharp, so horribly painful, that forever afterwards she preferred to forget it. It was as if she were shut up, boxed up, with hundreds of her race, closed up with that something in the racial character which had always been, to her, inexplicable, alien. Why, she demanded in fierce rebellion, should she be yoked to these despised black folk?

Back in the privacy of her own cubicle, self-loathing came upon her. "They're my own people, my own people," she kept repeating over and over to herself. It was no good. The feeling would not be routed. "I can't go on like this," she said to herself. "I simply can't."

There were footsteps. Panic seized her. She'd have to get out. She terribly needed to. Snatching hat and purse, she hurried to the narrow door, saying in a forced, steady voice, as it opened to reveal her employer: "Mr. Darling, I'm sorry, but I've got to go out. Please, may I be excused?"

At his courteous, "Certainly, certainly. And don't hurry. It's much too hot," Helga Crane had the grace to feel ashamed, but there was no softening of her determination. The necessity for being alone was too urgent. She hated him and all the others too much.

Outside, rain had begun to fall. She walked bare-headed, bitter with self-reproach. But she rejoiced too. She didn't, in spite of her racial markings, belong to these dark segregated people. She was different. She felt it. It wasn't merely a matter of color. It was something broader, deeper, that made folk kin.

And now she was free. She would take Uncle Peter's money and advice and revisit her aunt in Copenhagen. Fleeting pleasant memories of her childhood visit there flew through her excited mind. She had been only eight, yet she had enjoyed the interest and the admiration which her unfamiliar color and dark curly hair, strange to those pink, white, and gold people, had evoked. Quite clearly now she recalled that her Aunt Katrina had begged for her to be allowed to remain. Why, she wondered, hadn't her mother consented?

To Helga it seemed that it would have been the solution to all their problems, her mother's, her stepfather's, her own.

At home in the cool dimness of the big chintz-hung living-room, clad only in a fluttering thing of green chiffon, she gave herself up to daydreams of a happy future in Copenhagen, where there were no Negroes, no problems, no prejudice, until she remembered with perturbation that this was the day of Anne's return from her vacation at the sea-shore. Worse. There was a dinner-party in her honor that very night. Helga sighed. She'd have to go. She couldn't possibly get out of a dinner-party for Anne, even though she felt that such an event on a hot night was little short of an outrage. Nothing but a sense of obligation to Anne kept her from pleading a splitting headache as an excuse for remaining quietly at home.

Her mind trailed off to the highly important matter of clothes. What should she wear? White? No, everybody would, because it was hot. Green? She shook her head, Anne would be sure to. The blue thing. Reluctantly she decided against it; she loved it, but she had worn it too often. There was that cobwebby black net touched with orange, which she had bought last spring in a bit of extravagance and never worn, because on getting it home both she and Anne had considered it too *décolleté*, and too *outré*. Anne's words: "There's not enough of it, and what there is gives you the air of something about to fly," came back to her, and she smiled as she decided that she would certainly wear the black net. For her it would be a symbol. She was about to fly.

She busied herself with some absurdly expensive roses which she had ordered sent in, spending an interminable time in their arrangement. At last she was satisfied with their appropriateness in some blue Chinese jars of great age. Anne *did* have such lovely things, she thought, as she began conscientiously to prepare for her return, although there was really little to do; Lillie seemed to have done everything. But Helga dusted the tops of the books, placed the magazines in ordered carelessness, redressed Anne's bed in fresh-smelling sheets of cool linen, and laid out her best pale-yellow pajamas of *crêpe de Chine*. Finally she set out two tall green glasses and made a great pitcher of lemonade, leaving only the ginger-ale and claret to be added on Anne's arrival. She was a little conscience-stricken, so she wanted to be particularly nice to Anne, who had been so kind to her when first she came to New York, a forlorn friendless creature. Yes, she was grateful to Anne; but, just the same, she meant to go. At once.

Her preparations over, she went back to the carved chair from which the thought of Anne's home-coming had drawn her. Characteristically she writhed at the idea of telling Anne of her impending departure and shirked the problem of evolving a plausible and inoffensive excuse for its suddenness. "That," she decided lazily, "will have to look out for itself; I can't be bothered just now. It's too hot."

She began to make plans and to dream delightful dreams of change, of life somewhere else. Some place where at last she would be permanently satisfied. Her anticipatory thoughts waltzed and eddied about to the sweet silent music of change. With rapture almost, she let herself drop into the blissful sensation of visualizing herself in different, strange places, among approving and admiring people, where she would be appreciated, and understood.

BIBLIOGRAPHIC NOTES

Like Jessie Fauset, Nella Larsen has always been included in the literary canon as one of the Harlem Renaissance writers. Robert A. Bone, *The Negro Novel in America* (New Haven: Yale University Press, 1965), sees her as the only truly successful novelist of the 1920s who attempted the middle ground between traditional uplift literature and the radical visions of the Harlem Renaissance. Hugh M. Gloster in *Negro Voices in American Fiction* (Chapel Hill: University of North Carolina Press, 1948), comments on Rena of Charles Chestnutt's *House Behind the Cedars* as a predecessor to *Quicksand*'s Helga Crane. Arna Bontemps includes an essay by Hiroko Sako on Larsen and Fauset in *The Harlem Renaissance Remembered* (New York: Dodd, Mead, 1972), which praises Larsen for her "sophistication." Addison Gayle in *The Way of the New World: The Black Novel in America* (Garden City: Doubleday & Co., 1975), considers *Quicksand* as almost modern in its suggestion of the "serious psychological problems of spirit and soul" created by a world that is race mad. Gayle sees Helga Crane's psychic dilemma as a function of her privileged status as she searches for an identity in a world of race and class oppression.

Unfortunately, traditional literary criticism of Larsen ignores gender issues in her work. Emphasis has been placed on the tragic qualities of her mulatto heroines, with particular stress on Helga Crane's own participation in her isolation and frustration. The implication, particularly of Bone's analysis, is that Larsen and her heroines suffer from the inevitability of racial maladjustment. When critics do comment on Helga Crane's conflict with sexuality, it is in the Freudian, not feminist sense that her ambivalence is discussed.

There are now several excellent studies analyzing Larsen's work in a feminist context. Hortense Thornton's "Sexism as Quagmire: Nella Larsen's *Quicksand*," *College Language Association Journal* 16 (March 1973): 285–301, examines the sexual politics of *Quicksand*, arguing that Helga Crane's economic dependency as a woman, not her status as a mulatto, causes her entrapment. Barbara Christian in *Black Women Novelists: The Making of a Tradition, 1892–1976* (Westport, Conn.: Greenwood Press, 1980), identifies Crane's tragedy as a "female" situation in which her only options are as a self-centered oppressive neurotic or a downtrodden peasant. Linda Dittmar in her unpublished article, "When Privilege Is No Protection: Class, Race and Gender in Edith Wharton's *The House of Mirth* and Nella Larsen's *Quicksand*," also explores the social and political nature of Crane's ultimate defeat, emphasizing that in both *Quicksand* and *The House of Mirth* the protagonists are women whose privileged status disables them. Unlike many critics who have concentrated on the images of suffocation and frustration, Dittmar insists that rage and rebellion are the underlying impulses of these two novels.

Thadious M. Davis's unpublished essay, "Allegories of the Black Woman Artist: A Reading of Nella Larsen," gives excellent biographical information. Davis explores the retreat into obscurity which both Larsen and her characters used to escape from the social obstacles facing them as black women. She also discusses the psychological fragmentation that both Larsen and her heroes experienced. Mary Helen Washington's "Nella Larsen—Mystery Woman of the Harlem Renaissance," *Ms.* 9, no. 6 (December 1980): 44–50, also discusses these issues, focusing on Larsen's plots as disguises for Larsen's own sense of marginality and powerlessness in a male-dominated, middle-class black world.

In her introduction to a new edition of Nella Larsen's novels, *Quicksand* and *Passing* (New Brunswick, N.J.: Rutgers University Press, 1986), Deborah E. McDowell argues that a conflictual female sexual identity is a more urgent psychological problem than Helga's status as tragic mulatta. "Helga is divided psychically between a desire for sexual fulfillment and a longing for social respectability," a division that is mirrored in a series of "structural opposites on which the novel turns." (pp. xvii and xxi).

PART FOUR

i love the way Janie Crawford
left her husbands   the one who wanted
to change her into a mule
and the other who tried to interest her
in being a queen
a woman unless she submits is neither a mule
nor a queen
though like a mule she may suffer
and like a queen pace
the floor

—Alice Walker, "Janie Crawford,"

INTRODUCTION

"I Love the Way Janie Crawford Left Her Husbands": Zora Neale Hurston's Emergent Female Hero

In the past few years of teaching Zora Neale Hurston's *Their Eyes Were Watching God*,[1] I have become increasingly disturbed by this text, particularly by two problematic relationships I see in the novel: women's relationship to the community and women's relationship to language. *Their Eyes* has often been described as a novel about a woman in a folk community, but it might be more accurately described as a novel about a woman outside of the folk community. And while feminists have been eager to seize upon this text as an expression of female power, I think it is a novel that represents women's exclusion from power, particularly from the power of oral speech. Most contemporary critics contend that Janie is the articulate voice in the tradition, that the novel celebrates a women coming to self-discovery and that this self-discovery leads her ultimately to a meaningful participation in black folk traditions.[2] Perhaps. But before bestowing the title of "articulate hero" on Janie, we should look to Hurston's first novel, *Jonah's Gourd Vine*, to its main character, Reverend John Pearson, and to the power that Hurston is able to confer on a male folk hero.[3]

From the beginning of his life, John Pearson's relationship to the community is as assured as Janie's is problematic. Living in a small Alabama town and then in Eatonville, where Janie also migrates, he discovers his preaching voice early and is encouraged to use it. His ability to control and manipulate the folk language is a source of power within the community. Even his relationships with women help him to connect to his community, leading him to literacy and to speech while Janie's relationships with men deprive her of community and of her voice. John's friendship with Hambo, his closest friend, is much more dynamic than Janie and Pheoby's because Hurston makes the male friendship a deeper and more complex one, and because the community acknowledges and comments on the men's friendship. In his Introduction to *Jonah's Gourd Vine*, Larry Neal describes John Pearson's exalted function in the folk community:

> John Pearson, as Zora notes in her letter to [James Weldon] Johnson is a poet. That is to say, one who manipulates words in order to convey to others the mystery of that Unknowable force which we call God. And he is more; he is the intelligence of the community, the bearer of its traditions and highest possibilities.[4]

One could hardly make such an unequivocal claim for Janie's heroic posture in *Their Eyes*. Singled out for her extraordinary, anglicized beauty, Janie cannot "get but so close to them [the people in Eatonville] in spirit." Her friendship with Pheoby, occurring apart from the community, encapsulates Janie and Pheoby in a private dyad that insulates Janie from the jealousy of other women. Like the other women in the town, she is barred from participation in the culture's oral tradition. When the voice of the black oral tradition is summoned in *Their Eyes*, it is not used to represent the collective black community, but to invoke and valorize the voice of the black *male* community.[5]

As critic Margaret Homans points out, our attentiveness to the possibility that women are excluded categorically from the language of the dominant discourse should help us to be aware of the inadequacy of language, its inability to represent female experience, its tendency not only to silence women but to make women complicitous in that silence.[6] Part of Janie's dilemma in *Their Eyes* is that she is both subject and object—both hero and heroine—and Hurston, apparently could not retrieve her from that paradoxical position except in the frame story, where she is talking to her friend

and equal, Pheoby Watson. As object in that text, Janie is
often passive when she should be active, deprived of speech
when she should be in command of language, made powerless by her three husbands and by Hurston's narrative strategies. I would like to focus on several passages in *Jonah's
Gourd Vine* and in *Their Eyes* to show how Janie is trapped in
her status as object, as passive female, and to contrast the
freedom John Pearson has as subject to aspire to an heroic
posture in his community.

In both *Their Eyes* and in *Jonah's Gourd Vine* sexuality is
established in the early lives of Janie and John as a symbol of
their growing maturity. The symbol of Janie's emerging sexuality is the blossoming pear tree being pollinated by the
dust-bearing bee. Early in the text, when Janie is about fifteen, Hurston presents her stretched out on her back beneath a pear tree, observing the activity of the bees:

> She saw a dust-bearing bee sink into the sanctum of a
> bloom; the thousand sister-calyxes arch to meet the love
> embrace and the ecstatic shiver of the tree from root to
> tiniest branch creaming in every blossom and frothing
> with delight. So this was marriage! She had been sum-
> moned to behold a revelation. Then Janie felt a pain re-
> morseless sweet that left her limp and languid. (p. 24)

She leaves this scene of the pear tree looking for "an answer
seeking her" and finds that answer in the person of Johnny
Taylor who, in her rapturous state, looks like a golden glorious being. Janie's first sexual encounter is observed by her
grandmother and she is summarily punished.[7] To introduce
such a sexual scene at the age when Janie is about to enter
adulthood, to turn it into romantic fantasy, and to make it
end in punishment certainly limits the possibility of any
growth resulting from that experience.

John's sexual encounters are never observed by any adult
and thus he is spared the humiliation and the punishment
Janie endures for her adolescent experimentation. In an
early scene when he is playing a game called "Hide the

Switch" with the girl in the quarters where he works, he is the active pursuer, and, in contrast to Janie's romantic fantasies, John's experience of sexuality is earthy and energetic and confirms his sense of power:

> . . . when he was "it" he managed to catch every girl in the quarters. The other boys were less successful but girls were screaming under John's lash behind the cowpen and under sweet-gum trees around the spring until the moon rose. John never forgot that night. Even the strong odor of their sweaty bodies was lovely to remember. He went in to bed when all of the girls had been called in by their folks. He could have romped till morning. (p. 41)

A recurring symbol Hurston uses to represent John's sexuality is the train, which he sees for the first time after he meets Lucy, the woman destined to become his first wife. A country boy, John is at first terrified by the "panting monster," but he is also mesmerized by this threatening machine whose sides "seemed to expand and contract like a fiery-lunged monster." It looks frightening, but it is also "uh pretty thing" and it has as many destinations as John in his philandering will have. As a symbol of male sexuality, the train suggests power, dynamism, and mobility.[8]

Janie's image of herself as a blossom waiting to be pollinated by a bee transforms her figuratively and literally into the space in which men's action may occur.[9] She waits for an answer and the answer appears in the form of two men, both of whom direct Janie's life and the action of the plot. Janie at least resists her first husband, Logan, but once Jody takes her to Eatonville, he controls her life as well as the narrative. He buys the land, builds the town, makes Janie tie up her hair, and prescribes her relationship with the rest of the town. We know that Hurston means for Janie to free herself from male domination, but Hurston's language, as much as Jody's behavior, signifies Janie's status as an object. Janie's arrival in Eatonville is described through the eyes and speech of the men on the front porch. Jody joins the men, but Janie is seen "through the bedroom window getting settled." Not only are Janie and the other women barred from participation in the ceremonies and rituals of the community, but they become the objects of the sessions on the porch, included in the men's tale-telling as the butt of their jokes, or their flattery, or their scorn. The experience of having one's body become an object to be looked at is considered so demeaning that when it happens to a man, it figuratively transforms him into a woman. When Janie launches her most devastating attack on Jody in front of all the men in the store, she tells him not to talk about her looking old because "When you pull down yo' britches you look lak de change uh life." Since the "change of life" ordinarily refers to a woman's menopause, Janie is signifying that Jody, like a woman, is subject to the humiliation of exposure. Now that he is the object of the gaze, Jody realizes that other men will "look" on him with pity: "Janie had robbed him of his illusion of irresistible maleness that all men cherish." (p. 123)

Eventually Janie does speak, and, interestingly, her first speech, on behalf of women, is a commentary on the limitations of a male-dominated society:

> Sometimes God gits familiar wid us womenfolks too and talks His inside business. He told me how surprised He was 'bout y'all turning out so smart after Him makin' yuh different; and how surprised y'all is goin' tuh be if you ever find out you don't know half as much 'bout us as you think you do. (p. 117)

Speech does not lead Janie to power, however, but to self-division and to further acquiescence in her status as object. As her marriage to Jody deteriorates she begins to observe herself: "one day she sat and watched the shadows of herself going about tending store and prostrating itself before Jody, while all the time she herself sat under a shady tree with the wind blowing through her hair and her clothes." (p. 119)

In contrast to Janie's psychic split in which her imagination asserts itself while her body makes a show of obedience, John Pearson, trapped in a similarly constricting marriage with his second wife, Hattie, experiences not self-division but a kind of self-unification in which the past memories he has repressed seep into his consciousness and drive him to confront his life with Hattie: "Then too his daily self seemed to be wearing thin, and the past seeped thru and mastered him for increasingly longer periods. He whose present had always been so bubbling that it crowded out past and future now found himself with a memory." (p. 122) In this new state John begins to remember and visit old friends. His memories prompt him to confront Hattie and even to deny that he ever married her. Of course his memory is selective and self-serving, and quite devastating to Hattie, but it does drive him to action.

Even after Janie acquires the power of speech which allows her to stand up to Jody, Hurston continues to objectify her so that she does not take action. Immediately after Jody's death she goes to the looking glass where, she tells us, she had told her girl self to wait for her, and there she discovers that a handsome woman has taken her place. She tears off the kerchief Jody has forced her to wear and lets down her plentiful hair: "The weight, the length, the glory was there. She took careful stock of herself, then combed her hair and tied it back up again." (p. 135) In her first moment of independence Janie is not seen as autonomous subject but again as visual object, "seeing herself seeing herself," draping before herself that "hidden mystery" which attracts men and makes her superior to women. Note that when she turns to the mirror, it is not to experience her own sensual pleasure in her hair. She does not tell us how her hair felt to her—did it tingle at the roots? Did she shiver with delight?—no, she takes stock of herself, makes an assessment of herself. What's in the mirror that she cannot experience without it that imaginary other whom the mirror represents, looking on in judgment, recording, not her own sensations, but the way others see her.

Barbara Johnson's reading of *Their Eyes* suggests that once Janie is able to identify the split between her inside and outside selves, incorporating and articulating her own sense of self-division, she develops an increasing ability to speak.[10] I have come to different conclusions: that Hurston continues to subvert Janie's voice, that in crucial places where we need to hear her speak she is curiously silent, that even when Hurston sets out to explore Janie's internal consciousness, her internal speech, what we actually hear are the voices of men. Once Tea Cake enters the narrative his name and his voice are heard nearly twice as often as Janie's. He walks into Janie's life with a guitar and a grin and tells her, "Honey since you loose me and gimme privelege tuh tell yuh all about mahself. Ah'll tell yuh." (p. 187) And from then on it is Tea Cake's tale, the only reason for Janie's account of her life to Pheoby being to vindicate Tea Cake's name. Insisting on Tea Cake's innocence as well as his central place in her story, Janie tells Pheoby, "Teacake ain't wasted no money of mine, and he ain't left me for no young gal, neither. He give me every consolation in the world. He'd tell 'em so too, if he was here. If he wasn't gone." (p. 18)

As many feminist critics have pointed out, women do get silenced, even in texts by women, and there are critical places in *Their Eyes* where Janie's voice needs to be heard and is not, places where we would expect her as the subject of the story to speak. Perhaps the most stunning silence in the text occurs after Tea Cake beats Janie. The beating is seen entirely through the eyes of the male community, while Janie's reaction is never given. Tea Cake becomes the envy of the other men for having a woman whose flesh is so tender that one can see every place she's been hit. Sop-de-Bottom declares in awe, "wouldn't Ah love tuh whip uh tender woman ak Janie!" Janie is silent, so thoroughly repressed in this section that all that remains of her is what Tea Cake and the other men desire.

Passages which are supposed to represent Janie's interior consciousness begin by marking some internal change in

Janie, then gradually or abruptly shift so that a male character takes Janie's place as the subject of the discourse; at the
conclusion of these passages, ostensibly devoted to the reve-
lation of Janie's interior life, the male voice predominates.
Janie's life just before and after Jody's death is a fertile
period for such self-reflection, but Hurston does not focus
the attention of the text on Janie even in these significant
turning points in Janie's life. In the long paragraph that tells
us how she has changed in the six months after Jody's death,
we are told that Janie talked and laughed in the store at times
and was happy except for the store. To solve the problem of
the store she hires Hezikiah "who was the best imitation of
Joe that his seventeen years could make." At this point, the
paragraph shifts its focus from Janie and her growing sense
of independence to Hezikiah and his imitation of Jody,
describing Hezikiah in a way that evokes Jody's presence and
obliterates Janie. We are told at the end of the paragraph, in
tongue-in-cheek humor, that because "managing stores and
women store-owners was trying on a man's nerves,"
Hezikiah "needed to take a drink of liquor now and then to
keep up." Thus Janie is not only removed as the subject of
this passage but is subsumed under the male-defined category of worrisome women. Even the much-celebrated description of Janie's discovery of her split selves: "She had an
inside and an outside now and suddenly she knew how not to
mix them." (p. 112), represents her internal life as divided
between two men: her outside self exists for Joe and her
inside self she is "saving up" for "some man she had never
seen."[11]

Critic Robert Stepto was the first to raise the question
about Janie's lack of voice in *Their Eyes*. In his critique of
Afro-American narrative he claims that Hurston creates only
the illusion that Janie has achieved her voice, that Hurston's
strategy of having much of Janie's tale told by an omniscient
third person rather than by a first person narrator undercuts
the development of Janie's "voice."[12] While I was initially

resistant to this criticism of *Their Eyes*, my reading of *Jonah's Gourd Vine* suggests that Hurston was indeed ambivalent about giving a powerful voice to a woman like Janie who is already in rebellion against male authority and against the roles prescribed for women in a male dominated society. As Stepto notes, Janie's lack of voice is particularly disturbing in the courtroom scene, which comes at the end of her tale and, presumably, at a point where she has developed her capacity to speak. Hurston tells us that down in the Everglades "She got so she could tell big stories herself," but in the courtroom scene the story of Janie and Tea Cake is told entirely in third person: "She had to go way back to let them know how she and Tea Cake had been with one another." We do not hear Janie speaking in her own voice until we return to the frame where she is speaking to her friend, Pheoby.[13]

There is a similar courtroom scene in *Jonah's Gourd Vine*, and there is also a silence, not an enforced silence, but the silence of a man who deliberately chooses not to speak. John is hauled into court by his second wife, Hattie, on the grounds of adultery. Like the court system in *Their Eyes*, this too is one where "de laws and de cote houses and de jail houses all b'longed tuh white folks" and, as in Janie's situation, the black community is united against John. His former friends take the stand against him, testifying on Hattie's behalf in order to spite John, but John refuses to call any witnesses for his defense. After he has lost the trial, his friend Hambo angrily asks him why he didn't allow him to testify. John's eloquent answer explains his silence in the courtroom, but more than that, it shows that he has such power over his own voice that he can choose when and where to use it, in this case to defy a hypocritical, racist system and to protect the black community:

Ah didn't want de white folks tuh hear 'bout nothin' lak dat. Dey knows too much 'bout us as it is, but dey some things dey ain't tuh know. Dey's some strings on our harp

fuh us tuh play on and sing all tuh ourselves. Dey thinks
wese all ignorant as it is, and dey thinks wese all alike, and
dat dey knows us inside and out, but you know better. Dey
wouldn't make no great 'miration if you had uh tole 'em
Hattie had all dem mens. Dey wouldn't zarn 'tween uh
woman lak Hattie and one lak Lucy, uh yo' wife befo' she
died. Dey thinks all colored folks is de same dat way. (pp.
261–62)

John's deliberate silence is motivated by his political consciousness. In spite of the community's rejection of him, he
is still their defender, especially in the face of common ad-
versary. Hurston does not allow Janie the insight John has,
nor the voice, nor the loyalty to her people. To Mrs. Turner's racial insults, Janie is nearly silent, offering only a cold
shoulder to show her resistance to the woman's bigotry. In
the courtroom scene Janie is divorced from the other blacks
and surrounded by a "protecting wall of white women." She
is vindicated, and the black community humbled. Janie is the
outsider; John is the culture's hero, their "inspired artist,"
the traditional male hero in possession of traditional male
power.

But John's power in the community and his gift for words
do not always serve him well. As Robert Hemenway asserts
in his critical biography of Hurston, John is "a captive of the
community's need for a public giver of words."

His language does not serve to articulate his personal
problems because it is directed away from the self toward
the communal celebration. John, the man of words, becomes the victim of his bardic function. He is the epic poet
of the community who sacrifices himself for the group
vision.[14]

For John, words mean power and status rather than the
expression of feeling. When he first discovers the power of
his voice, he thinks immediately of how good he sounds and
how his voice can be exploited for his benefits:

Dat sho sound good . . . If mah voice sound *dat* good
de first time Ah ever prayed in, de church house, it sho
won't be de las'. (p. 93)

John never feels the call to preach until the day on Joe
Clarke's porch when the men tease John about being a
"wife-made man." One of his buddies tells him that with a
wife like Lucy any man could get ahead in life: "Anybody
could put hisself on de ladder wid her in de house." The
following Sunday in his continuing quest for manhood and
power, John turns to preaching. The dramatic quality of his
preaching and his showmanship easily make him the most
famous preacher and the most powerful man in the area.
John's inability to achieve maturity and his sudden death at
the moment of his greatest insight suggest a great deal about
Hurston's discomfort with the traditional male hero, with
the values of the community he represents, with the culture's privileging of orality over inward development. Janie
Starks is almost the complete antithesis of John Pearson,
"She assumes heroic stature not by externals, but by her
own struggle for self-definition, for autonomy, for liberation
from the illusions that others have tried to make her live by
or that she has submitted to herself."[15]

While Janie's culture honors the oral art, "this picture
making with words," Janie's final speech in *Their Eyes* actually
casts doubt on the relevance of oral speech:

Talkin' don't amount tuh uh hill uh beans when yuh can't
do nothin else . . . Pheoby you got tuh *go* there tuh *know*
there. Yo papa and yo' mama and nobody else can't tell
yuh and show yuh. Two things everybody's got tuh do fuh
theyselves. They got tuh go tuh God, and they got tuh find
out about livin' fuh theyselves. (p. 285)

Janie's final comment that experience is more important
than words is an implicit criticism of the culture that celebrates orality to the exclusion of inner growth. The language
of men in *Their Eyes* and in *Jonah's Gourd Vine* is almost always
divorced from any kind of interiority. The men are rarely

shown in the process of growth. Their talking is a game. Janie's life is about the experience of relationships. Logan, Jody, and Tea Cake and John Pearson are essentially static characters, whereas Pheoby and Janie allow experience to change them. John, who seems almost constitutionally unfitted for self-examination, is killed at the end of the novel by a train, that very symbol of male power he has been seduced by all of his life.[16]

Vladimir Propp, in his study of folklore and narrative, cautions us not to think that plots directly reflect a given social order but "rather emerge out of the conflict, the contradictions of different social orders as they succeed or replace one another." What is manifested in the tensions of plots is "the difficult coexistence of different orders of historical reality in the long period of transition from one to the other . . ."[17]

Hurston's plots may very well reflect such a tension in the social order, a period of transition in which the conflictual coexistence of a predominantly male and a more egalitarian culture is inscribed in these two forms of culture heroes. Both novels end in an ambiguous stance: John dies alone, so dominated by the ideals of his community that he is completely unable to understand his spiritual dilemma. And Janie, having returned to the community she once rejected, is left in a position of interiority so total it seems to represent another structure of confinement. Alone in her bedroom she watches pictures of "love and light against the walls," almost as though she is a spectator at a film. She pulls in the horizon and drapes it over her shoulder and calls in her soul to come and see. The language of this section gives us the illusion of growth and development, but the language is deceptive. The horizon represents the outside world—the world of adventure where Janie journeyed in search of people and a value system that would allow her real self to shine. If the horizon is the world of possibility, of journeys, of meeting new people and eschewing materialistic values, then Janie seems to be canceling out any further exploration of that world. In Eatonville she is a landlady with a fat bank account and a scorn for the people that ensures her alienation. Like the heroine of romantic fiction, left without a man she exists in a position of stasis with no suggestion of how she will employ her considerable energies in her now—perhaps temporarily—manless life.

Hurston was obviously comfortable with the role of the traditional male hero in *Jonah's Gourd Vine*, but *Their Eyes* presented Hurston with a problem she could not solve—the questing hero as woman. That Hurston intended Janie to be such a hero—at least on some level—is undeniable. She puts Janie on the track of autonomy, self-realization, and independence. She allows her to put on the outward trappings of male power: Janie dresses in overalls, goes on the muck, learns to shoot—even better than Tea Cake—and her rebellion changes her and potentially her friend Pheoby. If the rightful end of the romantic heroine is marriage, then Hurston has certainly resisted the script of romance by having Janie kill Tea Cake. (Though he exists in death in a far more mythical and exalted way than in life.) As Rachel Blau Du Plessis argues, when the narrative resolves itself in the repression of romance and the reassertion of quest, the result is a narrative that is critical of those patriarchal rules that govern women and deny them a role outside of the boundaries of patriarchy.[18]

While such a critique of patriarchal norms is obvious in *Their Eyes*, we still see Hurston's ambivalence about Janie's role as "hero" as opposed to "heroine."[19] Like all romantic heroines, Janie follows the dreams of men. She takes off after Jody because "he spoke for far horizon," and she takes off after Tea Cake's dream of going "on de muck." By the rules of romantic fiction, the *heroine* is extremely feminine in looks. Janie's long, heavy, Caucasianlike hair is mentioned so many times in *Their Eyes* that, as one of my students said, it becomes another character in the novel. A "hidden mystery," Janie's hair is one of the most powerful forces in her life, mesmerizing men and alienating the women. As a trope straight out of the turn-of-the-century "mulatto" novel, (*Clotel, Iola Leroy, The House Behind the Cedars*), the hair connects Janie inexorably to the conventional romantic heroine. Employing other standard devices of romantic fiction, Hurston creates the excitement and tension of romantic seduction. Tea Cake—a tall, dark, mysterious stranger—strides into the novel and wrenches Janie away from her prim and proper life. The age and class differences between Janie and Tea Cake, the secrecy of their affair, the town's disapproval, the sense of risk and helplessness as Janie discovers passionate love and the fear, desire, even the potential violence of becoming the possessed are all standard features of romance fiction. Janie is not the subject of these romantic episodes, she is the object of Tea Cake's quest, subsumed under his desires, and, at times so subordinate to Tea Cake that even her interior consciousness reveals more about him than it does about her.

In spite of his infidelities, his arrogance, and his incapacity for self-reflection, John Pearson is unambiguously the heroic center of *Jonah's Gourd Vine*. He inhabits the entire text, his voice is heard on nearly every page, he follows his own dreams, he is selected by the community to be its leader and is recognized by the community for his powers and chastised for his shortcomings. The preacher's sermon as he eulogized John at his funeral is not so much a tribute to the man as it is a recognition that the narrative exists to assert the power of the male story and its claim to our attention. Janie has, of course, reformed her community simply by her resistance to its values. The very fact of her status as outsider makes her seem heroic by contemporary standards. Unable to achieve the easy integration into the society that John Pearson assumes, she stands on the outside and calls into question her culture's dependence on externals, its lack of self-reflection, and its treatment of women. Her rebellion changes her and her friend Pheoby, and, in the words of Lee Edwards, her life becomes "a compelling model of possibility for anyone who hears her tale."[20]

NOTES

1. Zora Neale Hurston, *Their Eyes Were Watching God* (Urbana: University of Illinois Press, 1978).

2. Robert Hemenway, *Zora Neale Hurston: A Literary Biography* (Urbana: University of Illinois Press, 1977), p. 239. Hemenway says that Janie's "blossoming" refers personally to "her discovery of self and ultimately to her meaningful participation in black tradition." But at the end of *Their Eyes,* Janie does not return to an accepting community. She returns to Eatonville as an outsider, and even in the Everglades she does not have an insider's role in the community as Tea Cake does.

3. Zora Neale Hurston, *Jonah's Gourd Vine* (Philadelphia: J. B. Lippincott, 1971).

4. Ibid, p. 7.

5. Henry-Louis Gates, "Zora Neale Hurston and the Speakerly Text," in *The Signifying Monkey* (New York: Oxford University Press, 1987). Gates argues that *Their Eyes* resolves the implicit tension between standard English and black dialect, that Hurston's rhetorical strategies create a kind of new language in which Janie's thoughts are cast—not in black dialect per se but a colloquial form of standard English that is informed by the black idiom. By the end of the novel this language (or free indirect discourse) makes Janie's voice almost inseparable from the narrator's—a synthesis that becomes a trope for the self-knowledge Janie has achieved. While Gates sees the language of *Their Eyes* representing the collective black community's speech and thoughts in this "dialect-informed" colloquial idiom that Hurston has invented, I read the text in a much more literal way and continue to maintain that however inventive this new language might be it is still often used to invoke the thoughts, ideas, and presence of men.

6. Margaret Homans, "Her Very Own Howl," *SIGNS* 9 (Winter 1983): 186–205.

7. One of the ways women's sexuality is made to seem less dignified than men's is to have a woman's sexual experience seen or described by an unsympathetic observer. A good example of the double standard in reporting sexual behavior occurs in Ann Petry's "In Darkness and Confusion" in *Black Voices: An Anthology of Afro-american Literature,* ed. Abraham Chapman (New York: New American Library 1968), pp. 161–91. The young Annie Mae is observed by

her uncle-in-law who reports that her sexual behavior is indecent. In contrast, his son's sexual adventures are alluded to respectfully as activities a father may not pry into.

8. The image of the train as fearsome and threatening occurs in Hurston's autobiography, *Dust Tracks on a Road: An Autobiography,* ed. Robert Hemenway (Urbana: University of Illinois Press, 1984). When she is a young girl on her way to Jacksonville, Zora, like John Pearson, is at first terrified of its "big, mean-looking eye" and has to be dragged on board "kicking and screaming to the huge amusement of everybody but me." Later when she is inside the coach and sees the "glamor of the plush and metal," she calms down and begins to enjoy the ride which, she says "didn't hurt a bit." In both *Dust Tracks* and *Jonah's Gourd Vine* the imagery of the train is clearly sexual, but, while Zora sees the train as something external to herself, something that is powerful but will not hurt her, John imagines the train as an extension of his own power.

9. Teresa De Lauretis, *Alice Doesn't: Feminism, Semiotics, Cinema* (Bloomington: Indiana University Press, 1984), p. 143. De Lauretis notes that the movement of narrative discourse specifies and produces the masculine position as that of mythical subject and the feminine position as mythical obstacle, or, simply "the space in which that movement occurs."

10. I am indebted to Barbara Johnson for this insight which she suggested when I presented an early version of this paper to her class on Afro-American women writers at Harvard in the fall of 1985. I was struck by her comment that Jody's vulnerability makes him like a woman and therefore subject to this kind of attack.

11. Barbara Johnson, "Metaphor, metonymy and voice in *Their Eyes Were Watching God,*" in *Black Literature and Literary Theory,* ed. Henry Louis Gates, (New York: Methuen, 1984), pp. 204–19. Johnson' essay probes very carefully the relation between Janie's ability t speak and her ability to recognize her own self-division. Once Jani is able "to assume and articulate the incompatible forces involved i her own division," she begins to achieve an authentic voice. Arguin for a more literal reading of *Their Eyes,* I maintain that we hea precious little of Janie's voice even after she makes this pronounce ment of knowing that she has "an inside and an outside self." great deal of the "voice" of the text is devoted to the men in th story even after Janie's discovery of self-division.

12. Robert Stepto, *From Behind the Veil: A Study of Afro-American Narr tive* (Urbana: University of Illinois Press, 1979), pp. 164–67.

When Robert Stepto raised this issue at the 1979 Modern La guage Association Meeting, he set off an intense debate. While I c not totally agree with his reading of *Their Eyes* and I think he short-changes Hurston by alloting so little space to her in *From Behind the Veil*, I do think he is right about Janie's lack of voice in the courtroom scene.

13. More accurately the style of this section should be called *free indirect discourse* because both Janie's voice and the narrator's voice are evoked here. In his *Introduction to Poetics: Theory and History of Literature*, vol. I (Minneapolis: University of Minnesota Press, 1982), Tzvetan Todorov explains Gerard Genette's definition of free indirect discourse as a grammatical form that adopts the indirect style but retains the "semantic nuances of the 'original' discourse." (p. 28)

14. Hemenway, *Zora Neale Hurston*, p. 198.

15. Mary Helen Washington, "Zora Neale Hurston: A Woman Half in Shadow," in *I Love Myself When I Am Laughing . . . And Then Again When I Am Looking Mean and Impressive: A Zora Neale Hurston Reader*, ed. Alice Walker (Old Westbury, N.Y.: Feminist Press, 1979), p. 16. In the original version of this essay, I showed how Joseph Campbell's model of the hero, though it had been applied to Ralph Ellison's invisible man, could more appropriately be applied to Janie, who defies her status as the mule of the world, and, unlike Ellison's antihero, does not end up in an underground hideout.

Following the pattern of the classic mythological hero, defined by Campbell in *The Hero with a Thousand Faces*, (Princeton, N.J.: Princeton University Press, 1968), Janie leaves her everyday world to proceed to the threshold of adventure (leaves Nanny and Logan to run off with Jody to Eatonville); she is confronted by a power that threatens her spiritual life (Jody Starks and his efforts to make her submissive to him); she goes beyond that threat to a world of unfamiliar forces some of which threaten her and some of which give aid (Tea Cake, his wild adventures, and his ability to see her as an equal); she descends into an underworld where she must undergo the supreme ordeal (the journey to the Everglades; the killing of Tea Cake and the trial); and the final work is that of the return when the hero reemerges from the kingdom of dread and brings a gift that restores the world (Janie returns to Eatonville and tells her story to her friend Pheoby who recognizes immediately her communion with Janie's experience "Ah done growed ten feet higher from jus' listenin' tuh you, Janie").

16. Anne Jones, "Pheoby's Hungry Listening: Zora Neale Hurston's *Their Eyes Were Watching God*" (Paper presented at the National Women's Studies Association, Humboldt State University, Arcata, California, June 1982).

17. De Lauretis, *Alice Doesn't,* p. 113. In the chapter, "Desire in Narrative," De Lauretis refers to Vladimir Propp's essay, "Oedipus in the Light of Folklore," which studies plot types and their diachronic or historical transformations.

18. Rachel Blau Du Plessis, *Writing Beyond the Ending: Narrative Strategies of Twentieth-Century Women Writers* (Bloomington: Indiana University Press, 1985). Du Plessis asserts that "it is the project of twentieth-century women writers to solve the contradiction between love and quest and to replace the alternate endings in marriage and death that are their cultural legacy from nineteenth-century life and letters by offering a different set of choices." (p. 4)

19. Du Plessis distinguishes between *hero* and *heroine* in this way: "the female hero is a central character whose activities, growth, and insight are given much narrative attention and authorial interest." By *heroine* she means "the object of male attention or rescue." *(Writing Beyond the Ending,* n. 22), p. 200 Hurston oscillates between these two positions, making Janie at one time a conventional romantic heroine, at other times a woman whose quest for independence drives the narrative.

20. Lee R. Edwards, *Psyche As Hero: Female Heroism and Fictional Form* (Middletown, Conn.: Wesleyan University Press, 1984), p. 212.

ZORA NEALE HURSTON

His Over-the-Creek Girl

There was a strange noise that John had never heard. He was sauntering along a road with his shoes in his hand. He could see houses here and there among the fields—not miles apart like where he had come from. Suddenly thirty or forty children erupted from a log building near the road-side, shouting and laughing. He had been to big meeting but this was no preaching. Not all them li'l' chaps. A chunky stern-faced man stood in the door momentarily with a bunch of hickories in his hand. So! This must be the school house that he had heard about. Negro children going to learn how to read and write like white folks. See! All this going on over there and the younguns over the Creek chopping cotton! It must be very nice, but maybe it wasn't for over-the-creek-niggers. These girls all had on starchy little aprons over Sunday-go-to-meeting dresses. He stopped and leaned upon the fence and stared.

One little girl with bright black eyes came and stood before him, arms akimbo. She must have been a leader, for several more came and stood back of her. She looked him over boldly from his tousled brown head to his bare white feet. Then she said, "Well folks! Where you reckon dis big yaller bee-stung nigger come from?"

Everybody laughed. He felt ashamed of his bare feet for the first time in his life. How was he to know that there were colored folks that went around with their feet cramped up like white folks. He looked down at the feet of the black-eyed girl. Tiny little black shoes. One girl behind her had breasts,

---

"His Over-the-Creek Girl" from *Jonah's Gourd Vine* (1934)

must be around fourteen. He looked at her again. Some others were growing up too. In fact all were looking a little bit like women—all but the little black-eyed one. When he looked back into her face he felt ashamed. Seemed as if she had caught him doing something nasty. He shifted his feet in embarrassment.

"Ah think he musta come from over de Big Creek. 'Tain't nothin' lak dat on dis side," the little tormenter went on. Then she looked right into his eyes and laughed. All the others laughed. John laughed too.

"Dat's whar Ah come from sho 'nuff," he admitted.

"Whut you doin' over heah, then?"

"Come tuh see iffen Ah could git uh job uh work. Kin yuh tell me whar Marse Alf Pearson live at?"

The little girl snorted, "Marse Alf! Don't y'all folkses over de creek know slavery time is over? 'Tain't no mo' Marse Alf, no Marse Charlie, nor Marse Tom neither. Folks whut wuz borned in slavery time go 'round callin' dese white folks Marse but we been born since freedom. We calls 'em Mister. Dey don't own nobody no mo'."

"Sho don't," the budding girl behind the little talker chimed in. She threw herself akimbo also and came walking out hippily from behind the other, challenging John to another appraisal of her person.

"Ah calls 'em anything Ah please," said another girl and pulled her apron a little tight across the body as she advanced towards the fence.

"Aw, naw, yuh don't, Clary," the little black-eyed girl disputed, "youse talkin' at de big gate now. You jus' want somebody tuh notice yuh."

"Well, effen you calls 'em Mista, Ah kin call 'em Mista too," John talked at the little spitfire. "Whar at is Mista Alf Pearson's place?"

"Way on down dis road, 'bout uh mile uh mo'. When yuh git long dere by de cotton-gin, ast somebody and dey'll tell yuh mo' exact."

John shifted from one foot to another a time or two, then started off with the long stride known as boaging.

"Thankee, thankee," he threw back over his shoulder and strode on.

The teacher poked his head out of the door and all the other girls ran around behind the school house lest he call them to account for talking to a boy. But the littlest girl stood motionless, not knowing that the others had fled. She stood still akimbo watching John stride away. Then suddenly her hands dropped to her sides and she raced along the inside of the fence and overtook John.

"Hello agin," John greeted her, glad at her friendliness.

"Hello yuhself, want uh piece uh cawn bread look on de shelf."

John laughed boisterously and the girl smiled and went on in another tone, "Whyn't *you* come tuh school too?"

" 'Cause dey never sont me. Dey tole me tuh go find work, but Ah wisht dey had uh tole me school. Whut Ah seen of it, Ah lakted it."

From behind her the irate voice of a man called, "Lucy! Lucy!! Come heah tuh me. Ah'll teach yuh 'bout talkin' wid boys!"

"See yuh later, and tell yuh straighter," John said and walked off.

John strode on into Notasulga, whistling; his tousled hair every which away over his head. He saw a group of people clustered near a small building and he timidly approached.

"Dis heah mis' be de cotton-gin wid all dem folks and hawses and buggies tied tuh de hitchin' postes."

Suddenly he was conscious of a great rumbling at hand and the train schickalacked up to the station and stopped.

John stared at the panting monster for a terrified moment, then prepared to bolt. But as he wheeled about he saw everybody's eyes upon him and there was laughter on every face. He stopped and faced about. Tried to look unconcerned, but that great eye beneath the cloud-breathing smoke-stack glared and threatened. The engine's very sides seemed to expand and contract like a fiery-lunged monster. The engineer leaning out of his window saw the fright in John's face and blew a sharp blast on his whistle and John started violently in spite of himself. The crowd roared.

"Hey, dere, big-un," a Negro about the station called to John, "you ain't never seed nothin' dangerous lookin' lak dat befo', is yuh?"

"Naw suh and hit sho look frightenin'," John answered. His candor took the ridicule out of the faces of the crowd. "But hits uh pretty thing do. Whar it gwine?"

"Oh eve'y which and whar," the other Negro answered, with the intent to convey the impression to John that he knew so much about trains, their habits and destinations that it would be too tiresome to try to tell it all.

The train kicked up its heels and rattled on off. John watched after it until it had lost itself down its shiny road and the noise of its going was dead.

"You laks dat ole train Ah see," the Negro said to John, watching him as he all but fell down into the railroad cut, trying to keep sight of the tail of the train.

"Yeah, man, Ah lakted dat. It say something but Ah ain't heered it 'nough tuh tell whut it say yit. You know whut it say?"

"It don't say nothin'. It jes' make uh powerful racket, dass all."

"Naw, it say some words too. Ahm comin' heah plenty mo' times and den Ah tell yuh whut it say." He straightened up and suddenly remembered.

"Whar de cotton-gin at?"

"Hit's right over dere, but dey ain't hirin' nobody yit."

"Ain't lookin' tuh git hiahed. Lookin' fuh Mist' Alf Pearson."

"Dere he right over dere on de flat-form at de deepo', whut yuh want wid 'im?"

"Wants tuh git uh job."

"Reckon you kin git on. He done turned off his coachman fuh stovin' up one uh his good buggy hawses."

John stalked over to the freight platform.

"Is you Mist' Alf?" he asked the tall broad-built man, who was stooping over some goods.

"Why yes, what're you want?"

"Ah wants uh job uh work, please suh."

The white man continued to examine invoices without so much as a glance at the boy who stood on the ground looking up at him. Not seeing what he wanted, he straightened up and looked about him and saw John at last. Instead of answering the boy directly he stared at him fixedly for a moment, whistled and exclaimed, "What a fine stud! Why boy, you would have brought five thousand dollars on the block in slavery time! Your face looks sort of familiar but I can't place you. What's your name?"

"Mama, she name me Two-Eye-John from a preachin' she heered, but dey call me John Buddy for short."

"How old are you, John?"

"Sixteen, goin' on sebenteen."

"Dog damn! Boy you're almost as big as I am. Where'd you come from?"

"Over de Big Creek. Mama she sont me over here and told me tuh ast you tuh gimme uh job uh work. Ah kin do mos' anything."

"Humph, I should think you could. Boy, you could go bear-hunting with your fist. I believe I can make a lead plow-hand out of you."

"Yassuh, thankee, Mista Alf, Ah knows how."

"Er, who is your mama?"

"Amy Crittenden. She didn't useter be uh Crittenden. She wuz jes Amy and b'longed tuh you 'fo surrender. She say Ah borned on yo' place."

"Oh yes. I remember her. G'wan get in my rig. The bay horses with the cream colored buggy. Fetch it on over here and drive me home."

John went over by the courthouse to get the rig. It was some distance. As soon as he was out of earshot, one of Alf

Pearson's friends asked him, "Say, Judge, where'd you get the new house-nigger from?"

"Oh a boy born on my place since surrender. Mama married some stray darky and moved over the Big Creek. She sent him over here to hunt work and he ran into me and I'm hiring him. Did you ever see such a splendid specimen? He'll be a mighty fine plow hand. Too tall to be a good cotton-picker. Sixteen years old."

"Humph! plow-hand! Dat's uh house-nigger. His kind don't make good field niggers. It's been tried. In his case it's a pity, because he'd be equal to two hands ordinary."

"Oh well, maybe I can do something with him. He seems willing enough. And anyway I know how to work 'em."

When John brought the horses to a satisfactory halt before the white pillars of the Pearson mansion, his new boss got down and said, "Now John, take those horses on to the stable and let Nunkie put 'em away. He'll show you where the quarters are. G'wan to 'em and tell old Pheemy I said fix you some place to sleep."

"Yassuh, thankee suh."

"And John, I might need you around the house sometimes, so keep clean."

"Yassuh."

"Where's the rest of your clothes?"

"Dese is dem."

"Well, you'll have to change sometime or other. I'll look around the house, and perhaps I can scare you up a change or two. My son Alfred is about your size, but he's several years older. And er, er, I'll fetch 'em down to the quarters in case I find anything. Go 'long."

Ole Pheemy gave John a bed in her own cabin, "Take dis bed heah if hit's good 'nough fuh yuh," she said pointing to a high feather bed in one corner.

"Yassum, thankee ma'am. Ah laks it jes fine, and dis sho is uh pritty house."

He was looking at the newspapers plastered all over the walls.

Pheemy softened.

"Oh you ain't one uh dese uppity yaller niggers then?"

"Oh no ma'am. Ahm po' folks jes lak you. On'y we ain't got no fine houses over de Creek lak dis heah one."

"Whus yo' name?"

"John, but Zeke and Zack and dem calls me John Buddy, yassum."

"Who yo' folks is over de Big Creek?"

"Mama she name Amy Crittenden—she—."

"Hush yo' mouf, you yaller rascal, you! Ah knowed, Ah seed reckerlection in yo' face." Pheemy rushed upon John, beating him affectionately and shoving him around. "Well, Lawd a'mussy boy! Ahm yo' granny! Yo' nable string is buried under dat air chanyberry tree. 'Member so well de very day you cried." (First cry at birth.) "Eat dis heah tater pone."

The field hands came in around dusk dark, eyeing John suspiciously, but his utter friendliness prevented the erection of barriers on his birth place. Amy's son was welcome. After supper the young folks played "Hide the Switch" and John overtook and whipped most of the girls soundly. They whipped him too. Perhaps his legs were longer, but anyway when he was "it" he managed to catch every girl in the quarters. The other boys were less successful, but girls were screaming under John's lash behind the cowpen and under the sweet-gum trees around the spring until the moon rose. John never forgot that night. Even the strong odor of their sweaty bodies was lovely to remember. He went in to bed when all the girls had been called in by their folks. He could have romped till morning.

In bed he turned and twisted.

"Skeeters botherin' yuh, John Buddy?" Pheemy asked.

"No'm Ahm jes wishin' Mist' Alf would lak mah work and lemme stay heah all de time." Then the black eyes of the little girl in the school yard burned at him from out of the darkness and he added, "Wisht Ah could go tuh school too."

"G'wan tuh sleep, chile. Heah 'tis way in de midnight and

you ain't had no night rest. You gotta sleep effen you wanta
do any work. Whut Marse Alf tell yuh tuh do?"

"He ain't tole me nothin' yit."

"Well, you stay heah tuh de house. Ontell he send fuh yuh.
He ain't gwine overwork yuh. He don't break nobody down.
Befo' surrender he didn't had no whippin' boss on *dis* place.
Nawsuh. Come tuh 'membrance, 'tain't nothin' much tuh do
now. De crops is laid by, de ground peas ain't ready, neither
de cawn. But Ah don't speck he gointer put you in de fiel'
nohow. Maybe you hand him his drinks uh drive de carridge
fuh him and Ole Miss."

"Yassum," drifted back from John as he slid down and
down into sleep and slumber.

That night he dreamed new dreams.

"John."

"Yassuh."

"I see the clothes fit you."

"Yassuh, Ahm powerful glad dey do, cause Ah laks 'em."

"John, I don't reckon I'll have you to drive us again. I
thought to make a coachman out of you, but the mistress
thinks you're too, er, er—large sitting up there in front.
Can't see around you."

"Yassuh," John's face fell. He wasn't going to be hired
after all.

"But I've got another job for you. You feed the chickens
and gather the eggs every morning before breakfast. Have
the fresh eggs in the pantry at the big house before seven
o'clock so Emma can use some for our breakfast."

"Yassuh."

"And John, see to it that Ceasar and Bully and Nunkie
keep the stables, pig pens and the chicken houses clean.
Don't say anything to 'em, but when you find 'em dirty you
let me know."

"Yassuh."

"And another thing, I want you to watch all of my brood
sows. As soon as a litter is born, you let me know. And you
must keep up with every pig on the place. Count 'em every

morning, and when you find one missing you look around and find out what's become of it. I'm missing entirely too many shoats. I'm good to my darkies but I can't let 'em eat up all my hogs. Now, I'm going to see if I can trust you."

"Yassuh."

"Can you read and write, John?"

"Nawsuh."

"Never been to school?"

"Nawsuh, yassuh, Ah passed by dat one d'other day."

"Well, John, there's nothing much to do on the place now, so you might as well go on down to the school and learn how to read and write. I don't reckon it will hurt you. Don't waste your time, now. Learn. I don't think the school runs but three months and it's got to close for cotton-picking. Don't fool around. You're almost grown. Three or four children on this place go so you go along with them. Go neat. I didn't have slouchy folks on my place in slavery time. Mister Alfred, my son, is studying abroad and he's left several suits around that will do for you. Be neat. Let's see your feet. I don't believe you can wear his shoes but I'll buy you a pair and take it out of your wages. You mind me and I'll make something out of you."

"Yassuh, Mister Alf. Thankee. Youse real good tuh me. Mama said you wuz good."

"She was a well-built-up girl and a splendid hoe hand. I never could see why she married that darky and let him drag her around share-cropping. Those backwoods white folks over the creek make their living by swindling the niggers."

John didn't go to school the next day. He had truly been delighted at the prospect of attending school. It had kept him glowing all day. But that night the young people got up a game of "Hide and Seek." It started a little late, about the time that the old heads were going to bed.

Bow-legged, pigeon-toed Minnie Turl was counting, "Ten, ten, double ten, forty-five, fifteen. All hid? All hid?"

From different directions, as the "hiders" sought cover, "No!"

> "Three li'l' hawses in duh stable,
>   One jumped out and skint his nable.
>   All hid? All hid?"

"No!" from farther away.

John ran down hill towards the spring where the bushes were thick. He paused at a clump. It looked like a good place. There was a stealthy small sound behind it and he ran on. Some one ran down the path behind him. A girl's hand caught his. It was Phrony, the womanish fourteen-year-old who lived in the third cabin from Pheemy's.

"Ah'll show yuh uh good place tuh hide," she whispered, "nobody can't find yuh."

She dragged him off the path to the right and round and about to a clump of sumac overrun with wild grape vines.

"Right under heah," she panted from running, "nobody can't find yuh."

"Whar you goin' hide yuhself?" John asked as he crept into the arboreal cave.

"Iss plenty room," Phrony whispered. "Us bofe kin hide in heah."

She crept in also and leaned heavily upon John, giggling and giggling as the counting went on.

> "Ah got up 'bout half-past fo'
>   Forty fo' robbers wuz 'round mah do'
>   Ah got up and let 'em in
>   Hit 'em ovah de head wid uh rollin' pin.
>   All hid? All hid?"

"Yeah."

"All dem ten feet round mah base is caught. Ahm comin'!"

There were screams and shouts of laughter. "Dere's Gold-Dollar behind dat chany-berry tree. Ah got yuh."

"Whoo-ee! Ahm free, Minnie, Ah beat yuh in home."

"Less we run in whilst she gone de other way," John whispered.

"Naw, less we lay low 'til she git tired uh huntin' us and give us free base."

"Aw right, Phrony, but Ah loves tuh outrun 'em and beat 'em tuh de base. 'Tain't many folks kin run good ez me."

"Ah kin run good, too."

"Aw, 'tain't no girl chile kin run good ez me."

"Ah betcha 'tis. Lucy Potts kin outrun uh yearlin' and rope 'im."

"Humph! Where she at?"

"She live over in Pottstown. Her folks done bought de ole Cox place. She go to school. Dey's big niggers."

"She uh li'l' bitty gal wid black eyes and long hair plats?"

"Yeah, dat's her. She leben years ole, but she don't look it. Ahm fourteen. Ahm big. Maybe Ah'll git married nex' year."

"Ahm gwine race huh jes soon ez Ah gits tuh school. Mista Alf gwine lemme go too."

"Dat's good. Ah done been dere las' yeah. Ah got good learnin'. Reckon Ah'll git uh husban' nex'."

Cry from up the hill, "John and Phrony, come on in. You get free base!"

They scrambled out. John first, then Phrony more slowly, and trudged up the hill. A boy was kneeling at the woods chopping-block base when they came into the crowd. The crowd began to disperse again. John started off in another direction. He looked back and saw Phrony coming behind him, but Mehaley cut in from behind a bush and reached him first.

"Come on wid me, John, lemme show yuh uh good place." He started to say that he didn't want to hide out and talk as he had done with Phrony. He wanted to pit his strength and speed against the boy who was counting. He wanted to practise running, but he felt a flavor come out from Mehaley. He could almost sense it in his mouth and nostrils. He was cross with Phrony for following them. He let Mehaley take his hand and they fled away up the hill and hid in the hay.

"De hair on yo' head so soft lak," Mehaley breathed against his cheek. "Lemme smoothen it down."

When John and Mehaley came in, Minnie Turl was counting. Everybody was hid except Phrony who sat bunched up on the door step.

"Y'all better go hide agin," she said.

"Somebody else count and lemme hide," Minnie wailed. "Ah been countin' most all de time," she came and stood near John.

"G'wan hide, Minnie, Ah'll count some," John said.

"Heh! Heh!" Phrony laughed maliciously at Minnie. Minnie looked all about her and went inside the house and to bed.

"Haley, where mah hair comb you borried from me las' Sunday? Ah wuz nice enough tuh len' it tuh yuh, but you ain't got manners 'nough tuh fetch it back." Phrony advanced upon Mehaley and John.

"You kin git yo' ole stink hair comb any time. Ah'll be glad tuh git it outa mah house. Mama tole me not tuh comb wid it 'cause she skeered Ah'd git boogers in mah haid."

"Youse uh lie! Ah ain't got no boogers in mah haid, and if yo' mamy say so she's uh liar right long wid you! She ain't so bad ez she make out. Ah'll stand on yo' toes and tell yuh so."

"Git back outa mah face, Phrony. Ah don't play de dozens!" Mehaley shoved. Phrony struck, and John and all the hiders, who came running in at the sound of battle, had trouble stopping the rough and tumble.

"Did y'all had words befo' yuh fell out?" Charlie asked.

"We ain't had no words," said Mehaley.

"Whut y'all fightin' 'bout, if yuh ain't mad?"

"Aw, ole fish-mouf Phrony mad cause John wouldn't hide wid her and he took and hid wid me."

"Youse uh liar, madam! He did so hide wid me."

"He wouldn't stay, and Ah'll betcha Alabama wid uh fence 'round it he won't never hide wid yuh no mo'."

Mehaley preened herself akimbo and rotated her hips insolently.

"Sh-sh—" Charlie cautioned, "de old heads liable tuh

wake up, and dey'll haul off and take and frail everybody. Less all tip in tuh bed. Iss way after midnight anyhow."

So John overslept next morning and by the time that he had gathered the eggs and counted the hogs it was too late for school. He didn't want to see Lucy anyway. Not the way he felt that day, but late in the afternoon as he wandered over the place, he found a tiny clearing hidden by trees.

"Dis is uh prayin' ground," he said to himself.

"O Lawd, heah 'tis once mo' and again yo' weak and humble servant is knee-bent and body bowed—Mayh heart beneath mah knees and mah knees in some lonesome valley cryin' fuh mercy whilst mercy kinst be found. O Lawd! you know mah heart, and all de ranges uh mah deceitful mind—and if you find any sin lurkin' in and about mah heart please pluck it out and cast it intuh de sea uh fuhgitfullness whar it'll never rise tuh condemn me in de judgment."

That night John, deaf to Mehaley's blandishments, sat in the doorway and told tales. And Brer Rabbit and Brer Fox and Raw-Head-and-Bloody-Bones walked the earth like natural men.

Next morning, bright and soon he stood at the schoolhouse door. The teacher was a stodgy middle-aged man who prided himself on his frowns. Every few moments he lifted his head and glared about the room. He yearned to hold his switches in his hand. He had little ambition to impart knowledge. He reigned. Later John found out he was Lucy's uncle.

"Come heah, you," he pointed his ruler at John. "Don't you know no bettern to come in my school and sit yo'self down without sayin' a word to me?"

"Yassuh," he approached the deal table that went by the name of desk.

"If you know better, why did you do it? I ought to put forty lashes on yo' bare back. You come to school?"

"Yassuh."

"Don't say 'yassuh' to me. Say 'Yes suh.' "

The room tittered.

"What's yo' name?"

"John."

"John whut? You got some other name besides John."

"Mama, she name me Two-Eye John—"

They burst into loud laughter. John colored and he stole a glance at Lucy. She wasn't laughing. Her hands and lips were tense. She must be put out with him for being a fool. She wasn't laughing like the rest.

"But Mama and all of 'em at home calls me John Buddy."

"Buddy is a nick-name. What's yo' papa' name?"

John scratched his head and thought a minute.

" 'Deed Ah don't know, suh."

There was another short silence.

"Where do you live?"

"On Mista Alf Pearson's place."

"Was you born there?"

"Yessuh."

"Well, Ah'll jus' put you down as John Pearson and you answer by that, you hear?"

"Yes suh."

"Ever been to school before?"

"Naw suh."

"Well, you get over there in de A B C class and don't let me ketch you talkin' in school."

John was amazed at the number of things to be learned. He liked to watch Lucy's class recite. They put so many figures on the board and called it long division. He would certainly be well learnt when he could do that. They parsed sentences. They spelt long words.

He studied hard because he caught Lucy watching him every time he recited. He wrote on the ground in the quarters and in a week he knew his alphabet and could count to a hundred.

"Whut you learnin' in school, John—A, B, Ab's?" Charlie asked him.

"Ah already know dat, Charlie. Ah kin spell 'baker' too."

"Don't b'lieve it. Not dis quick, yuh can't."

"B-a-k-bak-e-r-er baker."

"Boy, you sho is eatin' up dat school!"

"Ain't ez smart ez some. Take Lucy Potts for instink. She almost uh 'fessor now. Nobody can't spell her down. Dey say she kin spell eve'y word in Lippincott's Blue-back Speller."

"Shucks! You ain't tryin' tuh buck up tuh her in book learnin', is yuh? Dey tell me she kin spell 'compresstibility,' and when yuh git dat fur 'tain't much mo' fuhther fur yuh tuh go."

"She sho kin spell it, 'cause Ah heered 'er do it. Some say she kin spell 'Constan-ti-nople' too."

"Ah b'lieve it. All dem Potts is smart. Her brother leads de choir at Macedony Baptis' Church, and she trebles right 'long wid dem grown women and kin sing all de notes—de square ones, de round ones, de triangles."

"Ah'll be dere tuh heah her do it nex' big meetin'. Charlie, Ah loves tuh heah singin'."

"Whyn't yuh join de choir? You oughter be able tuh sing lak git out wid all dat ches' you got."

"B'lieve Ah will, Charlie. Ah laks big meetin'."

It was three weeks from the time that John started to school 'til cotton-picking time. Prodded on all sides, he had learned to read a little and write a few words crudely.

He was sorry when school closed for the cotton-picking but he kept on studying. When the school re-opened for its final month he wanted to get promoted again. He found himself spelling out words on barns and wagons, almanacs, horse-medicine-bottles, wrapping-paper.

He had been to church; he hadn't enough courage to join the choir, but every meeting he was there. Lucy tossed her head and sang her treble and never missed a note.

When the cotton-picking began on his place, Alf Pearson said to John, "You better go across the Creek and let your mama know how you're getting along. If you see any good cotton pickers—anybody that can pick more than two hundred a day—tell 'em I need some hands, and you be back by tomorrow night. I bought a brood sow over round Chehaw and I want you to go get her."

There was great rejoicing in Amy's house when John climbed the hill from the Creek.

They didn't know him in his new clothes. They made great "'miration" over everything. Amy cried.

"Jes tuh think, mah boy gittin' book-learnt! Ned, de rest uh dese chillun got tuh go tuh school nex' yeah. Sho is."

"Whut fur? So dey kin lay in de peni'ten'ry? Dat's all dese book-learnt niggers do—fill up de jails and chain-gangs. Dese boys is comin' 'long all right. All dey need tuh learn is how tuh swing uh hoe and turn a furrer. Ah ain't rubbed de hair offa mah haid 'gin no college walls and Ah got good sense. Day ain't goin' tuh no school effen Ah got anythin' tuh say 'bout it. Jes' be turnin' 'em fools!"

Stormy weather. John cut in.

"Mama, Mista Alf say if Ah could find some good cotton-pickers tuh tell 'em he need hands. You know any? He payin' fifty cent uh hund'ed."

"Dat's more'n dey payin' over heah," Ned cut in eagerly, "Amy, whyn't you take Zeke and Zack and y'all g'wan make dat li'l' change? Ah'll take keer de li'l' chillun and pick up whut li'l' Ah kin git over heah. Cotton open dat side de Creek fust anyhow. By time y'll finish over dere hit'll jis' be gittin' in full swing over heah."

"Reckon us could make li'l' money. Tell 'im, 'Yeah,' John Buddy, we's comin'."

"Zack!" Ned called, "Take dis heah jug and run over tuh de Turk place and tell Ike tuh send me uh gallon. Pay 'im nex' week some time."

When the cotton was all picked and the last load hauled to the gin, Alf Pearson gave the hands two hogs to barbecue.

That was a night. Hogs roasting over the open pit of oak coals. Negroes from three other plantations. Some brought "likker." Some crocus sacks of yellow yam potatoes, and bushels of peanuts to roast, and the biggest syrup-kettle at Pearson's cane-mill was full of chicken perleau. Twenty hens and six water-buckets full of rice. Old Purlee Kimball was stirring it with a shovel.

Plenty of music and plenty of people to enjoy it. Three sets had been danced when Bully took the center of the hard-packed clay court upon which they were dancing. He had the whole rib of a two-hundred-pound hog in his hands and gnawed it as he talked.

"Hey, everybody! Stop de music. Don't vip another vop 'til Ah says so. Hog head, hog bosom, hog hips and every kind of hog there ever wuz is ready! Come git yourn. De chickens is cacklin' in de rice and dey say 'Come git it whilst iss fitten 'cause t'morrer it may be frost-bitten!' De yaller yams is spilin' in de ashes. It's uh shame! Eat it all up, and den we's gointer dance, 'cause we'll have somethin' tuh dance offa."

The hogs, the chickens, the yams disappeared. The old folks played "Ole Horse" with the parched peanuts. The musicians drank and tuned up. Bully was calling figures.

"Hey you, dere, us ain't no white folks! Put down dat fiddle! Us don't want no fiddles, neither no guitars, neither no banjoes. Less clap!"

So they danced. They called for the instrument that they had brought to America in their skins—the drum—and they played upon it. With their hands they played upon the little dance drums of Africa. The drums of kid-skin. With their feet they stomped it, and the voice of Kata-Kumba, the great drum, lifted itself within them and they heard it. The great drum that is made by priests and sits in majesty in the juju house. The drum with the man skin that is dressed with human blood, that is beaten with a human shin-bone and speaks to gods as a man and to men as a God. Then they beat upon the drum and danced. It was said, "He will serve us better if we bring him from Africa naked and thingless." So the bukra reasoned. They tore away his clothes that Cuffy might bring nothing away, but Cuffy seized his drum and hid it in his skin under the skull bones. The shin-bones he bore openly, for he thought, "Who shall rob me of shin-bones when they see no drum?" So he laughed with cunning and said, "I, who am borne away to become an orphan, carry my parents with me. For *Rhythm* is she not my mother and Drama is her man?" So he groaned aloud in the ships and hid his drum and laughed.

"Dis is jes' lak when Ah wuz uh girl," Amy told Pheemy and offered her body to the voice.

Furious music of the little drum whose body was still in Africa, but whose soul sung around a fire in Alabama. Flourish. Break.

> Ole cow died in Tennessee
> Send her jawbone back to me
> Jawbone walk, Jawbone talk
> Jawbone eat wid uh knife and fork.
> Ain't Ah right?

> CHORUS: Yeah!
> Ain't I right? Yeah!

Hollow-hand clapping for the bass notes. Heel and toe stomping for the little one. Ibo tune corrupted with Nango. Congo gods talking in Alabama.

> If you want to see me jabber
> Set me down to uh bowl uh clabber
> Ain't Ah right? Yeah!
> Now, ain't Ah right? Yeah!

> Ole Ant Dinah behind de pine
> One eye out and de other one blind
> Ain't Ah right? Yeah! Yeah!
> Now, ain't Ah right? Yeah!

"Looka dat boy uh yourn, Amy!" Zeke Turk urged. "Didn't thought he knowed how tuh dance. He's rushin' de frog tuh de frolic! And looka 'Big 'Oman,' dat gal dancin' wid 'im. Lawd, she shakin' yonder skirt."

> Wisht Ah had uh needle
> Fine ez Ah could sew
> Ah'd sew mah baby to my side
> And down de road Ah'd go.

Double clapping—

Down de road baby
Down de road baby
It's killing mama
Oh, it's killing mama.

Too hot for words. Fiery drum clapping.

"Less burn dat ole moon down to a nub! Is dat you, Pheemy?"

"Yeah Lawd. Mah head is tilted to de grave, but Ah'll show y'all Ah ain't fuhgit how. Come on out heah, Dink, and help ole Pheemy do de Parse me lah."

"Heel and toe. Don't call no figgers."

"Aw yeah, less call figgers. Go 'head Bully, but don't call it lak you call for white folks and dey go praipsin 'cross the floor lak dey steppin on eggs. Us kin dance. Call 'em, Bully."

"Awright, choose yo' partners."

"Couples tuh yo' places lak hawse tuh de traces."

"Sixteen hands up!"

"Circle four."

"Y'all ain't clappin' right. Git dat time.

Raccoon up de 'simmon tree
Possum on de ground
Raccoon shake dem 'simmons down
Possum pass 'em round."

The fire died. The moon died. The shores of Africa receded. They went to sleep and woke up next day and looked out on dead and dying cotton stalks and ripening possum persimmons.

As the final day of school closing drew near, John found life tremendously exciting. The drama of Pearson's plantation yielded to the tenseness around the school house. He had learned to spell his way thru several pages in his reader. He could add, subtract and divide and multiply. He proved his new power to communicate his thoughts by scratching Lucy's name in the clay wherever he found a convenient spot: with a sharp stick he had even scratched it on the back of Pheemy's chimney.

He saw Lucy at school every day. He saw her in church, and she was always in his consciousness, but he had never talked with her alone. When the opportunity presented itself he couldn't find words. Handling Big 'Oman, Lacey, Semmie, Bootsie and Mehaley merely called for action, but with Lucy he needed words and words that he did not have. One day during the practice for school closing he crowded near her and said, "Wisht Ah could speak pieces lak you do."

"You kin speak 'em better'n me," Lucy said evenly, "you got uh good voice for speakin'."

"But Ah can't learn no long ones lak you speaks. When do you learn 'em?"

"In de night time round home after Ah git thru wid mah lessons."

"You ain't got many mo' days tuh be studyin' of nights. Den whut you gwine do wid yo'self?"

"Mama always kin find plenty fuh folks tuh do."

"But Ah mean in de night time, Lucy. When youse thru wid yo' work. Don't you do nothin' but warm uh chair bottom?"

Lucy drew away quickly, "Oooh, John Buddy! You talkin' nasty."

John in turn was in confusion. "Whuss nasty?"

"You didn't hafta say 'bottom.'"

John shriveled up inside. He had intended to recite the rhymes to Lucy that the girls on the plantation thought so witty, but he realized that—

> Some love collards, some love kale
> But I loves uh gal wid uh short skirt tail.

would drive Lucy from him in disgust. He could never tell her that. He felt hopeless about her. Soon she was recalled to the platform to recite and John's chance was gone. He kept on thinking, however, and he kept on making imaginary speeches to her. Speeches full of big words that would make her gasp and do him "reverence." He was glad when he was selected as the soldier to sing opposite Lucy in the duet, "O

Soldier, Will You Marry Me?" It meant something more than singing with gestures beside a girl. Maybe she would realize that he could learn things too, even if she could read the letter. He meant to change all that as quickly as possible. One day he shyly overtook her on her way home.

"Dey tell me you kin run fast," he began awkwardly.

"Dey tole you right," Lucy answered saucily, "whoever tole you. Ah kin outrun most anybody 'round heah."

"Less we race tuh dat sweet-gum tree and see who kin beat," John challenged.

They were off. Lucy's thin little legs pumping up and down. The starchy strings of her blue sunbonnet fluttering under her chin, and her bonnet lying back of her neck.

"Ah beat yuh!" John gloated over the foot or two that he had gained with difficulty.

"Yeah, you beat me, but look how much mo' legs you got to run wid," Lucy retorted. "Bet if Ah had dem legs nobody couldn't never outrun me."

"Ah didn't mean tuh beat yuh. Gee, us done come uh good ways! How much further you live from heah, Lucy?"

"Oh uh little ways cross de branch."

"B'lieve Ah'll go see how yo' ole branch look. Maybe it got uh heap uh fish in it."

" 'Tain't got no fish in it worth talkin' 'bout. 'Tain't hardly knee deep, John, but iss uh great big ole snake down dere."

"Whut kinda snake?"

"Uh great big ole cotton-mouf moccasin. He skeers me, John. Everytime Ah go 'cross dat foot-log Ah think maybe Ah might fall in and den he'll bite me, or he might reah hisself up and bite me anyhow."

"How come y'all don't take and kill 'im?"

"Who you reckon goin' down in de water tuh strain wid uh moccasin? He got uh hole back under the bank where you kin see 'im, but you can't git 'im 'thout you wuz down in de branch. He lay all 'round dere on de ground and even on de foot-log, but when he see somebody comin' he go in his hole, all ready for yuh and lay dere and dare yuh tuh bother 'im."

"You jes show 'im tuh me. Ah can't stand tuh be aggravated by no ole snake and then agin Ah don't want 'im slurrin' *you.*"

"Sh-sh, watch out, John! He 'round heah somewhere. Can't you smell 'im? Dere he is goin' in his hole!"

John took a good look at the snake, then looked all about him for a weapon. Finding none he sat down and began to remove his shoes.

"You ain't goin' in dat branch!" Lucy gasped.

"Turn me go, Lucy. If you didn't want yo' ole snake kilt yuh oughta not showed 'im tuh me." He exulted, but pretended not to see her concern was for him.

He looked carefully to see that no other snakes were about, then stepped cautiously down into the water. The snake went on guard, slowly, insolently. Lucy was terrified. Suddenly, he snatched the foot-log from its place and, leaning far back to give it purchase, he rammed it home upon the big snake and held it there. The snake bit at the log again and again in its agony, but finally the biting and the thrashing ceased. John fished the snake out and stretched it upon the grass.

"Ooh, John, Ahm sho glad you kilt dat ole devil. He been right dere skeerin' folks since befo' Ah wuz borned."

"He won't skeer nobody else, lessen dey skeered uh dead snakes," John answered in the tone that boys use to girls on such occasions.

"Reckon his mate ain't gonna follow us and try tuh bite us for killin' dis one?"

"Lucy, he can't foller bofe us, lessen us go de same way."

"Thass right, John. Ah done forgot, you live over on de Alf Pearson place."

"Yeah, dat's right."

"Where M'haley and Big 'Oman live."

"Unh hunh, Ah speck dey do live dere. Ah seen uh lot u

bullet-size girl chillun 'bout de place. Nearly uh hund'ed head uh folks on dat plantation."

A heavy silence fell. Lucy looked across the shallow stream and said,

"You ain't put de foot-log back, John."

"Dat's right. Sho nuff Ah done fuhgot. Lemme tote you 'cross den. Ah kin place it back for de other folks."

"Doncha lemme fall, John. Maybe 'nother ole snake down dere."

"How Ahm gonna let uh li'l' bit lak you fall? Ah kin tote uh sack uh feed-meal and dat's twice big ez you. Lemme tote yuh. Ah 'clare Ah won't drop yuh."

John bore Lucy across the tiny stream and set her down slowly.

"Oh you done left yo' book-sack, Lucy. Got tuh take yuh back tuh git it."

"Naw, you hand it tuh me, John."

"Aw, naw, you come git it."

He carried Lucy back and she recrossed the stream the third time. As he set her down on her home side he said, "Little ez you is nobody wouldn't keer how fur he hafta tote you. You ain't even uh handful."

Lucy put herself akimbo, "Ahm uh li'l' piece uh leather, but well put t'gether, Ah thankee, Mist' John."

"Mah comperments, Miss Lucy."

Lucy was gone up the hill in a blue whirlwind. John replaced the foot-log and cut across lots for home.

"She is full uh pepper," John laughed to himself, "but ah laks dat. Anything 'thout no seasonin' in it ain't no good."

At home, Lucy rushed out back of the corn crib and tiptoed to see if her head yet touched the mark she had made three weeks before.

"Ah shucks!" She raged, "Ah ain't growed none hardly. Ah ain't never gointer get grown. Ole M'haley way head uh me!"

She hid and cried until Emmeline, her mama, called her to set the table for supper.

The night of school closing came. John in tight new shoes and with a standing collar was on hand early. Saw Lucy enter followed by the Potts clan. Frowning mama, placid papa, strapping big sister, and the six grown brothers. Boys with "rear-back" hair held down by a thick coating of soap. Boys hobbling in new shoes and tight breeches. Girls whose hair smelled of fresh hog-lard and sweet william, and white dresses with lace, with pink or blue sashes, with ruffles, with mothers searching their bosoms for pins to yank up hanging petticoats. Tearful girls who had forgotten their speeches. Little girls with be-ribboned frizzed-out hair who got spanked for wetting their starchy panties. Proud parents. Sulky parents and offspring. Whispered envy.

"Dere's Lucy Potts over dere in uh fluted dress. Dey allus gives her de longest piece tuh speak."

"Dat's 'cause she kin learn more'n anybody else."

"Naw 'tain't, dey muches her up. Mah Semmie could learn je' ez long uh piece ez anybody if de give it tuh her—in time. Ahm gwine take mah chillun outa school after dis and put 'em tuh work. Dey ain't learnin' 'em nothin' nohow. Dey makes cake outa some uh de chillun and cawn bread outa de rest."

Opening prayer. Song. Speech by white superintendent. Speeches rattled off like beans poured into a tin can.

"A speech by Miss Lucy Potts."

The shining big eyes in the tiny face. Lacy whiteness. Fierce hand-clapping. Lucy calm and self-assured.

"A chieftain to the highland bound, cried 'Boatman do not tarry' "—to the final. "My daughter, oh my daughter." More applause. The idol had not failed her public.

"She kin speak de longest pieces and never miss uh word and say 'em faster dan anybody Ah ever seed." It was agreed Lucy was perfect. Time and speeches flew fast.

> Little fishes in de brook
> Willie ketch 'em wid uh hook

Mama fry 'em in de pan
Papa eat 'em lak uh man.

"Duet—Miss Lucy Potts, bassed by Mr. John Pearson." They sang and their hearers applauded wildly. Nobody cared whether the treble was treble or the bass was bass. It was the gestures that counted and everybody agreed that John was perfect as the philandering soldier of the piece and that Lucy was just right as the over-eager maid. They had to sing it over twice. John began to have a place of his own in the minds of folks, more than he realized.

ZORA NEALE HURSTON

Janie Crawford

The years took all the fight out of Janie's face. For a while she thought it was gone from her soul. No matter what Jody did, she said nothing. She had learned how to talk some and leave some. She was a rut in the road. Plenty of life beneath the surface but it was kept beaten down by the wheels. Sometimes she stuck out into the future, imagining her life different from what it was. But mostly she lived between her hat and her heels, with her emotional disturbances like shade patterns in the woods—come and gone with the sun. She got nothing from Jody except what money could buy, and she was giving away what she didn't value.

Now and again she thought of a country road at sun-up and considered flight. To where? To what? Then too she considered thirty-five is twice seventeen and nothing was the same at all.

"Maybe he ain't nothin'," she cautioned herself, "but he is something in my mouth. He's got tuh be else Ah ain't got nothin' tuh live for. Ah'll lie and say he is. If Ah don't, life won't be nothin' but uh store and uh house."

She didn't read books so she didn't know that she was the world and the heavens boiled down to a drop. Man attempting to climb to painless heights from his dung hill.

Then one day she sat and watched the shadow of herself going about tending store and prostrating itself before Jody, while all the time she herself sat under a shady tree with the wind blowing through her hair and her clothes. Somebody near about making summertime out of lonesomeness.

"Janie Crawford" from *Their Eyes Were Watching God* (1937)

This was the first time it happened, but after a while it got so common she ceased to be surprised. It was like a drug. In a way it was good because it reconciled her to things. She got so she received all things with the stolidness of the earth which soaks up urine and perfume with the same indifference.

One day she noticed that Joe didn't sit down. He just stood in front of a chair and fell in it. That made her look at him all over. Joe wasn't so young as he used to be. There was already something dead about him. He didn't rear back in his knees any longer. He squatted over his ankles when he walked. That stillness at the back of his neck. His prosperous-looking belly that used to thrust out so pugnaciously and intimidate folks, sagged like a load suspended from his loins. It didn't seem to be a part of him anymore. Eyes a little absent too.

Jody must have noticed it too. Maybe, he had seen it long before Janie did, and had been fearing for her to see. Because he began to talk about her age all the time, as if he didn't want her to stay young while he grew old. It was always "You oughta throw somethin' over yo' shoulders befo' you go outside. You ain't no young pullet no mo'. You'se uh ole hen now." One day he called her off the croquet grounds. "Dat's somethin' for de young folks, Janie, you out dere jumpin' round and won't be able tuh git out de bed tuhmorrer." If he thought to deceive her, he was wrong. For the first time she could see a man's head naked of its skull. Saw the cunning thoughts race in and out through the caves and promontories of his mind long before they darted out of the tunnel of his mouth. She saw he was hurting inside so she let it pass without talking. She just measured out a little time for him and set it aside to wait.

It got to be terrible in the store. The more his back ached and his muscle dissolved into fat and the fat melted off his bones, the more fractious he became with Janie. Especially in the store. The more people in there the more ridicule he poured over her body to point attention away from his own.

So one day Steve Mixon wanted some chewing tobacco and Janie cut it wrong. She hated that tobacco knife anyway. I worked very stiff. She fumbled with the thing and cut way away from the mark. Mixon didn't mind. He held it up for a joke to tease Janie a little.

"Looka heah, Brother Mayor, whut yo' wife done took and done." It was cut comical, so everybody laughed at it. "Uh woman and uh knife—no kind of uh knife, don't b'long tuhgether." There was some more good-natured laughter at the expense of women.

Jody didn't laugh. He hurried across from the post office side and took the plug of tobacco away from Mixon and cut it again. Cut it exactly on the mark and glared at Janie.

"I god almighty! A woman stay round uh store till she get old as Methusalem and still can't cut a little thing like a plug of tobacco! Don't stand dere rollin' yo' pop eyes at me wid yo' rump hangin' nearly to yo' knees!"

A big laugh started off in the store but people got to thinking and stopped. It was funny if you looked at it right quick, but it got pitiful if you thought about it awhile. It was like somebody snatched off part of a woman's clothes while she wasn't looking and the streets were crowded. Then too Janie took the middle of the floor to talk right into Jody's face, and that was something that hadn't been done before.

"Stop mixin' up mah doings wid mah looks, Jody. When you git through tellin' me how tuh cut uh plug uh tobacco then you kin tell me whether mah behind is on straight or not."

"Wha—whut's dat you say, Janie? You must be out yo head."

"Naw, Ah ain't outa mah head neither."

"You must be. Talkin' any such language as dat."

"You de one started talkin' under people's clothes. Not me."

"Whut's de matter wid you, nohow? You ain't no young girl to be gettin' all insulted 'bout yo' looks. You ain't no young courtin' gal. You'se uh ole woman, nearly forty."

"Yeah, Ah'm nearly forty and you'se already fifty. How come you can't talk about dat sometimes instead of always pointin' at me?"

"T'ain't no use in gettin' all mad, Janie, 'cause Ah mention you ain't no young gal no mo'. Nobody in heah ain't lookin' for no wife outa yuh. Old as you is."

"Naw, Ah ain't no young gal no mo' but den Ah ain't no old woman neither. Ah reckon Ah looks mah age too. But Ah'm uh woman every inch of me, and Ah know it. Dat's uh whole lot more'n *you* kin say. You big-bellies round here and put out a lot of brag, but 'tain't nothin' to it but yo' big voice. Humph! Talkin' 'bout *me* lookin' old! When you pull down yo' britches, you look lak de change uh life."

"Great God from Zion!" Sam Watson gasped. "Y'all really playin' de dozens tuhnight."

"Wha—whut's dat you said?" Joe challenged, hoping his ears had fooled him.

"You heard her, you ain't blind," Walter taunted.

"Ah ruther be shot with tacks than tuh hear dat 'bout mahself," Lige Moss commiserated.

Then Joe Starks realized all the meanings and his vanity bled like a flood. Janie had robbed him of his illusion of irresistible maleness that all men cherish, which was terrible. The thing that Saul's daughter had done to David. But Janie had done worse, she had cast down his empty armor before men and they had laughed, would keep on laughing. When he paraded his possessions hereafter, they would not consider the two together. They'd look with envy at the things and pity the man that owned them. When he sat in judgment it would be the same. Good-for-nothing's like Dave and Lum and Jim wouldn't change place with him. For what can excuse a man in the eyes of other men for lack of strength? Raggedy-behind squirts of sixteen and seventeen would be giving him their merciless pity out of their eyes while their mouths said something humble. There was nothing to do in life anymore. Ambition was useless. And the cruel deceit of Janie! Making all that show of humbleness and scorning him all the time! Laughing at him, and now putting the town up to do the same. Joe Starks didn't know the words for all this, but he knew the feeling. So he struck Janie with all his might and drove her from the store.

After that night Jody moved his things and slept in a room downstairs. He didn't really hate Janie, but he wanted her to think so. He had crawled off to lick his wounds. They didn't talk too much around the store either. Anybody that didn't know would have thought that things had blown over, it looked so quiet and peaceful around. But the stillness was the sleep of swords. So new thoughts had to be thought and new words said. She didn't want to live like that. Why must Joe be so mad with her for making him look small when he did it to her all the time? Had been doing it for years. Well, if she must eat out of a long-handled spoon, she must. Jody might get over his mad spell any time at all and begin to act like somebody towards her.

Then too she noticed how baggy Joe was getting all over. Like bags hanging from an ironing board. A little sack hung from the corners of his eyes and rested on his cheek-bones; a loose-filled bag of feathers hung from his ears and rested on his neck beneath his chin. A sack of flabby something hung from his loins and rested on his thighs when he sat down. But even these things were running down like candle grease as time moved on.

He made new alliances too. People he never bothered with one way or another now seemed to have his ear. He had always been scornful of root-doctors and all their kind, but now she saw a faker from over around Altamonte Springs hanging around the place almost daily. Always talking in low tones when she came near, or hushed altogether. She didn't know that he was driven by a desperate hope to appear the old-time body in her sight. She was sorry about the root-doctor because she feared that Joe was depending on the scoundrel to make him well when what he needed was doctor, and a good one. She was worried about his not eating his meals, till she found out he was having old lady Davis to cook for him. She knew that she was a much better cook than the old woman, and cleaner about the kitchen. So she bought a beef-bone and made him some soup.

"Naw, thank you," he told her shortly. "Ah'm havin' uh hard enough time tuh try and git well as it is."

She was stunned at first and hurt afterwards. So she went straight to her bosom friend, Pheoby Watson, and told her about it.

"Ah'd ruther be dead than for Jody tuh think Ah'd hurt him," she sobbed to Pheoby. "It ain't always been too pleasant, 'cause you know how Joe worships de works of his own hands, but God in heben knows Ah wouldn't do one thing tuh hurt nobody. It's too underhand and mean."

"Janie, Ah thought maybe de thing would die down and you never would know nothin' 'bout it, but it's been singin' round here ever since de big fuss in de store dat Joe was 'fixed' and you wuz de one dat did it."

"Pheoby, for de longest time, Ah been feelin' dat somethin' set for still-bait, but dis is—is—oh Pheoby! Whut *kin* I do?"

"You can't do nothin' but make out you don't know it. It's too late fuh y'all tuh be splittin' up and gittin' divorce. Just g'wan back home and set down on yo' royal diasticutis and say nothin'. Nobody don't b'lieve it nohow."

"Tuh think Ah been wid Jody twenty yeahs and Ah just now got tuh bear de name uh poisonin' him! It's 'bout to kill me, Pheoby. Sorrow dogged by sorrow is in mah heart."

"Dat's lie dat trashy nigger dat calls hisself uh two-headed doctor brought tuh 'im in order tuh git in wid Jody. He seen he wuz sick—everybody been knowin' dat for de last longest, and den Ah reckon he heard y'all wuz kind of at variance, so dat wuz his chance. Last summer dat multiplied cock-roach wuz round heah tryin' tuh sell gophers!"

"Pheoby, Ah don't even b'lieve Jody b'lieve dat lie. He ain't never took no stock in de mess. He just make out he b'lieve it tuh hurt me. Ah'm stone dead from standin' still and tryin' tuh smile."

She cried often in the weeks that followed. Joe got too weak to look after things and took to his bed. But he relentlessly refused to admit her to his sick-room. People came and went in the house. This one and that one came into her house with covered plates of broth and other sick-room dishes without taking the least notice of her as Joe's wife. People who never had known what it was to enter the gate of the Mayor's yard unless it were to do some menial job now paraded in and out as his confidants. They came to the store and ostentatiously looked over whatever she was doing and went back to report to him at the house. Said things like "Mr. Starks need *somebody* tuh sorta look out for 'im till he kin git on his feet again and look for hisself."

But Jody was never to get on his feet again. Janie had Sam Watson to bring her the news from the sick room, and when he told her how things were, she had him bring a doctor from Orlando without giving Joe a chance to refuse, and without saying she sent for him.

"Just a matter of time," the doctor told her. "When a man's kidneys stop working altogether, there is no way for him to live. He needed medical attention two years ago. Too late now."

So Janie began to think of Death. Death, that strange being with the huge square toes who lived way in the West. The great one who lived in the straight house like a platform without sides to it, and without a roof. What need has Death for a cover, and what winds can blow against him? He stands in his high house that overlooks the world. Stands watchful and motionless all day with his sword drawn back, waiting for the messenger to bid him come. Been standing there before there was a where or a when or a then. She was liable to find a feather from his wings lying in her yard any day now. She was sad and afraid too. Poor Jody! He ought not to have to wrassle in there by himself. She sent Sam in to suggest a visit, but Jody said No. These medical doctors wuz all right with the Godly sick, but they didn't know a thing about a case like his. He'd be all right just as soon as the two-headed man found what had been buried against him. He wasn't going to die at all. That was what he thought. But Sam told her different, so she knew. And then if he hadn't, the next morning she was bound to know, for people began to gather in the big yard under the palm and chinaberry trees. People who would not have dared to foot the place before crept in and did not come to the house. Just squatted under the trees and waited. Rumor, that wingless bird, had shadowed over the town.

She got up that morning with the firm determination to go on in there and have a good talk with Jody. But she sat a long time with the walls creeping in on her. Four walls squeezing her breath out. Fear lest he depart while she sat trembling upstairs nerved her and she was inside the room before she caught her breath. She didn't make the cheerful, casual start that she had thought out. Something stood like an oxen's foot on her tongue, and then too, Jody, no Joe, gave her a ferocious look. A look with all the unthinkable coldness of outer space. She must talk to a man who was ten immensities away.

He was lying on his side facing the door like he was expecting somebody or something. A sort of changing look on his face. Weak-looking but sharp-pointed about the eyes. Through the thin counterpane she could see what was left of his belly huddled before him on the bed like some helpless thing seeking shelter.

The half-washed bedclothes hurt her pride for Jody. He had always been so clean.

"Whut you doin' in heah, Janie?"

"Come tuh see 'bout you and how you wuz makin' out."

He gave a deep-growling sound like a hog dying down in the swamp and trying to drive off disturbance. "Ah come in heah tuh git shet uh you but look lak 'tain't doin' me no good. G'wan out. Ah needs tuh rest."

"Naw, Jody, Ah come in heah tuh talk widja and Ah'm gointuh do it too. It's for both of our sakes Ah'm talkin'."

He gave another ground grumble and eased over on his back.

"Jody, maybe Ah ain't been sich uh good wife tuh you, but Jody—"

"Dat's 'cause you ain't got de right feelin' for nobody. You oughter have some sympathy 'bout yo'self. You ain't no hog."

"But, Jody, Ah meant tuh be awful nice."

"Much as Ah done fuh yuh. Holdin' me up tuh scorn. No sympathy!"

"Naw, Jody, it wasn't because Ah didn't have no sympathy. Ah had uh lavish uh dat. Ah just didn't never git no chance tuh use none of it. You wouldn't let me."

"Dat's right, blame everything on me. Ah wouldn't let you show no feelin'! When, Janie, dat's all Ah ever wanted or desired. Now you come blamin' me!"

" 'Tain't dat, Jody. Ah ain't here tuh blame nobody. Ah'm just tryin' tuh make you know what kinda person Ah is befo' it's too late."

"Too late?" he whispered.

His eyes buckled in a vacant-mouthed terror and she saw the awful surprise in his face and answered it.

"Yeah, Jody, don't keer whut dat multiplied cock-roach told yuh tuh git yo' money, you got tuh die, and yuh can't live."

A deep sob came out of Jody's weak frame. It was like beating a bass drum in a hen-house. Then it rose high like pulling in a trombone.

"Janie! Janie! don't tell me Ah got tuh die, and Ah ain't used tuh thinkin' 'bout it."

" 'Tain't really no need of you dying, Jody, if you had of— de doctor—but it don't do no good bringin' dat up now. Dat's just whut Ah wants tuh say, Jody. You wouldn't listen. You done lived wid me for twenty years and you don't half know me atall. And you could have but you was so busy

worshippin' de works of yo' own hands, and cuffin' folks
around in their minds till you didn't see uh whole heap uh
things yuh could have."

"Leave heah, Janie. Don't come heah—"

"Ah knowed you wasn't gointuh lissen tuh me. You
changes everything but nothin' don't change you—not even
death. But Ah ain't goin' outa here and Ah ain't gointuh
hush. Naw, you gointuh listen tuh me one time befo' you die.
Have yo' way all yo' life, trample and mash down and then
die ruther than tuh let yo'self heah 'bout it. Listen, Jody, you
ain't de Jody ah run off down de road wid. You'se whut's left
after he died. Ah run off tuh keep house wid you in uh
wonderful way. But you wasn't satisfied wid me de way Ah
was. Naw! Mah own mind had tuh be squeezed and crowded
out tuh make room for yours in me."

"Shut up! Ah wish thunder and lightnin' would kill yuh!"

"Ah know it. And now you got tuh die tuh find out dat you
got tuh pacify somebody besides yo'self if you wants any love
and any sympathy in dis world. You ain't tried tuh pacify
nobody but yo'self. Too busy listening tuh yo' own big voice."

"All dis tearin' down talk!" Jody whispered with sweat
globules forming all over his face and arms. "Git outa
heah!"

"All dis bowin' down, all dis obedience under yo' voice—
dat ain't whut Ah rushed off down de road tuh find out about
you."

A sound of strife in Jody's throat, but his eyes stared
unwillingly into a corner of the room so Janie knew the futile
fight was not with her. The icy sword of the square-toed one
had cut off his breath and left his hands in a pose of agonizing protest. Janie gave them peace on his breast, then she
studied his dead face for a long time.

"Dis sittin' in de rulin' chair is been hard on Jody," she
muttered out loud. She was full of pity for the first time in
years. Jody had been hard on her and others, but life had
mishandled him too. Poor Joe! Maybe if she had known
some other way to try, she might have made his face differ-

ent. But what that other way could be, she had no idea. She thought back and forth about what had happened in the making of a voice out of a man. Then thought about herself. Years ago, she had told her girl self to wait for her in the looking glass. It had been a long time since she had remembered. Perhaps she'd better look. She went over to the dresser and looked hard at her skin and features. The young girl was gone, but a handsome woman had taken her place. She tore off the kerchief from her head and let down her plentiful hair. The weight, the length, the glory was there. She took careful stock of herself, then combed her hair and tied it back up again. Then she starched and ironed her face, forming it into just what people wanted to see, and opened up the window and cried, "Come heah people! Jody is dead. Mah husband is gone from me."

BIBLIOGRAPHIC NOTES

Critical commentary on Zora Neale Hurston has never been lukewarm. For the first thirty years after she began writing, many Hurston critics were influenced as much by her personality and her politics as they were by her writing. Richard Wright thought her novel *Their Eyes Were Watching God* was counterrevolutionary, and in his 1937 review, " 'Between Laughter and Tears,' " for the leftist journal *New Masses* (5 October 1937):25–26, he accused her of voluntarily continuing the minstrel tradition, of exploiting the quaintness of Negro life in order to make white folks laugh. In his 1938 review of the literature of the race, Alain Locke in "Jingo, Counter—Jingo and Us," *Opportunity: Journal of Negro Life* 16, no. 2 (1938):10, dismissed the novel as one that failed to probe the inner psychology of its characters or to provide sharp social analysis. Locke called Hurston's characters oversimplified, "pseudo-primitives whom the reading public still loves to laugh with and weep over." Sterling Brown, the dean of Afro-American critics during the 1930s and 1940s, felt that Hurston avoided the harshness of Southern black life. Even in 1971, when Harlem Renaissance writers were being rediscovered and reinterpreted, Hurston was being subjected to harsh and unfair criticism. Nathan Huggins in *Harlem Renaissance* (New York: Oxford University Press, 1971) devotes much of his commentary on Hurston to Wallace Thurman's vitriolic satire on Hurston. Darwin Turner's 1971 study of Hurston, *In a Minor Chord: Three Afro-American Writers and Their Search for Identity* (Carbondale: Southern Illinois University Press, 1971), insists that Hurston's work be evaluated on the basis of her personality. Turner describes her as a quick-tempered woman, arrogant toward her peers, obsequious toward her superiors, desperate for recognition to assuage her feelings of inferiority. Then he concludes, "It is in reference to this image that one must examine her novels and her folklore."

Fortunately for Hurston, there is a new generation of scholars rereading and revising the critical commentary on her work. Among the best commentaries on *Their Eyes* are articles by Henry Louis Gates Jr., Anne Jones, Barbara Johnson, Robert Hemenway, and June Jordan—all of which are mentioned in this bibliography and all of which focus on Hurston's attempt to acknowledge the character of Janie Starks as an articulate voice in the Afro-American literary tradition. Gates, in his essay, "Zora Neale Hurston and the Speakerly Text," sees the novel as an evolution of black rhetorical strategy that culminates in the rejection of standard English and the reaffirmation of black dialect, the love affair with Tea Cake permitting and embodying that affirmation. Anne Jones, insisting on a more feminist reading in "Pheoby's Hungry Listening: Zora Neale Hurston's *Their Eyes Were Watching God*" (Paper presented at the National Women's Studies Association, Humboldt State University, Arcata Calif., June 1982) says that the novel revises the traditional male sermon: Janie preaches the sermon that her grandmother could not; she preaches it not from on high as traditional preacher, but to one eager friend whose hungry listening urges her on. Her sermon, says Jones, is about experience that ultimately makes words meaningful: "You got tuh *go* there tuh *know* there . . . talkin' don't amount tuh uh hill uh beans when yuh can't do nothin' else."

Barbara Johnson's essay, "Metaphor and metonymy and voice in *Their Eyes Were Watching God,*" in *Black Literature and Literary Theory,* ed. Henry-Louis Gates Jr., (New York: Methuen, 1984), pp. 205–19, also a feminist reading, focuses on a critical passage in the text, the two paragraphs in which Janie articulates her own self-division. When Janie is able to admit the incompatible forces within her, when she is able to recognize that "she had an inside and an outside now and suddenly she knew how to mix them," she is released from silence. From that point on in the novel, Johnson maintains, Janie paradoxically begins to speak. She is propelled into speech, not by a sense of unity or wholeness, but by the recognition of her own fragmentation. Lee R. Edwards discusses Janie's heroic power in her critical study of female heroism, *Psyche As Hero: Female Heroism and Fictional Form* (Middletown, Conn.: Wesleyan University Press, 1984), and concludes that Janie's heroic status at the end of the novel is unprecedented in women's fiction: "What she has, she shares with no other character we have considered: radiance, a complex and unshakable optimism, a capacity to stand alone without thereby abandoning a fully realized and never betrayed connection with another."

Robert Hemenway's excellent biography, *Zora Neale Hurston: A Literary Biography* (Urbana: University of Illinois Press, 1977), and Alice Walker's anthology of Hurston's work, *I Love Myself When I Am Laughing . . . And Then Again When I Am Looking Mean and Impressive: A Zora Neale Hurston Reader* (Old Westbury, N.Y.: The Feminist Press, 1979), are two of the texts that rescued Hurston from oblivion and restored her to her rightful place in American literature.

ADDITIONAL BIBLIOGRAPHY

Robert Hemenway, "Are You a Flying Lark or a Setting Dove?" in *Afro-American Literature: The Reconstruction of Instruction,* ed. Dexter Fisher and Robert B. Stepto (New York: Modern Language Association of America, 1979), pp. 122–52. Hemenway insists that in order to interpret Hurston's work one must have extensive knowledge of black folklore. As he demonstrates with his analysis of *Jonah's Gourd Vine,* one must understand the traditional metaphor and images of black poetic language in order to understand the novel's significance.

June Jordan, "On Richard Wright and Zora Neale Hurston," *Black World* 23 (August 1974): 4–8. Jordan's comparison of these two writers, a refutation of Wright's attack on Hurston, focuses on Hurston's novel as an affirmation of black life.

Ellease Southerland, "The Novelist-Anthropologist's Life/Works: Zora Neale Hurston," *Black World* 23 (August 1974): 20–30.

Mary Helen Washington, "Zora Neale Hurston: The Black Woman's Search for Identity," *Black World* 21 (August 1972): 68–74; and Mary Helen Washington, "A Woman Half in Shadow," in *I Love Myself When I Am Laughing . . . And Then Again When I Am Looking Mean and Impressive: A Zora Neale Hurston Reader,* ed. Alice Walker (Old Westbury, N.Y.: The Feminist Press, 1979), pp. 7–25.

PART FIVE

I see the mask, sense
the girl and the woman
you became, wonder
if mask and woman
are one, if pain is
the sum of all your
knowing, victim the
only game you learned.

—Sherley Anne Williams,
Some One Sweet Angel Chile

INTRODUCTION

"Infidelity Becomes Her":
The Ambivalent Woman in the Fiction
of Ann Petry and Dorothy West

Even though Ann Petry is still writing today, most of the criticism of her work has locked her into the 1940s tradition of social protest and the Richard Wright school of environmental determinism. But since her 1946 novel, *The Street*, and a 1947 novella, "In Darkness and Confusion," which clearly fit the mold of social protest fiction, Petry has written two novels, a book of short stories, and two biographies for young people.[1] As Petry's work moves away from the hostile environment of Harlem, the setting of her early work, her characters gain strength and stature. Her women and her men, especially in the stories set in New England *(Miss Muriel and Other Stories)*, are more firmly rooted in a sustaining community and are therefore less isolated and less likely to be defeated by external forces.

Certainly Petry's major work in the 1940s shows the environment as an overwhelming force determining people's lives. The protagonist of *The Street*, Lutie Johnson, is destroyed by economic and social forces that she is powerless to change. As she tries to speculate at the end of the story on what has caused her disastrous fate, she thinks, "It was that street. It was that god-damned street." In the short 1940s novella, "In Darkness and Confusion," the main character William Jones is constantly thinking about moving to a new apartment and a new street as if he is totally shaped by the place where he lives. The street in both of these stories seems almost more alive than the characters. When Petry was interviewed in the *Crisis*, following the success of *The*

Street, she insisted on the environment as a major factor in shaping the lives of her characters:

> In *The Street* my aim is to show how simply and easily the environment can change the course of a person's life. . . . I try to show why the Negro has a high crime rate, a high death rate, and little or no chance of keeping his family unit intact in large northern cities. There are no statistics in the book although they are present in the background, not as columns of figures but in terms of what life is like for people who live in over-crowded tenements.[2]

One of the reasons I am uneasy with Petry's insistence on environmental determinism as an explanation for her characters' dead-end lives is that this form of social protest fiction, while it diminishes the effectiveness of all human energy, threatens to marginalize and repress women in particular. What is hidden beneath the surface of deterministic fiction is an ideology that is mainly concerned with men. Identified with nature as one of the forces men must contend against, women have mysterious sexual power, capable of destroying men, turning them from their ideals. The revolt in this fiction is against racism, not sexism; its deep ideological conflict is between black men and white men. With its emphasis on a hostile physical environment, on crime, on suppressed aggression, on white exploitation of black life, deterministic fiction ignores many of the deeply felt realities of women's lives: their relationships with their families, their own suppressed creativity, and their conflicts with black men and with patriarchy.

This form of social protest is so inimical to women that they are often depicted in this fiction as victimizers. Valerie Smith points out in her recent study of narrative strategy in Afro-American fiction that because Richard Wright saw black women as implicated in the oppression of black men he sets up his male protagonists "to routinely reject their connections to black women as a stage in their search for liberation."[3] But women writers, attempting to write in this "borrowed" form, have also revealed, perhaps inadvertently, a similar bias against their women characters. As one of the few writers of social protest fiction to use a woman as the main character, Ann Petry does show Lutie Johnson's struggle as a single mother to hold her family together, to create a career as a singer, and to fight against male domination; but Lutie is also shown as the object of male desire, so that the reader is forced to assume the point of view of the male, objectifying the female, reducing her, in one case, to an object that can be weighed, bought, and sold—literally a marketable product.[4] At crucial points which could give the reader a sense of Lutie's internal life, Petry turns away from her and concentrates on male characters. As in a number of other women's novels of this period a young male—in this novel, Lutie's son Bub—remains at the end to represent the potential for change and growth in the future.[5]

Certainly, Petry meant for *The Street* and her other fiction of the 1940s to document the accumulation of evils that create the dead-end lives of the poor. The people she writes about experience racism in every aspect of their lives—from the hospitals that refuse to treat them, to the schools where their children are labeled stupid and dismissed. Poverty makes it impossible for the Jones family to move to a decent apartment. While protest fiction has been attacked as a literary genre with "little flexibility, no subtlety, and circumscribed possibilities," one that sacrifices the complexity of experience in order to score political points,[6] I think the current need to distance ourselves from political realities, the need to divorce literature and literary criticism from a social and historical context is part of what makes us uncomfortable with texts like "In Darkness and Confusion" and *The Street*. Petry's fiction engages us, in most unpleasurable ways, in the violence and brutality that result from poverty and discrimination. But I think our discomfort is also caused by the "circumscribed possibilities" of the text itself, its lack of subtlety and flexibility, its manipulation of characters to serve an ideological function, its refusal to give women a powerful point of view.

Petry moves away from social protest fiction in her 1953 novel *The Narrows* and her collection of short stories, *Miss Muriel and Other Stories* (1971), away from a world in which women and men are so completely dominated by external forces that they literally have no will of their own. On one level, however, women are still the entrappers in *The Narrows*. The main woman character, Abbie Crunch, ruins her adopted son's life by refusing maternal support; Camilo Treadway, the spoiled rich white woman, causes his death; and Mamie Powther, the subject of the excerpt included here, cuckolds her faithful and devoted husband, Malcolm.

While the larger social and political environment is no longer a powerful force in *The Narrows*, women in this novel are subjected to another kind of entrapment—perhaps typical of the 1950s. In her domestic role Mamie is so thoroughly framed in her husband's gaze that we know her only as he experiences her. When Malcolm sees Mamie for the first time, he is, in fact, reminded of the framed nudes in the paintings his wealthy employer owns: ". . . there in front of him coming down the stairs, in the flesh, was a woman exactly like the women in the great oil paintings with the ornately carved frames that hung in the long hall of Old Cooper's town house."[7]

The nude in Western art, as John Berger reminds us in his essay, *Ways of Seeing*, is always painted for a spectator, and the spectator is always a man—the owner who has the money to purchase the art object.[8] Mamie's body is such an experience for us. Always on display, its various parts are completely accessible to us. The deep reddish brown skin, the curve of the leg, the deep, big bosom, and her big behind as she bends over to open the oven door are as available to the reader as they are to Powther. Mamie's musical voice and sweet smell are so intrinsic to her being that to Powther they have become inextricably entwined with her presence. As Berger suggests, this sense of presence defines a woman in

terms of her flesh and assures her status as physical object.
Mamie's thoughts, desires, and motivations are not available
to us in this text. We do not know how she experiences
physical pleasure, only how others experience her. As an
object, Mamie cannot ever really express power. Powther
thinks a woman like Mamie would not be safe if she were to
be left around certain men—men like Bill Hod, the saloon
owner, or Link, Abbie's handsome nephew, or Copper, Powther's former employer—the implication being, of course,
that Mamie is powerless as well as amoral.

The attitude toward women in *The Narrows* would probably have gone unremarked in the 1950s since this view of
women was the same as the one depicted in most of the
popular culture of the day. Indeed it is such a conventional
notion even many contemporary readers will find Mamie a
"typical woman" and the emphasis on her physicality merely
appropriate. In his 1946 interview with Ann Petry in *Crisis*
magazine writer James W. Ivy quite routinely devotes an
entire paragraph to Petry's physical description: "In person
Mrs. Petry is of medium height, pleasant manners and intercourse and possessed of companionable good humor. She
has a creamy-brown complexion; alert smiling eye; and a
soft cultivated voice."[9] Like the other popular black magazines of the 1940s and 1950s, *Crisis* featured glamorous
photos of beauty queens on its covers and sponsored "cover
girl" contexts that depicted women in provocative poses and
various stages of undress. In the black Hollywood films of
the day, women always existed to affirm either masculine
privilege or white privilege. As cooks, maids, singers, or
entrepreneurs (in such films as *New Orleans* starring Billie
Holiday as a maid; *Stormy Weather* with Ethel Waters and Lena
Horne as singers and Louise Beavers as a business woman in
Imitation of Life), black women existed only in reference to
men or to whites. They were never autonomous and never
central to the text. As one film critic points out, in two of the
most popular black musicals of the 1950s, *Stormy Weather* and
Cabin in the Sky, neither Ethel Waters nor Lena Horne, in

spite of their superstar status, was ever permitted to occupy
the full range of center stage. They were almost always accompanied by men to whom they were romantically linked in
order to show visually that women do not exist outside of
male desire.[10]

Two aspects of Ann Petry's characterization of Mamie
Powther suggest Petry's own discomfort with the limits she
has prescribed for her women. In spite of Mamie's promis-
cuity and the anguish she causes her husband, she suffers no
punishment, no tragic end, no fatal repercussions. In fact,
toward the end of the novel, while Powther is suffering
shame over his complicity in the death of Link he marvels at
the perverse way Mamie's "infidelity becomes her":

. . . I used to take it for granted that a married woman
who has an affair with another man will have a depraved,
wornout look. But they don't. They grow younger and
there is an emanation of happiness from them that can be
sensed by other people, and it makes them more beautiful.
Like Mamie.[11]

But there is another, even more subtle way Mamie resists the
entrapment of this text, and this is how Petry shows a
deeper, perhaps unconscious, sense of alliance with Mamie.
The narrator of *The Narrows* tells us that Mamie is uncomfortable with and disdainful of writing. Her skill is speech—
laughing, singing, or talking, she is in control. Her songs are
about trains, mobility, love and sorrow; they connect her to
the tradition of women blues singers who were artists and
unconventional, independent women. She changes the
words to suit her feelings and, always, her voice is powerful,
commanding, and mesmerizing.

Allied with speech against writing, Mamie cannot be confined by the written word. Indeed, the first words of the
narrator's description of her undermine the attempt to
"write" Mamie into existence:

. . . Mamie was not the kind who would write a note.
Writing didn't come easy to her, and, even if it had, she

would have preferred the direct contact offered by speech, not the impersonal business of using a pen or a pencil, to inscribe an explanation or an apology, or an apologetic explanation, on a piece of paper, thus foregoing the pleasure and the excitement of an explosive violent scene.[12]

Mamie's intense need for pleasure and excitement and her defiance of conventional behavior make her the most vivid character in *The Narrows*. Modeled after the woman blues singer, Mamie is boldly assertive and arrogantly interested in her own sexual satisfaction. Even though Petry allows her husband to dominate her by telling her entire story through his point of view, Mamie's presence is always threatening and disruptive, calling our attention to her. The last voice we hear is Mamie's—and she is singing the blues.

But not until her "drugstore stories" in the *Miss Muriel* collection does Petry create a narrative situated entirely around female quest; predictably, the quester is an adolescent girl, young enough to be free from the claims of romance and still interested in exploring her own perceptions of the world. The switch to a first-person narrative with a female telling her story and to a female Bildungsroman that concentrates on female development shows Petry moving away from the male domination of her earlier texts and turning toward her woman characters with less ambivalence. Petry's own female relatives were the models for the women she creates in the *Miss Muriel* stories:

I think my view of myself was greatly affected by the women in my family. My mother was a chiropodist—one of my aunts was a pharmacist—she graduated from Brooklyn College of Pharmacy in 1908—the only woman in her class. Another aunt was a school teacher who created a very successful correspondence course. These women were role models for me. They left the world of the housewife in the early part of the 20th century—they became financially independent, successful women.[13]

Petry herself worked as a pharmacist in her home town of Old Saybrook, Connecticut, a predominantly white community where her father was the local druggist. Unlike the diminished, powerless lives of Petry's 1940s women, the characters in her "drugstore" stories exist in a social context that provides them with the resources for growth and choice.

Like the narrator of a traditional male Bildungsroman, the young girl in the title story "Miss Muriel" is a privileged member of a social order designed to maximize her opportunities for self-development. In the world outside of the home she is able to observe the behavior of many people, primarily men, engage in dialogue with them, listen to their storytelling, and finally, in an effort to establish her own identity, reject their narrow prejudices and assume loyalty to her own values. This strong, first-person female voice indicates an important change in Petry's presentation of women. We are involved in the girl's emerging comprehension of her world. We share her anger and outrage over the treatment of her friend. Like the young narrator, Claudia, in Toni Morrison's *The Bluest Eye*, this girl is permitted a psychic range not allowed the women in Petry's earlier tests.[14] Petry knows the social landscape of this New England world and she moves around in it freely, observing its rugged individualists, its eccentrics, its highly motivated aspiring black community. She wrote about Harlem as an outsider; here she is the insider, a vantage point of power which her characters share. In this tightly knit, protective community no one is defeated by the environment because the community, the family, and the individual are more potent forces.

NOTES

1. *The Street* (New York: Pyramid Publications, 1966); "In Darkness and Confusion," in *Black Voices: An Anthology of Afro-American Literature*, ed Abraham Chapman (New York: New American Library, 1968), pp. 161–91; *Country Place* (Chatham, N.J.: The Chatham

ookseller, 1947); *The Narrows* (New York: Pyramid Publications, 971); *Miss Muriel and Other Stories; Harriet Tubman: Conductor of the nderground Railroad* (New York: Harper & Row, 1955); *Tituba of lem Village* (New York: Harper & Row, 1964).

Interview with James Ivy in *Crisis* 53 (February 1946): 48–49.

Valerie Smith, *Narrative Authority in Twentieth-Century Afro-American ction* (Cambridge: Harvard University Press, 1987), p. 106.

As the black bandleader, Boots Smith, is trying to decide what ice he will have to pay to defy his white boss and to possess Lutie, s image of Lutie is described in terms that assert the male point of ew and make us, as readers, complicitious in his objectification of ero:

Balance Lutie Johnson. Weigh Lutie Johnson. Long legs and warm mouth. Soft skin and pointed breasts. Straight slim back and small waist. Mouth that curves over white, white teeth. Not enough. She didn't weigh enough when she was balanced against a life of saying "yes sir" to every white bastard who had the price of a Pullman ticket. Lutie Johnson at the end of a Pullman run. Not enough. One hundred Lutie Johnsons didn't weigh enough. *(The Street* [New York: Pyramid Publications, 1966], p. 165)

At the end of Dorothy West's novel *The Living Is Easy* (Old estbury, N.Y.: Feminist Press, 1982), Cleo, the main female char- ter, turns to her nephew, Tim, as the beacon of hope for a future. t the end of Ann Petry's *The Narrows* (1953) Mamie's son, J. C., is e one who represents hope and redemption for Abbie Crunch.

Marcus Klein, *After Alienation: American Novels in Mid-Century* leveland and New York: World Publishing Company, 1965), p. 73.

Petry, *The Narrows*, p. 219.

John Berger, *Ways of Seeing*, (London: British Broadcasting Com- ny and Penguin Books, 1972), pp. 45–64.

Interview with Ivy, *Crisis* 53 (February 1946): 48–49.

). Kathryn Kalinak, "Images of the Black Woman in the Holly- ood Musical" (Paper presented at the New York Conference on lm, June, 1985).

. Petry, *The Narrows*, p. 413.

. Ibid, p. 199.

. Interview with Mary Helen Washington, 1980.

. Although "Miss Muriel" does give the young girl a measure of wer and autonomy, the story still reveals ambivalence toward ult women. The narrator's curiosity, fearlessness, mobility, and dependence distance her from all the other women in the story. er mother and her aunt play more typically female roles. "At night e act just like other people's families," the narrator tells Mr. Bem-

back, see all the soft brown flesh waiting for him, see hims
laying his head between her breasts, soft, soft, soft, a
smell the strong sweet perfume she used.

That strong sweet smell came from a stick, a graywhi
stick, wrapped in tinfoil, the whole thing encased in a rou
glass bottle. He loved to watch her uncork the bottle, ca
fully unwrap the tinfoil, and then smear the stick perfume
her wrists, her elbows, the lobes of her ears, the back of h
neck. Everything smelt of it, her clothes, her body, her ha
the sheets and the pillowcases. He could never separate t
smell of that perfume from Mamie, the two inextricably e
twined; and all he asked in life, really, was—well, not to ke
his job, not long life and good health for himself and
family, not sufficient food, or ample clothing, all he ask
was that Mamie would, as long as they both should live,
him sleep with her on those nights when he was not
Treadway Hall, let him sleep with her so that he could
down, down, into sleep with the strong, toosweet perfu
all around him, tangible assurance of Mamie's presence.

Now that he had seen the pinkish light in the bedroc
windows, he started moving faster and faster, until he w
very nearly running when he went up the outside back sta
case. In the back entry, he stood still for a moment. He cou
smell pork chops frying on the stove, thought he could he
the spit-spatter of grease as the chops cooked, could sm
kale being cooked.

He opened the kitchen door, stepped inside, and had
shut his eyes for a moment, half blinded by the brilliant lig
from the hundred-watt bulbs Mamie used in the kitchen; a
it was hot, steam came from the open pot where the kale w
cooking, bubble, bubble, bubble, smell of kale. Mamie w
leaning over, bending over, opening the oven door, yams
the oven, corn muffins in the oven, fragrance issuing fr
the oven; and over it all the smell of her perfume, stro
heavy, toosweet, overriding the food smells, and he look
at Mamie bent over like that and could hear Old Coppe
big voice, roaring, "Get one with a big ass, Powther, get a

wench with a big ass, and by God, you'll be happy for the rest
of your life," could see Old Copper slapping his knee, could
hear him laughing, and there was Mamie, bent over, and he
looked away, because of the desire that rose in him, a sudden
emotion, that made him feel as though he were going to
choke, and he couldn't think straight, couldn't see, he
wanted to be on top of her, and he told himself there was a
fresh baked cake on the kitchen table, and he heard J.C.
whining, "I want cake. I want cake. I want cake."

Mamie closed the oven door, cuffed J.C. away from the
cake.

Shapiro yelled, "Hit him over the head again, Mamie.
Give him a good one this time."

"Ah, shut up, Shapiro," Kelly yelled back, "you big
mouth, you—"

"Whose a big mouth? Whose a big mouth?"

"You—you—you—"

They rolled over on the floor, over and over, clutching at
each other, shouting, faces contorted with anger.

Mamie hummed under her breath, turned the pork chops
in the frying pan with a longhandled fork, apparently unaware of the noise, the brilliant light, the sound of food
cooking, smell of food cooking. She was impervious to it,
Powther thought. No, a part of it, not ignoring, but enjoying,
liking, the heat, the light, the confusion, the noise, the boys
scuffling on the floor, J.C.'s yelps of rage.

Suddenly they were all looking at him, all silent, J.C.,
Shapiro, Kelly, Mamie. He supposed that he had brought
the cold wet air from the street in with him, the darkness of
the street, the silence of the street, brought it straight into
the hot, brilliantly lighted, filled-with-food-smell, noisy
kitchen; and their eyes questioned him, challenged his right
to enter this place that was the heartbeat of the house, heartbeat pulsing with heat, sound, life.

Mamie said, "Powther, you sure gave me a turn. Come on
in. Come on in and close that door. Supper'll be ready in a
minute."

He went through the kitchen, down the hall, into the bedroom. He always hurried to get here, inside the house, home, and yet he always felt as though he were an alien, a stranger, strangeness, a sense of strangeness, in the kitchen, here in this bedroom. It was always the same room no matter what the address, the room where a pink-shaded lamp shed warm pink light on the bed, on the table by the bed, on the pink taffeta spread, not too clean. Cupids on the bed.

He put his hat on the closet shelf, hung his overcoat on a hanger in the one closet—a closet jammed full of dresses which were paid for by Bill Hod. His coat would smell of Mamie's perfume, just as all these dresses did. He got a clothesbrush out of the one drawer of the chest which was reserved for his use, brushed his hat, his overcoat, then rehung them in the closet, and in a petty unreasoning kind of anger, born of what he could not say, he pushed the newestlooking dress from its hanger and watched it fall, in a heap, on the closet floor.

Tomorrow morning, if he had time, he would rearrange the closet before he went to work. Mamie liked having him fix up her clothes. He pressed her dresses, sewed on buttons, repaired the split seams under the arms. He couldn't leave that dress on the floor of the closet. He reached down, picked it up, shook it out, examined it for split seams, from force of habit. Mamie had put on quite a few pounds lately. Was she still dieting? He hoped not. True she lost weight, but she was so cross, so irritable, when she was dieting, slapping the children, swearing at him, that nobody could stay in the house with her. Two weeks ago, when he was off, he went to the movies and sat there dozing away the hours, those precious hours, of his days off, trying to think of something that would be so good to eat, so appealing, that she'd taste it and then eat it, and would be off the diet. He sat through two shows and then went home, walking warily around the side of the house, going quietly up the back stairs, sniffing the air, thinking that if she was cooking, at so early an hour, in the afternoon, she was still on the diet, still not eating.

When she went on these starvation diets, she seemed impelled to tortue herself by handling food, by cooking food that smelled to high heaven. She would sit at the table with a cup of black coffee and a package of cigarettes in front of her, sit there and sip the coffee; and smoke one cigarette after another, and watch them eat, watch forkfuls of the great round crusted roast of beef, and the browned potatoes and the beautiful fresh vegetables and the rich buttery dessert go into their mouths; her eyes followed the course of their forks and spoons from the plate to mouth, mouth to plate, her eyes eating the food with them, her lower lip thrust out, mouth a little open.

He imagined he saw saliva at the corner of her mouth, and would stare, fascinated, knowing that he was imagining it, but knowing, too, that it ought to be there, that the saliva glands were working overtime. Then Mamie would catch him staring and turn her belligerent baleful hungry eyes toward him, and he would look away, eating faster and faster, eating more than his stomach could possibly hold, afraid to stop eating.

It was a horrifying business to come home and find that Mamie was still on a starvation diet that might last anywhere from two days to a month. Once she'd held out for a whole month, a month during which she watched them eat cream puffs, chocolate éclairs, strawberry shortcakes piled up with whipped cream, all the rich sweet fattening food she loved most, while she drank black coffee, and wolfed down some kind of dry hard tasteless crackers.

For a whole month, they tiptoed around her, almost whispering, and she cooked from the time she got out of bed in the morning until she went back to bed at night, using up pounds of butter and quarts of cream and God only knew how much sugar and flour and vanilla. Kelly and Shapiro began to look like small round young pigs being fattened for the kill. J.C. gorged himself to the vomiting stage every night.

Night after night, Powther sneaked out to the corner drugstore for a large dose of sodium bicarb and oil of peppermint, afraid to mix it on the premises, even in the comparative privacy of the bathroom, because Mamie would have smelt the peppermint and known he'd eaten too much and been furious, with that quick unreasoning fury of the starving.

When she was hungry like that she couldn't sleep. He remembered the tenseness of her, lying there motionless beside him, flat on her back, as though she did not have the energy to turn over, not moving, tense, stiff, hungry. And he lay there beside her, afraid to touch her.

He had looked forward to this Saturday night, unexpected time off. A cold, rainy night. The kind of night a man needed a woman's arms around him. And now—

Hot in the house, he thought. Hot in the bedroom. He was sweating. Forehead wet with sweat. He'd get a clean handkerchief, mop his forehead. One of the old handkerchiefs. They were at the bottom of the pile in the top drawer of the chest.

Someone had been in the drawer, had mussed up the handkerchiefs, had put them back every which way. J.C. was getting completely out of hand, he would tell Mamie to get after him. He didn't ask much but he simply could not, would not, stand having anyone paw through his things. He'd rearrange them. He took them all out, turned the pile upside down, started to put them back, one by one. His hand touched something cold and metallic. He stood on tiptoe, looked in the drawer. There was a cigarette case in there. It had been under the handkerchiefs.

Perhaps it was a present, a surprise, from Mamie. He took it out, wondering why she had given it to him, because he didn't smoke. He turned it over. There were initials on it. L.W. picked out in brilliants. Who was L.W.? What was his cigarette case doing in this drawer?

He took the case over to the light. He turned it over, moving it back and forth, and the stones that formed the initials flashed, seemed to wink at him. It said Tiffany & Co. on the inside. A gold cigarette case. The initials were formed by small absolutely perfect diamonds. No question about their being diamonds. He used to see Old Copper's collection. Night after night the old man sat in the library holding a few of the stones in his hand, letting them trickle between his fingers. Old Copper told him about them, told him that finally you got so you could pick out the perfect ones without a glass, but a man ought always to carry a glass with him, just in case, just to verify what his naked eye told him. He went over to the closet, got a jeweler's glass out of his coat pocket, looked at the stones through it. Oh, yes, absolutely perfect, flawless, small stones. A gold cigarette case initialed in diamonds. L.W.

L.W.? Link Williams. Link Williams. Mrs. Crunch's nephew, or whatever he was, the tall arrogant young man who did not look like Bill Hod but resembled him, the way he held his head, the way he talked, even the eyes.

Bill Hod was no threat. At least he told himself that all the time; he told himself over and over again, as he hurried home on his days off, that Bill Hod would never encumber himself by permanently annexing a woman, not even Mamie Powther. And the closer he got to the house, the more convinced he became that Mamie had now, finally, gone off with Hod. But she hadn't. And then he would be certain that she never would, and the knowledge would last about a week or ten days and then he would begin to wonder and to doubt, and hurry home to make certain. But Link Williams, Mamie—.

He shivered. Perhaps she was telling him in this curious, subtle, not really to be understood, business of the cigarette case, had placed it where he would certainly find it, and thus would know that she and Link—

He put the case back in the drawer, piled the handkerchiefs on top of it, slowly, carefully, force of habit making him square them up, line them up, one on top of the other, taking a long time to do it because his hands were trembling. Mamie laughed whenever she saw him carefully arranging the contents of a drawer, "Law, Powther," she said, "you musta spent half your life in the army, must spent half your life puttin' things in piles."

He would pretend the cigarette case was not there. It would be the easiest way for everybody. It meant Mamie would have to figure out some more direct way of telling him whatever it was she was trying to tell him about herself and Link. If he had seen Link Williams before they moved in here, if Mrs. Crunch had said, "I have a very handsome young nephew, if you cherish your wife, your life, if you have a susceptible, loving wife, do not, under any circumstances, do not live under the same roof with my handsome unscrupulous young nephew."

Link Williams belonged to the Copper breed, so did Hod You could tell by looking at them, by listening to them, that they weren't to be trusted, that no woman was safe around them, not really. Mamie. For instance, it wouldn't have been safe to leave Mamie around Old Copper. What the dickens was he thinking about anyway, mind all in a jumble.

If Mrs. Crunch had only said, well, that day he stood wiping his feet so carefully on the doormat, instead of saying, "How did you know about the apartment?" she should have said, "I have a very handsome, very lawless young nephew."

Even if she had said it, he wouldn't have believed her Because looking at her he would have said that her nephew —Was Link Williams her nephew? He couldn't be, not with that handsome closed arrogant cruel gambler's face, with those expressionless gambler's eyes, he couldn't be her nephew, couldn't have in his veins any of the same blood that had produced short, plump, hawknosed, kindly faced kind-but-proud-faced, expressived-eyed Mrs. Abigail Crunch. It was a mobile face, a dead-give-away face, give away of whatever she was thinking, so were the plump, mo

g, always-in-motion, always gesturing hands. With that
hite hair piled on top of her head, with the very black
yebrows—well, it was a face and head you couldn't easily
orget. She had New England aristocrat written all over her,
n the straight back, in the quick but not hurrying short steps
he took that meant she covered a lot of ground but was
ever guilty of striding down the street, in the Yankee twang
o her speech. She wore the kind of clothes he liked, simple,
nadorned and yet completely feminine, white gloves on
undays, small black leather pocketbooks, carefully polished
hoes, pretty small hats, a feather the only gay note on her
est felt hat, and the seams in her stockings always straight.

He had met her, walked along Dumble Street with her,
hen she went marketing in the morning, tan cotton gloves
n her hands, the fingers so neatly, so cleverly darned, the
arning so beautiful that only an expert would notice that
he gloves had been darned; a market basket over her arm,
nd her pocketbook in the basket; and he knew just as
hough he had looked inside it that it contained a clean linen
andkerchief that would smell faintly sweet (violet or lilac or
avender), the front doorkey, and a billfold and small pencil
ith a pad; and on the pad would be a list, the grocery list,
ontaining all the items that she would want that particular
ay, so that this one trip, early in the morning, would take
are of all her needs.

In Mrs. Crunch's house, there would not be, say at five
'clock, that harumscarum running to the store for the thou-
and-and-one things that had been forgotten as there always
ere in his house. Mamie never knew what she was going to
ave for supper until the very last minute. She would start
or the store, forget her purse and hurry back to the house to
et it, laughing at herself, as she came in. He had seen her
hange her mind about an entire meal at the sight of a choice
ut of meat at the butcher's; she would hurry home with the
eat and ten minutes later she'd send Shapiro scurrying to
he store for potatoes and before Shapiro could get back in
he house, Kelly would be sent out to get butter and bread.

The only reason J.C. wasn't employed in this marathon
and from the store was because he couldn't be trusted on a
errand with or without money; J.C. just never bothered
come back at all and was usually found hanging over the
dock, looking down at the river, with that awful concentra
tion of the very young.

Breakfast was the same way; at least two members of the
family had to go to the corner store and back before the
Powthers could break their fast in the morning. He shoul
have married a woman like Mrs. Crunch, who never had
diet, who would never under any circumstances have permit
ted familiarities from a man to whom she was not married
whose every word, every look, every gesture told you tha

Then Mamie was standing in the doorway of the bedroom
tall, all soft flesh and curves, all soft warm flesh, sayin
"Pow-ther! Pow-ther! I've called you two times already."

"I was just getting—" he started to say getting a handke
chief, and said, "I was just getting ready to come out to the
kitchen."

He watched her walk down the hall toward the kitche
watched the rhythmic motion of her legs, her arms, an
thought, Yes, if I'd married Mrs. Crunch or someone like h
I would never have wondered if I'd come home and find th
she'd run off with another man; but then neither would
have known the absolute ecstasy and delight of Mamie,
the dark, in bed, the soft flesh yielding, yielding, the feel
those curves, the pressure of her arms around me.

He would never give her up, never, never. He was going
act as though Link Williams did not exist, as though th
cigarette case with its sparkling monogram did not exist,
though—Why had she put it under his handkerchiefs? Li
Williams. What was he doing with a cigarette case like tha
Why not? Hod probably gave it to him. Or a woman. Som
rich, dissolute, white woman. Link Williams was the typ
they fell in love with, it was the way he was built, it was h
height, and the breadth of his shoulders, and it was his fac
he looked like a brute, and women, white and colored, love

men with faces like that. Let's see, he thought, this is the
middle of January. So some rich dissolute white woman
probably gave it to him for a Christmas present.

Mamie said, from the kitchen, "Come along now, Powther. Supper's ready."

In the kitchen he blinked, the light was so brilliant. It was
hot. Steam came from the plates on the table. Mamie always
piled food on plates. J.C.'s plate was just as full of food as
Shapiro's or Kelly's or his own. And Mamie was still on a diet
because there was nothing at her place but a cup of black
coffee.

Shapiro and Kelly ate in silence. J.C. tried to talk with his
mouth crammed with food, so that no one understood what
he was saying, thus he carried on a monologue, a mumbling
mouth-full-of-food monologue, that was also an indication
of contentment because he swayed from side to side as he
ate and mumbled.

Mamie sat and glared at them as the pork chops and the
yams and the kale and the corn bread disappeared from their
plates. Occasionally she took a sip of the hot black bitter
coffee.

Powther threw small secret appraising glances at the coffee cup, lipstick all around the edges, brown stains on the
side where the coffee had dripped and spilled over, the
saucer splotched with a whole series of dark brown rings.
She used the same cup all day long, picking it up, sipping
from it, refilling it with hot coffee when the stuff cooled off.

J.C. said, "Missus Crunch—" and the rest of the sentence
was lost because he had crammed his mouth full of corn
bread and went on talking and chewing, talking and chewing.

Powther wondered how he could bring the conversation
around to Link Williams, how introduce his name, so that he
could see how Mamie acted when his name was mentioned.

J.C. pushed his chair away from the table, backed the
length of the room, still chewing, eying Mamie as he edged
toward the hall door, then he was through it, gone.

Powther said, "I don't think you ought to let J.C. go down-stairs to Mrs. Crunch's so much." He heard J.C.'s footsteps, thud, thud, on the inside staircase. It wasn't what he had planned to say, he hadn't really planned to say anything, he was just feeling his way, if he could get a conversation started about Mrs. Crunch then perhaps he could mention Link, easily, naturally.

Mamie glared at him. "Why not?" she said.

"Mrs. Crunch will get tired of him."

No answer. Perhaps she hadn't heard him. "Mrs. Crunch will get tired of him," he repeated. "I don't think you ought to let him go down there so much. It's late. He ought to be in bed."

"Oh, for God's sake, Powther, why don't you shut up?" She pushed the coffee cup away, with a sudden violent jerky motion, and got up from the table.

He watched her as she left the kitchen. She slammed the bedroom door and he listened, and could not tell whether she had turned the key in the lock.

Kelly said, "Mamie been like that all day, Pop. Me and Shapiro been outdoors in the rain the whole afternoon."

"It ain't safe to talk to her," Shapiro said. He stuffed his mouth full of cake, and cut himself another large wedge-shaped piece.

"J.C. left because he knew he'd get in trouble if he stayed around here," Kelly said. "Mamie been awful mean to him." He watched Shapiro gulp down the cake. "Mamie say he's got a tapeworm." He pointed at Shapiro.

Shapiro said, "I have not."

"You have too. Mamie say nobody could stuff their gut like you unless they got a tapeworm."

Shapiro picked up a fork with the evident intention of stabbing Kelly with it. Powther said, "That's enough of that."

He got up from the table, took a key out of his pocket, unlocked a cupboard high over the kitchen sink. "Here," he said, and handed them each a new comic book. He didn't

approve of comic books but as he evidently was going to
have to contend with the boys until bedtime, he didn't know
of anything else that would keep them from killing each
other while he did the dishes.

He found an apron, tied it tight around his waist, and set
to work, clearing the table, washing the dishes, scouring the
pots, then scouring the sink, boiling the dish towels. He
swept the kitchen and then mopped it, mopping carefully
around Shapiro and Kelly, who were lying flat on their stom-
achs, totally absorbed in the comic books, thinking that if
he'd been Old Copper, he would have taken the mop handle
and pushed and prodded them out of the way.

J.C. poked his head in through the door, looked around
the kitchen, "Where's Mamie?" he demanded.

"Gone to bed," Powther said. "Come on in and I'll tell
you a story."

J.C. loved fairy stories, and Powther, feeling suddenly
sorry for him, feeling that J.C. needed a mother and didn't
have one, and that he therefore be both mother and
father to him in this storytelling, said, "Here, you sit on my
lap and I'll tell you a new story."

Powther cleared his throat, said, slowly, "Once upon a
time," and Shapiro and Kelly looked up from the comic
books, and he thought, It's got to be extra good to hold their
attention.

"Once upon a time," he said again, "there was a princess
with golden hair who was kept chained deepdown in a dark
cold dungeon. The guardian of the door that led into the
dungeon was a wicked giant who was blind in one eye. The
princess cried all the time because she was hungry and the
giant beat her and the only food he gave her was dry hard
bread and water. But he brought her precious jewels to play
with, great diamonds and emeralds and rubies and sapphires
and pearls; and beautiful clothes to wear. When the giant left
to go about his dreadful business of robbing innocent people who passed through the woods, he would leave his dog
to guard the princess. The dog was a ferocious white bull-

dog, also blind in one eye, and if anyone ventured near the castle he would growl; and his growling was so fearful that they went on their way again.

"One day, Gaylord, the valet in the king's palace, a man who was small in stature but quick of movement, and noted for his kindness and the quickness of his thinking, was walking through the wood. As he neared the castle, he thought he heard sobs. He tried to enter, but he could not gain entrance because of the ferocious dog who guarded the entrance. He turned and walked away, puzzled, and he made up his mind to return again and explore the place when he had the golden needle with him. Gaylord was a persistent man, and not to be discouraged by danger or the threat of danger, for he was really a prince in disguise. He had been kidnaped and taken away from his kingdom at the orders of a jealous uncle. He was severely beaten and left for dead but an old peasant woman who lived on the edge of the forest where he had been left, found him, and nursed him back to health. After he recovered his health, he looked after the old woman, took such good care of her, that on her deathbed she gave him a small round silver case, almost like a tube, but heavily and curiously carved.

" 'Open it,' she said. 'Careful, now.' To his surprise he found a very fine golden needle inside the case.

" 'It will sew by itself,' she told him. 'You say, Stitch, Needle, stitch this leather, and it will stitch for you. It will stitch anything, water, wine, soap, wood, stone, fire. Guard it well. It has been in my family for five hundred years. I have no children to pass it on to so I will give it to you. You have been like a son to me. And whoever has this needle will always have whatsoever he wants.'

"A week later, Gaylord returned to the castle. This time he had the needle with him. The dog growled and would not permit him to pass the entrance. Gaylord said, 'Stitch, Needle,' The needle looked like a small flaming sunset flashing about the eyes of the dog, stitching up both eyes, just in case the blind eye was not blind, as so often happens in real life where a blind eye is often a fake, based on an old rumor that nobody knows whether or not it is true and it possibly isn't true, because most rumors are started by someone who has something to gain by it, and to be thought blind in one eye when you weren't would give a person an advantage over other people.

"The dog emitted piercing cries of pain, and ran and ran, put his head down to the ground and rubbed his eyes on the ground and the needle stitched the dog's heavy leather collar to the stone wall.

"Gaylord said, 'Well done, Needle,' and held out the small round silver tube and the needle came flashing through the air and settled inside the tube.

"He then went unmolested into the castle, and followed the sound of the sobs, and went down into the dungeon and found the beautiful goldenhaired princess chained there, with a great golden goblet beside her, half full of water. She said, 'Save me, save me, kind sir!'

"At that moment the giant entered the dungeon and lunged toward Gaylord. Gaylord said, 'Stitch, Needle! Stitch both his eyes, Needle!' and held out the small round silver tube and the needle flashed through the air, and stitched both the giant's eyes. The giant let out a roar of rage and pain; and started blundering around in the dungeon, hands outstretched before him. Gaylord said, 'Stitch, Needle! Stitch hand to stone!' The needle flashed through the air and when the giant blundered near one of the walls of the dungeon, the needle stitched the giant's hand to the stone.

"Gaylord said, 'Well done, Needle!' and the needle came flashing through the air and settled inside the small round silver tube that Gaylord held out.

"Gaylord then took the keys from the giant's girdle and unlocked the padlock, and released the beautiful princess with the long golden hair.

"They left the castle together, their arms clasped around each other's waists. Then they returned to Gaylord's rightful kingdom where they were married and lived happily forever after."

J.C. said, "Tell it again! Tell it again!"

Shapiro and Kelly had long since left the comic books on the kitchen floor. They were leaning against Powther now, and they said, together, "Whew! Tell it again, Pop. Tell it again."

"Not tonight. It's too late," Powther said. He felt a little glow of pride, of accomplishment, it was a good story. But he wouldn't tell it again.

He washed all three of them, helped all three into their night clothes, tucked them under the covers, opened the window, turned out the light. When he closed the door of the bedroom J.C. was saying, "All gold. She was all gold. She came right in the front door—Stitch stone to leather." But because he left the "s" sound off words, he was really saying, "Titch tone to leather."

Powther took his shoes off in the living room. He padded quietly down the hall in his stocking feet and tried the door of the bedroom that he shared with Mamie, turning the knob, slowly, cautiously. It was locked.

He had no blanket, nothing to cover himself with. If he should sleep on the sofa in the living room, with his clothes on, his trousers would be wrecked by morning. He undressed down to his underwear and went back to the boys' room and got in bed with J.C.

It was like trying to sleep with a dynamo. J.C.'s feet and knees were in his stomach, his chest, his back. He seemed all bone, all knobby knees and sharp elbows and hard round head, no flesh on him anywhere, though he was a plump child, his body putting a strain on every seam of his clothing.

Powther turned and twisted, trying to get comfortable, thinking of Old Copper, "Get one with a big ass, Powther, makes for happiness." Did it? The boy, the old man's youngest son, Peter, beat his wife, the miner's redheaded daughter, with a horsewhip. Did it? Mamie Powther locked Malcolm Powther out of the bedroom.

He remembered that the newspapers somehow got wind of that story about Peter and his wife and when the reporters came, Old Copper sat in his big leather chair in the library and laughed at them; and ordered whiskey and soda for them, whiskey and soda, whiskey and soda. That afternoon Powther mixed drinks, passed drinks to the thirstiest set of men he'd ever seen.

Old Copper kept bellowing, "True? How in hell do I know if it's true? Hope so, gentlemen. I certainly hope so. Ha, ha, ha. Funniest thing I ever heard. Ha, ha, ha."

The reporters were in a deliciously rosy state when they left, laughing, talking. Powther wondered when they would realize that they didn't have a story, that Old Copper had neither denied nor confirmed the story; and he supposed they would hold long confused discussions as to whether they should print his statement, "How in hell do I know?"

One of them, a short sharp-eyed young chap, who had politely refused the whiskey and soda, cornered Powther in the hall and said, "Look here, old man, what's this all about anyway?"

He had sidestepped out of the corner. He said, "I hope the whiskey was satisfactory, sir," and walked fast down the hall, the great hall lined with those tremendous oils of monstrously outsized, monstrously pinkfleshed females painted by a Dutchman. Old Copper was standing in the doorway of the library. He was grinning, looking up at one of the paintings, grinning at it. At that moment it occurred to Powther that those paintings belonged to Old Copper in a peculiarly intimate sort of way. He was always leering at them, and the big nude women in the paintings seemed to leer back at him.

He shoved J.C.'s knees out of his stomach again, and thought, Makes for happiness, and pursed his lips. The Copper boys fought with their big wives, filled the house in Baltimore with the sound and fury of their quarrels. And yet, because of the paintings, because of the blatant lecherousness of the old man, but especially because of the paintings, he, Powther, fell in love with a woman who might have been painted by the Dutchman.

One of the sons, the oldest one, came home for a visit, accompanied by his wife and his four-month-old son, and the wife's personal maid, and the baby's trained nurse, a lean fortyish looking and acting and sounding woman in a starched white uniform and cap. Old Copper met them in the hall. The nurse was holding the baby. The old man let out a roar, like a maddened bull, "Who's that?"

They stood there, in the hall, all of them, the oldest son, and his wife, and the nurse, and the maid, and Powther, all motionless, all frozen, frightened by the roar. The baby, probably sensing the consternation of the adults, began to wail.

Young Mrs. Copper, the mother of the child, said, bewildered, "Why it's the baby, Jonathan Copper Four."

"Dammit I know that," Old Copper roared. "Who's that lean-shanked witch that's holdin' him?"

"The nurse. His nurse. A trained nurse."

Old Copper bellowed, "Give me that baby." There was a kind of seesaw movement for a moment, the nurse trying to retain hold on the baby and Old Copper pulling at him, and the baby bellowing too, now.

"Powther," Old Copper shouted, "where's Powther?" He held the baby in his arms, glaring, cursing. "God dammit, why don't none of these people have any brains? Powther, go get a nurse for this baby. Go get a big fat colored woman." He turned on the nurse. "Here, you. You're fired. Get out."

The nurse said, "Mr. Copper, you can't, you mustn't. Give me the baby. You haven't washed your hands." She got quite excited and said, "Germs, germs, germs," as though she were talking to an idiot, and had to repeat one word, over and over, in the hope that something would trickle through the idiot's mind. "Germs," she said again.

Young Mrs. Copper said, "Oh, no. You can't do that. You can't do that. You mustn't. She's so wonderful."

"Shut up!" Old Copper shouted. "Powther, stop standin' there with your mouth open. Go get a big fat colored woman to look after this brat, a big fat colored woman that can sing. Don't stand there—"

He walked out the front door, hatless, thinking, A big fat colored woman. He was supposed to pull one out of thin air. Where in the city of Baltimore was he going to find a fat colored woman who was suitable? She had to be suitable.

He went, finally, and logically enough, to an employment agency. He explained to the thinfaced white woman who was in charge of the agency what type of nurse Mr. Jonathan Copper II wanted. She searched through the files and found a Mamie Smith who sounded promising.

The thinfaced woman called the number listed on the filing card and asked to speak to Mamie Smith. There was quite a delay, at least fifteen minutes, during which the employment agency woman grew impatient, threatened to hang up, bit her lip, tapped her foot, muttered under her breath something about colored people being so slow, until apparently Mamie Smith came to the phone; also apparently she explained with suitable apologies that she had a job, but that there was a lady who was highly suitable, who lived in the same rooming house, that said lady, a Mrs. Drewey, was expected back in a half-hour, and was listed at the agency under nursemaid's work. The thinfaced woman conveyed this information to Powther. He said he'd go right out there and interview her himself.

It was a big frame house, in need of paint, in need of repairs, in fact, as he rang the bell, he studied the house, and decided that what it really needed was to be torn down and rebuilt. It even needed a new foundation.

A lean, light-colored female opened the door a cautious crack. He knew instantly that she was the landlady, because of her eyes. She summed him up, all his potentialities and possibilities in one quick shrewd glance. He asked for Mrs.

Drewey. Mrs. Drewey was out, and the door started to close. Then he asked for Mamie Smith, and explained hastily and untruthfully that he had come about a job for Mamie Smith, and the door opened and the landlady said, "Step inside, and I'll call her."

He stood in the uncarpeted hall, waiting. He heard footsteps upstairs, somewhere; and then a woman came down the stairs. He stood, not moving, looking up at her. She came down the stairs slowly, the uncarpeted badly-in-need-of-paint stairs, of a rooming house in the least desirable part of Baltimore, and his heart started beating faster and faster, and he wished he had brought his hat with him, he needed something to hold in his hands. If he had brought his hat, he could have turned it around and around, as though shaping and reshaping the brim, brushing it off, because his hands needed something to do with themselves, desperately needed something to do, because there in front of him coming down the stairs, in the flesh, was a woman exactly like the women in the great oil paintings with the ornately carved frames that hung in the long hall of Old Copper's town house.

This woman was clothed, of course. She had on a dress, sleeveless, and short of skirt. She was wearing shoes, a flimsy kind of sandal, runover at the heel, but no stockings. The dress was a rather awful shade of brown. And her skin was brown, deep reddish brown, skin as smooth and flawless as that of Jonathan Copper IV with the same dewy quality, and it was just as though one of those big women in the paintings was coming down a staircase, the curve of the leg was the same, and the deepbosomed, big-bosomed look of her was the same.

"Yes?" she said. "You wanted to see me?"

Her voice was like music and it confused him even more, excited him even more, so that he swallowed twice and cleared his throat before he could answer her. "I'm Malcolm Powther," he said. "I'm the butler at the Coppers'. We need a nursemaid and the employment agency where I made inquiries phoned here about the job just a little while ago. I came straight here from the agency because a Miss Smith suggested a Mrs. Drewey."

"I'm Mamie," she said. "I was the one who suggested Drewey. She's good. She's about the best in the whole of Maryland. Come on in and sit. She'll be along pretty soon."

He couldn't get over her voice, and he kept asking her questions, just to hear her talk. It was more like listening to singing than listening to someone talk. He knew he shouldn't stare at her, that he ought to look away, and he tried to keep his eyes focused on some part of the room. But who could keep looking at a shabby, cheap rocking chair, at soiled badly fitted slipcovers on horrible overstuffed chairs, at sagging curtains in need of laundering, at a dreadful new-looking machine-made rug, all garish colors, and at dusty beaded lamp shades, when Mamie Smith was sitting on a sofa with her legs crossed, leaning her head back? He thought, I've got to have her. If it takes me the rest of my life, if it costs me my job, if it costs me all my savings, my life savings, I've still got to have her.

He asked her questions, just to keep her talking, just so he could keep hearing that voice that was like music. She lived in one of the upstairs rooms, across the hall from Mrs. Drewey. She had been married and was divorced. She didn't like Baltimore, it was too Southern a city for anybody like her who had been born in the North. She wanted to live North again, and as soon as she could leave, had enough money saved to tide her over the business of finding another job in a new place, she would go live in a small Northern city, any small Northern city.

He thought, Enough money. I'll be back here again. I can spend money, I've saved it all my life but I'm going to spend it now, spend and spend and spend, until I can buy Mamie Smith.

He said, "Miss Smith—"

"Oh," she said, and waved her hand in the air, waving his

words away, "don't be so formal. Everybody calls me Mamie."

"Mamie, will you, could you have dinner with me this
coming Thursday? Go out to dinner with me?"

"Sure," she said easily. "Any night you say. Thursday's
fine."

He was about to set the hour, when the front door opened
and Mamie said, "There's Drewey. Come on in, honey. I got
a job for you. Powther'll tell you all about it."

Drewey sat down in the parlor with them, on one of the
worn, sagging chairs. He thought, Suitable. Highly suitable.
She was more than that. She was exactly what Old Copper
wanted. She looked clean but not starchy. She was big, with a
lap made for sitting on and a feather-pillow bosom made for
laying the head on, and arms big enough to enfold and
cuddle the young Jonathan Copper in, for five or six years.

"Can you sing, Mrs. Drewey?" Powther asked.

"Sing?" Drewey repeated, frowning, "Course not. Is this a
singin' job? I didn't put in for no singin' job at the agency."

Powther explained about the job, about how he felt that
she was exactly what was wanted. He carefully avoided using
the old man's phrase "big fat colored woman," because after
all— Then he said, "I mean, can you, ah, sing enough to say,
sing a baby to sleep while rocking him in a rocking chair?"

"Lord, yes. I don't call that singin'. That's just a little hum-
a-byin'."

"Would you mind sitting in that rocking chair over there,
just, you understand, so I can get an idea, and do a little
hum-a-byin'?"

Mrs. Drewey looked as though she were going to refuse
and Mamie said, in that voice that was like singing, "Aw, go
on, Drewey, hum-a-by for Powther. It could mean a lot to
you workin' for them stinkin' rich Coppers."

Mrs. Drewey sat down in the shabby, cheap rocking chair,
her hands stiff on the arms, and glared at them. Then she
began to rock, back and forth, back and forth, and the chair
creaked a little every time she rocked. The glare subsided in

her eyes, and she closed them, her hands relaxed in her lap, and she began to hum, and the humming, at some point, Powther didn't know just when, became a soft singing. If there was a tune, it was not one he had ever heard before, if there were actual words they made no sense whatsoever, and he thought it was the most comforting, relaxing, beautiful sound he had ever heard.

His eyelids drooped over his eyes, and for the first time in his life he must have gone sound asleep sitting in a chair because when he opened his eyes, Mrs. Drewey was no longer in the rocking chair, she and Mamie Smith were sitting on the sofa, both of them looking at him, both of them laughing. It was evidently the sound of their laughter that woke him up. He felt like a fool, going to sleep like that in a chair, and he wondered if his mouth had been open, wished that he had teeth like Mamie Smith's, big, strong, evenly spaced teeth, very white in that coppery brown face.

He sat up straight. "I'm sure you'll do, Mrs. Drewey. Can you come for an interview right away?"

When Old Copper saw Mrs. Drewey, he promptly roared an order for a rocking chair, roared another order to the effect that Jonathan Copper IV be placed in Mrs. Drewey's lap. Young Jonathan was still howling his head off, and the instant Drewey tucked his head into the fleshy part of her arm, covered his little feet up with a blanket and started rocking and hum-a-byin', he stopped howling, sighed, and promptly went to sleep.

Mrs. Jonathan Copper III stared, amazed. "Why, he's asleep. He hasn't been asleep for six hours. He's done nothing but cry. I've never seen anything like it."

"Just wanted a big fat colored woman," Old Copper said. "Don't never give no male Coppers to no bony white women to bring up."

Powther told Mamie about Drewey and the baby when he took her to dinner on Thursday night. While he talked he studied her, trying to analyze her weaknesses. He decided that she would never be able to save the money to tide her over until she got a job in a small Northern city, that there would always be something that she wanted to buy. After all, the Northern city was an intangible, and the gaudy costume jewelry or the flimsy shoes were tangible, touchable, seeable, right there in a store window.

He knew, too, just by looking at her, that if she married him, he would always find gentlemen callers in his home. He couldn't foresee Bill Hod, and the general shape and size and viciousness of him, because he had led a life in the houses of the very rich which prevented him from being aware of the existence of the Bill Hods, but he could foresee jealousy and insecurity. Knowing this, he still intended to marry Mamie Smith, and so directed all his resources toward that end.

Whenever he saw her he talked about the disadvantages of living in rented rooms, about the luxury it was possible to enjoy in a small place of one's own.

He bought presents for her. Just before Christmas he sent to New York for three nightgowns, three such nightgowns as he was certain she had never dreamed could possibly exist. There was a gray one, because he knew the color would surprise her; a flaming red one, because she had a passion for red; and a peculiar yellowish one that would bring out the coppery tones of her skin. They were more like expensive evening gowns than like anything to sleep in.

But they were worth the price he paid for them because on Christmas Eve when she opened the box, she stared, and said, "What on earth—"

She took the nightgowns out of the big beautiful box, out of the layers of tissue paper, and sat with them in her lap, holding them, hugging them, spreading them out so that the long full pleated skirts foamed over the floor, covering part of the cheap, garish, machine-made rug.

He thought, If I had my choice I'd ask her to put on the yellowish one.

Mamie said, "Powther, you want me to try one of them on for you?"

He was suddenly overcome by emotion, a kind of shyness, and he nodded, holding his head down because he couldn't look at her.

"Which one?"

He pointed at the yellowish one, the almost mustard-colored yellow one, but not quite mustard, it had more green in it than that, a peculiar color. She swept all the gowns up in her arms, and he heard her going up that long uncarpeted staircase, walking swiftly.

A few minutes later, she said, "Powther!" from somewhere upstairs.

He stumbled on the stairs, striking his knee so that it hurt unbearably, and the pain halted him, halfway up. She called again, "Powther!" and he hurried up the stairs, his knee aching, stiff; and there she was standing in the doorway of a room, and the nightgown was made of a fabric so sheer that he could see through it, see all of her, and yet it was as though there were veiling over the flesh, and the flesh was so beautiful, that his eyes filled with tears; and that moment seemed to sum up all of his future relationship with Mamie, rapture, but pain, too.

After that he set to work to make himself indispensable to her. When he went to see her he brought choice crackers and old cheeses and beautiful fruit, in case she wanted something to eat late at night. He slipped the landlady ten dollars so that Mamie could cook in her room, which was against the rules. He bought a small electric icebox and an extremely efficient small electric stove so that she could bake and fry as much as she wanted to. He used all of his efficiency, all of his knowledge of the luxurious, and most of his bank account, in his courtship of Mamie Smith. He transformed that run-down dismal bedroom into a very comfortable one-room apartment.

Finally, he went to New York and registered with a high-class employment agency, explaining optimistically that he was going to get married, that his fiancée preferred to live in Connecticut. The Treadway job was offered to him and he went to Monmouth for an interview. He explained to Mrs. Treadway that his wife preferred not to live on the premises. Though he was certain Mamie would have gentlemen callers, he did not intend to have the Treadway chauffeur, cook, gardener included in their number. It would make for an impossible situation, all of them being white. Before he went back to Baltimore he rented an apartment for Mamie in the colored section of Monmouth. It wasn't what he wanted but it would do until he could locate something better.

When he told Old Copper that he was leaving, the old man let out one of those roars that made people jump back from him, startled, awed.

"Whatsamatter?" he bellowed. "I'll raise your pay. Is that the trouble? You want more money? You want more money?"

"No, oh, no, sir. It's just that I'm getting married."

"You are? Good God!" Old Copper looked at Powther half questioningly. "Has she got a big—"

Powther said hastily, "My fiancée don't like Baltimore, sir. The only way I can get her to marry me is to offer her the chance to live in Connecticut."

Old Copper snorted, "Connecticut! Of all the godforsaken swampy places to live," he shuddered. "It's got the goddamndest climate, the goddamndest weather in the whole United States. They got drought in August, flood in MarchApril, hurricanes in the fall, winds howlin' down the chimneys all winter long. The goddamndest—I know what I'm talkin' about, Powther. I was born there." He sighed, sank deeper in the leather chair. "When you leavin'?"

"In three weeks."

"I'll give you a weddin' present, Powther. Bring her around before you leave and I'll give you a weddin' present. And if those goddam farmers you're goin' to work for in Connecticut don't treat you right, you come back here and I'll pay you twice what they been payin' you."

Powther nodded, thinking, I may never go to Monmouth. I may be wrong about Mamie Smith. He stayed away from her until the day before he was to leave, stayed away for three weeks, hoping that she would wonder about him, miss him, become aware of the disorder in which she lived without him.

When he finally went to see her, he carried two big packages of food with him. He walked through that shabby down-attheheels crooked street where she lived, thinking, Too many people, too many dogs, too many smells. Spring of the year but already hot. Heat waves rising from the sidewalk, nearly naked children toddling down the street, crawling up and down the highstooped steps in front of the houses.

He would tell her about spring in Connecticut, about the dogwood and the laurel, about the smell of the river, the curve of the river, sunlight on the River Wye, about the grass, and the birds, the pigeons that strutted on every available patch of grass, about the friendliness of the people, about how clean Monmouth looked, how the houses, many of them, were painted white and the blinds were green, so that even though it was a city, it looked like a toy city compared to Baltimore with its dingy streets and its gray old buildings.

He wondered what Mamie had been doing these past three weeks while he had been completing his carefully thought out campaign. Had he made himself indispensable? He soon found out that in one way he had, and in another, perhaps more important, way, he hadn't. The bleak furnished room that he had turned into a colorful, rather luxurious, one-room apartment was in a state of dreadful disorder. He took off his coat, rolled up his shirt sleeves and set to work, washing dishes, making the bed, cleaning the room.

She must have been going to the movies rather often because there were innumerable stubs of tickets from the colored theatre, on the floor, on top of the chest of drawers. She hadn't bothered to fix a decent meal for herself because there wasn't a scrap of food in the icebox. She'd had a caller, or callers, there were six empty beer cans on the floor, and she didn't drink beer; two empty whiskey bottles, and several sticky glasses and innumerable empty ginger ale bottles. He found a man's socks, large size, loud red and green stripes, medium-priced, under the bed. Indispensable? For some things. Not needed for companionship, though. He held the socks in his hand, wondering, conjecturing, and then tossed them into the dustpan with the rest of the rubbish.

He had set the table, one of his gifts, a card table, very expensive, actually a folding table, heavy, unshakable, and the steak was just about ready to serve when Mamie came home from the restaurant where she worked.

She had a parcel under her arm, wrapped in brown paper, almost the color of the brown dress she wore. No stockings. No hat. Perspiration on her forehead. She looked hot and tired and so beautiful, so big and beautiful, that he swallowed twice, in an effort to get rid of the lump that rose in his throat. He didn't say anything to her because somehow he couldn't.

"Powther!" she said, pleasure in her voice. "My God! Ain't it hot!"

She looked all around the room, looked longest at the table set for two, at the white tablecloth, the carefully folded napkins, made no comment. He watched her cross the room, sit down in the chair by the front window, slip her feet out of her shoes, and then he turned back to the stove, stuck the French bread in the oven, served the plates, poured wine in the wine glasses.

She ate in silence, ate with a relish that made him wish he hadn't stayed away so long. She must have been hungry. He watched her with a tender, yearning feeling, and thought, surprised, That's the way mothers feel about their children. She ate four of the pastries he'd brought with him, drank coffee, and then nibbled at the white grapes.

"Powther," she said. "I haven't eaten a meal like this since the last time you was here. Where've you been?"

He leaned forward, grasped the edge of the table. "I've been getting a new job. In Monmouth. A small city in Connecticut. I've got an apartment there. And all you've got to do is to say the word, just say the word, and you can go with me. I leave tomorrow." He opened his wallet, took out two railroad tickets. "One's for you and one's for me."

"I couldn't," she said. "It was right sweet of you to get the ticket for me but I haven't got a job in Monmouth. I've tried and tried to save the money so I'd have enough to tide me over but I haven't got ten dollars to my name and that's the God's truth."

"That's just it," he said eagerly. "You won't need any job. I thought, well, will you marry me? I earn enough money to more than take care of both of us."

She threw her head back and laughed. "You're a funny little man," she said. "Here I been thinkin' I'd done something to hurt your feelings and you been away makin' plans." She was silent for a moment. "Suppose I said no?"

"I—" he began, and stopped. What would he do? He'd die. That's what he'd do. He couldn't live without her. "I'd —I'd just turn the unused ticket in when I got to the station tomorrow afternoon."

"You mean you'd go away? Without me?"

"I have to," he said. "I have a job there. I have to go."

She looked around the room again. He wished, afterwards, that she had looked at him, appraised him, studied him, but she didn't. She looked at the room, at the stove, at the table, at the chairs he'd bought, at the comfortable bed. He supposed she was weighing the comfort and luxury, the good food, the cleanliness, against the disorder and discomfort of the past three weeks. He knew that people got accustomed to luxury very quickly, accepting it finally as their due, and no matter what strain and struggle, what utter poverty they may have known, they soon forgot it, they soon reached the point where they could not survive whole without comfort, luxury. It softened them up. He knew that. He had used it to win Mamie with, but he couldn't help wishing that he, as a person, had been the one important factor in her decision.

Picking up one of the tickets, she started humming under her breath. "I'll wear that new navy hat," she said. "And that

new navy suit because it'll be cool up there and I've got some
new navy suedes and I've got a big red pocketbook that'll go
good with it. Let's see, what time's this train go anyway?"
She frowned at the ticket, examining it.

It was as simple as that, as quick as that. He couldn't quite
believe it, even while he packed her things, and made arrangements to have a moving van pick up the furniture.

On their way to the railroad station, the next day, they
stopped to see Old Copper. He stared at Mamie a long time
and to Powther's great discomfort, Mamie stared right back.

"You done well, Powther," Old Copper said. "If I was
younger I'd give you a run for your money." Then he got out
of the big leather chair, in the library, sat down at his desk,
wrote a note, made out a check, put the note and the check in
an envelope, and handed it to Powther. He handed the envelope to Powther, but he kept looking at Mamie, staring at
Mamie, and Mamie was staring right back. Powther felt more
and more uncomfortable, embarrassed.

Old Copper said, "Well! Good luck!" and shook Powther's hand, and patted his shoulder and said, again, "If
them goddamn farmers you're goin' to work for don't treat
you right, you come straight back here."

He followed them to the door, and once outside Powther
looked back and Old Copper was still staring at Mamie,
watching her go down the steps, and he knew a sudden rush
of sheer maleness such as he had never felt before, suddenly
hated the old man because of his wealth, the whiteness of his
skin, wanted to go back and punch him in the jaw. When Old
Copper saw Powther looking at him, he closed the door
suddenly.

While Mamie was in the ladies' room, on the train, he
opened the envelope. Old Copper's check was for a thousand dollars, and the note, written in that bold heavy hand,
sounded as though the old man had spoken to him:

*Watch what I tell you. Someday she'll leave you for another man.
If you're ever broke, ever need a job, ever need anything, just let me*

know, because God damn it, Powther, there's nobody else in the world can look after me like you done.

He was tempted to tell Mamie, after all they were married now, that he had to go back to Old Copper, that now that he had left, he knew he couldn't stand a new place, new people. And there was, too, the old man's warning, "She'll leave you for another man." In a new place it was much more likely to happen than in Baltimore.

It was all a dreadful mistake. He had spent money like a millionaire and his bank account had practically vanished. But he had Old Copper's check. That would serve as a stake, a kind of cushion against disaster. He folded the check and put it in his wallet, tore the letter into tiny pieces and thrust the pieces far under the seat.

Mamie came swaying down the aisle, swaying partially because of the motion of the train, but also because it was the way she walked. And he thought, Well, I can't go back to Old Copper's, not with Mamie. They had looked at each other, stared at each other, just as though they were testing each other out, as though they had immediately recognized some quality they had in common and were instantly defiant, instantly jockeying for position for some final test of strength.

He knew that he would have rivals, knew that he would find gentlemen callers in his house, but he could not, would not, make it possible for Old Copper to be included among them.

And now as he lay in this bed, beside J.C., turning and twisting, in vain, wasted effort to avoid the child's knees, elbows, head, he asked himself if he regretted that decision he'd made on the train. Should he have gone back to Old Copper? More important still, was it a mistake, the whole thing? Wouldn't he have been better off if he hadn't married Mamie? No. He had never known such delight as he had experienced with Mamie.

J.C. moved for the millionth time, turning over, and then

inching up in bed. He put his arm around him thinking to restrain his movements, and J.C.'s head caught him under the chin, hard, heavy, the impact was such that Powther thought his jaw was broken, then that he had cracked his bridge, but he had only bitten his tongue, viciously, painfully. It felt swollen and he lay there, pain along the edge of his tongue, moving it back and forth cautiously, exploratively, expecting to feel a gush of blood at any moment. J.C. muttered darkly to himself, under his breath. Kelly and Shapiro echoed his mutterings. They were talking in their sleep repeating words, phrases. Then they turned over, sighed groaned, kicked the covers off. He could hear their fee rejecting the covers, getting free of the covers.

I will never get to sleep, he thought. And I have to be a the Hall early tomorrow morning. He heard the clang-clang of the last trolley that went up Franklin Avenue. It seemed like a long time after that that the lights went off in The Las Chance. This room in the front of the house became suddenly darker, the pink-orange light from the neon sign wen out suddenly; and just before it went out, there was a littl eddy, a gust of talk in the street below, suggesting wind eddying, gone, as the last of the beer drinkers, and th seekers after Nirvana, left The Last Chance, heading reluc tantly toward home.

The Last Chance. The Last Chance. Last chance to d what? Get a drink? Burn in hell? Look at Bill Hod?

He sat up in bed, listening. He thought he heard footstep in the hall, then the click of a lock. He really couldn't tell, n in this room with its restless sleepers.

Getting out of bed, he covered J.C. carefully, closed th door of the boys' room behind him, and went down the ha slowly, quietly, in his bare feet, the floor cold to his feet. I stood outside the door of the bedroom, listening, and I thought he heard Bill Hod's voice. But he wasn't certain. I couldn't see anything except a thin thread of pinkish lig under the door.

The thread of pinkish light disappeared from under t

door and there was silence, no sound at all, nothing, just the
darkness and the cold floor under his feet. He stood there
waiting for some further sound. There was nothing at all, no
sound of voices, no movement. Silence.

He went back down the hall, opened the door of the boys'
bedroom, and got in bed with J.C., refusing to think about
what he thought he'd heard, thinking instead, I will not sleep
on that damn sofa in the living room, I will sleep in a bed, a
rightful bed, even if I cannot rest. I am not a refugee. I have a
right to a bed. I work all day and half the night, and come
home to—Bill Hod? Link Williams? Cigarette case incrusted
with diamonds.

At five o'clock the next morning he was dressing in the
living room. The boys were good for another two hours at
least. While he was putting on his shoes, he thought he
heard the thud-thud of the percolator in the kitchen, was
certain that he smelt coffee. But he didn't know how to greet
Mamie this morning, so he finished dressing and then went
down the hall. The bedroom door was open, the room was
empty.

Mamie called from the kitchen, "You up already, Powther?
Set the table for me, will you? Mebbe we can eat without
them starvin' Armenians sittin' in our laps."

He decided that he must have dreamed that business last
night, had a nightmare, a night horse, as his father used to
say. She was so gay this morning, her eyes sparkled, her lips
kept curving into a smile, and she sang as she turned the
bacon in the frying pan, cooked the pancakes.

"Soup's on," she said. He thought even her voice was
lovelier this morning, there was more music in it than ever.
And she was off the diet. She ate everything in sight.

When they finished eating, she leaned back in her chair,
sighed and lit a cigarette. "Let's leave the dishes," she said.
"And go get back in bed. It's too early for any poor black
sinners to be up."

He nearly tripped over his feet getting there, and later, he
went to sleep, relaxing into sleep, easily, quickly, content-

ment seeping all through him, so that he smiled in his sleep, aware just before he slid down into the total darkness, the blackout, the delicious oblivion of sleep that Mamie's soft warm naked body was pressed tight against him, and the strong sweet perfume was all around him, like a cloud.

When he woke up he looked around the room, trying to remember where he was, and how he got there, and then he smiled, remembering. He sat up in bed and saw that Mamie was up, and getting dressed.

She always put her shoes on first, she never wore any stockings in the house, and now she was leaning over, back turned, putting on a pair of green highheeled sandals. He liked to tease her about putting her shoes on first, telling her that she must have been born in the South, must have been a little barefoot pickaninny, and then she finally acquired a pair of shoes, sign of prosperity, mark of distinction, that set her apart from the rest of the black barefoot tribe, so precious a possession that she slept with them under her pillow her hand resting on them, like an old-time prospector with a small bag of gold dust never out of reach of his hand. When she woke up, she felt under her pillow for her shoes, and then got up, and put them on, just as she was doing now.

He changed the story each time he told it, changing the emphasis, changing the details, embellishing it, sometimes the shoes were scarlet, sometimes they were gold, sometimes she lost them and could not find them, but always on the mornings when she first got them, she went around singing, "All God's chillun got shoes."

Mamie straightened up and the new story about the first pair of shoes went out of his mind. She was shaped almost like a violin, like the base of a violin, big beautiful curve, and as she turned toward the bed, he thought, If she were standing inside a frame, naked like that, with that look of expectancy on her face, all the museums in the world would sell their Da Vincis and their Manets and their Rubens in order to own this one woman.

He said, "Mamie."

"Powther!" she said. "You awake? Here I been tippin' around—" She crossed over to the bed, sat down on the side of it, put her arms around him, hugged him close to her, and kissed his cheek.

He thought, I, I, I, cuckolded as I am, worried as I often am, after a night with you, you, you, soft warm flesh, smell of perfume, toosweet, toosweet, toostrong, deep-soft-cushion feel of you, feel of the arms, the legs, the thighs, me incased in your thighs, all joy, all ecstasy, all pleasure, not caring, forgetting, completely forget, not forgetting, not caring, who else does this to you, defying Bill Hod, conquering Bill Hod and you and the world, even I, an old man, sorrowful sometimes, frightened always, living forever afraid that you will leave me, don't ever leave me, even I can, could, walk for miles, could sing, could shout, could believe that I will live forever and ever, that I will never die, I am too alive, too filled with joy to die.

He had to get up, get dressed, get back to the Hall. He left Mamie, sitting on the side of the bed, singing:

> Tell me what color an' I'll tell you
> what road she took,
> Tell me what color an' I'll tell you
> what road she took.
> Why'n'cha tell me what color an' I'll
> tell you what road she took.

BIBLIOGRAPHIC NOTES

The majority of criticism on Ann Petry is devoted to her novels of the 1940s. Under the category of "Portrayals of Bitterness," Carl M. Hughes views her work as an illumination of the economic and social forces that overwhelm even intelligent, determined women characters. In *The Negro Novelist: A Discussion of the Writings of American Negro Novelists 1940–*

1950 (New York: The Citadel Press, 1953), Hughes contrasts Petry's novels with *Native Son*, demonstrating her adherence to the requirements of naturalist fiction.

Theodore Gross's "Ann Petry: The Novelist As Social Critic," in *Black Fiction: New Studies in the Afro-American Novel Since 1945*, ed. A. Robert Lee (London: Harper & Row, 1980), pp. 41–53 also views Petry as a social critic, commenting that "the landscape of her fiction tends to be more memorable than her characters." Gross discusses all of her work, but makes no distinction between her earlier novels and later short stories.

Addison Gayle's *The Way of the New World* (New York: Doubleday & Co., 1975) discusses Petry along the same lines as do Hughes and Gross. Comparison with Richard Wright is made, as well as comments on Petry's social determinism.

Even studies that focus on Petry's female characterizations tend to focus on the naturalistic novels. Barbara Christian's *Black Women Novelists: The Making of a Tradition, 1892–1976* (Westport, Conn.: Greenwood Press, 1980) analyzes Lutie Johnson's defeat in *The Street*. Thelma J. Shinn, "Women in the Novels of Ann Petry," *Critique: Studies in Modern Fiction* 16, no. 1 (1974): 110–20, asserts that Petry's focus is on the overwhelming forces that defeat women's attempts to gain personal development and social security.

Until Barbara Smith's unpublished manuscript, "The Relationships Between Men and Women in the Writing of Ann Petry" (Boston, fall 1971), there was little mention of *Miss Muriel and Other Stories* or *The Narrows*. Smith explores Petry's ambivalence toward women characters—her vacillation between showing them as powerful and weak—and concludes that despite her ambivalence toward her women, Petry's characters have more autonomy and power than do most female heroines of the time.

Two recent critiques continue Smith's efforts to examine Petry's work in the context of sexual as well as racial oppression. Bernard W. Bell, "Ann Petry's Demythologizing of American Culture and Afro-American Character," in *Conjur ing: Black Women, Fiction and Literary Tradition,* ed. Marjorie Pryse and Hortense J. Spillers (Bloomington: Indiana University Press, 1985), pp. 105–15. Bell says that Petry's fiction moves beyond the materialistic vision of Richard Wright and Chester Himes to deal more faithfully with the complexities of class and gender as well as race. One of the most interesting and insightful analyses of Petry's *The Street* is Marjorie Pryse, " 'Pattern Against the Sky': Deism and Motherhood in Ann Petry's *The Street,* " in *Conjuring.* Pryse argues that motherhood is the one design in the novel capable of sustaining the characters; its failure leads to the novel's ultimate sense of disintegration and alienation.

I Sign My Mother's Name:
Maternal Power in Dorothy West's
Novel, *The Living Is Easy*

Somewhere around 1926, when Dorothy West was not yet twenty years old, she went to New York and became a part of the group of younger Harlem Renaissance writers and artists which consisted of Wallace Thurman, Zora Hurston, Aaron Douglas, Augusta Savage, and Langston Hughes. West describes herself in the group as a quiet and shy spectator, a writer without a voice:

> I went to the Harlem Renaissance and never said a word. I was young and a girl so they never asked me to say anything. I didn't know I had anything to say. I was just a little girl from Boston, a place of dull people with funny accents.[1]

The "group" went to Wallace Thurman's loft regularly on Sunday nights, but one Sunday, instead of joining them, West went to visit a family of very proper black Bostonians who managed to do everything right. They had the correct manners, the proper dress and decorum; they even stood around the piano singing after dinner, trying to project the "proper" image of the happy family. In this one incident, a powerful transformation in West's sensibility occurred and she discovered the beginnings of her own creative voice by remembering her mother's voice:

> Our family was much more colorful and much less proper and at one point in the midst of all this proper behavior I saw my mother's disembodied face laughing at me for being with these people—these middle-class, proper folks. They were my class but not my people. I rushed out of there and went straight to Wally's loft, hoping wouldn't be too late. I could have gone home, but

couldn't. I had to be with them. And I went in and began
to tell them that story, making fun of those proper people
just as my mother would. All my mother's blood came out
in me. I was my mother talking. All of the things I thought
I admired and there I was making fun of them. I became
me. I thought I was a proper Bostonian until I met some.
It was the first time I had something to say.[2]

West is released from silence (both external and internal)
by the example of her mother's power and her mother's
voice. In her identification with her mother's sensibility—
her ironic view of pretentious blacks, her ability to satirize
their foibles, her magnificent storytelling gift—West's creative imagination comes alive.

There are other aspects of Rachel West's influence that
are not so positive. According to West, her light-skinned,
beautiful mother was never quite able to accept having a
plain, dark-skinned child like Dorothy. Class-conscious and
color-conscious, Rachel West tried to rear her daughter in
the same mold, but her domineering ways rankled and alienated her daughter. Once Dorothy complained angrily to her
father about her mother's tyrannical behavior, and he quietly took up for his wife, telling Dorothy, "I understand your
mother." West was not admitted to that inner circle. She
was, however, part of another circle as Rachel West gathered
into their large house sisters, nieces, and nephews whom she
ruled like a small potentate. Years later West understands
that her mother's purpose in creating this extended family
was to enable each child to draw from the strengths of the
others—under her command. In her autobiographical first
novel, *The Living Is Easy* (1948),[3] West tried to deal with this
complicated relationship with her mother, patterning its
protagonist, Cleo Jericho Judson, after Rachel West. Like
Rachel, Cleo assembles together in one large house her
three sisters and their children, destroying their marriages
and ruling over a small dynasty with a combination of manipulation, deceit, and willpower. Cleo seems to dominate
this community, but her powerful presence is constantly

undermined by a narrative perspective that is profoundly ambivalent toward her. In West's retelling of Rachel's story, it is the strange little dark-skinned daughter Judy who triumphs over a manipulative and domineering mother.

Physically and emotionally, Judy and Cleo are opposites, with Judy identified with the "masculine" and Cleo with the "feminine." Judy is the "deep rich color" of her father, Bart Judson, while Cleo is "bright skinned." Like her father, Judy is gentle, quiet, and intelligent with "strength and stability beneath [her] shy exterior." Cleo deplores Judy's gentleness and softness, confirming the absence of any shared emotional qualities between mother and daughter. Whereas Cleo tolerates and manipulates Bart, Judy genuinely loves and appreciates her kind and loving father. She forms an alliance with her cousin Tim, the only other male in the house, so that when she as the good little girl usurps the power of the bad mother she will have in Tim a miniature patriarch for her partner. In contrast to Cleo's dream of bringing up four little girls, Judy wants to have "four little boys exactly like Tim." At the end of the novel, Cleo is alienated from every member of the family, Bart has lost his business and must move to New York to find work, and Cleo is punished with the ultimate loss in patriarchal culture: she is left without a man: "He was gone. The door shut softly on her manlessness." (p. 346)

Except for the flashbacks to her childhood (chapters two and three which are included in this collection), which try sympathetically to account for Cleo's wild and rebellious nature, the narrative operates on several levels to keep us at a distance from her. The narrative begins with Judy's point of view, involving us immediately in her perceptions of Cleo even though Judy is only five: "She peeped at her mother from under the expensive brim of her leghorn straw. She knew what Cleo would look like. She looked mad." Our first experience of Judy is as a subject who is active: "she got up steam and propelled her stout body along like a tired scow straining in the wake of a racing sloop." In contrast to Judy obust movement, Cleo is depicted passively, as the object ooked at: we see her "slender buttocks," her "golden shoul-lers" gleaming through a thin shirtwaist, her hand gripping ler pocketbook. (p. 3) Even her underclothes are presented or us to observe, exposing Cleo in a way that suggests the unveiling yet to come.

Besides denying Cleo a point of view, the text distances us rom her in another even more powerful way by making her a romantic heroine. The object of domestic romance is to divert the female "hero" from heroic quest and to convert her into a "heroine" whose importance is measured by her ability to accommodate to the roles of wife, mother and/or sexual object.

When Cleo as a young girl is sent North to work as a house servant for Miss Boorum in Boston, she begins to dream of possibilities for her life—thrilled by the richness of her voice she plans to sing and dance on the stage. These possibilities are interrupted when Miss Boorum's nephew—a white man —falls in love with Cleo and begins to feel desire "growing n his loins," which, as the text makes clear, can lead only to Cleo's sexual seduction since marriage is impossible. His desire for Cleo diverts the story from her quest for a career o his quest for her. Once again we are forced to see Cleo as an object being looked at, this time by a male gaze so preda-ory that even Cleo's grief over her mother's death becomes or him an appealing sexual gesture:

> Cleo's grief was an inward thing that gave her a look of such purity that Miss Boorum's nephew was even further enmeshed. The enchantment of knowing that she was no one's was monstrous. He was seduced by her chastity. He would never be free as long as he knew he could be her first lover. Until he could see the face of her purity re-placed by the face of surrender, her image would lie on his lids to torment him. (p. 30)

We know that the language of romance and seduction is clearly designed to control and repress women and to make

them assume their "proper" subordinate roles in a male
dominated world. These early chapters of *The Living Is Easy*
so richly upholstered with the language and methods
domestic romance, set in motion from the beginning of the
text narrative practices that oppose Cleo's full developmen
Men fall instantly in love with her, seduced by her dar
streaming hair, her sparkling green eyes, her "appl
breasts." Her future husband, Bart, lies awake at night de
termined to make Cleo his wife; and, once he does, Cleo
expected by black middle-class culture and by the novel
designs to live up to the proper role of wife and mother. Fe
the rest of the text Cleo is seen as wife, mother, and car
taker of an extended family. But she defies our expectation
of how she is supposed to behave in those roles, and for h
defiance, she is severely punished. Rachel Blau Du Plessi
interpretation of Jane Eyre's transmogrification from "fe
male hero" to "heroine-wife" perfectly describes Cleo
plight in this text:

> Here as else where, the female character is embarked o
> heroic endeavors of resistance, mastery, self-realizatio
> and even personal independence in one of the very fe
> available professions. Yet by the end of the story, the pl
> has created a heroine, a character whose importance
> the society of the book lies in her status as an object
> choice, and as educative influence. Her integration wi
> kinship and family bonds is signaled by the production
> the infant of the next generation, which ends the story
> this one.[4]

There are only two chapters in this novel in which Cleo
allowed that position as heroic center of her own stor
Predictably it is when she is still a very young girl. In the
chapters which flashback to her childhood, Cleo ope
questions the paternalistic rules that deny her power a
autonomy.

In this section West tries to make us understand why
imaginative, adventurous, and rebellious child like Cl

eels such anger and frustration over her lesser status as a
girl. With her wild and boundless energy, eleven-year-old
Cleo tries unsuccessfully to exert her will against a world of
male prerogative. She wonders what intangible thing there
is in maleness that gives boys the automatic victory no mater how much a girl struggles for excellence. Once she gets
into a fight with a boy expecting her sisters to cheer her
victory over him and instead they rush to comfort the boy:

> She watched them with wonder. What was there to being a
> boy? What was there to being a man? Men just worked.
> That was easier than what women did. It was women who
> did the lying awake, the planning, the sorrowing, the
> scheming to stretch a dollar. That was the hard part, the
> head part. A woman had to think all the time. A woman
> had to be smart. (p. 21)

Cleo suffers a terrible despair at what happens inevitably to
the female world as girls grow up: "sisters turn into wives
. . . men take their women and ride away." Cleo's dreams
of her own glory, her inability to submit to these restrictions
on women's lives, her desire to maintain an all-female world
where women are central, are feminist concerns that oppose
and critique the antifemale patterns in other parts of this
text. Cleo does not see her world completed by a husband
but by her sisters as though only women can compensate for
her sense of lack. Her portrait reminds me of Toni Mor-
ison's Sula because, like Sula, Cleo does not have a structure or outlet for her considerable energies. They are both
"artists with no art form," but people gravitate toward them,
sensing excitement and danger in their presence. As Cleo
regales her sisters with her outrageous stories, they are stim-
ulated to life and movement simply by the sound of her
voice:

> Was it her voice? Did they like to listen to her talk just to
> hear the music sounds she made? Was it because she was
> so full of life that she made things move inside you, tears

or laughter or anger, and when she went out of a room something like something alive left with her? (p. 202)

We are made to understand how little that voice is appreciated outside this female community. Women in Cleo's class have little value in bourgeois culture except as their husband's showpieces. In the world of men even the powerful Cleo is silenced.

When men spoke, she knew that their worlds were larger than hers, their interests broader. She could not bear knowing that there were many things she didn't know; that a man could introduce a subject and she would have to be silent. Her defense was to shut out of her mind the didactic sound of their voices. (p. 140)

This array of feminist themes in *The Living Is Easy*—the silencing of women, the need for a female community, anger over the limitations and restrictions of women's lives—shows how sensitive Dorothy West was to a woman's story, especially to the ways societies thwart the energies of an extremely gifted, artistic girl child. Since she clearly feels the impossibility of narrating the story of woman as artist, West creates a novel that is in contradiction with itself: Cleo the girl artist becomes Cleo the woman monster.[5] The novel simply abandons its earlier attempts to represent Cleo's point of view. Punished for her willfulness, for her attempts to claim power, she is, at the novel's end, frightened, pathetic, uncomprehending—and in need of male support.

Marianne Hirsch writes in her very perceptive essay "Feminist Discourse/Maternal Discourse: 'Cruel Enough to Stop the Blood' " that mother-daughter stories are nearly always written from the daughter's point of view and the "great unwritten story" remains the story of the mother herself told in her own voice.[6] The mother in literature is silenced and oppressed by the discourse of the daughter because she may perceive the mother as both powerless in the world of men and overpowering in her domestic role. Our resistance to the maternal, Hirsch maintains, make us complicitous with the patriarchy in silencing the mother. The terrible discomfort in *The Living Is Easy* with the power of the mother, the ambivalence over whether to support the mother's position in a patriarchal world or to side with the father and thus claim at least a part of male power are the signs in his text of the daughterly distance from the mother's perspective. Judy, the daughter, is portrayed at the end of the novel with her two female cousins as "sufficient to each other," a sisterly community which has deposed the powerful mother.

In order to understand the ambivalent portrayal of the mother in West's novel, we have to look at her moving and loving portrait of Rachel West written twenty-five years after her mother's death, for it is in that portrait that we see the daughter struggling with the ambivalence, guilt, and awe she felt toward her mother but was unable to express in the novel. What is striking about this memoir is the recognition of a woman's life as separate from her roles as mother and wife and the greater recognition that that life still remains a mystery to the daughter:

> But I still cannot put my finger on the why of her. What had she wanted, this beautiful woman? Did she get it? I would look at her face when it was shut away, and I would long to offer her a penny for her thoughts. But I knew she would laugh and say, "I was just thinking it's time to start dinner," or something equally far from her yearning heart. ("My Mother, Rachel West")

In her attempts at reconciliation with her mother, the seventy-year-old Dorothy West does what the twenty-five-year-old novelist could not do. She admits not only an identification with the mother but comes to understand and appreciate how much of her power as a writer comes from her mother: "All my mother's blood came out in me. I was my mother talking." In their search for self and form, black women writers as diverse as Dorothy West, Alice Walker, and Paule Marshall have found in their mothers' legacies the key to the release of their creative powers. I think that either as conscious myth or literal reality the relation between mother and daughter and the daughter's decision to be a writer are, for many black women, essentially connected. Maybe it is the educated daughters' need to open the "sealed letter" their mothers "could not plainly read," to have their mothers' signatures made clear in their work, to preserve their language, their memories, their myths.[7] Before these signatures can be read clearly, we will have to free the mother from the domination of the daughter, representing her more honestly as a separate, individuated being whose daughters cannot even begin to imagine the mysteries of her life.

NOTES

1. Interview with Mary Helen Washington, Martha's Vineyard March 1980. Reprinted in Mary Helen Washington's "These Self Invented Women: A Theoretical Framework for a Literary History of Black Women" (Bunting Institute Working Paper, Radcliffe College Cambridge, Mass., 1980), p. 8. Also in Mary Helen Washington, "I Sign My Mother's Name: Alice Walker, Dorothy West and Paule Marshall," in *Mothering the Mind: Twelve Studies of Writers and Their Silent Partners*, ed. Ruth Perry and Martine Watson Broronley (New York: Holmes & Meier, 1984), pp. 150–54.

2. Interview with Mary Helen Washington reprinted in "I Sign My Mother's Name," p. 151.

3. Dorothy West, *The Living Is Easy* (New York: Arno Press and the New York Times, 1969).

4. Rachel Blau Du Plessis, *Writing Beyond the Ending: Narrative Strategies of Twentieth-Century Women Writers* (Bloomington: Indiana University Press, 1985), p. 11.

5. In one of the earliest comments on *The Living Is Easy*, novelist Paule Marshall acknowledges it as a forerunner in dealing with the psychological complexities of a black woman character. According to Marshall a sense of self-division is at the heart of Cleo's conflict

> Ruthless and despotic in her quest for acceptance, in constant terror that her lowly origins in the South will be found out, she is, at the same time, nostalgic for that past. She lives in perpetual conflict with the self she has assumed and the person she is.

"The Negro Woman in American Literature," a panel discussion held during a conference on "The Negro Writer's Vision of America" at the New School of Social Research in New York in 1965. Reprinted in Pat Crutchfield Exum, ed., *Keeping the Faith: Writings by Contemporary Black American Women* (Greenwich, Conn.: Faucett Publications, Inc., 1974), p. 37.

6. Marianne Hirsch, "Feminist Discourse/Maternal Discourse: 'Cruel Enough to Stop the Blood' " (Colloquium at the Bunting Institute, Cambridge, Mass., Spring 1985).

7. This idea of the mothers' signatures made plain in the daughters' art is taken from Alice Walker's essay, "In Search of Our Mothers' Gardens: The Creativity of the Black Woman in the South," *Ms.*, May 1974, 64–70, 105. Also quoted in Mary Helen Washington, "I Sign My Mother's Name," p. 161.

DOROTHY WEST

Cleo

I

"Walk up," hissed Cleo, somewhat fiercely.

Judy was five, and her legs were fat, but she got up steam and propelled her small stout body along like a tired scow straining in the wake of a racing sloop. She peeped at her mother from under the expensive brim of her leghorn straw. She knew what Cleo would look like. Cleo looked mad.

Cleo swished down the spit-spattered street with her head in the air and her sailor aslant her pompadour. Her French heels rapped the sidewalk smartly, and her starched skirt swayed briskly from her slender buttocks. Through the thin stuff of her shirtwaist her golden shoulders gleamed, and were tied to the rest of her torso with the immaculate straps of her camisole, chemise, and summer shirt, which were banded together with tiny gold-plated safety pins. One gloved hand gave ballast to Judy, the other gripped her pocketbook.

This large patent-leather pouch held her secret life with her sisters. In it were their letters of obligation, acknowledging her latest distribution of money and clothing and prodigal advice. The instruments of the concrete side of her charity, which instruments never left the inviolate privacy of her purse, were her credit books, showing various aliases and unfinished payments, and her pawnshop tickets, the expiration dates of which had mostly come and gone, constraining

---

"Cleo" from *The Living Is Easy* (1948)

her to tell her husband, with no intent of irony, that another of her diamonds had gone down the drain.

The lesser items in Cleo's pocketbook were a piece of chamois, lightly sprinkled with talcum powder, and only to be used in extreme necessity if there was no eye to observe this public immodesty, a lollipop for Judy in case she got tiresome, an Irish-linen handkerchief for elegance, a cotton square if Judy stuck up her mouth, and a change purse with silver, half of which Cleo, clandestinely and without conscience, had shaken out of Judy's pig bank.

Snug in the bill compartment of the bag were forty-five dollars, which she had come by more or less legitimately after a minor skirmish with her husband on the matter of renting a ten-room house.

She had begun her attack in the basement kitchen of their landlady's house, a brownstone dwelling in the South End section of Boston. Judy had been sent upstairs to play until bedtime, and Bart had been basking in the afterglow of a good dinner. Ten years before, he had brought his bride to this address, where they had three furnished rooms and the use of the kitchen and the clothesline at a rent which had never increased from its first modest figure. Here, where someone else was responsible for the upkeep, Bart intended to stay and save his money until he was rich enough to spend it.

Cleo had bided her time impatiently. Now Judy was nearing school age. She had no intention of sending her to school in the South End. Whenever she passed these schools at recess time, she would hustle Judy out of sight and sound. "Little knotty-head niggers," she would mutter unkindly, while Judy looked shocked because "nigger" was a badword.

These midget comedians made Cleo feel that she was back in the Deep South. Their accents prickled her scalp. Their raucous laughter soured the sweet New England air. Their games were reminiscent of all the whooping and hollering she had indulged in before her emancipation. These r'aring-

tearing young ones had brought the folkways of the South to
the classrooms of the North. Their numerical strength gave
them the brass to mock their timid teachers and resist attempts to make them conform to the Massachusetts pattern.
Those among them who were born in Boston fell into the
customs of their southern-bred kin before they were old
enough to know that a Bostonian, black or white, should
consider himself a special species of fish.

The nicer colored people, preceded by a similar class of
whites, were moving out of the South End, so prophetically
named with this influx of black cotton-belters. For years
these northern Negroes had lived next door to white neighbors and taken pride in proximity. They viewed their southern brothers with alarm, and scattered all over the city and
its suburbs to escape this plague of their own locusts.

Miss Althea Binney, Judy's private teacher, who for the
past three years had been coming four mornings weekly to
give Judy the benefit of her accent and genteel breeding, and
to get a substantial lunch that would serve as her principal
meal of the day, had told Cleo of a house for rent to colored
on a street abutting the Riverway, a boulevard which
touched the storied Fens and the arteries of sacred Brookline.

On the previous night, Thea's brother, Simeon, the im-
poverished owner and editor of the Negro weekly, *The Clarion,* had received a telephone call from a Mr. Van Ryper, who
succinctly advised him that he would let his ten-room house
for thirty-five dollars monthly to a respectable colored family. Notice to this effect was to be inserted in the proper
column of the paper.

Thea, *The Clarion*'s chronicler of social events, had urged
Simeon to hold the notice until Cleo had had first chance to
see the house. Cleo had been so grateful that she had promised Thea an extravagant present, though Thea could better
have used her overdue pay that Cleo had spent in an irresistible moment in a department store.

The prospect of Judy entering school in Brookline filled

her with awe. There she would rub shoulders with children whose parents took pride in sending them to public school to learn how a democracy functions. This moral obligation discharged, they were then sent to private school to fulfill their social obligation to themselves.

"It's like having a house drop in our laps," said Cleo dramatically. "We'd be fools, Mr. Judson, to let this opportunity pass."

"What in the name of common sense," Bart demanded, "do we went with a ten-room house? We'd rattle around like three pills in a box, paying good money for unused space. What's this Jack the Ripper want for rent?"

"Fifty dollars," Cleo said esaily, because the sum was believable and she saw a chance to pocket something for herself.

"That's highway robbery," said Bart, in an aggrieved voice. It hurt him to think that Cleo would want him to pay that extravagant rent month after month and year after year until they all landed in the poorhouse.

"Hold on to your hat," Cleo said coolly. "I never knew a man who got so hurt in his pocketbook. Don't think I want the care of a three-story house. I wasn't born to work myself to the bone. It's Judy I'm thinking of. I won't have her starting school with hoodlums. Where's the common sense in paying good money to Thea if you want your daughter to forget everything she's learned?"

Bart had never seen the sense in paying Thea Binney to teach his daughter to be a Bostonian when two expensive doctors of Cleo's uncompromising choosing could bear witness to her tranquil Boston birth. But he did not want Cleo to think that he was less concerned with his child's upbringing than she.

Slowly an idea took shape in his mind. "I'll tell you how I figure we can swing the rent without strain. We can live on one floor and let the other two. If we got fifteen dollars a floor, our part would be plain sailing."

"Uh huh," said Cleo agreeably.

He studied her pleasant expression with suspicion. It wasn't like her to consent to anything without an argument. "You better say what you want to say now," he advised her.

"Why, I like a house full of people," she said dreamily. "I've missed it ever since I left the South. Mama and Pa and my three sisters made a good-size family. As long as I'm the boss of the house, I don't care how many people are in it."

"Well, of course," he said cautiously, "strangers won't be like your own flesh. Matter of fact, you don't want to get too friendly with tenants. It encourages them to fall behind with the rent."

"I tell you what," she said brilliantly, "we can rent furnished rooms instead of flats. Then there won't be any headaches with poor payers. It's easier to ask a roomer to pack his bag and go than it is to tell a family to pack their furniture."

He saw the logic of that and nodded sagely. "Ten to one a roomer's out all day at work. You don't get to see too much of them. But when you let flats to families, there's bound to be children. No matter how they fell behind, I couldn't put people with children on the sidewalk. It wouldn't set right on my conscience."

Cleo said quietly, "I'd have banked my life on your saying that." For a moment tenderness flooded her. But the emotion embarrassed her. She said briskly: "You remind me of Pa. One of us had a sore tooth, Mama would tell us to go to sleep and forget it. But Pa would nurse us half the night, keeping us awake with kindness."

He accepted the dubious compliment with a modest smile. Then the smile froze into a grimace of pain. He had been hurt in his pocketbook.

"It'll take a pretty penny to furnish all those extra bedrooms. We don't want to bite off more than we can chew. Don't know but what unfurnished flats would be better, after all. We could pick settled people without any children to make me chicken-hearted."

She stared at him like an animal at bay. Little specks of

green began to glow in her gray eyes, and her lips pulled away from her even teeth. Bart started back in bewilderment.

"You call yourself a businessman," she said passionately. "You run a big store. You take in a lot of money. But whenever I corner you for a dime, it's like pulling teeth to get it out of you. You always have the same excuse. You need every dollar to buy bananas. And when I say, What's the sense of being in business if you can't enjoy your cash, you always say, In business you have to spend money to make money. Now when I try to advise you to buy a few measly sticks of bedroom furniture, a man who spends thousands of dollars on fruit, you balk like a mule at a racetrack."

He rubbed his mustache with his forefinger. "I see what you mean," he conceded. "I try to keep my store filled with fruit. I can't bear to see an empty storeroom. I guess you got a right to feel the same way about a house. In the long run it's better to be able to call every stick your own than have half your rooms dependent on some outsider's furniture."

She expelled a long breath. "That's settled then."

He thought it prudent to warn her. "We'll have to economize to the bone while we're furnishing that house."

She rolled her eyes upward. "We'll even eat bones if you say so."

He answered quietly: "You and the child will never eat less than the best as long as I live. And all my planning is to see to it that you'll never know want when I'm gone. No one on earth will ever say that I wasn't a good provider. That's my pride, Cleo. Don't hurt it when you don't have to."

"Well, I guess you're not the worst husband in the world," she acknowledged softly, and added slowly, "And I guess I'm the kind of wife God made me." But she did not like the echo of that in her ears. She said quickly, "And you can like it or lump it."

Bart took out an impressive roll of bills, peeled off a few of the lesser ones, and laid them on the table. The sight of the bank roll made Cleo sick with envy. There were so many things she could do with it. All Mr. Judson would do with it was buy more bananas.

She sighed and counted her modest pile. There were only forty-five dollars.

"It's five dollars short," she said frigidly.

"Yep," he said complacently. "I figure if this Jack the Ripper wants fifty dollars he'll take forty-five if he knows he'll get it every month on the dot. And if he ever goes up five dollars on the rent, we still won't be paying him any more than he asked for in the first place. In business, Cleo, I've learned to stay on my toes. You've got to get up with the early birds to get ahead of me."

II

Her eyes flew open. The birds were waking in the Carolina woods. Cleo always got up with them. There were never enough hours in a summer day to extract the full joy of being alive. She tumbled out of the big old-fashioned bed. Small Serena stirred, then lay still again on her share of the pillow. At the foot of the bed, Lily and Charity nestled together.

She stared at her three younger sisters, seeing the defenselessness of their innocent sleep. The bubbling mischief in her made her take one of Lily's long braids and double knot it with one of Charity's. She looked back at Serena, who tried so hard to be a big girl and never let anyone help her dress. She picked up Serena's little drawers and turned one leg inside out.

She was almost sorry she would be far away when the fun began. She could picture Lily and Charity leaping to the floor from opposite sides of the bed, and their heads snapping back, and banging together. As for Serena, surprise would spread all over her solemn face when she stepped into one leg of her drawers and found the other leg closed to her. She would start all over again, trying her other foot this time, only to find she had stepped into the same kettle of hot water. She would wrassle for fifteen minutes, getting madder and madder. Cleo had to clap her hand to her mouth to hush her giggles.

She would get a whipping for it. Mama would never see the joke. Mama would say it was mean to tease your sisters. You had to walk a chalkline to please her.

Sometimes Cleo tried to walk a chalkline, but after a little while, keeping to the strait and narrow made her too nervous. At home, there was nothing to do except stay around. Away from home, there were trees to climb, and boys to fight, and hell to raise with Josie Beauchamp.

She climbed out of the open window and dropped to the ground at the moment that Josie Beauchamp was quietly creeping down the stairs of her magnificent house. Some day Cleo was going to live in a fine house, too. And maybe some day Josie was going to be as poor as church mice.

They met by their tree, at the foot of which they had buried their symbols of friendship. Josie had buried her gold ring because she loved it best of everything, and Cleo best of everybody. Cleo had buried Lily's doll, mostly because it tickled her to tell her timid sister that she had seen a big rat dragging it under the house. Lily had taken a long stick and poked around. But every time it touched something, Lily had jumped a mile.

Cleo and Josie wandered over the Beauchamp place, their bare feet drinking in the dew, their faces lifted to feel the morning. Only the birds were abroad, their vivid splashes of color, the brilliant outpouring of their waking songs filling the eye and ear with summer's intoxication.

They did not talk. They had no words to express their aliveness. They wanted none. Their bodies were their eloquence. Clasping hands, they began to skip, too impatient of meeting the morning to walk toward it any longer. Suddenly Cleo pulled her hand away and tapped Josie on the shoulder. They should have chosen who was to be "It." But Cleo had no time for counting out. The wildness was in her, the

unrestrained joy, the desire to run to the edge of the world
and fling her arms around the sun, and rise with it, through
time and space, to the center of everywhere.

She was swift as a deer, as mercury, with Josie running
after her, falling back, and back, until Josie broke the magic
of the morning with her exhausted cry, "Cleo, I can't catch
you."

"Nobody can't never catch me," Cleo exulted. But she
spun around to wait for Josie. The little sob in Josie's throat
touched the tenderness she always felt toward those who
had let her show herself the stronger.

They wandered back toward Josie's house, for now the
busyness of the birds had quieted to let the human toilers
take over the morning. Muted against the white folks' sleeping, the Negro voices made velvet sounds. The field hands
and the house servants diverged toward their separate
spheres, the house servants settling their masks in place, the
field hands waiting for the overseer's eye before they
stooped to servility.

Cleo and Josie dawdled before the stables. The riding
horses whinnied softly, thrusting their noses to the day.
Josie's pony nuzzled her hand, wanting to hear his name
dripping in honey. And Cleo moved away. Anybody could
ride an old pony. She wanted to ride General Beauchamp's
roan stallion, who shied at any touch but his master's.

She marched back to Josie. "Dare me to ride the red
horse," she challenged. Her eyes were green as they bored
into Josie's, the gray gone under in her passion.

"No," said Josie, desperately trying not to flounder in the
green sea. "He'd throw you and trample you. He'd kill you
dead."

"He can't tromp me! I ain't ascairt of nothing alive. I dare
you to dare me. I double dare you!"

"I won't, I won't! I'm bad, but I'm not wicked."

"I'm not wicked neither! I just ain't a coward."

She streaked to the stall and flung open the barrier. The
wild horse smelled her wildness. Her green eyes locked with

his red-flecked glare. Their wills met, clashed, and would
not yield. The roan made a savage sound in his throat, his
nostrils flared, his great sides rippled. He lowered his head
to lunge. But Cleo was quicker than he was. She grasped his
mane, leaped on his broad neck, slid down his back, and dug
her heels in his flanks.

"Giddap, red horse!" she cried.

He flung back his head, reared, and crashed out of the
stall, with Josie screeching and sobbing and sidestepping
just in time.

Cleo hung on for ten minutes, ten minutes of dazzling
flight to the sun. She felt no fear, feeling only the power
beneath her and the power inside her, and the rush of wind
on which she and the roan were riding. When she was finally
thrown, she landed unhurt in a clover field. It never occurred to her to feel for broken bones. She never doubted
that she had a charmed life. Her sole mishap was a minor
one. She had split the seat of her drawers.

She got up and brushed off her pinafore, in a fever now to
get home and brag to her sisters. She knew that she ought to
let Josie see that she was still alive. The riderless horse
would return, and Josie would never tell who had ridden him
off. But she would be tormented by fear for as long as Cleo
stayed away.

Josie would not want to eat, no matter what fancy things
the white folks had for breakfast. She would not want to ride
in her pony cart, no matter how pretty a picture she made.
She would not want to go calling with her stylish mother, not
even if she was let to wear the dress that came all the way
from Paris. On this bright day the sun had darkened for
Josie, and nobody but Cleo could make it shine again.

The four sisters sat around the kitchen table, eating their
salt pork and biscuit and hominy, slupping down their but-
termilk. Charity was nine, two years younger than Cleo, Lily
was eight, Serena four. Their faces were tear-streaked.
Cleo's was not, though she was the one who had got the
whipping. Mama couldn't keep track of the times she had

tanned Cleo's hide, trying to bring her up a Christian. But the Devil was trying just as hard in the other direction.

There Cleo was this morning, looking square in Mama's eye, telling her she must have been sleepwalking again. Couldn't remember getting dressed or tying her sisters' braids together. Just remembered coming awake in a clover field. Mama had tried to beat the truth out of her, but Cleo wouldn't budge from her lie. Worst of all, she wouldn't cry and show remorse. Finally Mama had to put away the strap because her other children looked as if they would die if she didn't.

They couldn't bear to see Cleo beaten. She was their oldest sister, their protector. She wasn't afraid of the biggest boy or the fiercest dog, or the meanest teacher. She could sass back. She could do anything. They accepted her teasing and tormenting as they accepted the terrors of night. Night was always followed by day, and made day seem more wonderful.

Mama stood by the hearth, feeling helpless in her mind. Cleo was getting too big to beat, but she wasn't a child that would listen to reason. Whatever she didn't want to hear went in one ear and out the other. She was old enough to be setting an example for her sisters. And all they saw her do was devilment.

With a long blackened fireplace stick Mama carefully tilted the lid of the three-legged skillet to see if her corn bread was done. The rest of Pa's noon dinner—the greens, the rice, the hunk of fresh pork—was waiting in his bucket. Gently she let the lid drop, and began to work the skillet out of its covering of coals that had been charred down from the oak wood. As the skillet moved forward, the top coals dislodged. Their little plunking sounds were like the tears plopping in Mama's heart.

Sulkily Cleo spooned the hominy she hated because she mustn't make Mama madder by leaving it. Mama bleached her corn in lye water made from fireplace ashes. Pa spit tobacco juice in those ashes. He spit to the side, and Mama took her ashes from the center, but that didn't make them seem any cleaner. Mama thought everything about Pa was wonderful, even his spit.

Cleo made a face at Mama's back, and then her face had to smile a little bit as she watched the dimples going in and out of Mama's round arms. You could almost touch their softness with your eyes. A flush lay just under the surface, giving them a look of tender warmth. For all the loving in Mama's arms, she had no time for it all day. Only at night, when her work was done, and her children in bed, you know by Mama's silver laughter that she was finding time for Pa.

Mama loved Pa better than anyone. And what was left over from loving him was divided among her daughters. Divided even, Mama said whenever Cleo asked her. Never once would Mama say she loved one child the most.

On their straggling way to the mill with Pa's dinner, Cleo told her sisters about her wild ride. They were bewitched by her fanciful telling. Timid Lily forgot to watch where she was walking. Her toes uncurled. She snatched up a stick and got astride it.

Serena clung to Charity's hand to keep herself from flying. Cleo was carrying her away, and she wanted to feel the ground again. She wanted to take Pa his dinner, and go back home and play house.

Charity saw a shining prince on a snow-white charger. The prince rode toward her, dazzling her eyes with light, coming nearer and nearer, leaning to swoop her up in his arms. And Cleo, looking at Charity's parted lips and the glowing eyes, thought that Charity was seeing her riding the red horse into the sun.

Her triumphant tale, in which she did not fall, but grandly dismounted to General Beauchamp's applause, came to its thrilling conclusion. She turned and looked at Lily scornfully, because a stick was not a horse. Lily felt foolish, and let the stick fall, and stepped squish on an old fat worm. Serena freed her hand. Released from Cleo's spell, she felt indepen-

dent again. Charity's shining prince vanished, and there was
only Cleo, walking ahead as usual, forgetting to take back
the bucket she had passed to Charity.

Pa was waiting in the shade, letting the toil pour off him in
perspiration. His tired face lightened with love when they
reached him. He opened his dinner bucket and gave them
each a taste. Nothing ever melted so good in their mouths as
a bite of Pa's victuals.

He gave them each a copper, too, though he could hardly
spare it, what with four of them to feed and Mama wanting
yard goods and buttons and ribbons to keep herself feeling
proud of the way she kept her children. Time was, he gave
them kisses for toting his bucket. But the day Cleo brazenly
said, I don't want a kiss, I want a copper, the rest of them
shamefacedly said it after her. Most times Pa had to struggle
to dig down so deep. Four coppers a day, six days a week,
was half a day's pay gone up in smoke for candy.

Pa couldn't bring himself to tell Mama. She would have
wrung out of him that Cleo had been the one started it. And
Cleo was his eldest. A man who loved his wife couldn't help
loving his first-born best, the child of his fiercest passion.
When that first-born was a girl, she could trample on his
heart, and he would swear on a stack of Bibles that it didn't
hurt.

The sisters put their coppers in their pinafore pockets and
skipped back through the woods.

Midway Cleo stopped and pointed to a towering oak. "You
all want to bet me a copper I can't swing by my feet from up
in that tree?"

Lily clapped her hands to her eyes. "I doesn't want to bet
you," she implored. "I ain't fixing to see you fall."

Serena said severely, "You bust your neck, you see if
Mama don't bust it again."

Charity said tremulously, "Cleo, what would us do if our
sister was dead?"

Cleo saw herself dressed up fine as Josie Beauchamp,
stretched out in a coffin with her sisters sobbing beside it,

and Pa with his Sunday handkerchief holding his tears, and Mama crying, I loved you best, Cleo. I never said it when you were alive. And I'm sorry, sorry, I waited to say it after you were gone.

"You hold my copper, Charity. And if I die, you can have it."

Lily opened two of her fingers and peeped through the crack. "Cleo, I'll give you mine if you don't make me see you hanging upside down." It was one thing to hear Cleo tell about herself. It was another thing to see her fixing to kill herself.

"Me, too," said Serena, with a little sob, more for the copper than for Cleo, whom she briefly hated for compelling unnecessary sacrifice.

"You can have mine," said Charity harshly. Her sweet tooth ached for a peppermint stick, and she almost wished that Cleo was dead.

Cleo flashed them all an exultant smile. She had won their money without trying. She had been willing to risk her neck to buy rich Josie Beauchamp some penny candy. Now that it was too late to retrieve Josie Beauchamp's lost hours of anxiety, Cleo wanted to carry her a bag of candy, so that when Josie got through with being glad, and got mad, she wouldn't stay mad too long.

She held out her hand. Each tight fist poised over her palm, desperately clung aloft, then slowly opened to release the bright coin that was to have added a special sweetness to the summer day.

Cleo couldn't bear to see their woe-begone faces. She felt frightened, trapped by their wounded eyes. She had to do something to change their expressions.

"I'll do a stunt for you," she said feverishly. "I'll swing by my hands. It ain't nothing to be ascairt to see. You watch."

Quickly, agilely she climbed the tree and hung by her hands. Wildly, wildly she swung, to make them forget she had taken their money, to let them see how wonderful she was.

Then a boy came by, just an ordinary knotted-headed, knobby-kneed boy. He looked at her and laughed, because to him a girl carrying on so crazy cut a funny figure. She wanted to kill him. He made her feel silly. She climbed down, and she knew he was watching her, watching the split in her drawers.

When she reached the ground, she whirled to face him, and found his feet waving in front of her. He was walking on his hands. And her sisters were squealing with delight. They had seen her walk on her hands a thousand times. What was there so wonderful about watching a boy?

She flung herself upon him, and they fought like dogs, the coppers lost irrecoverably. Her sisters circled them, crying and wringing their hands. She had to win, no matter how. She bent her head and butted him in the groin, where the weakness of boys was—the contradictory delicacy.

The fight was knocked out of him. He lay very still, his hands shielding his innocent maleness from further assault, and the blood on his lips where his anguished teeth had sunk in.

Her sisters fluttered around him. They felt no pride for her victory. Instead they pitied him. She watched them with wonder. What was there to being a boy? What was there to being a man? Men just worked. That was easier than what women did. It was women who did the lying awake, the planning, the sorrowing, the scheming to stretch a dollar. That was the hard part, the head part. A woman had to think all the time. A woman had to be smart.

Her sisters weren't smart. They thought Pa was the head of the house. They didn't know the house was run by the beat of Mama's heart. There was an awful lonesomeness in Cleo when Mama went across the river to Grandma's. She did not want to be bad then. She wanted to be good so God would send Mama back safe. But she was wildly bad again the moment Mama returned. She could not bear the way she felt inside, like laughing and crying and kissing Mama's face.

She never kissed Mama. Kisses were silly. Pa kissed Mama

when he came home from work. There was sweat on him
from his labor, but Mama lifted her mouth to his. His mustache prickled against her lips, but Mama did not pull away.

Looking at her sisters, standing above the suffering boy,
she saw in each some likeness of Mama—in Charity the
softness and roundness, the flush just under the thin skin,
the silver laughter; in Lily the doe eyes, liquid and vulnerable, the plaited hair that kept escaping in curls; in small
Serena the cherry-red mouth, the dimpled cheeks. She knew
that she looked like Pa. Everyone said so. Everyone said she
was a beauty. What was wrong with their seeing? How could
looking like Pa, with his sweat and his stained mustache,
make anybody a beauty? Sometimes she would stare at herself in Mama's mirror and stick out her tongue.

Now, seeing her sisters, with their tender faces turned
toward the boy, a terrible sorrow assailed her. Some day
they would all grow up. They would all get married and go
away. They would never live together again, nor share the
long bright busy days. Mama, too, would go. Mama would
die. Didn't she always say that her side of the family were not
long livers? They were dead before they were fifty. Dead
with their loveliness alive in their still, smooth faces. When
Mama was gone in a last luminous moment, there would be
the look of her and the silver laughter in the children she had
blessed with her resemblance.

So long as her sisters were within sight and sound, they
were the mirrors in which she would see Mama. They would
be her remembering of her happy, happy childhood.

She flung herself down on the ground, and her torture
was worse than the boy's. For hers was spiritual suffering
and immeasurable frustration. All her terror of the future,
all her despair at knowing that nothing lasts—that sisters
turn into wives, that men take their women and ride away,
that childhood is no longer than a summer day—were in her
great dry sobs.

The boy staggered to his feet in complete alarm. He
thought he had hurt her in some dreadful way mysterious to

girls, her breast, her belly where the babies grew. Her father
would skin him alive. He made a limping dash across the
road and the trees closed in.

Then her sisters knelt beside her, letting their soothing
fingers caress her face. Her sobbing quieted. She jumped up
and began to turn cartwheels. A wildness was in her. She was
going to turn cartwheels all the way home, heretofore an
impossible feat.

Mama was in the doorway, watching her hurtle down a
dusty road, seeing a girl eleven years old turning upside
down, showing her drawers. Mama got the strap again and
laid it on hard and heavy. Cleo just grinned, and wouldn't
wipe the grin off, even with the whole of her on fire and
hurting. Mama couldn't bear such impudence from her own
flesh and blood. She let the strap fall and sat down and cried.

Mama didn't know what made Cleo so wild. Cleo got more
of her attention than all of her other children put together.
God help her when she grew up. God help the man who
married her. God help her sisters not to follow in her footsteps. Better for her sisters if Cleo had never been born.

Somewhere in Springfield, Massachusetts, at that moment, Bart Judson, a grown man, a businessman, too interested in the Almighty Dollar to give any thought to a wife
was certainly giving no thought to an eleven-year-old hell
raiser way down South. But for Bart, whose inescapable
destiny this unknown hoyden was to be, it might have been
better if her sisters had never been born.

III

Cleo arrived in Springfield three years later. She and Josie
reached their teens within a month of each other. Cleo became the Kennedy kitchen help and caught her hair up in a
bright bandana to keep it out of the cooking. Josie caught
her hair up, too, but with pins and combs in the fashion. She

out on a long dress and learned to pour tea in the parlor. Cleo learned to call her Miss Josephine, and never said anything that was harder.

Providence appeared as an elderly spinster, a northern lady seeking sun for her sciatica. Cleo's way home lay past her boarding place. She was entranced by Cleo's beauty as she returned from work, her hair flying free, the color still staining her cheeks from the heat of the cookstove and the fire in her heart, and her eyes sea-green from her sullen anger at working in the white folks' kitchen.

Miss Peterson, hating to see this sultry loveliness ripen in the amoral atmosphere of the South, urged Mama to let her take Cleo North. Mama considered it an answer to prayer. With Cleo getting so grown, Mama's heart stayed in her mouth. She didn't know what minute Cleo might disgrace herself. The wildness in the child might turn to wantonness in the girl. And that would kill Pa. Better for him if she sent Cleo North with this strict-looking spinster.

Cleo considered going North an adventure. Miss Josephine, who had never been outside of Carolina, would turn green with envy. In her secret sessions with her heartsick sisters, Cleo promised to send for them as soon as she got rich. She did not know how she was going to do it, but this boastful promise was more important than the performance.

She had thought she was going to night school when she reached the North. But her conscientious custodian, seeing that Cleo looked just as vividly alive in Springfield as she had looked in South Carolina, decided against permitting her to walk down darkened streets alone. There were too many temptations along the way in the guise of coachmen and butlers and porters.

Cleo's time, between her easy chores, was spent in training her tongue to a northern twist, in learning to laugh with a minimum show of teeth, and in memorizing a new word in the dictionary every day.

The things that Cleo never had to be taught were how to hold her head high, how to scorn sin with men, and how to

keep her left hand from knowing what her right hand wa
doing.

She saw Bart Judson six months after her arrival, on one (
the few occasions that she was let out of her cloister. Th
brief encounter, with a plate-glass window between then
made no impression on either participant. The wheels (
their inseparable destiny were revolving slowly. For short
thereafter Bart was to be on his way to Boston. And not fo
five years more was Cleo to follow, and then with no know
edge that Bart Judson had preceded her.

As they stared disinterestedly at each other, he seeing on
a pretty, half-grown, countrified girl, she seeing only a shir
sleeved man with a mustache, and neither recognizing Fat
the disappointed goddess had half a mind to change the
charted course. Then with habitual perversity thought bett
of it.

Cleo had come to a halt before a store front, where a
exquisite pile of polished fruit was arrayed on a silver tra
the sole and eye-compelling window display. Two men wei
busy inside the store, one, a fair-skinned man whom Cl
mistook for white and the proprietor, was waiting on th
customer, the other man, obviously the colored help, w
restocking the counters. The colored man stared briefly, a
did Cleo. Then her eyes moved to a wide arch which mad
convenient access to an ice-cream parlor next door.

Two retail stores on busy State Street was the distanc
Virginia-born Bart had come in his lucky boots on his way
the banana docks of the Boston Market. Cleo, with ten cen
burning a hole in her pocket and her throat parched for
fancy dish of ice cream, slowly walked away, because sh
wasn't certain that the owner wanted colored custome
And, as a matter of fact, Bart didn't.

When he and Cleo met five years later, again it was pu
chance. But this time Fate flung them headlong at ea
other, and for Bart, at least, there was no mistaking that
had met the woman he wanted for his wife.

Cleo was sent to Boston by the relatives of her Springfie

enefactress when the old lady's lingering illness was inevitably leading her to the grave. The relatives rallied around er, for there were always cases of elderly people deciding to eave their estates to faithful servants. They arrived *en masse*, or there were cases, too, of elderly people deciding that one evoted relative was more deserving than the rest.

They overflowed the small house. There was no room for Cleo, and also no need, for the women industriously cooked nd cleaned, went errands, and wrote letters. One of the etters was to a Boston friend of Miss Peterson, who knew Cleo slightly from her occasional visits to Springfield. She vas importuned to give shelter to this young Negro girl. With Christian charity, she promptly did so.

She shared her home with a nephew, whom she had raised nd educated. The young man, coming of age, was not rateful. He wanted to get married. He intended to leave tome. He was so obdurate about these matters that his aunt, Miss Boorum, was nearly resigned to spending her declining ears alone, regretting the sacrifice that had caused her spinterhood.

Cleo seemed a light in the gathering gloom. She was outhern, she was colored. From what Miss Boorum had ead of southern colored people they were devoted to what they quaintly called "my white folks," and quite disdainful of heir own kind, often referring to them as "niggers." They iked to think of themselves as an integral part of the family, nd preferred to die in its bosom rather than any place else. t was to be hoped that Cleo would show the same sterling oyalty.

In Boston Cleo settled into the same routine that she had ndured in Springfield. She was indifferent to the change. One old white woman looked just like any other old white voman to her. Only difference was Miss Boorum wore false eeth that slipped up and down when she talked. She paid he same five dollars a month, the sum that Cleo had been eceiving, obliquely, since she was sixteen. It was not considred wages. The amount was not the thing that mattered so

much as the spirit that prompted it. Though Cleo's duties
were similar to a servant's, she was considered a ward. She
was fed and clothed, and given a place at table and a chair in
the parlor, except when there was company. At such times
she put on an apron, held her proud head above the level of
everybody's eyes, and wished they would all drop dead.

Both her Springfield and Boston protectresses felt that
Cleo was better off without money. Each month Miss
Boorum, as had her predecessor, sent five dollars to Mama
affixed to a little note in an aging hand full of fancy flour-
ishes that Mama spent a day deciphering. These custodians
of Cleo's character had no wish to teach her to save. Nothing, they knew, is a greater inducement to independent action than knowing where you can put your hand on a bit of
cash.

Their little notes reported to Mama on Cleo's exemplary
behavior. But Cleo was neither good nor bad. She was in a
state of suspension. She knew she was paying penance for all
the joyous wildness of her childhood. She had been exiled to
learn the discipline that Mama's punishments had not taught
her. She did not mind these years of submission any more
than she had minded Mama strapping her. If you were bad,
you got punished. But you had had your fun. And that was
what counted. These meek years would not last forever. The
follies of childhood were sweet sins that did not merit eternal damnation. This was the period of instruction that was
preparing her for adulthood. Yet she knew she was not
changing. She was merely learning guile.

She was going to run away the minute she got her bearings
in Boston, leaving a sassy note saying, Thank you for nothing. Good-bye and good riddance. If I never see you again,
that will be too soon.

Then she was going on the stage. She was going to sing
and dance. That would be wickeder than anything she had
ever done, but almost as much fun as there had been in the
Carolina woods. Pa would disown her, and Mama would
pray for her soul. But she would fix up the house for Mama

with furniture and running water, and buy her some store
clothes and a horse to hitch the buggy to in place of Pa's old
mule.

She sat in Miss Boorum's parlor, reading *Little Women*
aloud, looking demure and gray-eyed, hearing the richness
of her own voice, being thrilled by its velvet sound, and
seeing herself singing and kicking her heels on a stage in a
swirl of lace petticoats. The only thing was she wasn't going
to have any partner. She wasn't going to sing an old love-
song with any greasy-haired coon. She wasn't going to dance
any cakewalk with him either, and let his sweaty hand ruin
her fancy costumes.

Miss Boorum's nephew, looking at Cleo across the table,
was profoundly disturbed by his emotions. He, too, had
heard about Negroes. He had heard mostly about Negro
women, and the information was correct. Desire was growing in his loins and there was nothing he could do to stop it.
All he could do was try to keep it from spreading to his heart.

He talked no more of marriage now, nor of moving away.
He rarely went out in the evening. He gloomed about the
house, staring moodily at Cleo. Miss Boorum supposed he
was beset by the jealous fear that her ward would supplant
him in her affections. To punish him for the pain he had
caused her, she made his ears ring with Cleo's praises. Cleo
supposed he was jealous, too, as the Springfield relatives
had been, and took a wicked delight in tormenting him by
being her most appealing in his presence.

Mama died. The letter came. Nobody down home had
sense enough to send a telegram. Mama was buried by the
time the letter reached Boston. She died bearing a dead
child. Pa had just as good as killed her.

Cleo hadn't seen Mama since she was fourteen. Mama
standing in the station saying, "God watch between me and
thee, while we are absent one from another." Mama with the
flush in her face from her fast-beating heart, and the tears
held tight in her searching doe eyes, her coral lip trembling
between her white teeth, and her arms reaching out, the

rounded arms with dimples. Mama was dead, and the lid was shut down. Now Mama could never say, Cleo, I loved you best of all my children.

Cleo's grief was an inward thing that gave her a look of such purity that Miss Boorum's nephew was even further enmeshed. The enchantment of knowing that she was no one's was monstrous. He was seduced by her chastity. He would never be free as long as he knew he could be her first lover. Until he could see the face of her purity replaced by the face of surrender, her image would lie on his lids to torment him.

He grew thin and wan. Cleo looked at him and thought indifferently that he was coming down with something, and hoped it wouldn't be catching.

Miss Boorum's nephew began his campaign. He bought Cleo a bicycle. Ostensibly it was to solace her sorrow. Actually it was because he could not afford to deck her in diamonds.

He did not ride with her, nor would he instruct her in the intricacies of balance. Subconsciously he had the bloody hope that she would break every bone in her body and destroy her beauty, if not herself.

She pedaled away as easily as if she had been cycling all her life, for she still did not know there was anything she was incapable of doing. In Norumbega Park she sped around a curve and rode unromantically into Mr. Judson's stomach.

The impact sent them sprawling on either side of the path, with the shiny new bicycle rearing like a bucking horse, flinging itself against a boulder, and smashing itself to pieces.

Because she had not long lost Mama, and now she had lost her new bicycle, Cleo burst into heartbroken howls. Her heretofore unshed tears flowed in a torrent. Mr. Judson sat and rubbed his upset stomach and felt himself drowning helplessly in her welling eyes and tumbled hair.

When she could speak, she sobbed accusations. Why didn't he look where he was going? Why hadn't he jumped out of her way? Look at her brand-new bicycle. Who did he think was going to get her another one?

He was, Mr. Judson assured her gallantly. He helped her to her feet, though she fought him all the way, jerking and twisting out of his unexploring hands. He asked her for her name and address, and she gave them to him defiantly. She knew this poor darky didn't have one thin dime to lay against another, but if he wanted to talk big, let him back up his promise. He told her his name, and she forgot it immediately. What did she want to know his name for? She wasn't going to give him a bicycle.

He offered to see her home. She refused so vehemently that he pictured her parents as martinets, and supposed that the courtship, on which he had decided the minute he got back his breath, would be long and hazardous.

She took the poor wreck of her bicycle and pushed off unaided. It was a painful journey, and she was often admonished to get a horse. She reached home footsore and furious. Miss Boorum's nephew flew to the door, for Cleo rang the bell so sharply that the unhappy young man had the rather pleasurable foreboding that a policeman had brought bad tidings.

It was Cleo. He had never seen her in a wild moment, and he was further undone. For now he saw her with all her aliveness, her dark hair streaming, her eyes sparking green stars, the blood in her cheeks with the tear streaks and dust streaks, and her apple breasts betraying the pulse of her angry heart. He knew God was punishing him for his desire to see her dead by sending her back more alive than ever.

That night Miss Boorum's nephew and Mr. Judson tossed and turned in their restless sleep, while Cleo slept like a rock from all the air she had imbibed on the long ride and the long walk.

Mr. Judson was ardently in love. Why it had come upon him like this, he could not have explained, except that he had reached the age for it. He had distrusted women until now. He thought all they saw in a man was his pocketbook.

When they asked him flattering questions, he imagined the
were prying into his affairs, trying to find out how much h
had that they would have if they married him. Artfully he ha
sidestepped them all, spending his days in such hard wor
that sleep came easily, and there were no wakeful hours c
aching loins. On Sunday afternoons he strolled in the city'
parks.

His excursions into society were infrequent and unsu
cessful. He did not look like a rich man, for he wore
disguise of ancient suits to confuse the predatory. He di
not resemble a Bostonian. His tongue was soft and liqui
He was dark. He was unimpressed by backgrounds. H
made it plain that if you were a State House attendant, yo
were only a porter to him, no matter how many of you
forebears had been freeborn.

The men with whom he had daily contact were unpreter
tious rich men, the bankers, the brokers, the shipowners, th
heads of wholesale houses. When he moved among colore
men, he was slightly contemptuous, though he thought h
was merely bored. He had been in business for himself sinc
he was ten, and was never wholly able to understand anyon
who was content to let someone else be the boss man.

Bart bought the finest bicycle he could find in Boston an
dispatched it next day, with a crate of oranges and two hanc
some hands of bananas that he hoped would impress Cleo
parents.

He called the following Sunday, and was surprised to fin
that Cleo worked in service, but rather pleased. She ought
consider herself a lucky girl to be courted by a man of sul
stance. Miss Boorum, herself, showed him into the parlo
and sat down with a colored man for the first time in her lif
Though she had not seen through her nephew, she sa
through Bart immediately. He was in love with Cleo. Th
did not surprise her. It was typical of colored men.

Her nephew, hearing a male voice below with a Negr
flavor, came down from his study in acute anxiety. Here wa
the stranger his common sense had commanded to com

Here was the man who would set him free. And his eyes were hot with hatred. Bart saw the young man's anguish. He saw that Cleo did not see it. Nor Miss Boorum. He had to get Cleo out of this house before the fever in the young man's eyes spread to his loins. He could not let her be lost in one wanton night. Or her image would lie on his eyelids for the rest of his life.

All the next day he worried like a hen with one helpless chick. When his picture-making grew too intolerable, he washed off his surface sweat and went to Miss Boorum's. He approached the house by way of the alley, hoping to find Cleo in the kitchen, where he could talk unheard. He had better luck than he bargained for. She was in the clothes yard. She had clothespins in her mouth, and was too surprised to take them out.

He began to whisper fiercely, and she only heard half of what he said, for he kept jerking his head around to see who might be coming. He told her hurriedly and harriedly that she was in great danger, a wolf was abroad in Miss Boorum's nephew's clothing. She was not safe, and never would be safe, so long as she stayed within reach of his clutches. She was too young to be alone in Boston. She had no mother to guide her. She needed a good man's protection. She needed a husband. He would marry her today if she would have him. If she would have him, he would apply for a licence today and marry her at City Hall at nine o'clock on Thursday morning.

If he had proposed to her any other way, if he had courted her for a longer time, she might have refused him, out of sheer contrariness. He had not frightened her with his fears. She felt that she could subdue any man with her scorn. But she wanted to get away. She couldn't stand seeing Miss Boorum's nephew moping around like a half-sick dog if woman hankering was what ailed him. If he ever came hankering after her, she'd stab him dead with an ice-pick. And no man on earth, let alone a white man, was worth going to hell for.

She was still so wrapped up in murderous thoughts and daring Miss Boorum's demoralized nephew to come within a foot of her that she married Bart without thinking about it. When she found herself in her marriage bed, she let him know straightaway that she had no intention of renouncing her maidenhood for one man if she had married to preserve it from another.

Bart had expected that he would have to lead her to love with patience. He was a man of vigor and could wait without wasting for Cleo's awakening. Some part of him was soothed and satisfied by the fact of his right to cherish her. It did not torment him to lie beside her and know that he could not possess her. He threw his energy into buying and selling. For he loved his fruit almost as much as he loved his wife. There was rich satisfaction in seeing it ripen, seeing the downiness on it, the blush on it, feeling the firmness of its flesh.

When Cleo was twenty, their sex battle began. It was not a savage fight. She did not struggle against his superior strength. She found a weapon that would cut him down quickly and cleanly. She was ice. Neither her mouth nor her body moved to meet his. The open eyes were wide with mocking at the busyness below. There was no moment when everything in her was wrenched and she was one with the man who could submerge her in himself.

Five years later, she conceived a child on a night when her body's hunger broke down her controlled resistance. For there was no real abhorrence of sex in her. Her need of love was as urgent as her aliveness indicated. But her perversity would not permit her to weaken. She would not face the knowledge that she was incomplete in herself.

Yet now, as she walked toward the trolley stop, she was determined not to live another year without her sisters.

DOROTHY WEST

My Mother, Rachel West

When my mother died, we who had sparred with her over the years of our growth and maturity said with relief, well, we won't have her intruding herself in our lives again. Our saying it may have been a kind of swaggering, or maybe we were in shock, trying to hide what was really inside us.

My mother had often made the declaration that she was never going to die. She knew what was here, she would say with a laugh, but she didn't know what was there. Heaven was a long way from home. She was staying right here.

So we just accepted it as fact that she would be the death of us instead. When her own death came first, we didn't know what to make of it. There was a thinness in the air. There was silence where there had been sound and fury. There was no longer that beautiful and compelling voice bending us to her will against our own.

The house that I grew up in was four-storied, but we were an extended family, continuously adding new members, and the perpetual joke was, if we lived in the Boston Museum, we'd still need one more room. Surrounded by all these different personalities, each one wanting to be first among equals, I knew I wanted to be a writer. Living with them was like living inside a story.

My mother was the dominant figure by the force of her vitality, and by the indisputable fact that she had the right to rule the roof that my father provided. She was a beautiful woman, and there was that day when I was grown, eighteen or so, ready to go off on my own, sure that I knew everything, that I said to her, "Well, your beauty was certainly wasted on you. All you did with it was raise children and run your sisters' lives."

My mother had done what she felt she had to do, knowing the risks, knowing there would be no rewards, but determined to build a foundation for the generations unborn. She had gathered us together so that the weakness of one would be balanced by her strength, and the loneliness of another eased by her laughter, and someone else's fears tempered by her fierce bravado, and the children treated alike, no matter what their degree of lovability, and her eye riveting mine if I tried to draw a distinction between myself and them.

We who had been the children under her command, and then the adults, still subject to her meddling in our intimate affairs, were finally bereaved, free of the departed, and in a rush to divorce ourselves from any resemblance to her influence.

When one of us said something that Mother might have said, and an outraged chorus shouted, "You sound just like her," the speaker, stung with shame and close to tears, shouted back, "I do not!"

Then as time passed, whoever forgot to watch her language and echoed some sentiment culled from my mother responded to the catcalls with a cool, "So what?"

As time increased its pace, although there were diehards who would never relent, there were more of us shifting positions, examining our ambivalent feelings, wondering if the life force that had so overwhelmed our exercise of free will, and now no longer had to be reckoned with, was a greater loss than a relief.

When a newborn disciple recited my mother's sayings as if they were gospel, the chiding came from a scattered chorus of uninspired voices.

Then there was the day when someone said with wonder, "Have you noticed that those of us who sound just like her are the ones who laugh a lot, love children a lot, don't have any hangups about race or color, and never give up without trying?"

"Yes, I've noticed," one of us answered, with the rest of us adding softly, "Me, too."

I suppose that was the day and the hour of our acknowledgment that some part of her was forever imbedded in our psyches, and we were not the worst for it.

But I still cannot put my finger on the why of her. What had she wanted, this beautiful woman? Did she get it? I would look at her face when it was shut away, and I would long to offer her a penny for her thoughts. But I knew she would laugh and say, "I was just thinking it's time to start dinner," or something equally far from her yearning heart.

I don't think she ever realized how often she made the remark, "Speech was given man to hide his thoughts." At such times I would say to myself, she will die with her secrets. I had guessed a few, but they had been only surface deep, easy to flush out. I know that the rest went with her on her flight to heaven.

—1982

BIBLIOGRAPHIC NOTES

The Living Is Easy has almost always been excluded from the Afro-American literary canon. It is not mentioned in Addison Gayle's *The Way of the New World* (New York: Doubleday & Co., 1975) nor in Richard Barksdale and Keneth Kinnamon's *Black Writers of America* (New York: Macmillan, 1972) nor in Barbara Christian's *Black Women Novelists: The Making of a Tradition, 1892–1976* (Westport, Conn.: Greenwood Press, 1980). Although Robert Bone *The Negro Novel in America* (New Haven: Yale University Press, 1965), pp 187–91, includes West's novel, his analysis is condescending and sexist. He describes the main character, Cleo, as a "castrating female" whose "bitchery" satirizes the social ambitions of black Boston women. Her "manipulative" and "domineering" behavior are traced in a pseudo-Freudian manner to her troubled relationship with her mother, which allows Bone to overlook Cleo's conflict with the traditional female role. Even Judith Berzon, "The Mulatto as Black Bourgeois," in *Neither White nor Black: The Mulatto Character in American Fiction* (New York: New York University Press, 1978), tends to see Cleo in a purely psychological context. Paraphrasing Bone, Berzon states that Cleo is "compelled to mutilate her Rabelaisian soul, her creativity," in order to gain social acceptance by the black bourgeoisie. Although Berzon concedes Cleo's tragedy stems from her ignorance of alternative forms of success, she does not analyze the construction of the female role Cleo is forced to play.

In the 'Afterword' to the reprinted edition of *The Living Is Easy* (Old Westbury, N.Y.: The Feminist Press, 1982), Adelaide Cromwell writes an appreciative essay using a recent interview with West. She gives biographical and social context to the history of West's literary achievements and comments on the uniqueness of Cleo's characterization. The thesis of my essay on West "I Sign My Mother's Name: Alice Walker, Dorothy West, Paule Marshall," in *Mothering the Mind: Twelve Studies of Writers and Their Silent Partners*, ed. Ruth Perry and Martine Watson Brownley (New York: Holmes and Meier, 1984) is that many black women writers, including West, find their own literary voices through a rediscovery of their mother's power and sensibilities. West's relationship with her mother, Rachel West, helps to illuminate the complexity of forces that make up the protagonist of *The Living Is Easy*.

PART SIX

Think of thaumaturgic lass
Looking in her looking-glass
At the unembroidered brown;
Printing bastard roses there;
Then emotionally aware
Of the black and boisterous hair,
Taming all that anger down.

—Gwendolyn Brooks
"The Anniad" from *Annie Allen*

INTRODUCTION

"Taming All That Anger Down": Rage and Silence in the Writing of Gwendolyn Brooks

When Gwendolyn Brooks's autobiographical first novel, *Maud Martha*, was published in 1953, it was given the kind of ladylike treatment that assured its dismissal.[1] Reviewers invariably chose to describe the novel in words that reflected what they considered to be the novel's appropriate feminine values. The young black woman heroine was called a "spunky Negro girl," as though the novel were a piece of juvenile fiction. Reviewers, in brief notices of the novel, insisted on its optimism and faith: Maud's life is made up of "moments she loved," she has "disturbances," but she "struggles against jealousy" for the sake of her marriage. There is, of course, "the delicate pressure of the color line," but Maud has the remarkable "ability to turn unhappiness and anger into a joke." Brooks's style was likened to the exquisite delicacy of a lyric poem. The New York *Times* reviewer said the novel reminded him of imagist poems or "clusters of ideograms from which one recreates connected experience."[2]

In 1953 no one seemed prepared to call *Maud Martha* a novel about bitterness, rage, self-hatred, and the silence that results from suppressed anger. No one recognized it as a novel dealing with the very sexism and racism that these reviews enshrined. What the reviewers saw as exquisite lyricism was actually the truncated stutterings of a woman whose rage makes her literally unable to speak. Maud Martha rarely speaks aloud to anyone else. She has learned to conceal her feelings behind a mask of gentility, to make her hate silent and cold, expressed only in the most manipulative and deceptive ways. When she is irritated with her husband, Paul, who pinches her on the buttocks, trying to interest her in the activities of the book he is reading, *Sex in the Married Life*, she rises from the bed as though she is at a garden party, and says, "pleasantly," "Shall I make some cocoa? . . . And toast some sandwiches?" (p. 67). That she is aware of this pattern and its destructiveness, and her need to change, is clearly part of the novel's design: "There were these scraps of baffled hate in her, hate with no eyes, no smile, and—this she especially regretted, called her hungriest lack—not much voice" (p. 176). But the silence of Maud Martha is also Brooks's silence. The short vignetted chapters enact Maud Martha's silence. Ranging in length from one and a half to eighteen pages, these tightly controlled chapters without information about Maud, just as she withholds her feelings, they leave her frozen in an arrested moment so that we are left without the reactions that are crucial to our understanding of her. With no continuity between one chapter and the next, the flow of Maud's life is checked just as powerfully as she checks her own anger. The short, declarative sentences, with few modifiers and little elaboration, are as stiff, unyielding, and tight-lipped as Maud Martha herself.

An example of Brooks's tendency to check Maud's activity (and thus her growth) is chapter 5, ironically entitled "you're being so good so kind." As the teenage Maud awaits a visit from a white schoolmate named Charles, she begins to feel embarrassed by the shabbiness of her home and worried that her house may have the unpleasant smell that "colored people's houses necessarily had." It is a moment of pure terror. She is the whole "colored" race and "Charles was the personalization of the entire Caucasian plan" (p. 18) about to sit in judgment on her. Charles never actually materializes. The chapter ends with a freeze-frame of Maud hiding in the bathroom, experiencing an emotion worse than fear:

> What was this she was feeling now? Not fear, not fear. A sort of gratitude! It sickened her to realize it. As though Charles in coming gave her a gift.

Recipient and benefactor.
It's so good of you.
You're being so good. (p. 18)

These last few lines, set off from the rest of the text, are a
commentary by a black consciousness more aware and more
removed from the event than is the teenage Maud. While the
commentator's indignation is reassuring, we can only imagine how the visit would have affected Maud: whether Charles
continues to have such power when he appears, or whether
Maud is as truly defeated in the encounter as her position
behind closed doors intimates.

In all the chapters covering Maud's girlhood on the south
side of Chicago in the 1930s and 1940s, Brooks continues to
silence Maud Martha, to leave her frozen in an enigmatic
pose that silences Maud and denies her any expression of
her real feelings. In chapter 1, "description of Maud
Martha," for example, Maud decides on a personal metaphor for herself: she is a dandelion, a sturdy flower of demure prettiness, but, just as a puff of wind can destroy it, so
her belief in its—and her—power to allure is easily shaken,
for "it was hard to believe that a thing of only ordinary
allurements—if the allurements of any flower could be said
to be ordinary—was as easy to love as a thing of heart-
catching beauty" (p. 2). Maud's wish to be alluring is dashed
in the last two sentences of this chapter by a sudden shift to a
description of her prettier sister, Helen: "her sister Helen!
who was only two years past her own age of seven, and was
almost her own height and weight and thickness. But oh, the
long lashes, the grace, the little ways with the hands and
feet" (p. 3). Once, at the age of ten, when Maud is trying to
appear more daring than she feels, she calls out "Hi handsome" to the little boy Emmanuel riding by in his wagon. He
scowls back: "I don't mean you, old black gal" (p. 34), and
he offers the ride to her sister Helen. In this chapter Maud
tries to account for the mysterious, implacable design that
has determined her inferior status and the greater worthi-

ness of light-skinned beauties like Helen. In the short, staccato sentences that characterize much of the novel's narration, she tries to be nobly superior about her family's
preference for Helen: "It was not their fault. She understood. They could not help it. They were enslaved, were
fascinated, and they were not at all to blame" (p. 35). Yet it is
not her problem that we feel in these sentences but her
anger—or, rather, her inability to express that anger.

The painful awareness of herself as an undesirable object
whose worth cannot be gauged by eyes accustomed to dis-
missing the commonplace mystifies the child Maud. She is
disdainful of her family's failure to see that she is smarter
than Helen, that she reads more, that old folks like to talk to
her, that she washes as much and has longer and thicker (if
nappier) hair. But from the age of seventeen to the birth of
her first child (chapters 10–19) her own self-perception is
dismissed while she abandons herself to the obligatory quest
for a man. When she is finally chosen by one of "them," or,
in her words, when she "hooks" Paul, she shifts from being
interested in her own perceptions to seeing herself entirely
through Paul's eyes. In the chapter called "Low Yellow"
Maud engages in a grotesque act of double-consciousness in
which she fantasizes about Paul's negative view of her:

> He wonders, as we walk in the street, about the thoughts
> of the people who look at us. Are they thinking that he
> could do no better than—me? Then he thinks, Well, hmp!
> Well, huh!—all the little good-lookin' dolls that have
> wanted *him*—all the little sweet high-yellows that have
> ambled slowly past *his* front door—What he would like to
> tell those secretly snickering ones!—That any day out of
> the week he can do better than this black gal. (p. 53)

After Maud settles down to "being wife to him, salving him,
in every way considering and replenishing him," we begin to
see how Maud is the one who's been "hooked," who feels
hemmed in, cramped, and "unexpressed" in this marriage.
Although she is as disappointed as he in their life together,

she evades her feelings. Once, in a classic example of self-abnegation, she worries that he is tired of her.

> She knew that he was tired of his wife, tired of his living quarters, tired of working at Sam's, tired of his two suits . . . He had no money, no car, no clothes, and he had not been put up for membership in the Foxy Cats Club . . . He was not on show . . . Something should happen . . . She knew that he believed he had been born to invade, to occur, to confront, to inspire the flapping of flags, to panic people. (p. 147)

Maud's lack of voice and her indirectness become more troubling for us when, as a grown woman confined to a small apartment and to being Mrs. Paul Phillips, she seems to have become an accomplice to her own impotence. Maud's passivity in the face of the persecutory actions of others inhibits her growth and reflects her resistance to facing her anger.[3] When Maud and Paul are invited to the Foxy Cats Club Ball, where acceptance requires sophistication and good looks, Maud is once again up against the image of the "little yellow dream girl." Thinking about how she will forestall her old feelings of inferiority, she prepares for the event in language that we know will defeat her:

> "I'll settle," decided Maud Martha, "on a plain white princess-style thing and some blue and black satin ribbon. I'll go to my mother's. I'll work miracles at the sewing machine."
> "On that night, I'll wave my hair. I'll smell faintly of lily of the valley." (p. 82)

The words she uses to refashion herself—*white, princess, wavy, lily*—all suggest how complete a transformation she imagines she needs in order to be accepted. At the club, Paul goes off with the beautiful, "white-looking," curvy Maella, leaving Maud on a bench by the wall. Maud imagines how she might handle the interloper: "I could," considered Maud Martha, "go over there and scratch her upsweep down. I could spit on her back. I could scream. 'Listen,' I could scream, 'I'm making a baby for this man and I mean to do it in peace' " (p. 88).

Instead of asserting herself, however, Maud chooses to say nothing. The scraps of rage and baffled hate accumulate while she resists the words of power as though she has subjected her language to the same perverted standards by which she judges her physical beauty. In one of the early chapters she describes the "graceful" life as one where people glide over floors in softly glowing rooms, smile correctly over trays of silver, cinnamon, and cream, and retire in quiet elegance. She imagines herself happy and caressed in these cool, elegant (white) places, and she aspires to the jeweled, polished, calm lives the people live there. This life, as she imagines it, is like a piece of silver, silent and remote and behind bright glass. The black world, as symbolized by the Foxy Cats Ball, is, by comparison, hot, steamy, sweaty, and crowded. Far from caressing her, this real world batters her until she retreats into her imagination, refusing to speak in it because it does not match the world of her fantasies. She conceals her real self behind the bright glass of her strained gentility.

All of this pretense, this muted rage, this determination to achieve housewifely eminence, the desire to protect herself "to keep herself to herself," masks so much of Maud's real feelings that we are compelled to consider what is missing in *Maud Martha*. Are there places in the novel where the real meaning of the character's quest is disguised? Are there "hollows, centers, caverns within the work—places where activity that one might expect is missing . . . or deceptively coded?"[4]

Something is missing in *Maud Martha*, something besides the opportunity to speak, something we have the right to expect in Maud's life because Maud herself expects it. She has already, in the first chapter, begun to chafe at the domestic role, and yet Brooks suggests that Maud has no aspirations beyond it. When Maud asks in the last chapter, "What what, am I to do with all this life?" she is expressing the same

sense of perplexity that her readers have been feeling
throughout the novel. How is this extraordinary woman going to express herself? She claims not to want to be a star
because she once saw a singer named Howie Joe Jones
parade himself before an audience, foolishly "exhibiting his
precious private identity," and she has vowed that she will
never be like that—"she was going to keep herself to herself" (p. 21). The artist's role, she says, is not for her. But the
fact that she has considered and dismissed the possibility is
revealing.

"To create . . . a role, a poem, picture, music, a rapture
in stone: great. But not for her.

What she wanted was to donate to the world a good Maud
Martha. That was the offering, the bit of art, that could not
come from any other.

She would polish and hone that" (p. 22).

Everywhere in the novel, however, Maud's artistic intentions are indirectly revealed. She perceives the world sensu-
ously: she responds to the complexity of beauty: "What she
wanted to dream, and dreamed, was her affair. It pleased her
to dwell upon color and soft bready textures and light, on a
complex beauty, on gem-like surfaces. What was the matter
with that?" What, indeed, is the matter with a woman having
some subversive ideas? In an article on the sexist images of
woman in modernist texts, Joyce Carol Oates maintains that,
by aspiring to art, women violate the deeply conservative
and stereotypical images of men. The autonomy of the artist
is considered unnatural for women, unfeminine and threatening.[5] Maud uses the language of the artist as she surren-
ders her claim to be an artist: her language betrays her.
Maud's gifts are words, insight, imagination. She has the
artist's eye, the writer's memory, that unsparing honesty that
does not put a light gauze across little miseries and monoto-
nies but exposes them, leaving the audience as ungauzed as
the creator.

It is natural to wonder why Brooks, in her "autobiographical novel," did not allow Maud the same independence and

creative expression that she herself had as a writer. After all, Brooks was her own model of a black woman artist in the 1950s. In her autobiography, *Report from Part One* (1972), she describes the exuberance she felt as she waited for books she would review to arrive in the mail, the "sassy brass" that enabled her to chide Richard Wright for his clumsy prose, and her eager sense of taking on the responsibility of a writer. But Maud, who craves something "elaborate, immutable, and sacred," who wants to express herself in "shimmering form," warm, but "hard as stone and as difficult to break," is never allowed to fulfill these cravings.

The novelist Paule Marshall has pointed out that women often make their first woman protagonist a homebody, as if to expiate their own "deviance" in succeeding in the world of men. There is, she says, some need to satisfy the domestic role, and so they let their characters live it. *Maud Martha* ends with a pregnancy, not a poem, but, if Maud has no life outside marriage, she has a child, through whom she begins to hear her own voice.

The pregnancy actually becomes a form of rebellion against the dominance of both her mother and her husband. She screams at Paul in the midst of her labor pains: "*Don't you go out of here and leave me alone!* Damn! Damn!" When her mother, who is prone to faint over blood, comes in the door, Maud sets her straight about who's important in this drama: "Listen. If you're going to make a fuss, go on out. I'm having enough trouble without you making a fuss over everything." In that one vital moment of pulling life out of herself, Maud experiences her own birth and hears in the cries of her daughter, Paulette, something of her own voice: "a bright delight had flooded through her upon first hearing that part of Maud Martha Brown Phillips expressing itself *with a voice of its own.*" (p. 99, Emphasis mine) Shortly after the birth of her child, Maud speaks aloud the longest set of consecutive sentences she has so far uttered. For a woman who has hardly said more than a dozen words at one time, this is quite a speech: " 'Hello, Mrs. Barksdale!' she hailed. 'Did you hear the news? I just had a baby, and I feel strong enough to go out and shovel coal! Having a baby is *nothing*, Mrs. Barksdale, Nothing at all.' "(p. 98) Pregnancy and the birth of a child connect Maud to some power in herself, some power to speak, to be heard, to articulate feelings.

Yet, however powerful the reproductive act is, it is not the same as the creative process: a child is a separate, independent, individualized human being, not a sample of one's creative work. Without the means to satisfy her deeper cravings, Maud's life remains painfully ambiguous. Brooks must have felt this ambiguity, for when she imagined a sequel to *Maud Martha* she immediately secured some important work for Maud and dispensed with the role of housewife. In a 1975 interview, Brooks was asked to bring Maud Martha up to the present day. With obvious relish, Brooks eliminates Maud's husband:

> Well, she has that child and she has another child and then her husband dies in the bus fire that happened in Chicago in the fifties. One of those flammable trucks with a load of oil ran into a street car and about thirty-six people burned right out on Sixty-third and State Streets. So I put her husband in that fire. Wasn't that nice of me? I had taken him as far as I could. He certainly wasn't going to change. I could see that.[6]

Brooks insists that Maud feels some regret at the loss of her husband, but returning from the funeral Maud is thinking passionately about the cake that's going to be at the wake and how good it's going to be. Having safely buried Paul, Brooks proceeds to explain how Maud Martha will get on with her own adventures. She will be chosen as a guide to accompany some children on a trip to Africa and will use her slender resources to help them. She will live her life with herself at the center of it.

Brooks actually did begin to write a sequel to *Maud Martha,* and in 1955 published an initial chapter called "The Rise of Maud Martha."[7] As she indicates in the 1975 interview, Maud's husband, Paul, does die in a bus fire and Maud, at the funeral, thinks back on the sight of her dead husband's body "black with a more 'dreadful' blackness than that which he had ever known and despised"; and then she thinks ahead to life with her children, without Paul: "She held the destinies of herself and her children in her individual power—all was up to her." In this chapter, anger is neither repressed nor disguised. Maud's grisly satisfaction over the gruesome details of Paul's death, her fantasy that as Paul is lowered into the grave she herself is actually rising, her anticipation of how good the after-funeral cake is going to taste, are explicitly angry responses to whatever her life with Paul has meant. Brooks does not pull back from the intensity of Maud's reactions, nor does she end the chapter ambiguously as she does in many of the earlier chapters of the first book. In allowing Maud the full emotional intensity of her feelings, Brooks seems to have found a way to give Maud the authority to carry an act through to its completion. Brooks's tone in the sequel—so freewheeling and aggressive and self-assured —reveals by comparison the uncertainties and tensions of the 1953 version.

One wonders if Brooks also denies Maud a more dynamic role in the novel by her own ambivalence (understandable in view of the restrictions on women in the 1950s) toward women as heroic figures. In her poetry all the heroes are men. From the dapper hustler Satin-Legs Smith to the renegade Way-out Morgan or the soldier in "Negro Hero" or the armed Rudolf Reed defending his family against a white mob, Brooks selects the heroic strategies of men and the ritual grounds on which men typically perform. Even a plain man like Reed has a moment of glory as he runs out into the street "with a thirty-four/and a beastly butcher knife." He dies in defense of his family, while his wife, who has been passive throughout the entire ballad, stands by mutely and does nothing "But change the bloody gauze."

Brooks, in her poetry, seldom endows women with the power, integrity, or magnificence of her male figures. The

passive and vulnerable Annie Allen, the heroine of her Pulitzer-prize-winning poem, is deserted by her soldier husband
and left pathetically mourning in her little kitchenette,
"thoroughly/Derelict and dim and done." Sometimes
Brooks's women manage to be "decently wild" as girls, but
they grow up to be worried and fearful, or fretful over the
loss of a man. They wither in backyards, afraid to tackle life,
they are done in by dark skin, and, like "estimable Mable,"
they are often incapable of estimating their worth without
the tape measure of a man's interest in them.[8]

Brooks does allow Maud to grow in some ways, to become
more in control of her life and to speak out against the racist
violence of her life. When Maud moves away from the domestic sphere of her little kitchenette apartment and out
into a larger social and political world, she feels more urgently the need to speak. There are three racial encounters
leading up to Maud's self-affirmation. Each encounter in-
volves a change in the language Maud has available to her,
each moves her closer to experiencing and expressing her
rage. In the last of these three encounters Maud makes the
longest speech of the novel: she tries to explain to her child,
Paulette, that Santa Claus loves her as much as any white
child.

> Listen, child. People don't have to kiss you to show they
> like you. Now you know Santa Claus liked you. What have
> I been telling you? Santa Claus loves every child, and on
> the night before Christmas he brings them swell presents.
> Don't you remember, when you told Santa Claus you
> wanted the ball and bear and tricycle and doll he said
> "Um-hm"? That meant he's going to bring you all those.
> You watch and see. Christmas'll be here in a few days.
> You'll wake up Christmas morning and find them and then
> you'll know Santa Claus loved *you* too. (p. 175)

From Maud Martha, this is a veritable torrent of words, but
the problem with her words is that they are still part of her
subterfuge. She denies Santa Claus's rejection of Paulette

and insists that Paulette deny her own perception of Santa's cold indifference.

The honest voice in this chapter is Paulette's:

> "Why didn't Santa Claus like me?"
>
> "Baby, of course he liked you."
>
> "He didn't like me. Why didn't he like me?"
>
> "It maybe seemed that way to you. He has a lot on his mind, of course."
>
> "He liked the other children. He smiled at them and shook their hands."
>
> "He maybe got tired of smiling. Sometimes even I get—"
>
> "He didn't look at me, he didn't shake *my* hand." (p. 174)

In the chapter "a birth" Maud has said that her daughter's voice is part of her own. Mother and child are locked in a conversation that forces Maud out from behind the bright glass of her pretense. Now Maud admits rage, laments her lack of voice, speaks aloud, and bites back the tears as she looks down at her child's trusting face, knowing she cannot keep for her a fairy-tale land where no Santa Claus ever hates a black child. Brooks does not leave Maud frozen in this chapter; we do see her acting and speaking. But perhaps the most important change is that Maud is given her most aggressive role when she confronts the racism of that cool, elegant, white, fantasy world.

If Brooks's novel seems fragmentary and incomplete, undoubtedly it is because the knowledge of oneself as a black woman was fragmented by a society that could not imagine her. I am thinking specifically of the 1940s and 1950s, those postwar decades that enshrined the Great American Domestic Dream of a housewife and a Hoover in every home. If the housewife in that dream was a white woman, the servant was always a black woman—simple and unsophisticated, as the reviews called *Maud Martha.* The leading black magazines of those years—*Ebony, Negro Digest,* and *Crisis*—contributed their share of images of black women as idealized, childlike creatures and assumed that their basic role was to satisfy the male imagination. *Crisis* alternated pictures of cute babies and "cute" women on its covers, while the covers of *Negro Digest* featured bathing beauties, tennis beauties, homecoming queens, and pinups in various stages of undress. In contrast to these pictures of black women, the back page of *Digest* spotlighted "Men of Achievement," so that back to back with the smiling faces and exposed bodies of black women were ministries about the first black man to enter a prestigious college, to excel in athletics, or to perform valiantly in some war. The August 1947 issue of *Digest* featured on its back page the bravery of Negro volunteers (all men) during the Civil War, on the front cover there is a picture of a fan "girl" whose partially nude body is coyly hidden behind a polka-dot umbrella. Beneath the fan girl's picture is the title of the opening article by Era Bell Thompson, "What's Wonderful About Negro Men."

The articles about black women in these magazines range from the condescending to the obscene. The titles themselves reveal extreme hostility: "What's Wrong with Negro Women?" "Are Black Women Beautiful?" "The Care and Feeding of Negro Women." This last article, based on the metaphor of cultivating a fine pet, claims that a properly trained female will develop the loyalty of a German shepherd and the cleverness of a Siamese cat and will provide many hours of diversion and relaxation for her owner. The article "What's Wrong with Negro Women?" lists among the many shortcomings of black women their lack of cultural interests, their sense of inferiority to white women, and their lack of militancy: "Where are the Negro women of self-sacrifice and courage in the cause of the race?" the writer Roi Ottley wonders. "There is not one woman to rank with the distinguished Harriet Tubman."[9]

Brooks entered into this male-female debate that the *Negro Digest* encouraged in the 1940s and 1950s with an angry essay called "Why Negro Women Leave Home."[10] As in *Maud Martha,* questions of female autonomy, male domination, and the constriction of women's freedom in marriage

are at issue in this essay. The essay, published the year afte
Simone de Beauvoir's *The Second Sex*, tries to explain wh
many black women were choosing to leave their marriage
and work. Being able to support herself, says Brooks, make
a woman feel "clean, straight, tall, and as if she were part o
the world." With the "good taste of financial independence'
still fresh, black women, according to Brooks, were refusin
to settle for marriages that deprived them of dignity an
self-respect. In this outspoken critique of male dominance i
marriage, there is none of the indirection we find in *Mau
Martha*, none of the self-abnegation nor subordination. Th
women described in this essay have no problem with actior
each paragraph depicts a different woman leaving her hus
band for a different reason. None of these women seems a
all interested in pleasing a husband but rather in getting o
with the action that will give her greater freedom and greate
control over her life.

Though Maud is silenced in fiction in ways that Brooks i
nonfiction is not, she too leaves husband and home and goe
looking for a way to be straight and tall in the world. Leadin
us to believe that she is ready to shed the domestic lif
Maud thinks that the fallible romantic love of a man and
woman "could not be heavily depended on." Leaning on
man was "work." Then, in the novel's final chapter, poise
on the edge of self-creation, just when we expect the "illum
nation of her gold," Maud announces that she is pregnar
again, and happy. My initial reaction to this ending wa
critical of Brooks for precluding any growth beyond th
domestic life. But that disappointment ignores the novel'
intention that we read Maud's life in tone, in images, and i
gestures. Released from an incapacitating anger, Maud be
comes exhilarated and full of energy. In the last chapter sh
is out of doors with her daughter on a glorious day. She i
outside all the spaces that have enclosed her—the bec
rooms, the kitchens, the male clubs, the doctors' offices, th
movie theaters, the white women's houses, the dress shop
the beauty parlors, out of the psychic confines that left he

preoccupied with her "allurements" and presumed deficiencies. Free from destructive self-concern, Maud thinks of the people around her, of the glory and bravery in their ability to continue life amid the reality of city streets, lynchings in Mississippi and Georgia, and the grim reminder of death as the soldiers, back from war, march by with arms, legs, and parts of faces missing. Maud says she is ready for anything. So this catalogue of evils (including the Negro press's preoccupation with pale and pompadoured beauties) has to be seen as Maud's growing sense of relation to the social and political problems of her world. Perhaps even Maud's pregnancy can be seen as a powerful way of being in the world. For in the midst of destruction and death, she will bring forth life.

Sandra Gilbert and Susan Gubar in *Madwoman in the Attic* write about the woman writer's need to heal herself by "assaulting and revising, deconstructing and reconstructing those images of women inherited from male literature."[11] Maud announces this process of revision in the last chapter as she parenthetically refers to those "usual representatives of womanly beauty, pale and pompadoured" that are featured in the pages of the Negro press. Casual and parenthetical as that reference appears, it tells us something about Maud's rejection of what black American society values in women; it is a criticism of the standards of womanhood set by all patriarchal institutions in the black world—the black press, clubs, sororities, fraternities, colleges. When you examine the black magazines of the 1950s, it is clear that *Maud Martha* stands as an "exorcism of the infection": Maud's presence in the black world as well as in the white world is profoundly disturbing—a plain, dark-skinned black woman with sharp insight and a probing mind that cut through and exposed the powerlessness and self-contempt inherent in the world's negative assessment of her.

Sharp as this insight may have been, it provided no safe refuge for the mind it belonged to. In this novel we see evidence of a deeply divided self, of loneliness, of fear, of a deep muted rage—of everything we suspect is problematic for the woman attempting self-definition. Part of the problem is the privateness of Maud's story. Her constant self-analysis and self-consciousness emphasize her solitariness. She lives alienated from the two blood-related women in her life—the fussy, domineering mother and the vain sister. She has no women friends. Although she succeeds through heroic individual effort in rejecting others' definitions of her, she is still unable to express the full meaning of her growth. True, the presence of another "woman-in-embryo" allows her her first move toward freedom, but she does not have the advantage of Zora Neale Hurston's Janie of telling her story to an eager, loving listener whose life is changed by hearing Janie's tale.

Rereading *Maud Martha* is a necessary step in revising the male-dominated Afro-American canon, not only because this unusual text requires a different set of interpretative strategies but because it suggests a different set of rituals and symbols for Afro-American literature and a different set of progenitors. Current feminist theories that insist that we have to learn how to read the coded messages in women's texts—the silences, the evasions, the repression of female creativity—have helped me to reread *Maud Martha,* to read interiority in this text as one of the masks Maud (and Brooks) uses to defend herself against rage. But if Maud cannot rely on the spoken word for help, Brooks has certainly given her power in more concealed ways—she writes Maud's husband out of the text midway, she reduces her mother to a vain, pretentious fool, and she assigns her beautiful sister to a static end in a compromising marriage—thus the victim becomes superior to her victimizers. The reconstruction of scenes in which condescending others (white women and black and white men) are shown dominating Maud, while the reader is aware of her internal resistance, is another indirect way of giving Maud power. However oblique Maud's (and Brooks's) methods might seem, they are somewhat effective, for her manipulation of power in the narrative finally erupts into speech when she confronts the white Santa Claus.

If *Maud Martha* is considered an integral part of the Afro-American canon, we will have to revise our conception of power and powerlessness, of heroism, of symbolic landscapes and ritual grounds. With his access to middle-class aspirations, to a public life and to male privilege, the Invisible Man is not so easily defined out of existence as the physically vulnerable and speechless Maud. He may experience himself as invisible but he is not inert; he can imagine personal accomplishment, public recognition, political activism—Maud first has to rescue herself from the terrible passivity that is imposed on women. Yet, in spite of her greater powerlessness, she is not at the end of her text submerged in a dark hole, contemplating her invisibility in isolation. She is outside, in the light, with her daughter by the hand, exhilarated by the prospect of new life. Her ritual grounds are domestic enclosures, where we have rarely looked for heroic gestures, her most heroic act is one defiant declarative sentence, and yet she has changed in enough small ways for us to hope that "these little promises, just undercover" may, as she says earlier in the novel, in time, fulfill themselves.

The real significance of *Maud Martha* for the literary canon is that its discontinuous and truncated chapters, its short, angry sentences, its lack of ornamentation and freeze-frame endings represent structurally the entrapment of women expressed thematically in the earlier narratives of writers like Nella Larsen, Zora Neale Hurston, Ann Petry, Dorothy West, and Harriet Jacobs. Helga Crane's thwarted creativity, Janie Starks concealed inner self, Lutie Johnson's checked rage, Cleo Judson's frustrated maneuverings, Linda Brent's self-effacement are literally enacted in *Maud Martha*. While the novel looks back to the past, it also prefigures the themes of silence, repressed creativity, and alienation from language in the novels of Alice Walker and Toni Morrison. Paule Marshall has said that *Maud Martha* is the first novel she read that permitted a black woman a rich interior life, that it provided the inspiration for her own writing about black women. Perhaps these "little promises, just under cover" are, in fact, fulfilling themselves in the vibrant novels of contemporary black women.

NOTES

1. Gwendolyn Brooks, *Maud Martha* (Boston, Mass.; Atlantic Press, 1953). In her autobiographical statement, *Report from Part One* (Detroit, Mich.: Broadside Press, 1972), Brooks says that *Maud Martha* is not autobiographical in the usual sense. "Much that happened to Maud Martha has not happened to me—and she is a nicer and better coordinated creature than I am. But it is true that much in the 'story' was taken out of my own life, and twisted, highlighted or dulled, dressed up or down." (p. 191)

2. 1953 reviews of *Maud Martha: New Yorker* (October 10, 1953), 160 words; Hubert Creekmore, "Daydreams in Flight," *New York Times Book Review* (October 4, 1953), 400 words; Nicolas Monjo "Young Girl Growing Up," *Saturday Review* (October 31, 1953), 140 words Coleman Rosenberger, *New York Herald Tribune* (October 18, 1953) 600 words.

3. Roy Schafer, "Narration in the Psychoanalytic Dialogue," in *On Narrative,* ed. W. J. T. Mitchell (Chicago: University of Chicago Press, 1980), pp. 25–49. Schafer says that in the psychoanalytic process as the analysand begins to become more responsible, he or she "comes to construct narratives of personal agency ever more readily" and to deemphasize narratives that highlight the persecutory actions of others.

4. Sandra M. Gilbert and Susan Gubar, *The Madwoman in the Attic: The Woman Writer and the Nineteenth-Century Literary Imagination* (New Haven: Yale University Press, 1979), p. 75. In this passage the authors are referring to ideas in Patricia Meyer Spacks's *The Female Imagination* (New York: Avon Books, 1976) and to discussions of women's literature by Carolyn Heilbrun and Catherine Stimpson.

5. Joyce Carol Oates, " 'At Least I Have Made a Woman of Her' Images of Women in Twentieth-Century Literature," *Georgia Review* 38 (Spring 1983): 7–30.

6. Gloria T. Hull and Posey Gallagher, "Update on *Part One:* A Interview with Gwendolyn Brooks," *College Language Association Journal* 21 (September 1977): 26.

7. Gwendolyn Brooks, "The Rise of Maud Martha," in *We Be Word Sorcerers: Twenty-five Stories by Black Americans*, ed. Sonia Sanchez (New York: Bantam Books, 1973), pp 13–16.

8. These references to Brooks's poetry are from the following poems in *The World of Gwendolyn Brooks* (New York: Harper & Row, 1971); "The Ballad of Randolph Reed," p. 12; "The Anniad," p. 84; "obituary for a living lady," p. 18; and "a song in the front yard," p. 12. "Estimable Mable" is from Gwendolyn Brooks, *Family Pictures* (Detroit, Mich.: Broadside Press, 1970), p. 20.

9. Roi Ottley, "What's Wrong with Negro Women?" *Negro Digest* 8 (December 1950): 71–75; E. Simms Campbell, "Are Black Women Beautiful?" *Negro Digest* 9 (June 1951): 16–20; and Louie Robinson, "The Care and Feeding of Negro Women," *Negro Digest* 10 (September 1951): 9–12.

10. Gwendolyn Brooks, "Why Negro Women Leave Home," *Negro Digest* 9 (March 1951): 26–28.

11. Gilbert and Gubar, *Madwoman in the Attic*, p. 76.

GWENDOLYN BROOKS

The Courtship and Motherhood
of Maud Martha

LOW YELLOW

I know what he is thinking, thought Maud Martha, as she sat
on the porch in the porch swing with Paul Phillips. He is
thinking that I am all right. That I am really all right. That I
will do.

And I am glad of that, because my whole body is singing
beside him. And when you feel like that beside a man you
ought to be married to him.

I am what he would call—sweet.

But I am certainly not what he would call pretty. Even with
all this hair (which I have just assured him, in response to his
question, is not "natural," is not good grade or anything like
good grade) even with whatever I have that puts a dimple in
his heart, even with these nice ears, I am still, definitely, not
what he can call pretty if he remains true to what his idea of
pretty has always been. Pretty would be a little cream-
colored thing with curly hair. Or at the very lowest pretty
would be a little curly-haired thing the color of cocoa with a
lot of milk in it. Whereas, I am the color of cocoa straight, if
you can be even that "kind" to me.

He wonders, as we walk in the street, about the thoughts
of the people who look at us. Are they thinking that he could
do no better than—me? Then he thinks, Well, hmp! Well,
huh!—all the little good-lookin' dolls that have wanted *him*

"The Courtship and Motherhood of Maud Martha" from *Maud
Martha*" (1953)

—all the little sweet high-yellows that have ambled slowly past *his* front door—What he would like to tell those secretly snickering ones!—That any day out of the week he can do better than this black gal.

And by my own admission my hair is absolutely knappy.

"Fatherhood," said Paul, "is not exactly in my line. But it would be all right to have a couple or so of kids, good-looking, in my pocket, so to speak."

"I am not a pretty woman," said Maud Martha. "If you married a pretty woman, you could be the father of pretty children. Envied by people. The father of beautiful children."

"But I don't know," said Paul. "Because my features aren't fine. They aren't regular. They're heavy. They're real Negro features. I'm light, or at least I can claim to be a sort of low-toned yellow, and my hair has a teeny crimp. But even so I'm not handsome."

No, there would be little "beauty" getting born out of such a union.

Still, mused Maud Martha, I am what he would call—sweet, and I am good, and he will marry me. Although, he will be thinking, that's what he always says about letting yourself get interested in these incorruptible virgins, that so often your manhood will not let you concede defeat, and before you know it, you have let them steal you, put an end, perhaps, to your career.

He will fight, of course. He will decide that he must think a long time before he lets that happen here.

But in the end I'll hook him, even while he's wondering how this marriage will cramp him or pinch at him—at him, admirer of the gay life, spiffy clothes, beautiful yellow girls, natural hair, smooth cars, jewels, night clubs, cocktail lounges, class.

EVERYBODY WILL BE SURPRISED

"Of course," said Paul, "we'll have to start small. But it won't be very long before everybody will be surprised."

Maud Martha smiled.

"Your apartment, eventually, will be a dream. The *Defender* will come and photograph it." Paul grinned when he said that, but quite literally he believed it. Since he had decided to go ahead and marry her, he meant to "do it up right." People were going to look at his marriage and see only things to want. He was going to have a swanky flat. He and Maudie were going to dress well. They would entertain a lot.

"Listen," said Paul eagerly, "at a store on Forty-third and Cottage they're selling four rooms of furniture for eighty-nine dollars."

Maud Martha's heart sank.

"We'll go look at it tomorrow," added Paul.

"Paul—do you think we'll have a hard time finding a nice place—when the time comes?"

"No. I don't think so. But look here. I think we ought to plan on a stove-heated flat. We could get one of those cheap."

"Oh, I wouldn't like that. I've always lived in steam."

"I've always lived in stove—till a year ago. It's just as warm. And about fifteen dollars cheaper."

"Then what made your folks move to steam, then?"

"Ma wanted to live on a better-looking street. But we can't think about foolishness like that, when we're just starting out. Our flat will be hot stuff; the important thing is the flat, not the street; we can't study about foolishness like that; but our flat will be hot stuff. We'll have a swell flat."

"When you have stove heat, you have to have those ugly old fat black pipes stretching out all over the room."

"You don't just have to have long ones."

"I don't want any ones."

"You can have a little short one. And the new heaters they got look like radios. You'll like 'em."

Maud Martha silently decided she wouldn't, and resolved to hold out firmly against stove-heated flats. No stove-heated flats. And no basements. You got T.B. in basements.

"If you think a basement would be better—" began Paul.

"I don't," she interrupted.

"Basements are cheap too."

Was her attitude unco-operative? Should she be wanting to sacrifice more, for the sake of her man? A procession of pioneer women strode down her imagination; strong women, bold; praiseworthy, faithful, stout-minded; with a stout light beating in the eyes. Women who could stand low temperatures. Women who would toil eminently, to improve the lot of their men. Women who cooked. She thought of herself, dying for her man. It was a beautiful thought.

THE KITCHENETTE

Their home was on the third floor of a great gray stone building. The two rooms were small. The bedroom was furnished with a bed and dresser, old-fashioned, but in fair condition, and a faded occasional chair. In the kitchen were an oilcloth-covered table, two kitchen chairs, one folding chair, a cabinet base, a brown wooden icebox, and a three-burner gas stove. Only one of the burners worked, the housekeeper told them. The janitor would fix the others before they moved in. Maud Martha said she could fix them herself.

"Nope," objected Paul. "The janitor'll do it. That's what they pay him for." There was a bathroom at the end of the hall, which they would have to share with four other families who lived on the floor.

The housekeeper at the kitchenette place did not require a reference. . . .

The *Defender* would never come here with cameras.

Still, Maud Martha was, at first, enthusiastic. She made plans for this home. She would have the janitor move the bed and dresser out, tell Paul to buy a studio couch, a desk chest, a screen, a novelty chair, a white Venetian blind for the first room, and a green one for the kitchen, since the wallpaper there was green (with little red fishes swimming about). Perhaps they could even get a rug. A green one. And green drapes for the windows. Why, this *might* even turn out to be their dream apartment. It was small, but wonders could be wrought here. They could open up an account at L. Fish Furniture Store, pay a little every month. In that way, they could have the essentials right away. Later, they could get a Frigidaire. A baby's bed, when one became necessary, could go behind the screen, and they would have a pure living room.

Paul, after two or three weeks, told her sheepishly that kitchenettes were not so bad. Theirs seemed "cute and cozy" enough, he declared, and for his part, he went on, he was ready to "camp right down" until the time came to "build." Sadly, however, by that time Maud Martha had lost interest in the place, because the janitor had said that the Owner would not allow the furniture to be disturbed. Tenants moved too often. It was not worth the Owner's financial while to make changes, or to allow tenants to make them. They would have to be satisfied with "the apartment" as it was.

Then, one month after their installation, the first roach arrived. Ugly, shiny, slimy, slick-moving. She had rather see a rat—well, she had rather see a mouse. She had never yet been able to kill a roach. She could not bear to touch one with foot or stick or twisted paper. She could only stand helpless, frozen, and watch the slick movement suddenly appear and slither, looking doubly evil, across the mirror before which she had been calmly brushing her hair. And why? Why was he here? For she was scrubbing with water containing melted American Family soap and Lysol every other day.

And these things—roaches, and having to be satisfied with the place as it was—were not the only annoyances that had to be reckoned with. She was becoming aware of an oddness in color and sound and smell about her, the color and sound and smell of the kitchenette building. The color was gray, and the smell and sound had taken on a suggestion of the properties of color, and impressed one as gray, too. The sobbings, the frustrations, the small hates, the large and ugly hates, the little pushing-through love, the boredom, that came to her from behind those walls (some of them beaverboard) via speech and scream and sigh—all these were gray. And the smells of various types of sweat, and of bathing and bodily functions (the bathroom was always in use, someone was always in the bathroom) and of fresh or stale love-making, which rushed in thick fumes to your nostrils as you walked down the hall, or down the stairs—these were *gray*.

There was a whole lot of grayness here.

THE YOUNG COUPLE AT HOME

Paul had slept through most of the musicale. Three quarters of the time his head had been a heavy knot on her shoulder. At each of her attempts to remove it, he had waked up so suddenly, and had given her a look of such childlike fierceness, that she could only smile.

Now on the streetcar, however—the car was in the garage —he was not sleepy, and he kept "amusing" Maud Martha with little "tricks," such as cocking his head archly and winking at her, or digging her slyly in the ribs, or lifting her hand to his lips, and blowing on it softly, or poking a finger under her chin and raising it awkwardly, or feeling her muscle, then

putting her hand on his muscle, so that she could tell th
difference. Such as that. "Clowning," he called it. And be
cause he felt that he was making her happy, she tried not t
see the uncareful stares and smirks of the other passenger
—uncareful and insultingly consolatory. He sat playfull
upon part of her thigh. He gently kicked her toe.

Once home, he went immediately to the bathroom. He di
not try to mask his need, he was obvious and direct about i

"He could make," she thought, "a comment or two o
what went on at the musicale. Or some little joke. It isn't tha
I'm unreasonable or stupid. But everything can be done wit
a little grace. I'm sure of it."

When he came back, he yawned, stretched, smeared hi
lips up and down her neck, assured her of his devotion, an
sat down on the bed to take off his shoes. She picked up *C
Human Bondage*, and sat at the other end of the bed.

"Snuggle up," he invited.

"I thought I'd read awhile."

"I guess I'll read awhile, too," he decided, when his shoe
were off and had been kicked into the kitchen. She got u₁
went to the shoes, put them in the closet. He grinned at he
merrily. She was conscious of the grin, but refused to look ;
him. She went back to her book. He settled down to his. Hi
was a paper-backed copy of *Sex in the Married Life*.

There he sat, slouched down, terribly absorbed, happy i
his sock feet, curling his toes inside the socks.

"I want you to read this book," he said, "—but at the righ
times: one chapter each night before retiring." He reache
over, pinched her on the buttock.

She stood again. "Shall I make some cocoa?" she aske
pleasantly. "And toast some sandwiches?"

"Say, I'd like that," he said, glancing up briefly.

She toasted rye strips spread with pimento cheese an
grated onion. She made cocoa.

They ate, drank, and read together. She read *Of Huma
Bondage*. He read *Sex in the Married Life*. They were silent.

Five minutes passed. She looked at him. He was asleep

His head had fallen back, his mouth was open—it was a good thing there were no flies—his ankles were crossed. And the feet!—pointing confidently out (no one would harm them). *Sex in the Married Life* was about to slip to the floor. She did not stretch out a hand to save it.

Once she had taken him to a library. While occupied with the card cases she had glanced up, had observed that he, too, was busy among the cards. "Do you want a book?" "No-o. I'm just curious about something. I wondered if there could be a man in the world named Bastard. Sure enough, there is."

Paul's book fell, making a little clatter. But he did not wake up, and she did not get up.

MAUD MARTHA SPARES THE MOUSE

There. She had it at last. The weeks it had devoted to eluding her, the tricks, the clever hide-and-go-seeks, the routes it had in all sobriety devised, together with the delicious moments it had, undoubtedly, laughed up its sleeve—all to no ultimate avail. She had that mouse.

It shook its little self, as best it could, in the trap. Its bright black eyes contained no appeal—the little creature seemed to understand that there was no hope of mercy from the eternal enemy, no hope of reprieve or postponement—but a fine small dignity. It waited. It looked at Maud Martha.

She wondered what else it was thinking. Perhaps that there was not enough food in its larder. Perhaps that little Betty, a puny child from the start, would not, now, be getting fed. Perhaps that, now, the family's seasonal house-cleaning, for lack of expert direction, would be left undone. It might be regretting that young Bobby's education was now at an end. It might be nursing personal regrets. No more the mysterious shadows of the kitchenette, the uncharted twists, the unguessed halls. No more the sweet delights of the chase, the charms of being unsuccessfully hounded, thrown at.

Maud Martha could not bear the little look.

"Go home to your children," she urged. "To your wife or husband." She opened the trap. The mouse vanished.

Suddenly, she was conscious of a new cleanness in her. A wide air walked in her. A life had blundered its way into her power and it had been hers to preserve or destroy. She had not destroyed. In the center of that simple restraint was— creation. She had created a piece of life. It was wonderful.

"Why," she thought, as her height doubled, "why, I'm good! I am *good.*"

She ironed her aprons. Her back was straight. Her eyes were mild, and soft with a godlike loving-kindness.

WE'RE THE ONLY
COLORED PEOPLE HERE

When they went out to the car there were just the very finest bits of white powder coming down with an almost comical little ethereal hauteur, to add themselves to the really important, piled-up masses of their kind.

And it wasn't cold.

Maud Martha laughed happily to herself. It was pleasant out, and tonight she and Paul were very close to each other.

He held the door open for her—instead of going on around to the driving side, getting in, and leaving her to get in at her side as best she might. When he took this way of calling her "lady" and informed her of his love she felt precious, protected, delicious. She gave him an excited look of gratitude. He smiled indulgently.

"Want it to be the Owl again?"

"Oh, no no, Paul. Let's not go there tonight. I feel too good inside for that. Let's go downtown?"

She had to suggest that with a question mark at the end.

always. He usually had three protests. Too hard to park. Too much money. Too many white folks. And tonight she could almost certainly expect a no, she feared, because he had come out in his blue work shirt. There was a spot of apricot juice on the collar, too. His shoes were not shined. . . . But he nodded!

"We've never been to the World Playhouse," she said cautiously. "They have a good picture. I'd feel rich in there."

"You really wanta?"

"Please?"

"Sure."

It wasn't like other movie houses. People from the Studebaker Theatre which, as Maud Martha whispered to Paul, was "all-locked-arms" with the World Playhouse, were strolling up and down the lobby, laughing softly, smoking with gentle grace.

"There must be a play going on in there and this is probably an intermission," Maud Martha whispered again.

"I don't know why you feel you got to whisper," whispered Paul. "Nobody else is whispering in here." He looked around, resentfully, wanting to see a few, just a few, colored faces. There were only their own.

Maud Martha laughed a nervous defiant little laugh; and spoke loudly. "There certainly isn't any reason to whisper. Silly, huh."

The strolling women were cleverly gowned. Some of them had flowers or flashers in their hair. They looked—cooked. Well cared-for. And as though they had never seen a roach or a rat in their lives. Or gone without heat for a week. And the men had even edges. They were men, Maud Martha thought, who wouldn't stoop to fret over less than a thousand dollars.

"We're the only colored people here," said Paul.

She hated him a little. "Oh, hell. Who in hell cares."

"Well, what I want to know is, where do you pay the damn fares."

"There's the box office. Go on up."

He went on up. It was closed.

"Well," sighed Maud Martha, "I guess the picture has started already. But we can't have missed much. Go on up to that girl at the candy counter and ask her where we should pay our money."

He didn't want to do that. The girl was lovely and blonde and cold-eyed, and her arms were akimbo, and the set of her head was eloquent. No one else was at the counter.

"Well. We'll wait a minute. And see—"

Maud Martha hated him again. Coward. She ought to flounce over to the girl herself—show him up. . . .

The people in the lobby tried to avoid looking curiously at two shy Negroes wanting desperately not to seem shy. The white women looked at the Negro woman in her outfit with which no special fault could be found, but which made them think, somehow, of close rooms, and wee, close lives. They looked at her hair. They liked to see a dark colored girl with long, long hair. They were always slightly surprised, but agreeably so, when they did. They supposed it was the hair that had got her that yellowish, good-looking Negro man.

The white men tried not to look at the Negro man in the blue work shirt, the Negro man without a tie.

An usher opened a door of the World Playhouse part and ran quickly down the few steps that led from it to the lobby. Paul opened his mouth.

"Say, fella. Where do we get the tickets for the movie?"

The usher glanced at Paul's feet before answering. Then he said coolly, but not unpleasantly, "I'll take the money."

They were able to go in.

And the picture! Maud Martha was so glad that they had not gone to the Owl! Here was technicolor, and the love story was sweet. And there was classical music that silvered its way into you and made your back cold. And the theater itself! It was no palace, no such Great Shakes as the Tivoli out south, for instance (where many colored people went every night). But you felt good sitting there, yes, good, and as if, when you left it, you would be going home to a sweet-smelling apartment with flowers on little gleaming tables; and wonderful silver on night-blue velvet, in chests; and crackly sheets; and lace spreads on such beds as you saw at Marshall Field's. Instead of back to your kit'n't apt., with the garbage of your floor's families in a big can just outside your door, and the gray sound of little gray feet scratching away from it as you drag up those flights of narrow complaining stairs.

Paul pressed her hand. Paul said, "We oughta do this more often."

And again. "We'll have to do this more often. And go to plays, too. I mean at that Blackstone, and Studebaker."

She pressed back, smiling beautifully to herself in the darkness. Though she knew that once the spell was over it would be a year, two years, more, before he would return to the World Playhouse. And he might never go to a real play. But she was learning to love moments. To love moments for themselves.

When the picture was over, and the lights revealed them for what they were, the Negroes stood up among the furs and good cloth and faint perfume, looked about them eagerly. They hoped they would meet no cruel eyes. They hoped no one would look intruded upon. They had enjoyed the picture so, they were so happy, they wanted to laugh, to say warmly to the other outgoers, "Good, huh? Wasn't it swell?"

This, of course, they could not do. But if only no one would look intruded upon. . . .

IF YOU'RE LIGHT AND HAVE LONG HAIR

Came the invitation that Paul recognized as an honor of the first water, and as sufficient indication that he was, at last, a social somebody. The invitation was from the Foxy Cats Club, the club of clubs. He was to be present, in formal dress, at the Annual Foxy Cats Dawn Ball. No chances were taken: "Top hat, white tie and tails" hastily followed the "Formal dress," and that elucidation was in bold type.

Twenty men were in the Foxy Cats Club. All were good-looking. All wore clothes that were rich and suave. All "handled money," for their number consisted of well-located barbers, policemen, "government men" and men with a lucky touch at the tracks. Certainly the Foxy Cats Club was not a representative of that growing group of South Side organizations devoted to moral and civic improvements, or to literary or other cultural pursuits. If that had been so, Paul would have chucked his bid (which was black and silver, decorated with winking cats faces) down the toilet with a yawn. "That kind of stuff" was hardly understood by Paul, and was always dimissed with an airy "dicty," "hincty" or "high-falutin'." But no. The Foxy Cats devoted themselves solely to the business of being "hep," and each year they spent hundreds of dollars on their wonderful Dawn Ball, which did not begin at dawn, but was scheduled to end at dawn. "Ball," they called the frolic, but it served also the purposes of party, feast and fashion show. Maud Martha, watching him study his invitation, watching him lift his chin, could see that he considered himself one of the blessed.

Who—what kind soul had recommended him!

"He'll have to take me," thought Maud Martha. "For the envelope is addressed 'Mr. and Mrs.,' and I opened it. I guess he'd like to leave me home. At the Ball, there will be only beautiful girls, or real stylish ones. There won't be more than a handful like me. My type is not a Foxy Cat favorite. But he can't avoid taking me—since he hasn't yet thought of words or ways strong enough, and at the same time soft enough—for he's kind: he doesn't like to injure— to carry across to me the news that he is not to be held permanently by my type, and that he can go on with this marriage only if I put no ropes or questions around him. Also, he'll want to humor me, now that I'm pregnant."

She would need a good dress. That, she knew, could be a

problem, on his grocery clerk's pay. He would have his own
expenses. He would have to rent his topper and tails, and he
would have to buy a fine tie, and really excellent shoes. She
knew he was thinking that on the strength of his appearance
and sophisticated behavior at this Ball might depend his
future admission (for why not dream?) to *membership*, actually, in the Foxy Cats Club!

"I'll settle," decided Maud Martha, "on a plain white prin-
cess-style thing and some blue and black satin ribbon. I'll go
to my mother's. I'll work miracles at the sewing machine.

"On that night, I'll wave my hair. I'll smell faintly of lily of
the valley."

The main room of the Club 99, where the Ball was held,
was hung with green and yellow and red balloons, and the
thick pillars, painted to give an effect of marble, and stretching from floor to ceiling, were draped with green and red
and yellow crepe paper. Huge ferns, rubber plants and
bowls of flowers were at every corner. The floor itself was a
decoration, golden, glazed. There was no overhead light;
only wall lamps, and the bulbs in these were romantically
dim. At the back of the room, standing on a furry white rug,
was the long banquet table, dressed in damask, accented by
groups of thin silver candlesticks bearing white candles, and
laden with lovely food: cold chicken, lobster, candied ham
fruit combinations, potato salad in a great golden dish, corn
sticks, a cheese fluff in spiked tomato cups, fruit cake, angel
cake, sunshine cake. The drinks were at a smaller table
nearby, behind which stood a genial mixologist, quick with
maraschino cherries, and with lemon, ice and liquor. Wines
were there, and whiskey, and rum, and eggnog made with
pure cream.

Paul and Maud Martha arrived rather late, on purpose.
Rid of their wraps, they approached the glittering floor.
Bunny Bates's orchestra was playing Ellington's "Solitude."

Paul, royal in rented finery, was flushed with excitement.
Maud Martha looked at him. Not very tall. Not very hand-

somely made. But there was that extraordinary quality of maleness. Hiding in the body that was not *too* yellow, waiting to spring out at her, surround her (she liked to think)—that maleness. The Ball stirred her. The Beauties, in their gorgeous gowns, bustling, supercilious; the young men, who at other times most unpleasantly blew their noses, and darted surreptitiously into alleys to relieve themselves, and sweated and swore at their jobs, and scratched their more intimate parts, now smiling, smooth, overgallant; the drowsy lights; the smells of food and flowers, the smell of Murray's pomade, the body perfumes, natural and superimposed; the sensuous heaviness of the wine-colored draperies at the many windows; the music, now steamy and slow, now as clear and fragile as glass, now raging, passionate, now moaning and thickly gray. The Ball made toys of her emotions, stirred her variously. But she was anxious to have it end, she was anxious to be at home again, with the door closed behind herself and her husband. Then, he might be warm. There might be more than the absent courtesy he had been giving her of late. Then, he might be the tree she had a great need to lean against, in this "emergency." There was no telling what dear thing he might say to her, what little gem let fall.

But, to tell the truth, his behavior now was not very promising of gems to come. After their second dance he escorted her to a bench by the wall, left her. Trying to look nonchalant, she sat. She sat, trying not to show the inferiority she did not feel. When the music struck up again, he began to dance with someone red-haired and curved, and white as a white. Who was she? He had approached her easily, he had taken her confidently, he held her and conversed with her as though he had known her well for a long, long time. The girl smiled up at him. Her gold-spangled bosom was pressed— was pressed against that maleness—

A man asked Maud Martha to dance. He was dark, too. His mustache was small.

"Is this your first Foxy Cats?" he asked.

"What?" Paul's cheek was on that of Gold-Spangles.

"First Cats?"

"Oh. Yes." Paul and Gold-Spangles were weaving through the noisy twisting couples, were trying, apparently, to get to the reception hall.

"Do you know that girl? What's her name?" Maud Martha asked her partner, pointing to Gold-Spangles. Her partner looked, nodded. He pressed her closer.

"That's Maella. That's Maella."

"Pretty, isn't she?" She wanted him to keep talking about Maella. He nodded again.

"Yep. She has 'em howling along the stroll, all right, all right."

Another man, dancing past with an artificial redhead, threw a whispered word at Maud Martha's partner, who caught it eagerly, winked. "Solid, ol' man," he said. "Solid, Jack." He pressed Maud Martha closer. "You're a babe," he said. "You're a real babe." He reeked excitingly of tobacco, liquor, pinesoap, toilet water, and Sen Sen.

Maud Martha thought of her parent's back yard. Fresh. Clean. Smokeless. In her childhood, a snowball bush had shone there, big above the dandelions. The snowballs had been big, healthy. Once, she and her sister and brother had waited in the back yard for their parents to finish readying themselves for a trip to Milwaukee. The snowballs had been so beautiful, so fat and startlingly white in the sunlight, that she had suddenly loved home a thousand times more than ever before, and had not wanted to go to Milwaukee. But as the children grew, the bush sickened. Each year the snowballs were smaller and more dispirited. Finally a summer came when there were no blossoms at all. Maud Martha wondered what had become of the bush. For it was not there now. Yet she, at least, had never seen it go.

"Not," thought Maud Martha, "that they love each other. It oughta be that simple. Then I could lick it. It oughta be that easy. But it's my color that makes him mad. I try to shut my eyes to that, but it's no good. What I am inside, what is really me, he likes okay. But he keeps looking at my color, which is like a wall. He has to jump over it in order to meet and touch what I've got for him. He has to jump away up high in order to see it. He gets awful tired of all that jumping."

Paul came back from the reception hall. Maella was clinging to his arm. A final cry of the saxophone finished that particular slice of the blues. Maud Martha's partner bowed, escorted her to a chair by a rubber plant, bowed again, left.

"I could," considered Maud Martha, "go over there and scratch her upsweep down. I could spit on her back. I could scream. 'Listen,' I could scream, 'I'm making a baby for this man and I mean to do it in peace.' "

But if the root was sour what business did she have up there hacking at a leaf?

A BIRTH

After dinner, they washed dishes together. Then they undressed, and Paul got in bed, and was asleep almost instantly. She went down the long public hall to the bathroom, in her blue chenille robe. On her way back down the squeezing dark of the hall she felt—something softly separate in her. Back in the bedroom, she put on her gown, then stepped to the dresser to smear her face with cold cream. But when she turned around to get in the bed she couldn't move. Her legs cramped painfully, and she had a tremendous desire to eliminate which somehow she felt she would never be able to gratify.

"Paul!" she cried. As though in his dreams he had been waiting to hear that call, and that call only, he was up with a bound.

"I can't move."

He rubbed his eyes.

"Maudie, are you kidding?"

"I'm not kidding, Paul. I can't move."

He lifted her up and laid her on the bed, his eyes stricken. "Look here, Maudie. Do you think you're going to have that baby tonight?"

"No—no. These are just what they call 'false pains.' I'm not going to have the baby tonight. Can you get—my gown off?"

"Sure. Sure."

But really he was afraid to touch her. She lay nude on the bed for a few moments, perfectly still. Then all of a sudden motion came to her. Whereas before she had not been able to move her legs, now she could not keep them still.

"Oh, my God," she prayed aloud. "Just let my legs get still five minutes." God did not answer the prayer.

Paul was pacing up and down the room in fright.

"Look here. I don't think those are false pains. I think you're going to have that baby tonight."

"Don't say that, Paul," she muttered between clenched teeth. "I'm not going to have the baby tonight."

"I'm going to call your mother."

"Don't do that, Paul. She can't stand to see things like this. Once she got a chance to see a still-born baby, but she fainted before they even unwrapped it. She can't stand to see things like this. False pains, that's all. Oh, GOD, why don't you let me keep my legs still!"

She began to whimper in a manner that made Paul want to vomit. His thoughts traveled to the girl he had met at the Dawn Ball several months before. Cool. Sweet. Well-groomed. Fair.

"You're going to have that baby *now*. I'm going down to call up your mother and a doctor."

"DON'T YOU GO OUT OF HERE AND LEAVE ME ALONE! Damn. DAMN!"

"All right. All right. I won't leave you alone. I'll get the woman next door to come in. But somebody's got to get a doctor here."

"Don't you sneak out! Don't you *sneak* out!" She was

pushing down with her stomach now. Paul, standing at the foot of the bed with his hands in his pockets, saw the creeping insistence of what he thought was the head of the child.

"Oh, my Lord!" he cried. "It's coming! It's coming!"

He walked about the room several times. He went to the dresser and began to brush his hair. She looked at him in speechless contempt. He went out of the door, and ran down the three flights of stairs two or three steps at a time. The telephone was on the first floor. No sooner had he picked up the receiver than he heard Maud Martha give what he was sure could *only* be called a "bloodcurdling scream." He bolted up the stairs, saw her wriggling on the bed, said softly, "Be right back," and bolted down again. First he called his mother's doctor, and begged him to come right over. Then he called the Browns.

"Get her to the hospital!" shouted Belva Brown. "You'll have to get her to the hospital right away!"

"I can't. She's having the baby now. She isn't going to let anybody touch her. I tell you, she's having the baby."

"Don't be a fool. Of course she can get to the hospital. Why, she mustn't have it there in the house! I'm coming over there. I'll take her myself. Be sure there's plenty of gas in that car."

He tried to reach his mother. She was out—had not returned from a revival meeting.

When Paul ran back up the stairs he found young Mrs. Cray, who lived in the front apartment of their floor, attending to his shrieking wife.

"I heard 'er yellin', and thought I'd better come in, seein' as how you all is so confused. Got a doctor comin'?"

Paul sighed heavily. "I just called one. Thanks for coming in. This—this came on all of a sudden, and I don't think I know what to do."

"Well, the thing to do is get a doctor right off. She's goin' to have the baby soon. Call *my* doctor." She gave him a number. "Whichever one gets here first can work on her. Ain't no time to waste."

Paul ran back down the stairs and called the number. "What's the doctor's address?" he yelled up. Mrs. Cray yelled it down. He went out to get the doctor personally. He was glad of an excuse to escape. He was sick of hearing Maudie scream. He had had no idea that she could scream that kind of screaming. It was awful. How lucky he was that he had been born a man. How lucky he was that he had been born a man!

Belva arrived in twenty minutes. She was grateful to find another woman present. She had come to force Maud Martha to start for the hospital, but a swift glance told her that the girl would not leave her bed for many days. As she said to her husband and Helen later on, "The baby was all ready to spill out."

When her mother came in the door Maud Martha tightened her lips, temporarily forgetful of her strange pain. (But it wasn't pain. It was something else.) "Listen. If you're going to make a fuss, go on out. I'm having enough trouble without you making a fuss over everything."

Mrs. Cray giggled encouragingly. Belva said bravely, "I'm not going to make a fuss. You'll see. Why, there's nothing to make a fuss *about*. You're just going to have a baby, like millions of other women. Why should I make a fuss?"

Maud Martha tried to smile but could not quite make it. The sensations were getting grindingly sharp. She screamed longer and louder, explaining breathlessly in between times, "I just can't help it. Excuse me."

"Why, go on and scream," urged Belva. "You're supposed to scream. That's your privilege. I'm sure *I* don't mind." Her ears were splitting, and over and over as she stood there looking down at her agonized daughter, she said to herself, "Why doesn't the doctor come? Why doesn't the doctor come? I know I'm going to faint." She and Mrs. Cray stood, one on each side of the bed, purposelessly holding a sheet over Maud Martha, under which they peeped as seldom as they felt was safe. Maud Martha kept asking, "Has the head come?" Presently she felt as though her whole body were having a bowel movement. The head came. Then, with a little difficulty, the wide shoulders. Then easily, with soft and slippery smoothness, out slipped the rest of the body and the baby was born. The first thing it did was sneeze.

Maud Martha laughed as though she could never bear to stop. "Listen to him sneeze. My little baby. Don't let him drown, Mrs. Cray." Mrs. Cray looked at Maud Martha, because she did not want to look at the baby. "How you know it's a him?" Maud Martha laughed again.

Belva also refused to look at the baby. "See, Maudie," she said, "see how brave I was? The baby is born, and I didn't get nervous or faint or anything. Didn't I tell you?"

"Now isn't that nice," thought Maud Martha. "Here I've had the baby, and she thinks I should praise her for having stood up there and looked on." Was it, she suddenly wondered, as hard to watch suffering as it was to bear it?

Five minutes after the birth, Paul got back with Mrs. Cray's doctor, a large silent man, who came in swiftly, threw the sheet aside without saying a word, cut the cord. Paul looked at the new human being. It appeared gray and greasy. Life was hard, he thought. What had he done to deserve a still-born child? But there it was, lying dead.

"It's dead, isn't it?" he asked dully.

"Oh, get out of here!" cried Mrs. Cray, pushing him into the kitchen and shutting the door.

"Girl," said the doctor. Then grudgingly, "Fine girl."

"Did you hear what the doctor said, Maudie?" chattered Belva. "You've got a daughter, the doctor says." The doctor looked at her quickly.

"Say, you'd better go out and take a walk around the block. You don't look so well."

Gratefully, Belva obeyed. When she got back, Mrs. Cray and the doctor had oiled and dressed the baby—dressed her in an outfit found in Maud Martha's top dresser drawer. Belva looked at the newcomer in amazement.

"Well, she's a little beauty, isn't she!" she cried. She had not expected a handsome child.

Maud Martha's thoughts did not dwell long on the fact of the baby. There would be all her life long for that. She preferred to think, now, about how well she felt. Had she ever in her life felt so well? She felt well enough to get up. She folded her arms triumphantly across her chest, as another young woman, her neighbor to the rear, came in.

"Hello, Mrs. Barksdale!" she hailed. "Did you hear the news? I just had a baby, and I feel strong enough to go out and shovel coal! Having a baby is *nothing*, Mrs. Barksdale. Nothing at all."

"Aw, yeah?" Mrs. Barksdale smacked her gum admiringly. "Well, from what I heard back there a while ago, didn't seem like it was nothing. Girl, I didn't know anybody *could* scream that loud." Maud Martha tittered. Oh, she felt fine. She wondered why Mrs. Barksdale hadn't come in while the screaming was going on; she had missed it all.

People. Weren't they sweet. She had never said more than "Hello, Mrs. Barksdale" and "Hello, Mrs. Cray" to these women before. But as soon as something happened to her, in they trooped. People were sweet.

The doctor brought the baby and laid it in the bed beside Maud Martha. Shortly before she had heard it in the kitchen —a bright delight had flooded through her upon first hearing that part of Maud Martha Brown Phillips expressing itself with a voice of its own. But now the baby was quiet and returned its mother's stare with one that seemed equally curious and mystified but perfectly cool and undisturbed.

POSTS

People have to choose something decently constant to depend on, thought Maud Martha. People must have something to lean on.

But the love of a single person was not enough. Not only was personal love itself, however good, a thing that varied from week to week, from second to second, but the parties to it were likely, for example, to die, any minute, or otherwise be parted, or destroyed. At any time.

Not alone was the romantic love of a man and a woman fallible, but the breadier love between parents and children; brothers; animals; friend and friend. Those too could not be heavily depended on.

Could be nature, which had a seed, or root, or an element (what do you want to call it) of constancy, under all that system of change. Of course, to say "system" at all implied arrangement, and therefore some order of constancy.

Could be, she mused, a marriage. The marriage shell, not the romance, or love, it might contain. A marriage, the plainer, the more plateaulike, the better. A marriage made up of Sunday papers and shoeless feet, baking powder biscuits, baby baths, and matinees and laundrymen, and potato plants in the kitchen window.

Was, perhaps, the whole life of man a dedication to this search for something to lean upon, and was, to a great degree, his "happiness" or "unhappiness" written up for him by the demands or limitations of what he chose for that work?

For work it was. Leaning was a work.

GWENDOLYN BROOKS

The Rise of Maud Martha

The pastor stood in the small areaway, his coat on, and looked after the ladies carrying flowers and at the speeding casket (whose lid had been closed as quietly as possible, to avoid jarring the family), his hands together, closing and unclosing behind him. It was impossible to tell just what he was thinking. It could have been about the look of the deceased, or the quality of the casket, or death itself, or strawberries.

Maud Martha, the children, Mama—and *his* mama—sat in the first car, the longest and shiny-blackest of the long black cars. They waited. Eventually, the assistant at the funeral parlor came to the end of his lists, all the doors were shut as if forever, the motors made their little noise, and the funeral procession began.

Maud Martha had not seen him in the casket. No one had. For the casket was sealed beforehand. Banked upon it were flowers, fresh and barely fresh, and in front of it were wreaths, big and little and few.

What the fire had done to the little man Paul. Exhaled at him. Teased him, touched him, pleaded with him, put its swelling arms around him. It ate what it desired. Of him and 30-odd. It was strange to think of—that streetcar (the new green model with the sealed windows—the "Green Hornet") after the collision with the gas truck (INFLAMMABLE—in big white letters) standing there, patiently, while the invader ate at the flesh of 30-odd. It almost seemed as tho the street-

---

car might have done something, something to help itself and its little faint charges.

The women in the street. Would she ever forget the women? To think that women could turn into ripped-open wounds, and into sores that cankered before the eyes. Pretty women, begrimed, with stretching slits for mouths. Ugly women, grown almost beautiful in their grief. Herself. Herself, with nothing to feel but surprise.

This was what gripped her still. That, at that moment, thru the sick smoke, the boiling air above it, the strict stench, when the policeman lifted up the grimmest piece of cloth she had even seen and exposed her husband—black with a more "dreadful" blackness than that which he had ever known and despised—hairless, eroded chin outthrust, and with never one more dream of sophistication remaining, all she could feel was a big surprise that this was happening to her.

A high-school girl with glossy braids behind her ears and pretty clothes to sweeten the half-charm of her face, and books in one arm and a boyfriend in the other, was standing just inside the curb, searching her eyes. The girl had been positively fascinated. Enjoying herself. Seeing Life. At school the next day: There was this hag. You should've seen her bending over what was left of her man. Maud Martha had thought, as she turned her gaze from the sight beneath her: Why should I envy her, that little girl. Her time is coming. There isn't a woman alive can hope to escape a something bad.

"He was sure a good boy," suddenly choked Paul's mother, "that he was, and whoever says no is a liar." She looked at Maud Martha, who looked straight ahead at the mole on the neck of the driver.

"Always a-laughin', and a-jokin', and a-makin' you feel good, that's what he was always a-doin'," went on Mrs. Phillips, "and when I think of him on that streetcar, screamin',

and tryin' to dodge the fire, and burnin' up alive, I could just
—oh, I could just—"

Here, what Mrs. Phillips could just do, she did, and with
such energy that the man with the mole jumped, and for a
moment the car slowed down. Mrs. Phillips reached over
and, wiping her wet face with one hand, patted Maud Martha's knee with the other. "Nobody can say you didn't do
pretty good by my boy," she declared. "You didn't fix him
hot meals all the time. They should be hot enough so that
the steam rises up thru his nostrils. That's what makes for a
healthy man. And I always thought it wouldn't have hurt you
to get a little job, to help out, and left them little ones with
Paulette, wouldn't have hurt her to miss a year or two out of
school—"

"Paulette being ten," interrupted Maud Martha, "the
Board of Education mightn't have liked it."

"But take her all in all, Mrs. Brown," went on Mrs. Phillips, directing her eye-swords at Maud Martha's mother,
"she did about as well as most of these young gals." Belva
Brown said nothing. She did part her lips. But she snapped
them shut again.

"Now, Maudie," said Mrs. Phillips, "now, Maudie, you
know I want to see those children. They're mine just as much
as they're your mother's. I want you to bring them to see
their grandmother every few days. Do you understand?"

"I understand," said Maud Martha.

But she was listening only a little, because there was something else she was about to begin to understand. It was fuzzy,
she could not yet see it properly, or properly finger it. But a
hint nudged her, promised her that very soon a reality more
horrible than that fact of her first surprise would establish
itself, would command her recognition.

The hint got larger, louder, more palpable. By the time
they stood beside the grave, she had it by the hand and it
talked to her. It was willing to tell her what was cold and
rude.

It told her this: When you love a man, he becomes more
than a body. His physical limits expand, and his outlines
recede, vanish. Suddenly he has no bowels, his eliminatory
functions seem unimportant or beautiful. He is rich and
sweet and right. He is part of the world, the atmosphere, the
blue sky and the blue water. If he happens to be dead, he is
still what you love, and your big pity is for yourself, not for
him.

It told her this—that for her now, none of this was true.

At what point it had all stopped being true she did not
know. Perhaps when vicissitudes were no longer adventures
but only vicissitudes. Perhaps when he had made her feel
like a pumpkin for the least little minute too long. She could
not locate that little minute. She had been feeling like a
pumpkin for a very long time.

Her pity was all for him. He, who had so loved physical
beauty, in the end a fire-used, repulsive thing.

But for herself (she did not think of groceries, she did not
think, as yet, a certain, old, child-helplessness of the eyes)—
why, she could actually feel herself rising. She felt higher
and more like a citizen of—what?

A road was again clean before her. She held the destinies
of herself and of her children in her individual power—all
was up to her.

Down and down they sent her Paul. The relatives, for
some time worried, looked on her with approval at last. For
she was crying.

Crying because she could not stop herself from thinking
about the after-funeral white cake that waited in her mother's home.

—1955

GWENDOLYN BROOKS

Afterword

No, it is not *Native Son, Invisible Man, Jubilee, Roots*. Pauline Hopkins is not Richard Wright, Ralph Ellison, Margaret Walker, Alex Haley. Unlike Margaret Walker, in the fire of *For My People*, Pauline Hopkins is not herein urging that "martial songs be written"; she is often indignant, but not indignant enough to desire Margaret's "bloody peace." It is true that Pauline Hopkins can and does involve herself with black anger, but the texture range, scope, the slashing red and scream and curse and *out-there* hurt that overwhelm us as Wright, Ellison and Haley deal with us, are not to be found in *Contending Forces*. I am not prepared to say that they are not "necessary." However, this quaint little "romance"—as the author likes to call it—keeps us with it, keeps us trotting, with quite some tension, too, down its elder dust, and through its quizzical mist.

Words do wonderful things. They pound, purr. They can urge, they can wheedle, whip, whine. They can sing, sass, singe. They can churn, check, channelize. They can be a "*Hup* two three four." They can forge a fiery army out of a hundred languid men. Pauline Hopkins, had we met, might have said in answer to my questions that her interest was *not* in Revolution *nor* exhaustive Revision. But it is perfectly obvious that black fury invaded her not seldom and not softly, and if she has not chosen from her resources words and word jointures that could make changes in the world, she has given us a sense of her day, a *clue* collection, and we can use the light of it to clarify our understanding and our

---

"Afterword" to *Contending Forces* (1968)

intuition. We can take the building blocks she does supply us and use them to fill in old gaps. After association with her, some of our concepts won't be quite as wobbly.

Pauline Hopkins had, and this is true of many of her brothers and sisters, new and old, a touching reliance on the dazzles and powers of anticipated integration. But she would have been remarkable indeed if, enslaved as she was by her special time and special temperament, she had been forward enough to instruct blacks not to rely on goodies coming from any source save personal heart, head, hand. To ask them, to entreat them to address themselves, rather than whites, to cherish, champion themselves, rather than whites, to trust, try, traipse with themselves, was not her inspiration nor motivation.

Often doth the brainwashed slave revere the modes and idolatries of the master. And Pauline Hopkins consistently proves herself a continuing slave, despite little bursts of righteous heat, throughout *Contending Forces*. She tells us, for example, what she really thinks of "black beauty" over and over again, in passages like this description of our paper-doll heroine, Sappho Clark: "Tall and fair, with hair of a golden cast, aquiline nose, rosebud mouth, soft brown eyes veiled by long, dark lashes which swept her cheek, just now covered with a delicate rose flush . . . a combination of 'queen rose and lily in one.'" To which vision an *ordinary* black, Sarah Ann, (fat, colloquial, ebony-hued), responds: "That's somethin' *God* made, honey." (The accepted understanding being that one of the lower devils made the ilk of Sarah Ann.) We are also treated to such outrages as "there might even have been a strain of African blood polluting the fair stream of Montfort's vitality"; and "In many cases African blood had become diluted from amalgamation with the higher race"; *and* "that justice of heart and mind for my people which the Anglo-Saxon in America never withholds from suffering humanity."

In her preface, the author suggests that *her* desire is to give us the kind of "simple, homely tale . . . which cements the bond of brotherhood among all classes and all complexions." But like most blacks, of whatever persuasion, self-delusion, perverse ambition, or approximate "transformation," Pauline is unable to keep a certain purely "native" rage *steadily* stomped down. Certain things she does not mind us suffering through, any more than does Alex Haley or Margaret Walker. We get "cruelties . . . such as to sicken the most cold-hearted and indifferent. For instance: causing a child to whip his mother until the blood ran; if a slave looked his master in the face, his limbs were broken; women in the first stages of their accouchement, upon refusing to work, were placed in the treadmill where terrible things happened, too dreadful to relate." And she is able to make Will say—calmly—that agitation—never Revolution—"will do much. It gave us freedom; it will give us manhood. The peace, dignity, and honor of this nation rises or falls with the Negro."

As she says, and with more desperate truth than she knows she says or feels, the reader is left to "draw conclusions."

And what conclusions would Pauline Hopkins draw, if she were alive, and looking, and writing novels today? It is to be supposed that most of the agitation she suffered during the composition of *Contending Forces* would be distinct in her today. I believe she would be angrier today. I believe she would scream to herself and to whatever listeners she could muster: "What! This is all that has been achieved in the minds and morals of men and women?" (For she could not fail to observe that when the mobs assemble to deprive the weak of their shreds, here and there in our fair country—in Chicago, in Boston, in Rhode Island, in Georgia, and in Mississippi still—the "gentler" sex is amply represented, clarion-mouthed, furnace-eyed, and armed with spittle, brick, stick, and obscenity.)

"What!" Pauline Hopkins would declaim. "Beautiful, warm-faced, soft-eyed citizens are *still* gathering, physically to deplore, deride, and devastate that which is 'different' (and *imported*); physically and mentally and spiritually to check, inhibit, cripple those who are here only because of fierce Invitations to come?"

Pauline Hopkins would look about her and discover that cruelty, once at least to some degree impulsive or random or spasmodic, is now deliberate, massively and cleverly organized, steady, fundamental, *national.* And she would look beyond shores to the "far reaches" of the world. She would understand that when the American flag was registered on the moon, racism, the proper definition of which is "prejudice with oppression," had its automatic representation in that simple planting.

And our author would see, certainly, somewhat closer to "home," that what is happening to the "weak" on the Afrikan continent can by all means be called rape and slave-driving and lynching. She would agree with the wise among our scholars today that added to old rape, old slave-driving, old lynching are many refinements and ingenious extensions.

However, she would question, would investigate that word *weak.* So many millions of the "weak"—in the grip of a comparative handful of the "strong"! I believe she would have cared to predict that the "weak" would, finally, perceive the impressiveness of their numbers, perceive the quality and legitimacy of their essence, and take a *sufficiency* of indicated steps toward their definition, clarification, and indisputable salvation. Querulous though some of Pauline's notions may be (she was understandably a daughter of her time) she had spirit, flexible spirit, and I do not think she would "fault" that ultimate salvation for being "different"— for differing from the European ideal of salvation.

Indeed, Pauline Hopkins would take note of glitterings of promise on the horizon. She would note that many of the "weak"—not all—are raising their voices and their fists, fists in which often may be found "means necessary"; are circulating *their* word *outside* their seduced arena, knowing pretty well, at last, that only the squeaky wheel gets the grease of notice and empathy from the preoccupied, obsessed, self-honeying, self-crowned Editors of our world.

But how important is the gift of this testimonial! We need the essential Black statement of defense and definition. Of course, we are happiest when that statement is not dulled by assimilationist urges, secret or overt. However, there is in "the soul of Black folk"—even when inarticulate and crippled—a yearning toward black validation.

And!—the better-meaning members of the *white* dispensation, with a thousand counts against their doing anything *costly* to abet it, respect the courage, the cutting edge of the Voice That Means Business.

Wherefore our inevitable indebtedness to the author of *Contending Forces.*

BIBLIOGRAPHIC NOTES

Until very recently, only Gwendolyn Brooks's poetry has received serious critical attention. Even though *Maud Martha* was published in 1953, current studies and collections of black writers usually omit the novel from consideration. The anthology, Richard Barksdale and Keneth Kinnamon, eds., *Black Writers of America* (New York: Macmillan, 1972), focuses only on her poetry. And even as a poet, Brooks is often neglected. In Addison Gayle's *The Way of the New World: The Black Novel in America* (New York: Doubleday & Co., 1975), only her name is mentioned among several other poets who redefined the black aesthetic between 1952 and 1972.

Critics who do discuss *Maud Martha* usually emphasize the novel's poetic techniques. Annette Shank's "Gwendolyn Brooks as Novelist," *Black World* (June 1973): 22–30 discusses themes shared by both Brooks's poetry and fiction. Harry Shaw's *Gwendolyn Brooks* (Boston: Twayne, 1980), devotes an entire chapter to *Maud Martha,* but it ignores social and political realities as an ingredient in her literary concerns and techniques. His discussion of Maud Martha's conflict with norms of feminine beauty demonstrates his dismissal of feminist thought, for here he characterizes Maud as "insecure" and "self-disparaging." He traces Brooks's absence of plot and her use of vignettes to her poetic sensibilities. Barbara Christian in *Black Women Novelists: The Making of a Tradition, 1892–1976* (Westport, Conn.: Greenwood Press, 1980), also devotes several pages to *Maud Martha*, commenting on how Brooks defeats the "mystique of heroism" forced on earlier black women characters by concentrating on the ordinariness of daily life which allows Maud Martha to escape from the pressures of "heroism."

An analysis of the critical reception of *Maud Martha* is found in Mary Helen Washington's articles, "Taming All That Anger Down: Rage and Silence in Gwendolyn Brooks's *Maud Martha*," in *Black Literature and Literary Theory*, ed. Henry Louis Gates, Jr., (New York: Methuen, 1984), pp. 249–62; and "Plain, Black, and Decently Wild: The Heroic Possibilities of *Maud Martha*," in *The Voyage In: Fictions of Female Development*, ed. Elizabeth Abel, Marianne Hirsch, and Elizabeth Langland (Hanover, N.H.: University Press of New England, 1983), pp. 270–86. Both articles link the "silences" that characterize the critics' neglect of *Maud Martha* to the heroine's "silence." Washington finds evidence of these silences in Brooks's truncated syntax and abbreviated chapters. Both articles place Brooks in a pivotal role in the Afro-American literary tradition.

INDEX